CRIME, POLICE, AND PE

Clive Emsley is Emeritus Professor of History and former Co-Director of the International Centre for Comparative Criminological Research at the Open University.

Crime, Police, and Penal Policy

European Experiences 1750–1940

CLIVE EMSLEY

OXFORD

UNIVERSITY PRESS

OXFORD

UNIVERSITY PRESS

Great Clarendon Street, Oxford OX2 6DP

Oxford University Press is a department of the University of Oxford.
It furthers the University's objective of excellence in research, scholarship,
and education by publishing worldwide. Oxford is a registered trade mark of
Oxford University Press in the UK and in certain other countries

British Library Cataloguing in Publication Data

Data available

Library of Congress Cataloging in Publication Data

Data available

ISBN 978–0–19–920285–0 (Hbk.)
ISBN 978–0–19–966947–9 (Pbk.)

For Martha Elizabeth

Preface

THE origins of this book lie in an academic career during which my research has continually come back to questions of crime and policing and how similar institutions have developed in different national contexts. The incentive to write it was a suggestion, by my friend and colleague Peter King writing in the *British Journal of Criminology*, that, given a generation of research, we have reached a point where someone should attempt a comparative textbook on the history of crime, policing, and penal policy. The opportunity to start writing it was provided by a generous three-month fellowship at the Humanities Research Centre at the Australian National University. Jokes about Australia being the perfect place to study crime and criminals are misplaced, at least in this case. The HRC is a wonderful institution providing opportunities to read, to think, and to exchange ideas in a genuine academic environment; specifically an environment that is far away from the jargon of quality assessments, research assessments, 'customers', 'products', 'targets', and 'training' that infests and stultifies so much of contemporary British university life.

In addition to the HRC, I must also thank the large number of colleagues and friends who have shared their ideas with me over the last few years at various conferences and seminars. In particular, for their advice, help, and generous response to queries that I have raised in preparing this book, I must thank Martin Bergman, Alexander Böhm, Alyson Brown, Francis Dodsworth, Jonathan Dunnage, Christine Frasch, Annika Mombauer, Nicolas Pitsos, Mark Pittaway, Xavier Rousseaux, Marie Vogel, Klaus Weinhauer, Jim Whitfield, and Chris Williams. René Lévy and Renée Zauberman have also always been generous with advice and suggestions, and above all with their hospitality in Paris. Peter King, Paul Lawrence, and René Lévy kindly read a draft of the whole book and made corrections and valuable suggestions; the errors and infelicities that remain are mine entirely.

Two caveats are necessary about the range of what follows, first on my use of 'Europe' and second on my decision to restrict the text to 'Europe'. Any historian has to draw on what sources are available. This book is essentially a work of synthesis and I have been reliant on what others have written and on what I can read of what others have written. Some European countries do not get a mention in what follows. And if much of the emphasis is on England, France, Germany, and Italy this is because it is, as far as I am aware, in these countries where most of the recent work on the history of crime, policing, and penal policy has been done. My decision on the second matter was similarly pragmatic. There has been interesting and important work on how these issues developed in North America, in Australia, and in New Zealand, but I considered that focusing on 'Europe' would just about keep the text manageable and, I hope, maintain the reader's patience.

Patience is a virtue that, among others, my wife has in spades. I cannot conclude this preface without an acknowledgement of, and thanks for her love and support while I struggled with this book. The dedication is to our granddaughter.

Contents

Abbreviations

APP	Archives de la Préfecture de Police, Paris
AN	Archives Nationales, Paris
BJC	*British Journal of Criminology*
CHS	*Crime, histoire et sociétés/Crime, history and societies*
CJH	*Criminal Justice History*
IAHCCJ	International Association for the History of Crime and Criminal Justice
MO	Mediathèque d'Orléans
NA	National Archives, Kew, London

1

Introduction

THE changes in penal policy and policing from the mid-eighteenth to the mid-twentieth centuries are relatively well known, but they have generally been written up with the focus of the subject matter limited by the boundaries of separate nation states, of local regions or even of individual cities or towns. The changes, however, and the ideas and models that guided them were not restricted to nation states, even though different cultural, political, and social contexts led to them taking unique forms in different countries and regions. A chronological narrative of these changes is the subject matter of this book. This introduction is designed to provide a broad, brief survey of what follows and, more particularly, to give an outline of the theories that some deploy to explain the changes but which can be used, more profitably, as tools for structuring questions that need to be posed of the historical evidence.

A key element in any historical study is assessing change over time, the causes and the pattern of that change. Certain behaviours by and between individual human beings have a degree of constancy. One individual's actions directed against another individual can be regarded by the latter as a 'wrong'. Sometimes these wrongs are acknowledged as such beyond the individuals involved in them. Thus a community can perceive a particular wrong as an infringement of its socially accepted norms and in some instances the wrong can be categorized as an offence within a written criminal code. This is essentially what is meant by the statement that crime is constructed by society.

Criminal laws vary between different societies. While certain offences, most obviously forms of homicide and theft, have been regarded and categorized as crimes by the law in Western societies for centuries, on the fringes the criminal law is constantly changing. Similarly perceptions of what is and is not criminal, or acceptable, are constantly shifting. This means that crime is not an absolute. It is now readily recognized, at least in academic circles, that the ways in which societies have defined and dealt with crime and criminals have changed significantly over time. Moreover, different geographical areas, economic conditions, population, and social structures have provided contexts for different forms of offending. As these contexts have changed, so too have forms of criminal behaviour.

The period from the late eighteenth to the early twentieth centuries witnessed enormous changes in the perception of crime and criminality and in the ways in which these issues were addressed by states through their laws and through administrative and institutional structures. The process of change was not linear; historical change rarely is. Perhaps the most obvious example of this is the way in which the emphasis in penal policies shifted, pendulum-like, from retribution to reform and back across the period. Similarly, in the face-to-face communities of the old regime and rural world it was common for courts to make decisions based on some personal knowledge of the offender. The rational legal theorists of the Enlightenment, in contrast, sought uniformity of punishment according to the crime. Then, at the close of the nineteenth century, as the offender began to be seen as a fallible individual, often with mental and social problems, so the courts tended to make decisions that were perceived as relevant to the particular offender.

There were considerable variations in the perceptions of offenders and in the creation and use of new institutions between states, across states, and across regions. There were also variations amongst individuals who were members of the same polity. The state jurist, for example, commonly dealt with abstract situations but explored the issues consistently and regularly. Jurists and other official actors also became more secular in their outlook across the period; they made growing claims of professionalism and unique expertise in the exercise of their duties. Their numbers grew with the increasing bureaucratization and regulation imposed during the nineteenth century and beyond. Crime was their business. The victim of a wrong, or a crime, in contrast, had to deal with something that was usually unpleasant and upsetting, but probably he or she was a victim only once in a lifetime.

Across Europe during the nineteenth century new legal codes were prepared for nation states and empires. There was the development of professional, bureaucratic police institutions and the replacement of public, physical punishment on the body of an offender by the closed institution of the prison. Throughout the whole period there were shifts in the ideas about what caused crime and about those who were responsible for committing it. In the religious environments of the Middle Ages and the Reformation, crime was commonly equated with sin and with temptation prompted by supernatural powers. But from the Enlightenment especially, the criminal was increasingly perceived as an individual making rational decisions about his behaviour. In the rational, scientific, and increasingly secular age that emerged during the nineteenth century, however, heredity and forms of mental illness were seen as significant causes of criminal activity. Such shifting perceptions were accompanied by a growing faith in the idea that social problems might be resolved in large measure by the state. Increasingly from the late eighteenth century many at the centre of political power considered that the state and its agencies were the only authoritative bodies capable of acting upon the relationships between offenders and their victims. These shifts and developing beliefs affected both policing practices and strategies, and also the attitudes of the courts when it came to decisions on guilt and sentencing. Yet, at the same time, in some areas there continued to be a dynamic relationship between the burgeoning state and private philanthropy; this was especially apparent in the responses to juvenile offending and the correction of 'fallen' women.

A variety of explanations have been deployed to explain these changes, some carefully articulated and others much less so. Several of the prominent social theorists who lived during the two centuries covered here formulated ideas and theories that helped to shape different understandings of crime and responses to it. Karl Marx and Émile Durkheim are the obvious examples. Recent historical research has also turned to more recent theorists, notably to the German sociologist Norbert Elias and to the French philosopher Michel Foucault. But a theoretical underpinning for action or interpretation is not always articulated either by historical actors or by historians. Throughout the period penal and police reformers considered themselves as progressive and humanitarian. These beliefs fed into the early historical surveys and created a Whig interpretation of change, generally assumed rather than articulated, that tended to take reformers at their word, to see changes in penal policy and policing as progressive and to portray opponents and critics of the changes as foolish or reactionary. The idea of the Whig interpretation of history was delineated in the 1930s by Herbert Butterfield and with reference to explanations of political change in late eighteenth- and nineteenth-century Britain.[1] Whig ideas remain embedded in many of the popular histories of crime and the institutional histories of police and penal policy in Britain and they are implicit also in much of the traditional understanding of the

[1] Herbert Butterfield, *The Whig Interpretation of History*, London: G.Bell and Sons, 1931.

changes in other countries. They commonly presuppose a social order based on consensus in which the criminal is an identifiable, alien 'other' that preys upon ordinary, law-abiding citizens.

Karl Marx, in contrast, considered that class conflict, emanating from economic relationships, was at the heart of society. Yet, somewhat surprisingly, outside of a series of articles for the *Rheinische Zeitung* on the debates in the Rhenish Parliament on wood theft during the autumn and winter of 1842 to 1843, he made relatively little reference to crime.[2] The most extensive and authoritative Marxist account of the relationship between economic conditions and crime was written by a Dutch Professor of Law, Willem Adriaan Bonger, a decade before the First World War.[3] But Marx's work inspired some of the early criminologists such as the Italian Enrico Ferri who used 'scientific socialism' to delineate how each phase of civilization has its own form of criminality:

> As there was a criminality of violence and bloodshed in feudal society, a criminality of robbery and fraud in bourgeois society, so the society of the future will have its own appropriate character. . . . [N]atural crime passes more and more from material forms of violence into the intellectual forms of cunning and fraud. It thus reproduces the evolution by which man ceaselessly gets further and further away from his animal and savage origin. Crimes against property, especially in the numerous forms of indirect robbery, become more and more numerous in comparison with crimes of bloodshed. Even the latter assume forms more and more intellectual, and homicide itself is contrived with craft instead of with violence.[4]

This perspective can be seen also as an early form of the *violence au vol* concept that, towards the close of the twentieth century, became particularly popular with French historians surveying crime over the *longue durée* and describing the change from medieval to modern. This concept suggested a shift in the pattern of crime from one in which violence predominated to one in which the principal form of offending was some form of theft.[5]

---

[2] Pierre Lascoumes and Hartwig Zander, *Marx: du 'vol de bois' à la critique du droit*, Paris: Presses Universitaires de France, 1984; see also Paul Phillips, *Marx and Engels on Law and Laws*, Oxford: Martin Robertson, 1980.

[3] Willem Adriaan Bonger, *Criminalité et conditions économiques*, was first published in Amsterdam in 1905. There was an English translation, *Criminality and Economic Conditions*, Boston: Little, Brown, 1916, and a much edited version, Bloomington: Indiana University Press, 1969.

[4] Enrico Ferri, *Criminal Sociology*, Boston: Little, Brown, 1917, 179; repr. New York: Agathon Press, 1967.

[5] Emmanuel Le Roy Ladurie, 'Violence, délinquence, contestation; de la violence à la filouterie', in Georges Duby and Armand Wellon, eds., *Histoire de la France rurale*, ii. *L'Âge classique des paysans 1340–1789*, Paris: Seuil, 1975.

Marx's theories also inspired one of the earliest attempts to explain the changing patterns of punishment. For Georg Rusche and Otto Kirchheimer punishment was a social phenomenon the form of which was structured in accordance with the dominant mode of production during the period in question. Penal punishment, in their reading, appears as another element within the broad strategy of ruling groups for controlling and managing the poor. Rusche and Kirchheimer's book had a long gestation, was eventually published on the eve of the Second World War but remained relatively unknown until a new edition, together with Italian and German versions, appeared at the close of the 1960s.[6] The new edition appeared at the same time as both a radical critique of prisons systems and the first wave of the recent research into the history of crime, which, while not necessarily Marxist, was underpinned by a perception of societies divided by class conflict.

In a detailed study of suicide the sociologist Émile Durkheim developed the notion of *anomie* by which he meant the disruption, even disappearance of value systems among individuals in the expanding cities of the nineteenth century. *Anomie* was subsequently applied by some criminologists as a way into explanations of crime. The idea that immigrants moved into burgeoning nineteenth-century cities and resorted to crime because they lacked any welfare assistance or traditional support networks was popular during the period itself and it has underpinned some of the work on nineteenth-century crime, though not always with any genuflection towards Durkheim.[7] It is much the same with certain of Durkheim's other ideas. He stressed, for example, that crime was something normal within society. Indeed it had a useful function to the extent that it enabled a society to identify and maintain its norms. The identification and subsequent punishment of an offender was a statement of a society's common indignation and common morality. And, at a time when penologists were claiming to develop rational punishments to reform the convict, he had no qualms about identifying passion as something at the heart of the punishment of offenders.[8]

---

[6] Georg Rusche and Otto Kirchheimer, *Punishment and Social Structure*, New York: Russell and Russell, 1968. The origin and history of the book, which was first published 1939, are explored in the extensive introduction to the French edition by René Lévy and Hartwig Zander, *Peine et structure sociale*, Paris: CERF, 1994.

[7] See e.g., J. J. Tobias, *Crime and Industrial Society in the Nineteenth Century*, Harmondsworth: Penguin, 1972.

[8] Howard Zehr, *Crime and the Development of Modern Society: Patterns of Criminality in Nineteenth-Century Germany and France*, London: Croom Helm, 1976, is significant for the way in which it begins and ends with Durkheim. For the significance of Durkheim's concept of punishment

Like Rusche and Kirchheimer's book, Norbert Elias's concept of the civilizing process was first published on the eve of the Second World War but did not achieve significant recognition until much later. The notion of a 'civilizing process' might appear to fit easily with the Whig interpretation but Elias's intention was more wide-ranging and complex. He did not understand civilization as a linear process of progress. It was constantly evolving, but ideas of material and humanitarian progress were largely irrelevant. Elias's principal focus was on the early modern period. His main concern was how the warlike culture of knights evolved into courtly society and the processes by which, initially among elite groups, a variety of human behaviours and experiences were pushed into the private sphere.[9] While not specifically focused on crime and punishment Elias's work has been influential in recent research in the area. It can be seen to fit with the *violence au vol* concept and as a theoretical framework for assessing the long-term decline of homicide. But it has also had a particular impact on attempts to explain changes in punishment. The Dutch historian Pieter Spierenburg has been most notable in picking up upon Elias's ideas in arguing that the brutalities of the scaffold decreased and eventually disappeared as elite groups became more and more sensitive to suffering and death.[10]

Without subscribing to a Whiggish perspective it is possible to argue that the period explored in the chapters that follow did indeed experience a degree of humanitarian progress in at least parts of the subject matter under investigation. The fact that the modern state in Europe no longer inflicts violent physical punishment in public on offenders, and the fact that there is no serious chance, as yet, of such punishment being reintroduced for crime, even in private, can readily be understood as progress. It is a similar situation in those states that no longer employ the death penalty. The role of state functionaries and the courts in seeking to suppress domestic violence, specifically the chastisement of

see David Garland, *Punishment and Modern Society: A Study of Social Theory*, Oxford: Clarendon Press, 1990.

[9] Norbert Elias, *The Civilizing Process: Sociogenetic and Psychogenetic Investigations*, rev. edn., Edmund Jephcott, Oxford: Blackwell, 2000.

[10] Pieter Spierenburg, *The Spectacle of Suffering: Executions and the Evolution of Repression*, Cambridge: Cambridge University Press, 1984. For a combative defence of the use of Elias's theories in explaining patterns of inter-personal violence see Pieter Spierenburg, 'Violence and the Civilizing Process: Does it Work?', *CHS* 5, 2 (2001), 87–105; and for a comparison and contrast of the explanatory values of Elias and Foucault, see idem, 'Punishment, Power and History: Foucault and Elias', *Social Science History*, 24, 4 (2004), 607–36.

wives, children, and servants, was and continues to be similarly progressive. Elias's theories have considerable explanatory value in all of this. But then the use of such theories presupposes an idea of some form of successive change in history and Michel Foucault, one of the most influential thinkers of the late twentieth century, suggested that this may not be the case.

The theories of Foucault provide a sharp challenge to the comfortable Whig perspective as well as to accepted concepts of change in history.[11] A moral philosopher and committed political activist, Foucault challenged traditional ideas of development over time, arguing that knowledge in a different period was bound by limits generated within that period alone. He sought also to highlight the shifting development of power relationships, and, across a variety of publications but most significantly in his book *Discipline and Punish*, he argued that there had been a shift from judicial to disciplinary modes of power particularly over the eighteenth and nineteenth centuries. The former system centred on the force of the monarch's will and the law and was characterized by harsh punishments inflicted on the body of the offender. Disciplinary modes of power, in contrast, regulated behaviour, movement, and thought by working on the mind rather than the body. They were characterized, metaphorically, by the all-seeing gaoler in Jeremy Bentham's model prison, the Panopticon. They were sustained largely by the scientific discourse of criminologists, doctors, and psychiatrists who specified symptoms and thus diagnosed subjects. The prison, in Foucault's analysis of the modern world, was the institution in which modern techniques for controlling human beings were at their most powerful and given free rein. Moreover, criminals brought together in new prisons could be assessed by experts who drew conclusions about what distinguished the criminal from the law-abiding and then presented solutions to the problem. Foucault's history is largely French in its orientation and its source material, but since the last quarter of the twentieth century his ideas have been particularly important in generating research and debate. Marie-Christine Leps, for example, has sought to develop his work through a discourse analysis of how the apprehension of crime and criminals contributed to the spread of a cheap daily press, and to the development of education and of welfare policies that were established, at

---

[11] In his review of *Discipline and Punish*, Clifford Geertz feared that with the kinds of ideas emanating from Foucault 'we seemed to be faced with a kind of Whig History in reverse—a history, in spite of itself, of the Rise of Unfreedom'. *New York Review of Books*, 26 January 1978.

least in part, to combat criminality.[12] But perhaps the most significant use and development of Foucault's ideas in this area have been made by Peter Becker.

Focusing on German sources, but with a clear eye on developments elsewhere, Becker has used Foucault's concept of discursive practice to delineate a shift during the nineteenth century from a master narrative concerning 'fallen men' (*gefallene Menschen*) to a master narrative of 'impaired men' (*verhinderte Menschen*). This shift also involved a gradual change in the kinds of men responsible for assessing the criminal. At the beginning of the century they were commonly practical men, police officers and judges, *Kriminalisten* who interacted with the criminal in public arenas and who were keen to chart his biography and to find the trigger for his descent into crime. By the end of the century the *Kriminalisten* had been largely superseded by the *Kriminologen*. The latter were anthropologists, medical men, and scientists, now described as criminologists, who saw the criminal as an object for experiment and investigation in the confines of an asylum, clinic, lecture hall, or prison. *Kriminalisten* considered the criminal as one of a group, a member of a criminal underworld who had joined that underworld by personal choice. *Kriminologen*, in contrast, were interested in the criminal as an individual and, particularly, in the extent to which he, and less commonly she, had been influenced by environment and heredity. By the end of the century the criminal was perceived as a threat to the social order not merely because of his activities but also because he was passing on his hereditary deficiencies to his offspring.[13]

Foucault's ideas have also contributed to sharpened gender awareness and a new cultural perspective in history. Crime has long been recognized as, overwhelmingly, a problem involving men, and usually young men. Female offending, at least in the period covered by this volume, was generally linked with prostitution, and much of the early work on women's crimes often focused on this issue. More recently, historians have been drawn to the ways in which women's bodies became central to any explanations of female criminality, and considerable attention has also been paid to domestic violence. This, in turn, has led to explorations of the support networks for such victims developed within communities. There have also been reviews

---

[12] Marie-Christine Leps, *Apprehending the Criminal: The Production of Deviance in Nineteenth-Century Discourse*, Durham, NC: Duke University Press, 1992.
[13] Peter Becker, *Verderbnis und Entartung:eine Geschichte der Kriminologie des 19. Jahrhunderts als Diskurs und Praxis*, Göttingen: Vandenhoeck und Ruprecht, 2002. See also Peter Becker and Richard F. Wetzell, *Criminals and their Scientists: The History of Criminology in International Perspective*, New York: Cambridge University Press, 2006.

of the gender variations in property crime, contrasting the ways in which men and women often stole for different reasons and took advantage of their physical presence or form of clothing to facilitate their behaviour.[14]

The cultural turn in history has shifted interest away from measurements, processes, and structures—the driving forces behind much social history—towards representations and narratives. History has always required a close reading of texts and the need to explore their unwitting testimony, but the new cultural history, often drawing on literary theory, has brought a greater sensitivity to the reading of texts and put new emphasis on debates about truth and objectivity. For the history of crime this has sometimes meant a focus on a particular kind of source or on a particular crime or criminal which could be explored in detail as a way into a set of social relationships at a specific moment. But the cultural turn has also emphasized the great variety of texts that were used by contemporaries and that are now used by historians to construct, analyse, and seek to understand criminal events and behaviours, and their corollaries. Recent research has also emphasized how these various texts—police reports, trial narratives, and various forms of popular culture—inter-react and draw from one another. And without wishing to fetishize the text too much, there are interesting issues and complexities about many of the narratives used by historians of crime and criminal justice. Police and trial narratives often depend on the memories of individuals angered, shocked, and even traumatized by the events that they experienced or witnessed. The narratives and texts of popular culture were constructed with very different motives, yet they commonly drew on the same events; moreover, the power of various forms of culture to help formulate stereotypes often appears reflected in what might be termed the official narratives.[15]

The role and significance of power play an important part in the work of Marx, Elias, and Foucault. There is a common assumption that power is in the hands of the elite within society, and in many respects it is impossible to quarrel with this. Under the old regime the powerful were those possessing privilege and property; in the modern bureaucratic state power has spread rather more to, in particular, governments, ministers, judges, police chiefs.

[14] Much of this work has focused on the English experience; see e.g., Shani D'Cruze, *Crimes of Outrage: Sex, Violence and Victorian Working Women*, London: UCL Press, 1998; Deirdre Palk, *Gender, Crime and Judicial Discretion, 1780–1830*, Woodbridge: Boydell Press/Royal Historical Society, 2006; Tammy C. Whitlock, *Crime, Gender and Consumer Culture in Nineteenth-Century England*, Aldershot: Ashgate, 2006.

[15] Amy Gilman Srebnick and René Lévy, eds., *Crime and Culture: An Historical Perspective*, Aldershot: Ashgate, 2005, provides a useful introduction; see in particular Srebnick's chapter, 'Does the Representation Fit the Crime? Some Thoughts on Writing Crime History as Cultural Text'.

If the system is working as the elite expects it to work, then, when a crisis emerges, the final decisions are made, and outcomes are decided by members of the ruling elite. But in the day-to-day functioning of society, power is delegated to a range of functionaries, magistrates, police, prison officers, and so on. Such delegated power can also be deployed in the interests of these functionaries as much as in the interest of the ruling elite. Finally, there are what James C. Scott described as the weapons of the weak which provide some degree of power to the poor and those with little or no say in the running of affairs.[16] The use of local dialects, of informal customary laws and sanctioning systems, and of kin networks can keep the state and its functionaries at arm's length. This was especially the case before the development of the bureaucratic nation state with its attempt to impose a unified law and language, but it was never completely suppressed during the nineteenth century. Recognition of this fragmentation of power does not negate the fact that a ruling elite, whatever its form, has the most authority and influence within a polity. But it serves to emphasize that the will of an elite, in penal policy for example, is mediated through a variety of relationships as it works down to street level, to the courts, and to the prisons.

An eclectic use of theory upsets and infuriates many purists. But a single theory rarely provides a convincing explanation for every single change and development. In particular, the major theories that seek to contribute to an understanding of changes in penal policy over time do not necessarily explain what historical actors thought they were doing. A key criticism that can be levelled at the Whig historians is that they took what penal and police reformers claimed they were doing at face value. More recently the term 'moral entrepreneur' has been appropriated to help understand such reformers. Moral entrepreneurs make a career out of identifying and raising alarm about a problem, proposing specific remedies, and offering themselves as the individuals to introduce and carry through the remedies.[17] The concept of the moral entrepreneur allows human agency; it also allows sincerity and genuine commitment on the part of human actors. On occasions, the deployment of some metahistories has reduced human actors to ciphers who acted in specific ways largely because they were required so to do because of deeper structures. A penal reformer of the

---

[16] James C. Scott, *Weapons of the Weak: Everyday Forms of Peasant Resistance*, New Haven: Yale University Press, 1987.

[17] The term was coined in Howard Becker, *Outsiders: Studies in the Sociology of Deviance*, New York: Free Press of Glencoe, 1963, ch. 8.

late eighteenth century might have thought that he was seeking to dissuade offenders from re-offending and remove what he considered to be brutal, degrading spectacles of punishment from public view. He (and I use the male pronoun advisedly since most public actors in this field were men) may indeed have considered his actions and aspirations as part of a civilizing process, though probably with much less nuance and with a rather different perception of such a process from Elias. But he would not have understood his efforts to be part of the development of what Foucault termed 'the carceral archipelago'. He may have been anxious about criminal and dangerous classes in burgeoning towns and cities, and keen to see these classes controlled, educated, and encouraged to an awareness of what he understood to be their role and their place in society. He may have had some perception of an idealized bourgeois order, but it is unlikely that his perception was of a well theorized, economically determined social structure of the kind delineated by Marx.

Historical actors generally work on a very different level to those historians and social scientists that subsequently interpret their actions in broad conceptual theories of change. Broad theories of historical change often have earnest disciples. They do not go unchallenged, not least by empiricists who charge them with inaccuracies and oversimplifications. But grand narratives can provide even the most severe empiricist or sceptic with useful hypotheses for interrogating patterns of change over time and the reasons for that change. Historians test their hypotheses and probe the past with the traces that remain of that past. What the historical actors did, created, wrote, said, and what can be deduced of what they thought, are essential to a historical understanding that keeps people at the heart of descriptions of social change and recognizes the role of chance, contingency, and compromise in both individual events and longer-term developments. At the beginning of his account of Louis Napoleon's *coup d'état* Marx commented that men make their own history 'but not of their own free will; not under circumstances they themselves have chosen but under the given and inherited circumstances with which they are directly confronted'.[18] He might also have added that things often do not turn out quite as intended. The aim of what follows here is to describe changes over time and how they have been interpreted, but also to endeavour to draw out what people thought they were doing and what they wanted to do within the pattern of change.

---

[18] Karl Marx, 'The Eighteenth Brumaire of Louis Bonaparte', in Karl Marx, *Political Writings*, ii. *Surveys from Exile*, ed. David Fernbach, Harmondsworth: Penguin, 1973, 146.

Two further points that appear often to become obscured in the search for theories of police and penal development are important to emphasize. First, laws are made by one set of actors but enforced by another. The policeman and the courts employ discretion in the ways that they use the law; indeed, there have been times when enforcers of the law significantly reshaped and remade it.[19] Second, it is important to remember that institutions created in one period are forced to adapt to changing circumstances that their creators almost certainly could never have envisaged. The courts and the police forces developed at the beginning of the nineteenth century, for example, were, by the close of the century, dealing with much bigger and more complex cities and towns, and with larger populations that had the potential for more rapid mobility. The institutions adapted, but these adaptations could push them in new directions with unexpected consequences.

Dates are important for history, especially political history, but they are not as important in the movements and patterns explored by cultural or social historians. In the case of law enforcement there can be changes in behaviour among the functionaries responsible for enforcement and implementation that stem from broad shifts in attitudes from both below, that is from the public, and above, that is from the functionaries' political masters. Setting any precise date on such changes is rarely possible. Nevertheless, political events can and did have an impact on the changes discussed in this book. The French Revolution, for example, facilitated new legal structures; the wars that followed the Revolution appeared to foster a new wave of offending and also enabled the spread of the new centralized French administrative model. Thus the chapters that follow are divided chronologically. But the point is stressed throughout that not every region in a country followed the same trajectory. Not only were the developments discussed here not linear, but what might be termed traditional community systems of norm enforcement continued in some regions while largely disappearing in other regions of what was, politically, the same state.

The changes discussed here also inter-reacted with and took place in the context of other significant developments, most notably the rise of the nation state and the emergence of a significant and increasingly literate public. Nineteenth-century Europe was divided into nation states and empires whose rulers were jealous of their authority and who largely achieved the aspirations of their Enlightenment predecessors to extinguish the alternative legal and

---

[19] Peter King, *Remaking Justice from the Margins: The Courts, the Law and Patterns of Lawbreaking, 1750–1840*, Cambridge: Cambridge University Press, 2006.

political structures of church and nobility. As will be discussed below, they also established policing systems that secured their centres, generally their capital cities, and proclaimed their presence in the more remote peripheries. Those bodies that were well integrated into, and subservient to the state were permitted to maintain certain of their penal and policing institutions. The larger municipalities are the best example here, though there were exceptions as, most notably perhaps, is demonstrated by the case of Italy.

When the French old regime authorized communities to draft *cahiers des doléances* on the eve of the Revolution it genuflected, reluctantly, to the emergence of public opinion. During the seventeenth and eighteenth centuries chapbooks and scaffold broadsides entertained the literate public, as well as those who could hear the stories recounted, with the adventures and crimes of highwaymen and murderers; the literature also warned against following the offenders' lifestyles. Gradually this kind of literature was replaced by novels, often written as gripping part-works, and by a popular, sensationalist daily press that provided true histories of real murders and robberies often luridly illustrated. Alongside the popular literature there was a steady growth in publications produced by experts in crime and criminality—penal reformers, police officers, and, by the close of the nineteenth century, members of the embryonic academic community of criminologists. Particularly interesting in this change of media form over time was the way that, consistently, the same group was stigmatized under different labels. The vagrants and beggars of the eighteenth century became the dangerous and criminal classes of the early nineteenth century. Their faults were their refusal to do an honest day's work, their love of luxury and drink, their feckless parents, and their own feckless parenting. By the end of the century the same group, with largely the same faults, were being assessed by an increasingly medical and psychiatric discourse that portrayed them as victims of their heredity. The similarity in ideas across frontiers of the European world meant that, while nation states and empires jealously guarded their independence and separateness, their penal experts often maintained the cosmopolitanism of the Enlightenment and were prepared to read each others' work, to exchange ideas, and to believe that they were developing rational, scientific, and humane structures. Yet, as the following chapters show and as the inter-war period demonstrates most acutely, even when the discourse remained similar, political ideology and contingency could generate very different practices and outcomes.

The ways in which different national contexts adopted, exploited, and reshaped ideas common across Europe is a recurrent issue in this book.

But to reiterate a point made in the preface, the book does not cover every country in Europe in equal measure. It seeks to describe the major changes in understanding crime and criminals, and the major institutional developments that were established to deal with crime and criminals. In the process, a series of key themes recur. First, and perhaps most obvious, is the increase of state intrusion and the erosion, though not necessarily the eradication, of local control and authority in matters of criminal justice. The book also highlights the tensions between ideas, usually for some kind of reform, and pragmatism—a tension that is not unique to the field of criminal justice. Third, while it has to be recognized that crime could be a terrifying and traumatic experience for victims and, at times, for their family and friends, the concept of the criminal was commonly one by which articulate commentators—many of whom had no direct experience of either crime or its perpetrators—sought to categorize and to stigmatize social groups whose lifestyle and experience they frowned upon and failed to comprehend.

PART I

THE OLD REGIME AND THE ENLIGHTENMENT

2

Laws and Punishments

MICHEL FOUCAULT began his account of the birth of the prison with a description of the execution of the would-be regicide Robert-François Damiens in March 1757. The violence inflicted on Damiens by the executioner and his assistants was horrific. Flesh was torn from his body with red-hot pincers. A mixture of molten lead, oil, sulphur, and wax was poured into the wounds. His limbs were then harnessed to horses so that they could be ripped off; but the latter was not as easy as had been assumed and the long-suffering Damiens had to have his joints severed with knives before the horses could do their job. Finally, his trunk was reduced to ashes. Foucault followed this account by printing the daily timetable of a young offenders' institution in Paris eighty years later. The execution and the timetable, he argued, each 'define a certain penal style'.[1] Reformers and the Whig historians of penal change would not have challenged Foucault's delineation of penal styles. But while the reformers and the Whigs thought in terms of the change as indicating humanitarian progress, for Foucault the styles showed something different. This was not humanitarian progress but a shift from penal repression being a spectacle and something directed at the body of the offender to penal repression as the deprivation of liberty and attempts to work on the 'soul' of the prisoner. Damiens's execution and the prison timetable thus become ideal types in two contrasting understandings of the shift in penal policy.

Ideal types are useful for the historian, but like any conceptualization they need to be probed. They can only provide a single representation to stand for a multiplicity of events, and the historian, who is always as concerned with the specific as with the general, needs to make further exploration of the complexities and varieties of the events that the ideal type is used to define. Damiens's torture and execution might stand for violence against the body, yet this event was unique in its violence. To find a parallel in the France

---

[1] Michel Foucault, *Discipline and Punish: The Birth of the Prison*, tr. Alan Sheridan, London: Allen Lane, 1977, 7.

of the old regime it is necessary to go back to 1610 and to the execution of François Ravaillac, the man who had assassinated Henri IV.[2] Damiens's judges themselves went back to this execution to assess what should be done with the man that they had sentenced. But, over the century and a half since Ravaillac's execution, the public executioner appears to have lost some of the 'skills' of his trade—hence the problem with the horses. Normally, those offenders executed in the century before the Revolution in France were either broken on the wheel or hanged. The former was brutal, but it was a much shorter ritual than the savagery inflicted on Damiens and, while it involved offenders having their limbs broken with an iron bar before the *coup de grâce*, arguably it was less grotesque. Hanging during the old regime was also horrific and prolonged. The victim strangled rather than having his or her neck broken by a drop and a well-placed knot. Nevertheless this slow strangulation at the end of a rope was still a very different procedure from the cruelty meted out to Damiens. So too was beheading, carried out with a sword or an axe depending upon regional or state traditions. Beheading, however, was something generally reserved for members of the nobility. It may well be that, during the old regime, there was a penal style that involved an assault on the body of the offender; after all, in addition to execution, there were various forms of corporal punishment and mutilation, notably branding and whipping. There were still shaming punishments that required an offender to be exhibited on the scaffold during an execution, bound to a post with an iron collar and a placard stating his or her offence, set in the stocks or the pillory. But the point of departure in this chapter is to emphasize that a violent assault on an offender's body was not the only penal style of the old regime. The aim here is to explore what jurists during the Enlightenment thought the criminal law was doing and what they thought it should be doing.[3]

Criminal law in continental Europe was based largely on Roman Law. The law of Ancient Rome had been revived in Italian universities during the

[2] Pascal Bastien, 'Usage politique des corps et rituel de l'exécution publique à Paris, XVII–XVIII siècles', *CHS* 6, 1 (2002), 31–56; 39.

[3] There is an excellent discussion of the situation in pre-revolutionary France that challenges many of Foucault's broad assertions in part 2 of Richard Mowery Andrews, *Law, Magistracy and Crime in Old Regime Paris, 1735–1789*, i. *The System of Criminal Justice*, Cambridge: Cambridge University Press, 1994. Pieter Spierenburg, 'Punishment, Power, and History: Foucault and Elias', *Social Science History*, 28, 4 (2004), 607–36, acknowledges that Foucault's overall perspective is not particularly contentious. Nevertheless, he emphasizes the complexities in the development of punishment by beginning with the description of a public execution in Paris in 1939 and contrasting it with the regulations for a prison in Amsterdam in 1595.

twelfth century and through the unity of medieval Christendom it spread and was developed by different jurisdictions. The most recognized formulation of the Roman Law was the *Consitutio Criminalis Carolina*. The *Carolina* had been issued by the Emperor Charles V in 1532 for use in imperial courts and it was recommended for those courts in the imperial territories where the emperor had no prescriptive rights. The *Carolina* established precise rules for criminal proceedings. These rules were inquisitorial, with the accused being the subject of a secret investigation by judges. There was no open court. The procedure of each case was carefully written up. The judges heard witnesses on oath, interrogated the accused, and could use torture to achieve a confession if there were sufficient grounds to suspect guilt. Since the accused could be convicted and sentenced only either on the evidence of two reliable witnesses who had actually seen the offence or on the evidence of a confession, then regulated torture became a key element of the trial. The problem was that in the plethora of jurisdictions within the Holy Roman Empire—electors, princes, free imperial cities, and so on—a variety of systems and practices functioned under the broad umbrella of the *Carolina*. Jurisdictions that were relatively close or even neighbours could act in different ways. In south-western Germany at the close of the seventeenth century, the court of the Catholic convent of St Peter in the Black Forest prosecuted offences against religion more often than offences against property. But in the Protestant, free imperial city of Ulm, the reverse was the case.[4] In Hungary there was a maze of legal codes and the gentry possessed some of the most extensive authority over the peasantry of anywhere in Europe. Hungarian serfs had no rights other than to obey their seigneur. The seigneur was responsible for protecting the lives and property of his serfs, but he also had complete jurisdiction over them and was bound by no rules of precedent. His powers could include *jus gladii*, the right of life and death. Even when the peasant was the plaintiff and the seigneur the defendant, the initial judgment was made in the seigneur's court. Any appeal, and an appeal was a complex process, was to a district judge answerable to a county assembly. This assembly (*megye*), in turn, was accountable to the local nobility. This situation survived the reforms of Joseph II during the 1780s and remained operative until the upheaval of 1848, at which time the *jus gladii* was held by 304 individuals and 167 corporations.[5]

---

[4] Bernd Roeck, 'Criminal Procedure in the Holy Roman Empire in Early Modern Times', *IAHCCJ Bulletin*, 18 (1993), 21–40.
[5] Béla K. Király, *Hungary in the Late Eighteenth Century: The Decline of Enlightened Despotism*, New York: Columbia University Press, 1969, 87–8 and n. 11. Király describes an extremely

Further east, and far beyond the bounds of the *Carolina*, the Russian elite boasted of customs that prohibited the killing of serfs. But the land-owning Russian nobility and gentry also considered themselves to be unfettered by law in their treatment of serfs and the kinds of ferocious punishments that they ordered for their peasantry could be tantamount to a death sentence. The tsar rarely challenged noble and gentry behaviour unless mass killing and brutality became so extreme as to suggest that some corrective, such as detention of the offending landowner in a monastery, was required.[6]

No human system is likely to remain static for long. The term 'the old regime' conjures an image of rigid, hierarchical, and unchanging structures. Yet the legal structures of the old regime were constantly shaped and reshaped in response to different pressures and changing ideas. In Denmark, for example, over the eighteenth century there was a gradual shift from an accusatorial procedure, that involved some sort of confrontation between accuser and accused in open court, to the inquisitorial system in which the accused ceased to be an active party and became the object of secret investigation by court officials. This change began with the appointment of a chief constable for Copenhagen in 1682. It was extended with the creation of the Inquisition Commission in 1686 that was intended to deal with military offences but which also took responsibility for cases of theft in Copenhagen. It culminated with an ordinance of 1796 that introduced the inquisitorial procedure formally into Danish Law.[7] In Russia a mishmash of old laws was made even more confused by Peter the Great's attempts to impose laws inspired by western European examples. Both accusatory and inquisitorial systems were in operation, often to the confusion of those involved. In 1767 Catherine the Great issued her celebrated *Nakaz* or Instruction to a commission established for preparing a new code of laws. This also drew on inspiration from the west, this time from Enlightenment ideas. The *Nakaz* did not lead to a new criminal code but some of its ideas appear to have trickled down into the way that certain, liberal-minded individuals interpreted the laws and made decisions about how to deal with offenders.[8] From the early

arbitrary system and I am grateful to my colleague Mark Pittaway for drawing my attention to the right and possibility of appeal.

[6] John P. LeDonne, *Absolutism and the Ruling Class: The Formation of the Russian Political Order 1700–1825*, New York: Oxford University Press, 1991, 209–10.

[7] Ditlev Tamm et al., 'The Law and the Judicial System', in Eva Österberg and Sølvi Bauge Sogner, eds., *People Meet the Law: Control and Conflict-Handling in the Courts. The Nordic Countries in the Post-Reformation and Pre-Industrial Period*, Oslo: Universitetsforlaget, 2000, 41–4.

[8] Isabel de Madariaga, *Politics and Culture in Eighteenth-Century Russia*, London: Longman, 1998, ch. 3; LeDonne, *Absolutism and the Ruling Class*, ch. 11.

eighteenth century some of the principalities and dukedoms in Italy and Germany sought, not always successfully, to simplify the complexities of their laws and to reduce the number of conflicting jurisdictions. Often this was a result of the prince or duke seeking to strengthen his own power and authority. But it was also the case that many princes became firmly wedded to ideas of legal and penal reform in keeping with the humanitarian and rational principles of the Enlightenment. Such ideas were both implicit and explicit in the work of a range of contrasting, but influential, thinkers such as the German moral philosopher Christian Wolff, the Italian scholar-priest Ludovico Muratori, and the celebrated French *philosophes*.[9]

During the final century of the old regime even a single state, possessed with what in the context of the time was a powerful monarch and centralized administration, did not necessarily have a single legal system in operation. France, a model for many absolutist princes, provides the best example. It had a legal structure based on Roman Law and the courts employed inquisitorial practice. The king was the ultimate source of law and his law took precedence over the *coutumes* of the provinces, but the centralization of the seventeenth century had failed to establish a single legal code. The *coutumes* agreed on broad categories within offences such as several different forms of theft: *vol simple* (petty larceny), *vol avec effraction* (breaking and entering), *vol en grand chemin* (highway robbery), and so on. They did not necessarily agree on how the different forms of theft should be treated.[10] But if the *coutumes* were varied and confusing, they were also widespread and popular with local seigneurs, not least because they were a manifestation of local particularism. They gave status to the seigneurs and some share in sovereignty. During the eighteenth century, moreover, a significant school of jurists spent time poring over the *coutumes* intent on establishing general principles from them. Again this was popular with the seigneurs since it buttressed their position with reference both to their vassals and to the monarch.

Seigneurial justice still existed in eighteenth-century France, with various nobles and gentry holding rights of high, medium, and low justice. Much of the justice administered by these courts concerned civil and feudal matters. The courts of low justice could also hear criminal cases for which the maximum punishment was a fine of around 10 *sous*; the precise amount

---

[9] See, e.g., Yves Cartuyvels, 'Éléments pour une approche généalogique du code pénal', *Déviance et Société*, 18, 4 (1994), 373–96.
[10] Olwen H. Hufton, *The Poor of Eighteenth-Century France, 1750–1789*, Oxford: Clarendon Press, 1974, 248–9.

appears to have varied according to the local *coutumes*. By the mid-eighteenth century inflation had rendered such justice all but meaningless. The medium courts could hear criminal cases for which punishment could be a larger fine but, again, inflation had whittled away at their relevance. A seigneurial court with the power of high justice might hear serious cases and order the death penalty, though the monarchy increasingly insisted that certain serious offences, notably murder, rebellion, rape, counterfeiting, were *cas royales* that might only be heard in royal courts. Also, from 1670 royal tribunals were able to take over any case that they considered to be taking too long in a seigneurial court.

The seigneurial courts functioning towards the end of the old regime have generally received a bad press and there is no doubt that there were problems. The exercise of high justice, for example, required the seigneur to maintain both a courthouse and a prison. The expense of such buildings, together with other costs that arose from the administration of justice, led many seigneurs to relinquish their rights or to economize in some fashion. In Brittany between 1650 and 1750 around 1,000, some 30 per cent, of the seigneurial courts disappeared.[11] On occasions seigneurs were known to refuse to pursue thieves and to avoid any involvement in criminal cases even when the *Maréchaussée*, the military police that patrolled the countryside, had identified the offender and made an appropriate arrest.[12] But in the twenty years before the Revolution royal advisers recognized these courts as offering considerable potential for the provision of lesser royal justice at a local level. In one respect their aspirations were swept away by the Revolution's abolition of feudalism; but in another they were met with the creation, in 1790, of a new local legal officer, the *juge de paix*.[13]

Similar seigneurial courts, with similar problems, existed outside France. In Piedmont, for example, the costs of enforcing law and order appear to have led the *signori* who possessed such powers to ignore them. The issue was one of several raised by a local legal thinker, Carlo Denina, in his *Dell'impiego delle persone*, written in 1777. The book was promptly banned by the Savoyard

---

[11] Anthony Crubaugh, *Balancing the Scales of Justice: Local Courts and Rural society in Southwest France, 1756–1800*, University Park: Pennsylvania State University Press, 2001, 18–21; Steven G. Reinhardt, *Justice in the Sarladais, 1770–1790*, Baton Rouge: Louisiana State University Press, 1991, 56–64; Olwen H. Hufton, 'Crime in Pre-Industrial Europe', *IAHCCJ Newsletter*, 4 (1981), 8–35; 16.

[12] Eric Hestault, *La Maréchaussée de Nantes (1770–1791)*, Maisons Alfort: Service historique de la *Gendarmerie* nationale, 2002, 371.

[13] Alain Follain, 'De la justice seigneuriale à la justice de paix', in Jacques-Guy Petit, ed., *Une justice de proximité, la justice de paix (1790–1958)*, Paris: Presses Universitaires de France, 2003.

monarchy.[14] While the French monarchs allowed inflation to whittle away at the nobles' preparedness to run their own courts, both Frederick the Great and Joseph II made more decisive moves in Prussia and Austria respectively. They each sought to ensure that no one should act as a judge in a seigneurial court unless he had successfully completed some legal training. In Austria, Joseph also required that the judges be paid in money rather than getting their remuneration from fines, taxes, and payment in kind such as 'cheese, sausages, and pickled tongues'. Arguably such requirements improved the system, but it is also the case that in Prussia at least, when an unqualified seigneur appointed a qualified judge for his patrimonial court, that judge invariably remained the seigneur's man.[15]

The royal courts in France had been growing in importance since the late Middle Ages as the monarchy and its jurists, determined to enhance royal authority, increasingly asserted the power of the crown over potential rivals. In some instances this was done in relatively quiet ways, such as allowing inflation to reduce the value of the fines that could be imposed by the seigneurial courts and thus making much of their judicial authority meaningless. At other times it was done in a public, assertive fashion through royal ordinances that limited the powers of, for example, municipal and church courts and extended the role of royal courts and royal judges. Most notable among the courts established by the monarchy to deal with criminal offences were the *bailliage* courts (in the north) and the *sénéchaussée* courts (in the south). Similarly the *prévôtés des maréchaux*, the courts of the military police (the *Maréchaussée*), that functioned across the whole of the kingdom, acquired increasing jurisdiction over civilian offenders. By the eighteenth century the royal courts were responsible for trying most criminal offences. But France under the old regime was home to a society rigidly segregated into distinct social orders and there was no understanding of equality before the law in the courts. Indeed, the social divisions in the country were reinforced in the law and by the application of the law. Members of the respectable classes who were accused of criminal offences commonly appeared before a *bailliage* or a *sénéchaussé* court. Poor offenders, and especially those with no fixed abode, commonly appeared before the *prévôté* courts. The latter,

[14] Michael Broers, *Napoleonic Imperialism and the Savoyard Monarchy, 1773–1821*, New York: Edwin Mellen Press, 1997, 132–3.
[15] Edith Murr Link, *The Emancipation of the Austrian Peasant, 1740–1798*, New York: Columbia University Press, 1949, 120–1; Robert M. Berdahl, *The Politics of the Prussian Nobility: The Development of a Conservative Ideology, 1770–1848*, Princeton: Princeton University Press, 1988, 60–2.

unlike the *bailliage* or *sénéchaussée* courts, had the power to pass a death sentence. Moreover, while the cases heard at a *bailliage* or *sénéchaussée* might be appealed to the local *parlement*, there was no appeal from the courts of the *Maréchaussée*.[16]

There were thirteen *parlements* in France. These were also foci for regional pride and independence, particularly among the elite. The position of magistrate in one of these institutions was venal but was commonly purchased by the eldest sons of previous members. These magistrates were supposed to have a law degree and to be over the age of 25. Some were very competent in the law, but it would appear that others had never been particularly diligent in their studies and it was usually possible to get dispensation so as to bypass the age requirement. The *parlements* were lawcourts but they also held some administrative authority and exercised an autonomous legislative power. The king's law was not promulgated in a region until it had been inscribed in the registers of the *parlements*, and the *parlements* had the right to challenge such a law, point out defects, and suggest improvements. Alongside the requirement to hear all cases brought before them and to validate capital offences in the region, the magistrates of the *parlements* regularly used their administrative powers to challenge the monarchy and the king's ministers in the closing decades of the old regime.

The *parlements*, and especially that of Paris, increasingly liked to think of themselves as a tribune for popular opinion. This posture appears to have contributed unwittingly to a shift in the understanding of the responsibility of criminals for their actions. During the old regime there was no requirement for the reasons behind any judgment in a criminal trial to be published. The argument was threefold. Challenges to verdicts were extremely limited, if not impossible, when no details were offered of how and why the judges had reached a verdict. Secrecy ensured that judges would not be bound by precedent in resolving a case; and secrecy was felt to ensure the independence of judges from any external pressure. However, from early on in the eighteenth century the *parlement* of Paris began to publish judgments (*arrêts criminels*) in criminal cases. From the middle of the century, at the moment when intellectual criticism of arbitrary justice was becoming more apparent, the *arrêts* became more frequent and provided more and more detail regarding the offender. The publication and frequency of these judgments increasingly

[16] Hufton, *The Poor of Eighteenth-Century France*, ch. 9; Julius R. Ruff, *Crime, Justice and Public Order in Old Regime France: The Sénéchaussées of Libourne and Bazas, 1696–1789*, London: Croom Helm, 1984, ch. 2.

directed the attention of the public away from punishment as a demonstration of the power of the king and his law, and towards the offender and his or her responsibility for a criminal act.[17]

England was different. Here there was no dominance of Roman Law, no inquisitorial system, no myriad of local jurisdictions; there was a significant degree of equality before the law and there was little secrecy. The criminal law, which has subsequently been labelled 'the Bloody Code', was a steady accretion of statutes authorizing the death penalty; some of these statutes covered the same types of offences as others but related to specific venues. Changes in economic and social relations also led to new offences, most significantly with new capital legislation for forgery. The polite and commercial English people could not afford to have their expanding economy undermined by the concerns about financial credit and commercial trust that such an offence implied. Legislation against embezzlement was introduced for similar reasons, though this offence was rather more difficult to define in legal terms.[18] The king's courts covered the whole country and local, private jurisdictions had very little authority. Criminal offences were dealt with by royal judges who sat at the Old Bailey in London or in the assize courts that, in most counties, met twice a year. Magistrates heard other criminal cases either in the quarter sessions, that were held four times a year to administer all of the administrative business of a county, or, more frequently, in summary courts. In contrast to the inquisitorial system of the Continent, the trials at the Old Bailey, at assizes, and at quarter sessions were held in public. Eighteenth-century newspapers reported trials at quarter sessions and assizes and the records of the Old Bailey were published at the close of each session from the late seventeenth century. The accused and the accuser confronted each other face to face in court and in the presence of a jury. England was divided socially, but, unlike the situation in many European states, the social division was rarely carried formally into the criminal law; the game laws were the exception that proved the rule. While people of wealth and social standing had considerable advantages in the English courts, they were subject to the same laws and the same procedures. The public execution and anatomical

---

[17] Pascal Bastien, 'Private Crimes and Public Executions: Discourses on Guilt in the *Arrêts Criminels* of the Eighteenth-Century Parliament of Paris', in Amy Gilman Srebnick and René Lévy, eds., *Crime and Culture: An Historical Perspective*, Aldershot: Ashgate, 2005.

[18] Randall McGowen, 'From Pillory to Gallows: The Punishment of Forgery in the Age of the Financial Revolution', *Past and Present*, 165 (1999), 107–40; John P. Locker, '"This most pernicious of crimes": Embezzlement in its Public and Private Dimensions, 1850–1930', Ph.D., Keele University, 2004, 95–107.

dissection of Laurence, Lord Ferrers for the murder of his steward in 1760 may have been an exceptional incident—lords of the realm did not make a habit of murdering their stewards, and the overwhelming majority of the people hanged at Tyburn were poor and untitled—but it could be used to demonstrate a form of equality before the law. In its way Ferrers's execution provided as significant a metaphor for the English assertion of equality before the law as the execution of Damiens was, subsequently, to provide for Foucault's assertion of the old regime's use of the body for punishment. Moreover, for all the exceptionality of the Ferrers case, eighteenth-century Englishmen appear to have believed that they enjoyed a degree of equality before the law quite distinct from their continental neighbours.

Eighteenth-century 'freeborn Englishmen', as they liked to proclaim themselves, took pride in this equality before the law and there were distinguished foreign observers who flattered them in their beliefs.[19] The English also enjoyed considerable latitude when it came to abusing their monarch and their government in cartoon and print. There were abuses when it came to reporting crime; one provincial newspaper appears to have concocted a string of highway robberies simply to boost its sales. In a notorious forgery case involving the twin brothers Daniel and Robert Perreau and Margaret Rudd there were concerns that press reporting made an impartial trial impossible. The case of the 'London Monster', who attacked women in the metropolis in the early 1790s, was reported with all of the lurid sensationalism generally associated with the newspapers of a later century.[20] All of this constituted a freedom of the press on a scale unknown on continental Europe. Moreover there were legal safeguards that protected the subject from the king, his ministers, and other powerful individuals. Most significant here was the Habeas Corpus Act which prevented the arrest and holding of any individual without a specific charge. The act could be suspended, wide-ranging general warrants could still facilitate the arrest of a large number of people who were not named on the warrant, and certain forms of prosecution, such as the ex-officio information, could still put an individual in court with little idea of his offence. But these practices were exceptional and English

---

[19] See e.g. Montesquieu, *De l'esprit des lois*, bk. 6, ch. 3; Voltaire, *Lettres philosophiques* (usually translated as *Letters on the English*), esp. Letter VIII, On Parliament, and Letter IX, On Government.

[20] Peter King, 'Newspaper Reporting, Prosecution Practice and Perceptions of Urban Crime: The Colchester Crime Wave of 1765', *Continuity and Change*, 2, 3 (1987), 423–54; Donna T. Andrew and Randall McGowen, *The Perreaus and Mrs Rudd: Forgery and Betrayal in Eighteenth-Century London*, Berkeley: University of California Press, 2001; Jan Bondeson, *The London Monster: A Sanguinary Tale*, Cambridge, Mass.: Da Capo, 2002.

liberty stood out particularly in contrast to the situation in France where the *lettre de cachet*, in particular, became a symbol of the arbitrariness of the regime.

The *lettre de cachet* was an order of the king that enabled the imprisonment of an individual for an unspecified time and without any specific charge. Such letters were often prepared by officials such as the *Lieutenant générale de police de Paris* and were most often used by families seeking to control dissolute, drunken, or libertine family members, rather than by the king and his ministers acting against political opponents or critics. Nevertheless it was the latter, sinister image that came to symbolize the *lettre* and make it a target for the critics of French absolutism.[21] The sinister image was also maintained by attempts to silence critics of the regime who had chosen to live outside France. A series of attempted kidnappings, and possible attempts at murder, of exiles living in Britain reinforced the complaints that the Bourbon monarchy was despotic and, at the same time, reinforced English boasts about their liberties.[22]

During the eighteenth century French critics of the old regime commonly started their analyses by questioning what had first prompted humans to enter into societies. Many concluded, drawing their inspiration from John Locke, that society had been established for the safety and the security of persons and property. And if such was its origin, then it was incumbent on society to provide such safety and security. Inflicting harm on an individual by an assault or by damage to, or appropriation of his or her property became perceived as a breach of the social contract. Security, moreover, in the understanding of these thinkers meant freedom from arbitrary arrest and equality before the law. Denis Diderot argued, for example, that a society would be truly happy if liberty and property were secure, if taxes were fairly apportioned, if talent and virtue were rewarded, and 'if all citizens are equally subjected to the laws'.[23] At the same time the old medieval fusion of the spiritual and the temporal worlds was disintegrating under the combined pressure of rational thought and the emergence of states that jealously asserted their authority over the church. People educated in the ideas of the Enlightenment

[21] Claude Quétel, *De par le Roy: Essai sur les lettres de cachet*, Paris: Privat, 1981; Arlette Farge and Michel Foucault, *Le désordre des familles: lettres de cachet des Archives de la Bastille*, Paris: Gallimard/Julliard, 1982.
[22] Simon Burrows, 'Despotism within Bounds: The French Secret Police and the Silencing of Dissent in London, 1760–1790', *History*, 84, 4 (2004), 525–48.
[23] 'Observations sur le Nakaz', in Denis Diderot, *Political Writings*, tr. and ed. John Hope Mason and Robert Wokler, Cambridge: Cambridge University Press, 1992, 124; see also his article 'Autorité politique' in *L'encyclopédie*.

considered human beings to be largely responsible for their own behaviour and for their successes and failures in life. And if some peasants, particularly, still thought in terms of God's will or the Devil's temptation encouraging actions, businessmen increasingly saw profit as the result of good sense and management, while losses were the result of miscalculation or an individual's malfeasance.

This shift from heaven to earth was not uniform; religion remained central for the understanding and implementation of law in Russia, for example, and it continued to play an important role elsewhere.[24] But the shift was increasingly apparent in attitudes towards punishment and the use of the law to maintain religious orthodoxy. In the German lands a religious element was to be found less and less in the ritual of the public execution and in the reporting of executions.[25] Increasing calls for the toleration of minority faiths and increasing criticism of the prosecution of moral and religious offences were exemplified in France by the cases of Jean Calas and the Chevalier de La Barre. The former involved an elderly Protestant of Toulouse who was broken on the wheel for allegedly murdering a son who wished to convert to Catholicism. The latter involved a young nobleman, tortured, mutilated, and then beheaded for alleged blasphemy. Both cases provoked an outcry, especially that of Calas. Royal judges eventually declared him to have been innocent, and within a decade public opinion in Toulouse, helped by the appointment of a new archbishop, had swung to a liberal perspective critical of the execution. The shift was symptomatic of a changing attitude among much educated public opinion in France; this opinion was increasingly uncomfortable with the use of the secular arm to establish religious uniformity.[26] As these cases suggest, the church and its ideology remained influential and powerful but princes were increasingly establishing their supremacy in the extended conflict between church and state in the same way that they were establishing supremacy over their nobles and independent cities. France was not exceptional in witnessing such developments. The new legal code introduced into Tuscany in 1786, for example, was unquestionably liberal and 'enlightened' but it was also a

[24] LeDonne, *Absolutism and the Ruling Class*, 202–3.

[25] Richard J. Evans, *Rituals of Retribution: Capital Punishment in Germany 1600–1987*, Oxford: Oxford University Press, 1996, pp. 124–5 and 154–6.

[26] David D. Bien, *The Calas Affair: Persecution, Toleration and Heresy in Eighteenth-Century Toulouse*, Princeton: Princeton University Press, 1960; Max Gallo, *Que passe la justice du roi: vie, procès et supplice du chevalier de La Barre*, Paris: Robert Laffont, 1987; John McManners, *Church and Society in Eighteenth-Century France*, 2 vols., Oxford: Clarendon Press, 1998, ii. ch. 45.

significant act in the struggle over independent authority between the Grand Duke and the Pope.[27]

The shifting attitudes towards religion also involved a move away from the understanding of God as a figure of wrath and a greater focus on him as the God of love. Fashionable sermons contained more references to consolation and put less emphasis on eternal punishment. Fashionable clergy indulged in that conversation and literature which was becoming infused with Romantic sensibility and, in a climate that considered appeals to the heart as more persuasive than threats of hellfire, there was a growing disquiet about the use of torture and the public infliction of pain and death. For those clergy and for others who subscribed to the new sensitivities, moreover, a death on the scaffold focused attention on the sufferings of the offender rather than on the crime. It also raised questions about God's ultimate intentions for human beings as well as about the potential for an individual's improvement.[28]

There were still those who, throughout eighteenth and even at the beginning of the nineteenth century, considered torture to be essential for the criminal process and hence for the general good. Without torture, its advocates insisted, guilty men would go unpunished. When Catherine the Great ordered that it be used only with the utmost caution, there were large numbers of landowners and gentry who objected. Her enlightened comments on the topic in the great *Nakaz* were no better received.[29] The Austrian legal code of 1768 contained illustrated instructions of how various methods of torture should be administered.[30] Yet, across Europe, concerns about the use of torture were becoming apparent at least by the end of the seventeenth century. It has been convincingly argued that by then both judges and jurists were increasingly regarding its use as an unsatisfactory means of securing proof in criminal cases. Judges, in consequence, began to permit offenders to be convicted and sentenced for less serious crimes that did not require such strict forms of proof and, hence, the use of torture.[31] Where it continued to be used, torture continued to produce awkward anomalies and

[27] John A. Davis, *Conflict and Control: Law and Order in Nineteenth-Century Italy*, Basingstoke: Macmillan, 1988, 128–9.

[28] McManners, *Church and Society*, ii. 73–5; Randall McGowen, 'The Changing Face of God's Justice: The Debate over Divine and Human Punishment in Eighteenth-Century England', *CJH* 9 (1988), 63–98.

[29] Madariaga, *Politics and Culture*, 107.

[30] Evans, *Rituals of Retribution*, 110 and 112–13; Gordon Wright, *Between the Guillotine and Liberty: Two Centuries of the Crime Problem in France*, Oxford: Oxford University Press, 1983, 14–15.

[31] John H. Langbein, *Torture and the Law of Proof: Europe and England in the Ancien Régime*, Chicago: University of Chicago Press, 1977.

ammunition for its critics. In Amsterdam in 1766 Nathaniel Donker and his lover, Dorothea (known as Dora) Bosselman, murdered Nathaniel's wife. Before being tortured Nathaniel confessed to the murder; he was convicted and was broken on the wheel. But Dora resisted first the shin screws and then a whipping while suspended by her arms with weights on her feet. She could not be sentenced for murder as she had not confessed; nevertheless the judges were able to sentence her to fifty years in the Spinhouse, a prison for women in Amsterdam, to be followed by eternal banishment from the city. But the judges were worried. Visitors came into the public ward of the prison to view the inmates. Dora was young and attractive; she was also partly paralysed as a result of the torture. Some visitors to the public ward shunned the sight of tortured criminals. But the judges feared that Dora might tell visitors that she had been maltreated and so they ordered that she be kept in the secret ward.[32]

Even though judges and jurists may have been turning their backs on the use of judicial torture, the opportunity to abolish it provided several eighteenth-century princes with a way of demonstrating their personal commitment to the Enlightenment and its humanitarian ideals. Frederick the Great, for example, condemned torture as cruel and useless; he protested that hardened offenders might withstand it while an innocent but weak individual might yield to it.[33] He restricted the use of torture shortly after succeeding his father to the throne in 1740; he abolished it in 1754. A generation later Gustavus III of Sweden abolished torture as one plank in his raft of policies that aimed to establish what he considered to be a more humane and rational penal system with justice administered more speedily and more equitably. In Austria, Baden, Bavaria, Saxony, Württemberg, and other lesser German states, torture was restricted or simply ceased to be used as a prelude to abolition. But formal abolition sometimes had to await French domination early in the nineteenth century. In Hanover it was used as late as 1818 but abolished four years later.[34] In France from at least the late seventeenth century there had been expressions of doubt about the use of torture as a means of identifying the guilty from the innocent. The Ordinance of 1670 authorized judges to pass sentences, though not of death, on any accused against whom there was significant circumstantial evidence but who had

---

[32] Pieter Spierenburg, *Written in Blood: Fatal Attraction in Enlightenment Amsterdam*, Columbus: Ohio State University Press, 2004, esp. 104–5 and 112–13.

[33] 'Dissertation sur les raisons d'établir ou d'abroger les lois', in F. D. E. Preuss, ed., *Œuvres de Frédéric le Grand*, 30 vols., Berlin, 1846–56, ix. 28–9.

[34] Evans, *Rituals of Retribution*, 115.

refused to confess even under torture. As a result, the use of torture appears to have declined markedly in many parts of France during the eighteenth century. In 1780 *la question préparatoire*, by which the accused was tortured to provide a confession, was abolished. Eight years later *la question préalable*, by which an offender was tortured to reveal his or her accomplices, was also abolished.[35]

Torture was part of the judicial process rather than part of the punishment, and punishments themselves changed in the last century of the old regime, but not always for the same reasons. Those who could pay were often punished with a fine; petty offenders from the poorer sections of society were commonly subjected to some form of corporal punishment such as a whipping or a mutilation, most commonly branding on some part of the body. The latter enabled recidivists to be identified and then subjected to a harsher punishment for subsequent offending. Individuals might be banished from their home communities for a fixed period of years or subjected to the shame of the pillory. In England the use of the pillory gradually declined, partly, it appears, because the authorities were concerned that they could no longer control it. For some offenders, notably homosexuals, the pillory could be tantamount to a capital sentence with very severe injuries and even death inflicted by the missiles hurled by a hostile crowd. For others, such as those who caught the imagination of the crowd by publishing a critique of an unpopular ministry or a popular, but legally seditious, political pamphlet, the pillory could be a coronation. In these instances the condemned was feted by the crowd, showered with flowers, and even rewarded with a public collection. But arguably also shaming punishments in England were ceasing to have much impact in a society where reputation was beginning to depend less and less on public show and more and more on the written word, on an individual's position and profession, and on their good works.[36] Where noble and gentry caste were involved, however, shaming punishments were contentious. In Vienna, in the name of legal equality, Joseph II instructed that the offenders from the gentry should be required to work on the chain gangs charged with cleaning and repairing the streets and sewers. His noble subjects were outraged, regarding the order as a shaming of their entire estate. 'This severe justice levelling everybody before the law, seemed to me

---

[35] Wright, *Between the Guillotine and Liberty*, 9 and 15.

[36] Robert Shoemaker, 'Male Honour and the Decline of Public Violence in Eighteenth-Century London', *Social History*, 26 (2001), 190–208; idem, 'Street of Shame? The Crowd and Public Punishments in London, 1700–1820', in Simon Devereaux and Paul Griffiths, eds., *Penal Practice and Culture, 1500–1900: Punishing the English*, London: Palgrave, 2004.

unfair' recalled one gentlewoman; 'to condemn a count, a councillor, or a distinguished citizen to street sweeping, just as if they were ordinary workers or domestics.'[37]

Joseph II's penal policy, like that of his younger brother Leopold when Grand Duke of Tuscany, echoed some of the proposals of the Italian savant Cesare Beccaria. *Dei delitti e delle pene* (On Crimes and Punishments) was published by Beccaria in 1764. The pamphlet has been considered as heralding a sea-change in attitudes to punishment and fostering a new humanitarian perspective. It has also been criticized as ambiguous, contradictory, and ultimately conservative. The ambiguities may have been generated by Beccaria's personal difficulty in putting pen to paper or by the common practice of thinkers of the Enlightenment to employ obscurity in the hope of avoiding the censor. The conservative elements of the pamphlet, such as Beccaria's unstinting support for property, industry, and the authority of the prince, made the work acceptable to monarchs and governments who could subscribe to liberal and humanitarian penal reform while, at the same time, hoping to develop more effective systems of control. Essentially Beccaria encapsulated and crystallized much Enlightenment thinking rather than presenting a great number of original ideas. The pamphlet was rapidly translated and it had an immediate impact across Europe.[38]

Beccaria opposed the death penalty and, rather more ambiguously, torture. Criminal laws were necessary for society but the existing laws, he believed, had been created in previous centuries in moments of passion. They needed to be reconstructed dispassionately and rationally, by individuals guided by principles of utility and determined to ensure the greater happiness and security of the majority. Punishment, he insisted, should be perceived as the logical outcome of committing a crime; it should be administered in proportion to the seriousness of the crime, and it should be administered equally, whatever an offender's social rank. To ensure that

---

[37] Quoted in Saul K. Padover, *The Revolutionary Emperor: Joseph II of Austria*, 2nd edn., London: Eyre and Spottiswoode, 1967, 139; see also T. C. W. Blanning, *Joseph II*, London: Longman, 1994, 82.

[38] The literature on Beccaria is considerable. For a recent, favourable perspective see Michel Porret, *Beccaria: le droit de punir*, Paris: Éditions Michalon, 2003; for the spread of his pamphlet across Europe see Michel Porret, ed., *Beccaria et la culture politique des lumières*, Geneva: Droz, 1997. For more critical perspectives see Philip Jenkins, 'Varieties of Enlightenment Criminology', *BJC* 24 (1984), 112–30; Graeme Newman and Pietro Marongiu, 'Penological Reform and the Myth of Beccaria', *Criminology*, 28 (1990), 325–46. The two latter articles are reprinted in Piers Beirne, ed., *The Origin and Growth of Criminology: Essays on Intellectual History, 1760–1945*, Aldershot: Dartmouth Publishing, 1994.

punishment followed rapidly on a crime, and that punishment was correspondingly associated as a logical outcome, there were to be no long drawn out legal processes. Those awaiting trial should not be incarcerated with those already convicted. If murder was wrong, then so too was killing authorized by the courts; in place of the death penalty, Beccaria proposed perpetual slavery (*schiavitù perpetua*). The image of convicted offenders forced to work in the public gaze would, he reasoned, be a much greater deterrent than the scaffold since executions were over fairly rapidly.

Moves towards the abolition of torture were, as described above, already well developed by the time of the publication of Beccaria's book. His stand on the death penalty was much more controversial. Some princes, jurists, and *philosophes* were sympathetic from both humanitarian and utilitarian perspectives: death, after all, robbed a society of a man's productive labour. Joseph II in Austria and Grand Duke Leopold in Tuscany both abolished the death penalty in their new legal codes, but they maintained fearsome punishments. This was especially the case with Joseph's *Allgemeines Gesetz über Verbrechen und deren Bestrafung* (1787) which authorized public floggings, branding with hot irons, and lifelong periods of imprisonment, sometimes in chains in tiny cells. In Russia the situation was much the same. The Empress Elizabeth had announced her determination never to confirm a death sentence when she seized the throne in 1741. Her temporary *Ukaz* of 1754 abolished the death penalty until a new criminal code was established. A flogging with the whip known as the knout, however, could be tantamount to a death sentence. Catherine the Great's *Nakaz* of 1767 drew directly on Beccaria with its emphases on punishments fitting the crime and the deterrent requirement of punishment. But although Elizabeth's abolition of the death penalty remained in force and while Catherine was critical of torture, Catherine made no attempt to limit the potential for death under the knout. Voltaire was obsequious and full of admiration for her penal proposals; Diderot's observations, in contrast, revealed a personal ambivalence towards the death penalty:

In [Paris] fewer than 150 men are put to death each year. In all the courts of France scarcely that number are tortured. That is, 300 men in 25 million, or one man in 83,000. Is not more damage done by vice, exhaustion, a ball, parties, danger, a ruined courtesan, a carriage, mischance, cold or a bad doctor? To save the life of a man is always an excellent deed, even though there may be a presumption against this man which does not apply to the victim of a bad doctor. From this I only draw the conclusion that there are many disadvantages [to Beccaria's ideas] which are in different ways serious and which have not received any attention.[39]

Others among those who claimed 'enlightenment' supported the continuance of the death penalty. In Prussia Frederick the Great considered that there were some offenders, notably arsonists and murderers, who deserved to be executed and whose death should be public because of the impression that this made. But the death sentence also concerned him. He looked for alternatives when offenders were young. He aspired to remove the stigma that prompted some young, unmarried women to murder their newborn children for the sake of preserving their honour and continuing in employment. And always he urged that the greatest thought and care be taken when passing a death sentence.[40]

Plenty of jurists and churchmen could be called upon to defend the status quo. Catholic Spain contained some of the most fervent critics of Enlightenment thought, and especially of legal reform and the abolition of torture. The Spanish translation of Beccaria's *Dei delitti* first appeared with a warning after the title page that it was not intended to subvert the laws of the kingdom; even so, it took only three years for the Inquisition to add the book to the Index of prohibited works.[41] In France the leading jurist Pierre-François Muyart de Vouglans condemned Beccaria and argued that capital punishment remained an important deterrent. Leniency, he believed, bred crime.[42] In England Archdeacon William Paley defended the death penalty as providing deterrence through terror. Paley stressed that the law was not administered mechanically and indiscriminately in England. Large numbers of those condemned to death were reprieved by the royal prerogative of mercy that was available to any who appeared deserving. Human justice, in Paley's eyes, could not be like God's justice and if the English executed more it was because this was preferable to the French system of control and surveillance by police.[43]

---

[39] 'Observations sur le Nakaz', 119; Diderot also took the utilitarian principle in a sinister direction. In the article on Anatomy in the *Encyclopédie*, Diderot suggested that the death of a felon would be of more use to society if it occurred under the knife of a surgeon anatomist rather than at the hands of an executioner on a scaffold. Jeremy Bentham took a rather similar approach: see Janet Semple, *Bentham's Prison: A Study of the Panopticon Penitentiary*, Oxford: Clarendon Press, 1993, 30–1

[40] Frederick to Condorcet, 24 October 1785, in Preuss, ed., *Œuvres de Frédéric*, xxv. 379–80; Frederick to Voltaire, 11 October 1777, in Theodore Bestermann, ed., *Voltaire's Correspondence*, 103 vols. Geneva: Insitut et Musée Voltaire, 1953–65 xcvii. 122–3.

[41] Richard Herr, *The Eighteenth-Century Revolution in Spain*, Princeton: Princeton University Press, 1958, 60–2, 205–6 and 215.

[42] Wright, *Between the Guillotine and Liberty*, 15.

[43] V. A. C. Gatrell, *The Hanging Tree: Execution and the English People, 1770–1868*, Oxford: Oxford University Press, 1994, 202–3 and 517–19.

Technically death remained the punishment for felony in England through-out the eighteenth century, but concerns about the number of offenders who might fall into the category and the belief that it was impossible simply to keep increasing the numbers executed had led to the development of the secondary punishment of transportation. In the half-century following the Transportation Act of 1718 some 50,000 convicts were shipped across the Atlantic, principally to the southern colonies of Maryland and Virginia.[44] Combinations of exile and labour were tried elsewhere. The idea of exil-ing an offender had a long pedigree and in the early modern period exile from a city state had been a significant punishment. In Russia punishment required penance and redemption; the former might be achieved through a flogging but from the eighteenth century subsequent redemption might mean banishment and banishment, always for perpetuity, was a means of populating Siberia. Peter the Great developed these practices using convicts, as well as serfs and prisoners of war, for building St Petersburg as well as a variety of factories, fortresses, roads, and ships. In 1722 he ordered further that criminals be sent with their wives and children to the region of the silver mines in eastern Siberia. The practice, known as *katorga* (derived from the Greek verb 'to force'), was regarded as a great success and was continued for more than two centuries by his successors.[45] Mediterranean countries, which had war fleets of galleys, sometimes sent petty offenders or rounded up able-bodied vagrants to serve as oarsmen on the ships. Spain and several of the Italian states acted in this way; so too did France, which sent a mixture of offenders—army deserters, Protestants, smugglers, and thieves as well as vagabonds—to be oarsmen on the galley fleet based in Marseilles. The decline of the galley as a ship of war required alternative postings and, following an Ordinance of 1748, the French *galériens* began to be dispatched to construct projects such as the Canal du Midi. But, particularly, they were set to work in the great naval arsenals of Brest, Rochefort, and Toulon. In Brest, between 1750 and 1753, a massive stone structure known as the *bagne* was built for the convicts and their work. By the mid-1770s the Protestants had been released, the numbers of army deserters and smugglers had declined, and the overwhelming majority of the

---

[44] A. Roger Erkich, *Bound for America: The Transportation of British Convicts to the Colonies, 1718–1775*, Oxford: Clarendon Press, 1987; Gwenda Morgan and Peter Rushton, *Eighteenth-Century Criminal Transportation: The Formation of the Criminal Atlantic*, Houndmills, Basingstoke: Palgrave, 2004.

[45] Le Donne, *Absolutism and the Ruling Class*, 205; Anne Applebaum, *Gulag: A History of the Soviet Camps*, London: Allen Lane, 2003, 16–17.

galériens were petty thieves.[46] Across the eighteenth century the number of food thieves sentenced to deprivation of liberty rose steadily from 15 per cent between 1700 and 1724, to 20 per cent between 1725 and 1749, to 39 per cent from 1750 to 1774 and to 45 per cent in the next fifteen years.[47] The increase was particularly marked in those sentenced to the galleys, but the courts, and others, were also beginning to give serious consideration to the prison as the place of punishment and also the reformation of criminal offenders.

The idea of depriving offenders of their liberty and of requiring them to work was not something new to the eighteenth century. There is a broad distinction, particularly used in the United States, between gaols, where people awaiting trial were held, and prisons, where those who had been before a court of some sort served a sentence. A similar kind of division existed in the eighteenth century, with debtors included amongst those held in gaols, though the distinction was often blurred as the complaints about the mixing of offenders made by Beccaria, and many others, testified. Some nobles and people who were held for political offences were commonly put in fortresses such as the notorious Bastille situated on the eastern edge of Paris. But confinement, with labour within that confinement, was reserved for offenders from the poorer classes. 'Houses of correction', often called Bridewells in England and sometimes 'houses of discipline' (*tuchthuizen*) in the Netherlands and (*Zuchthäuser*) in Germany, had been established, particularly in northern Europe, during the sixteenth century as a way of dealing with specific individuals, notably vagrants, petty thieves, and prostitutes. The church and private philanthropic organizations were especially involved in the creation of asylums for prostitutes. In all of these institutions the intention was to reform the offenders and inculcate industrious habits. Other kinds of offender were sometimes incarcerated, such as libertine members of well-to-do families confined at their family's request; but these particular individuals were kept separate from their social inferiors, were excused labour, and were paid for by their embarrassed families. In France the *hôpitaux généraux* set up during the seventeenth century performed similar functions, but opened their doors also to widows and orphans as well as the various kinds of offender. On the eve of the Revolution the ten units of the *hôpital* in Paris housed some 10,000

---

[46] Jacques-Guy Petit, Nicole Castan, et al., *Histoire des galères, bagnes et prisons, XIIIe–XXe siècles*, Toulouse: Privat, 1991, ch. 3 and 6 (both by André Zysberg); Andrews, *Law, Magistracy and Crime*, 330–43.

[47] Arlette Farge, *Délinquence et criminalité:le vol d'aliments à Paris au XVIII siècle*, Paris: Plon, 1974, 84–5.

persons with 2,000 staff which, in total, was about 2 per cent of the city's population.[48] The complexity of these different institutions, the mixing of different groups, the separation of others, together with the appalling physical state and the abuses found in many of them were exposed by the work of an Englishman, John Howard in 1777.

Howard's book, *The State of the Prisons in England and Wales*, was published at a moment of particular difficulty for the British government with regard to penal policy. The war in America had effectively ended transportation until an alternative could be found. A stopgap had been provided by the use of old warships, the hulks, to confine convicts and, even after the decision to renew transportation to a new penal colony in Australia, reformers continued to urge an alternative direction for punishment. The reformers took their cue from Howard's comprehensive study of the situation in England and Wales, which he augmented with continental European examples. Like Beccaria's book, Howard's work crystallized much contemporary thinking, but unlike Beccaria he provided a wealth of detailed example to support his arguments. Howard was shocked by the abuses, disorder, neglect, and squalour that he found in many gaols and prisons. He wanted the prison to be informed with ideas of Christian charity and this meant gaolers and the magistrates who were responsible for supervising them should accept the responsibility for running honest, reforming institutions. In developing these ideas Howard formulated the concept of the prison as the natural shape for punishment. Some local magistrates took up his ideas and began to reform and rebuild their local gaols; forty-two new gaols and houses of correction were built in England between 1779 and 1787. The British Parliament agreed to establish two model penitentiaries, one for women and one for men, though it took over thirty years to deliver. Howard's work had a similar impact beyond Britain. There was already a network of reformers in discussion with each other and circulating their ideas on both sides of the English-speaking Atlantic. But his work was also translated and eagerly consumed by similar reformers in continental Europe.[49]

Several of the individuals who have described the birth of the prison have suggested that the development of incarceration with labour was linked with the development of a new bourgeois-capitalist society and, in Marxian terms, the new mode of production. The interpretation provides a broad,

---

[48] Andrews, *Law, Magistracy and Crime*, 345–74.
[49] See e.g. John Howard, *L'état des prisons, des hôpitaux et des maisons de force en Europe au XVIII siècle* tr, and ed. Christian Carlier and Jacques-Guy Petit, Paris: editions de l'Atelier, 1994.

provocative framework. But it can also flatten out contrasts and complexities and ultimately deny human agency by portraying individuals as ciphers for a political class. Thus, Jeremy Bentham, the utilitarian philosopher who proposed an ideal prison—the Panopticon—which would enable a single observer to supervise a large number of prisoners from a central point, becomes 'a major representative of the ascendant English bourgeoisie'—a title that begs rather a lot of questions about both Bentham and an 'ascendant bourgeoisie'.[50] Foucault's arguments about the great incarceration that began with the houses of correction, as well as other closed institutions notably the asylum, are important for focusing attention on power and control within society, but again human agency is lost as is any recognition that men such as Howard could possess sincere humanitarian motives. This is not to deny that both reformers and conservatives during the Enlightenment were interested in the control of society, fearful of those who appeared outside of control, such as vagrants and brigands, and keen to prevent robbery and other forms of offending. But because there was a variety of agendas, no doubt within the mind of each individual involved in the debates, this does not mean that appeals to humanity were hypocritical and meant nothing to those seeking change. Moreover, change and reform were not easy.

Much of the administration of the old regime was geared towards profit for the officeholder. The administration of justice, like much else, was entrepreneurial. Why should men who had often paid for their position (and this could be a small sum or it could be a large one) provide a service that was free at the point of delivery? In England there was an ideology of civic duty, and contemporary thinkers conceived of public service in the sense of acting as a magistrate or constable as an obligation on citizens of a free state. Nevertheless this concept began to be challenged from a variety of perspectives.[51] The outlay to be JP was relatively small; outlay to be a constable non-existent, but, in the latter case, if a man did not wish to serve then he had to provide a substitute to act in his place and the substitute cost money. The individuals who ran the houses of correction and the gaols commonly profited from their posts; they sold any goods made by their charges; they profited from any services that they could provide such as separate rooms, food, and drink; and they even pocketed the release fees.

[50] Dario Melossi and Massimo Pavarini, *The Prison and the Factory: Origin of the Penitentiary System*, tr. Glynis Cousin, London: Macmillan, 1981, 40; see also Georg Rusche and Otto Kirchheimer, *Punishment and Social Structure*, New York: Russell and Russell, 1968.

[51] Francis M. Dodsworth, ' "Civic" Police and the Condition of Liberty: The Rationality of Governance in Eighteenth-Century England', *Social History*, 29, 2 (2004), 199–216.

In France the purchase of, and profit from, judicial and police offices was significant. These offices gave some prestige; they provided a regular, though probably relatively small income on the investment, and they provided also the chance of receiving fees for services. There had been proposals for free justice and the abolition of venality by a succession of individuals during the final century of the old regime, though it would be quite wrong to assume that, because there was venality and nepotism among magistrates and the judiciary, many of them did not have strong notions of public duty, principles about adherence to the law, honesty, and probity.

In the early 1770s, during the extended conflict between Louis XV and the *parlements*, Chancellor Maupeou, more by blunder than design, attempted major changes, establishing new lawcourts, abolishing venality, and promising, though never delivering, a new law code and free justice. These were not reforms driven by a liberal agenda. Indeed, with reference to the criminal law Maupeou declared that he was 'not one of those who believe that all that which is old is corrupt practice and who suddenly take the axe to the foot of the tree because the tree does not always bear propitious fruits'.[52] Moreover, in his determination to enforce his changes, he resorted to many of the abuses that the liberal reformers condemned, notably the *lettre de cachet* and the arrest of opposition publicists. Such tactics served to highlight what critics declared to be wrong with the regime, but they also served to show how difficult it could be to confront the judiciary and the magistracy and to seek to change the way that they did things.[53] Ultimately Maupeou's reforms failed, and so too did those of Joseph II in Austria, providing a warning of what might be necessary to establish major changes in the system even in the leading absolutist powers of the late eighteenth century. And there was a related problem. John Howard had urged that gaolers should be salaried, but salaries required that someone provide the money. Jurists, *philosophes*, and others might argue the merits and demerits of existing systems, but major changes were certain to be costly. In addition to the costs for any new functionaries and buildings, those who had purchased office and took fees in the old system were likely to demand compensation. Lawyers and judges in the old regime were, after all, commonly drawn from the gentry and nobility; and while their loyalty might be expected by a prince, it was not guaranteed,

---

[52] Quoted in John A. Carey, *Judicial Reform in France before the Revolution of 1789* Cambridge, Mass.: Harvard University Press, 1981, 96.

[53] For the outcry see e.g. Marie Singham Shanti, ' "A Conspiracy of Twenty Million Frenchmen": Public Opinion, Patriotism and the Assault on Absolutism during the Maupeou years, 1770–1775', Ph.D., Princeton University, 1991.

particularly when money and prestige were at stake. Both the Whig histories
and those inspired by Foucault generally have ignored questions of the costs
of reform. The princes and ministers of the old regime did not enjoy that
luxury. The attempted reforms introduced by Chancellor Maupeou and
Joseph II demonstrated the potential difficulties when absolutist monarchs
offended elements of the nobility and the legal estate. Moreover, towards the
end of the eighteenth century the French state, in spite of its pre-eminence,
was bankrupt.

Debates about laws, punishments, and the administrative and fiscal problems of reform were fierce and significant, but these were not issues that often
went far beyond the ruling elites of eighteenth-century Europe. It is easy
to become sidetracked by the debates and their underlying ideologies,
and to forget the activities that the criminal laws and punishments were
meant to address. Criminal behaviour itself could affect people from all social
classes; moreover, the definition of what was criminal behaviour itself might
also, on occasions, be a matter of dispute.

3

The Understanding and Nature of Crime

THE definitions of crime and criminals in the large encyclopaedias that began to appear during the eighteenth century were literal, common-sense explanations. According to *l'Encyclopédie* of Diderot and d' Alembert, a criminal was quite simply someone who had been convicted of a crime. Crimes were of two varieties, public and private. The seriousness of a crime, however, was to be assessed by the intent and malice of the offender and by the cost to society.

It is necessary therefore to put at the top those crimes that interest human society in general; after these come those that trouble the order of civil society, and finally those that affect individuals. These latter have to be rated according to the evil that they cause and the rank and relationship of the victim to the offender, etc. Thus, the person who kills their father commits a homicide more criminal than one who kills a stranger; a sacrilegious priest is more criminal than a lay offender; a thief who attacks people is more criminal than one who simply fleeces them; a domestic servant who steals is more criminal than a stranger, etc.

The 'Law' article in the second edition of the *Encyclopaedia Britannica*, published in Edinburgh a few years later, took a similar line. 'A *crime*, or *misdemeanour*, is an act committed or omitted, in violation of a public law either forbidding or commanding it.' Moreover, 'all persons are *capable* of committing crimes unless there be in them a *defect* of *will*: for to constitute a legal crime there must be in them both a vitious will, and a vitious act.' There was no suggestion in any of this that crime was a way of life for some individuals or that criminals were a distinct social group. Nevertheless, the way in which people understood crime and criminals during the eighteenth century suggests that particular types of individuals and specific social groups were stigmatized as criminals or potential criminals. The growth of houses of correction and of discipline from the sixteenth century has already been described. In the eighteenth century too, offenders continued to be situated among the poor, and especially among beggars and vagabonds, that is to say those who appeared to be fit enough to work yet had no work.

Henry Fielding, the novelist and London magistrate, divided the poor into three groups. The smallest group, he believed, consisted of those who were unable to work; then came those who were prepared to work, but who could not find any employment; the largest of the three groups was made up of those who, while perfectly capable, simply would not work.[1] What especially concerned Fielding were the crimes of the poor. He considered that the poor were being brought to crime through idleness, love of luxury, gambling, and other forms of vice. Unsupervised institutions such as cheap lodging houses and pawnbrokers' shops fostered and encouraged crime. In his analysis of 'the late increase of robbers', published in 1751, he expressed particular anxiety about the wandering poor.

Where then is the Redress? Is it not *to hinder the Poor from wandering*, and this by compelling the Parish and Peace Officers to apprehend such Wanderers and Vagabonds, and by empowering the Magistrate effectually to punish and send them to their Habitations? Thus if we cannot discover, or will not encourage a Cure for Idleness, we shall at least compel the Poor to starve or beg at home: for there it will be impossible for them to steal or rob, without being presently hanged or transported out of the way.[2]

Other commentators, contemporaries of Fielding such as Sir William Blizard and Jonas Hanway, took a similar line. George Barrett went so far as to propose an annual census to be completed by householders, and a registration system with everyone holding a certificate giving details of their name, date and place of birth, residence, and so forth.

[I]t will infallibly detect all swindlers and all other persons whatever, who through fear of receiving those just rewards which they might at the hands of justice, have been necessitated to abscond from their usual place of residence, and who still subsist by committing depredations on the public, and by assuming a feigned name.[3]

On continental Europe the police and other officials of the princes shared such perceptions of who was to blame for crime. The policy, introduced in the sixteenth century, of incarcerating beggars, vagrants, and prostitutes to

---

[1] Henry Fielding, *An Enquiry into the Causes of the Late Increase of Robbers, and Related Writings*, ed. Malvin R. Zirker, Oxford: Clarendon Press, 1988, 108–11. The *Enquiry* was first published in 1751.

[2] Ibid. 144.

[3] George Barrett, *An Essay Towards Establishing a System of Police, on Constitutional Principles*, London, 1786, 13–19; 17–18.

instil discipline and to instruct them in industrious habits was continued and developed by both princes and private philanthropists. The fitting out of houses of correction in Baden and Leipzig, for example, was rooted in concerns that beggars and vagrants were also petty offenders.[4] In Naples during the 1780s the official categories of dangerous individuals began with 'the idle, vagabonds, and adventurers' (*oziosi, vagabondi, avventurieri*). At the beginning of his rule as Grand Duke of Tuscany, Leopold considered that he faced a major security problem with hundreds of destitute peasants camped outside the gates of Florence. Attempts to force them back to whence they came failed and, as a result, a system of public works was established, and beggars were registered and required to carry papers identifying their parish of origin.[5] The police in Maria Theresa's Vienna were expected to round up beggars and suppress mendicancy. Johann Anton von Pergen, who subsequently took control of the city's police, informed Joseph II that the principal cause of crime was public idleness (*Müßiggang*). The police of Paris maintained a vigorous surveillance of the lodging houses (*maisons garnies*) that were frequented by the poorer migrants and that acquired sinister reputations as the haven for all kinds of thieves and scoundrels.[6] The police considered that the inactivity of vagabonds and beggars was a kind of theft in that it deprived agriculture and industry of labour. They believed that most of the assaults and thefts in the city were committed by beggars and vagabonds, often acting in gangs. The point was stressed in the *Dictionnaire de Police* published shortly before the Revolution by the lawyer Nicolas Des Essarts:

Who are the instruments of these public calamities? Always men whose names and abode are unknown; individuals who seem strangers even in the city which succours them; beings who live only for the moment and who disappear as easily as they appear. In short, men without roots.[7]

---

[4] Helmut Bräuer, *Der Leipziger Rat und die Bettler. Quellen und Analysen zu Bettlern und Bettlerwesen in der Messestadt bis ins 18. Jahrhundert*, Leipzig: Universitäts Verlag, 1997; Bernhard Stier, *Fürsorge und Disziplinierung im Zeitalter der Absolutismus. Das Pforzheimer Zucht- und Waisenhaus und die badische Sozialpolitik im 18. Jahrhundert*, Sigmarigen: Thorbecke, 1988.

[5] Giorgia Alessi, *Giustizia e Polizia: Il controllo di una capitale, Napoli 1779–1803*, Naples: Jovene, 1992, 7; Mario Sismondi, *Classi povere e strategie del controllo sociale nel Granducato di Toscana (1765–1790)*, Florence: Dipartimento Statistico, Università degli Studi di Firenzi, 1983.

[6] Vincent Milliot, 'L'accueil sous surveillance: le contrôle des lieux d'herbergement parisiens sous l'Ancien Régime', in Claire Levy-Vroelant, ed., *Logements de Passage*, Paris: L'Harmattan, 2000, 185–6.

[7] Quoted in Daniel Roche, *Le peuple de Paris*, Paris: Aubier, 1981, 23. See also Thomas Brennan, *Public Drinking and Popular Culture in Eighteenth-Century Paris*, Princeton: Princeton University Press, 1988, 280 and 282–3.

Again the distinction was made between those who were forced to beg and those who chose an idle life, though Jean-Charles-Pierre Lenoir, one time police chief of Paris, admitted that it was not always easy to distinguish the deserving poor from those who were habitually idle.[8] Moreover, the police, and others, were fully aware that during periods of high prices and food shortages many of the poor were driven to crime simply to survive; and the police began increasingly to play a significant role in poor relief. In the bleak and hungry autumn of 1768, for example, Antoine-Gabriel de Sartine, the *lieutenant général de Police* in Paris, persuaded the finance minister to provide funds for public works to assist the city's poor. Rumours also spread that the police were registering names for the distribution of assistance. The poor flocked to the offices of the *commissaires de police* and continued to do so even after they had been sympathetically advised to look to their parish priests for help.[9]

In the provinces the military police, the *Maréchaussée,* were charged with rounding up vagrants and beggars, something that they did with particular zeal when there were bounties offered for each individual apprehended. Jacques-François Guillauté, an officer of the corps, suggested that the police of Paris should be extended across the whole country to deal with the vagrancy problem. He also proposed a system of identity certificates for the whole population, rather as George Barrett was to do for England some years later.[10] In the administrative context of old-regime France the possibility of such a widespread scheme of identification was probably unworkable. Nevertheless in 1781, motivated principally by concern about industrial unrest among urban workers, a royal decree required that every such worker carry a passbook (*livret*) that had to be endorsed by his successive employers.[11] For the next century and more '*Je demande à voir tes papiers*' appear to have been the

[8] MO Fonds anciens, manuscrit 1400, Mémoires de J.C.P. Lenoir, ancien Lieutenant générale de Police de Paris, écrits en pays étrangers dans les années 1790 et suivantes, fo. 678/1.

[9] David Garrioch, *Neighbourhood and Community in Paris, 1740–1790,* Cambridge: Cambridge University Press, 1986, 155; Steven L. Kaplan, *Bread, Politics and Political Economy in the Reign of Louis XV,* 2 vols., The Hague: Martinus Nijhoff, 1976, i. 322–3.

[10] Jacques-François Guillauté, *Mémoire sur la Réformation de la Police de France* (introduced and annotated by Jean Seznec), Paris: Hermann, 1974.

[11] Steven Kaplan, 'Réflexions sur la police du monde de travail, 1700–1815', *Revue historique,* 529 (1979), 17–77; 56–7. In some trades the passbook was established in the mid-1770s. Various papers were supposed to be carried by people on the roads in Germany, but it does not appear to have been difficult to get forgeries that would fool officials, many of whom had little education. See Otto Ulbricht, 'The World of a Beggar around 1775: Johann Gottfried Kästner', *Central European History,* 27, 2 (1994), 153–84; 156–62.

opening words of any conversation between gendarmes and poor men on the roads of provincial France.[12]

Vagrants appeared to be a problem on the roads of eighteenth-century Europe. There were always artisans on the tramp, young men seeking to develop their skills before trying to settle down. There were others such as entertainers, knife-grinders, and pedlars whose business put them on the road. At the beginning of the agricultural year young men and women walked to various fairs and gatherings hoping to be hired as labourers or maidservants for the coming twelve months. Others travelled to nearby cities and towns looking for work, often returning in the dead winter months. Others were pushed on to the roads by sheer poverty. It has been suggested that 5 per cent of the population of the German lands were on the road at the beginning of the eighteenth century because of demographic pressure.[13] Throughout the century the population of continental Europe increased faster than the economy could bear. During the 1760s, in France, the adoption of physiocratic policies made the situation worse. Grain prices increased and seigneurial landlords were permitted to take over areas of common land. The *gibier de prévôt*—literally the wild game of the *Maréchaussée* courts—increased accordingly. When people were stigmatized and targeted by police organizations, it is not surprising that they sometimes clung together either in families or in such groups as came together for mutual support and camaraderie. But groups of poor travellers, who may or may not have been beggars, appeared more frightening than people travelling in ones and twos. Indeed, even beggars travelling alone or in pairs appear to have been welcomed at times since they brought news and might do some work for payment in cash or kind. Groups of itinerant beggars were different, especially if they seemed to include former soldiers, and while most groups appear never to have journeyed great distances from their place of origin, they commonly provoked a fear of brigands among country dwellers. Desperate individuals committed robberies or might burn the property of someone who rejected their requests (sometimes demands) for assistance. Some groups did involve themselves in banditry or else they bullied and threatened small communities into giving them alms. It was claimed that, towards the end of the eighteenth

[12] In his short story *Le bon gendarme*, Léon Bloy (1846–1917), the ardent Catholic social reformer and novelist, has his eponymous hero, retired *brigadier* Dussutour, confronting the invading Prussians with these words in 1870.

[13] Uwe Danke, 'Bandits and the State: Robbers and the Authorities in the Holy Roman Empire in the Late Seventeenth and Early Eighteenth Century', in Richard J. Evans, ed., *The German Underworld: Deviants and Outcasts in German Society*, London: Routledge, 1988, 98.

century, some German villagers were spending as much on such 'alms' as they spent on their own families.[14]

There is a romance about bandits. The spread of broadsides and chapbooks during the eighteenth century may have contributed to the image of the bandit hero. The notoriety of most bandits rarely spread beyond their native region. Some, however, rapidly acquired the mantle of a Robin Hood, such as Diego Corrientes, the 'generous bandit' of Andalusia, and 'the famous Poulailler' of France.

> Diego Corrientes, el ladrón de Andalucía,
> Que a los ricos robaba y a los pobres socorria.

(Diego Corrientes, the robber of Andalusia, | Who took from the rich and helped the poor.)[15]

> Chacun dit que Poulailler,
> Ne detruit personne.
> Quand il vient pour vous arrêter,
> Si ver lui vous vous plaignez
> De l'argent—il vous donne,
> Ayant de vous pitié

(Everyone says that Poulailler | Never killed anyone. | When he comes to stop you | If you tell him you lack | Money—he will give you some | Taking pity on you.)[16]

A generation ago Eric Hobsbawm conceptualized and defined what he called the 'social bandit'. Such bandits were 'peasant outlaws whom the lord and the state regard as criminals' but who still lived in their communities and were regarded in those communities 'as heroes, as champions, avengers, fighters for justice, perhaps even leaders of liberation'. They were quite distinct from 'the professional "underworld" [and] . . . mere freebooters ("common robbers")'. The latter saw the peasantry merely as 'prey'.[17] Hobsbawm's work generated new research and debate. Carsten Küther's examination of southern Germany during the old regime suggested the existence of a parallel society among parts of the peasantry and among those on the roads; this, in turn, fostered 'criminal bandits' who often looked rather similar to Hobsbawm's social bandits.[18] Uwe

---

[14] Ulbricht, 'The World of a Beggar', 171–3; Jerome Blum, *The End of the Old Order in Rural Europe*, Princeton: Princeton University Press, 1978, 190–1.

[15] Peter Burke, *Popular Culture in Early Modern Europe*, London: Temple Smith, 1978, 165–6.

[16] Julius R. Ruff, *Violence in Early Modern Europe, 1500–1800*, Cambridge: Cambridge University Press, 2001, 21–2.

[17] E. J. Hobsbawm, *Bandits*, London: Weidenfeld and Nicolson, 1969, 13–14.

[18] Carsten Küther, *Räuber und Gauner in Deutschland: Das organisierte Bandenwesen in 18. und frühen 19. Jahrhundert*, Göttingen: Vandenhoeck und Ruprecht, 1987.

Danke, however, also focusing on southern Germany but in a slightly earlier period, concluded that bandits were a much more modest phenomenon than the contemporary literature suggested. This literature, which in Germany required the sanction of church and state for publication, emphasized the bandit's evil nature, portrayed him as challenging the divinely ordained social order, and stressed the attacks on peaceable citizens and churches. In Danke's estimation the emergent state used the idea of the bandit to consolidate its own power and to foster its legitimacy among ordinary people who felt threatened by banditry.[19] Anton Blok, an anthropologist and historian, whose research has ranged from eighteenth-century bandits in the Low Countries to the emergence of the Sicilian mafia, made a frontal assault on Hobsbawm's ideas. Blok argued that the whole concept of the social bandit 'overemphasizes the element of social protest while . . . obscuring the significance of the links which bandits maintain with established power-holders.'[20]

These issues will all recur in what follows in much the same way that bandits recurred across Europe throughout the eighteenth and nineteenth centuries. But overall the evidence would appear to suggest that the romance of the bandit appears to have stemmed more from a popular wish for social justice rather than from any experience of the behaviour of most bandits. Few bandits ever seem to have emulated Robin Hood's altruism in robbing the rich to give to the poor, and an individual bandit's popularity often appeared in ballad literature only after his death. 'Bandit' itself was a label that was applied to individuals who committed a variety of offences that ranged from highway robbery to burglary and from the pillaging of farms to large-scale smuggling. Moreover, while banditry was probably less of a problem in the eighteenth century than before, and while the authorities were capable of making sweeps of bandit-infested areas and picking up suspects (who probably spent longer in prison under investigation than they had done on the roads), some areas remained notorious for the danger.

Parts of southern and south-eastern Europe were particularly noted for banditry. In Greece, for example, there was a tradition of banditry among the migratory shepherds who crossed and recrossed the mountains. The bandits were usually young men who, when in trouble with the authorities or facing

---

[19] Uwe Danke, *Räuberbanden im Alten Reich um 1700: Ein Beitrag zur Geschichte von Herrschaft und Kriminalität in der frühen Neuzeit*, Frankfurt am Main: Suhrkamp, 1988. There is an English summary in Uwe Danke, 'Bandits and the State: Robbers and the Authorities in the Holy Roman Empire in the Late Seventeenth and Early Eighteenth Centuries', in Richard J. Evans, ed., *The German Underworld: Deviants and Outcasts in German History*, London: Routledge, 1988.

[20] Anton Blok, *Honour and Violence*, Cambridge: Polity Press, 2001, 22.

other difficulties, took to robbery, kidnap, and ransom. The large flocks of sheep, sometimes including goats and even horses, destroyed the crops of settled peasants and in such cases the strong arm of the shepherd bandit was useful for defending the transhumant community against angry cultivators. The waning authority of the Ottoman Empire that had never properly controlled these mountain regions aggravated the problems. Some of the bandits, known as *klefts* since the end of the fifteenth century, subsequently acquired the mantle of a primitive national resistance since they attacked Ottoman tax collectors and other symbols of Ottoman rule. But they were also prepared to attack and rob wealthy Greeks. The Ottomans recruited local irregulars, *armatoloi*, to fight the *klefts*, but the line between the two groups was fuzzy. If Ottoman pay was not forthcoming, then *armatoloi* became bandits. If the pickings from banditry were slim, then *klefts* were known to enlist as *armatoloi*; and it was even possible for a successful bandit leader to become a commander of local police and to rise from there to be a figure with significant regional authority.[21]

The Lower Meuse and the rural area around Aix-la-Chapelle and Maastrict was another, but quite different, centre of banditry. This was a bustling commercial crossroads and a district that had long been fought over. It was a region where the peripheries of France, the Netherlands, and the German Empire met, where there was a clutch of semi-autonomous statelets, and where there was a boundary between Catholicism and Protestantism. During the eighteenth century the area was periodically plundered by the bandits known as the *Bokkeryders*—the Billy-goat riders. These were neither noble nor social bandits. They drew their strength from mobile groups of skinners who tended to be marginalized because of their trade; these were reinforced rather more by local artisans than by agricultural workers and their targets tended to be principal symbols of hierarchy and wealth within the local community, namely churches and farms.[22] In France bandits were to be found in a range of regions from the wealthy grain-producing Beauce to the poverty-stricken Forez. What made both of these regions attractive to robbers were travellers on busy roads: the main roads through the Beauce ran between Paris and Orleans; roads in the Forez were travelled by people involved in the silk trade of Lyons. Banditry in these regions was not a

---

[21] Richard Clogg, *A Short History of Modern Greece*, 2nd edn. Cambridge: Cambridge University Press, 1986, 26–8; John S. Koliopoulos, *Brigands with a Cause: Brigandage and Irredentism in Modern Greece, 1821–1912*, Oxford: Clarendon Press, 1987; Thomas W. Gallant, *Modern Greece*, London: Arnold, 2001, 16–18.

[22] Blok, *Honour and Violence*, ch. 2 *passim*.

full-time occupation. The Beauce had few peasant proprietors and large numbers of landless labourers. The poor people on the roads and those who might engage in banditry often did harvest work in the summer and early autumn; harvest pay was, at least for a period, steadier and more profitable than robbery.[23]

Beggars and vagrants might have instilled fear in rural communities and been targeted by such forces of law and order as were available, but not every beggar and vagrant was a bandit. The point has been stressed with reference to the Dutch Republic during the eighteenth century that banditry and criminality were not simply the result of what individuals lacked in the way of jobs, permanent residence, social status, and so forth. They depended also on certain positive elements such as an awareness of, and access to, certain local resources, a familiarity with weapons, family or other group solidarity, and perhaps also some family tradition of marginality, resistance, and criminality.[24] Some bandit groups were reported to have been very large. The broadside of 1796 celebrating the career of Poulailler and published ten years after his execution, claimed, erroneously, that his band had 500 men. The biggest band in the Beauce, that of Charles Hulin, may have had 300 members and *la bande de Forez* about 100. But probably most gangs, including that of Poulailler, rarely numbered more than a dozen individuals. Moreover, the very big bands did not live communally, did not raid all together, and seem only to have assembled for big social occasions.

Other large gangs were established for entrepreneurial lawbreaking rather than robbery. Customs barriers and taxes encouraged smugglers. In England this could be big business when it came to smuggling tea and produce from continental Europe; on a much smaller scale it could be a profitable sideline for fishermen. The mass of tiny states in Italy and parts of Germany fostered smuggling, as did the customs due, the *octroi*, levied on many goods entering French towns. France was also divided internally by customs barriers, notably with different regional levies on salt—the *gabelle*. The smuggling of salt in old regime France could involve solitary individuals, families, and even whole villages. The Cottereau family of the Breton hamlet of Closerie des Poiriers, whose father took the alias of 'Chouan' in the 1770s, formed a smuggling coterie a generation before the name was adopted, during the 1790s, as

[23] Olwen H. Hufton, *The Poor of Eighteenth-Century France 1750–1798*, Oxford: Clarendon Press, 1974, 266–83.
[24] Florike Egmond, *Underworlds: Organized Crime in the Netherlands, 1650–1800*, Cambridge: Polity Press, 1993.

the *nom de guerre* of counter-revolutionary, royalist rebels.[25] And just as
the smuggling of tea into Britain was big business involving large gangs of
armed men so, in France, was the smuggling of contraband such as tobacco.
The best known of the big smuggling gangs was that of Louis Mandrin.
Mandrin specialized in running into France tobacco and cloth purchased
cheaply in Switzerland. On the occasion of these raids his gang may have
consisted of as many as 200 men. Local populations could be ambivalent
towards smugglers. They wanted necessities like salt and luxuries like alcohol
and tobacco without having to pay the taxes. In addition, the smuggling
gangs could provide job opportunities for young men down on their luck or
for discharged and unemployed soldiers who knew how to handle firearms.
They provided work for small artisans and tradesmen such as blacksmiths,
saddlers, and gunsmiths as well as trade for innkeepers. But the smuggling
gangs could also be violent towards anyone who crossed them and they could
bring trouble and upheaval to local communities in the shape of pursuing
police and soldiers. Mandrin's gang fought a pitched battle with troops in
the neighbourhood of the village of Gueunaud in December 1754. Fifteen
soldiers and nine smugglers were killed, and another five or six smugglers
were captured. The troops celebrated their success by pillaging the village,
though the villagers do not appear to have complained too vociferously,
possibly because they still managed to hold on to some of the smugglers'
contraband.[26]

In the same way that smuggling could involve a local community as willing
participants, so too could the looting of shipwrecks. Wrecking was not the
work of entrepreneurial criminal gangs or bandits, though it was often alleged
that the coastal communities involved in the looting of wrecked ships for
their profit had lured those ships to destruction. In France it was known for
local priests to be asked to pray for bad weather likely to cause a wreck; in
England, at best, there were local clergy who received goods knowing them
to have come from a wreck.[27]

There were some criminal gangs active in towns, but the concept of the
gang and the different styles of group offending need to be unpicked. Fielding

[25] Bernard Briais, *Contrebandiers du sel: la vie des faux sauniers au temps de la gabelle*, Paris: Aubier, 1984, 47–8, 94–7, and 101–7.
[26] Bernard Lesueur, *Le Vrai Mandrin*, Paris: édition Spéciale, 1971, 221–2.
[27] John McManners, *Church and Society in Eighteenth-Century France*, 2 vols., Oxford: Clarendon Press, 1998, ii. 257; John G. Rule, 'Wrecking and Coastal Plunder', in Douglas Hay, Peter Linebaugh, E. P. Thompson, et al., *Albion's Fatal Tree: Crime and Society in Eighteenth-Century England*, London: Allen Lane, 1975, 184–5.

wrote of a 'great Gang of Robbers' in London. Lenoir wrote of a similar gang whose membership spread into Paris from Montargis and the Orléannais and that took years to unearth and bring before the courts.[28] Elsewhere other criminal networks linked banditry with other forms of criminal offending and were active in both town and country. Ecology, landscape and the density of population were all important to the form that criminality took. Thus in the heavily populated province of Holland, where the distances between communities were small and where communication by road or canal were good, criminality tended to be quiet and sneaky. In the province of Brabant, in contrast, where communities were small and widely scattered and where there were few roads, the gangs that robbed the large and isolated farms could take their time and could torture their victims for information, or even for sadistic pleasure, with little fear of disturbance.[29] In the mountainous regions of southern Piedmont, where the local *signori* were reluctant to spend money on running their courts and where the state had no police to deploy, criminality tended to be rooted in villages with large gangs of smugglers. They traded particularly in salt and easily crossed the frontier into the even less well policed territories of Liguria. In the foothills and in the Po valley, in contrast, criminality appears more to have been the activity of desperate, landless labourers sometimes robbing on the highways and sometimes robbing vineyards and orchards.[30]

Criminal gangs in the urban environment also took a variety of forms. There was a tradition dating back to the Middle Ages that certain parts of towns or cities were populated entirely by criminal communities—the so-called Court of Miracles in Paris is the best-known example. In Germany in the early eighteenth century there was already a word to describe criminals—*Gauner*. This is generally translated today as 'crook' or 'trickster', but in the eighteenth-century German lands it was used commonly to describe a member of a distinct and separate criminal community, the *Gaunertum*. There is evidence of some such communities formed by trade, family, or kin groups that were marginalized and stigmatized. Across much of Europe certain trades were considered to be dishonourable and polluting. In some instances it was possible to make a reasonable living when involved in such a trade; the public executioner is an obvious example. But executioners, skinners,

---

[28] Fielding, *An Enquiry*, 76; MO Fonds anciens, manuscrit 1400, Mémoires de J.C.P. Lenoir, fos. 678/1 and 678/2.

[29] Egmond, *Underworlds*.

[30] Michael Broers, *Napoleonic Imperialism and the Savoyard Monarchy, 1773–1821*, New York: Edwin Mellen Press, 1997, 128–30 and 140–1.

knackers, molecatchers, and the like were relegated to the margins, or to the rougher parts of towns. In Bologna, for example, the *sbirri* acted as a kind of police, but they were stigmatized as 'vile' because they administered corporal punishment, carried shackles, and led prisoners to prison. They were required to live in a remote street supposedly marked by the plague. Some of the people involved in these polluting trades, even those employed to do the prince's dirty work, seem to have extended their social stigmatization by undertaking criminal activities. Minorities such as Gypsies and Jews were similarly stigmatized, and while some of the claims about the extent of their offending were exaggerated, they appear to have played a disproportionate role in some criminal behaviour, often working in gangs. By the end of the eighteenth century, however, the Dutch evidence, at least, suggests a considerable mixing with, and integration between Jews and marginal groups among Christians in the formation of criminal gangs. Elsewhere other gangs were formed by friends or workmates acting opportunely to commit a theft or sometimes with planning, particularly if the offence was some form of protest or assault on a master or an employer. Rather like some of the rural gangs, the criminal gangs in towns might come together to carry out a particular crime and split up immediately afterwards. This might be done on a regular basis, especially where links could be developed with others who could fence stolen goods. Finally, there seem to have been some gangs that got together as the result of an opportunity for a theft, or possibly following a chance meeting in a pub or tavern.[31]

There is a problem here, however, of when two, three, or more individuals acting in concert can really be said to constitute a criminal gang. Just over a third of food thefts in eighteenth-century Paris were committed by people acting in pairs or in slightly bigger groups.[32] At the same time there appears to have been a particularly high proportion of migrants involved in theft in eighteenth-century cities and towns.[33] If recent migrants lost their employment or could not find work, then, with no networks to fall back on, they became particularly vulnerable economically. But migrants were not

[31] See e.g. Steven C. Hughes, 'Fear and Loathing in Bologna and Rome: The Papal Police in Perspective', *Journal of Social History*, 21, 1 (1987), 97–116; Küther, *Räuber und Gauner*; Egmond, *Underworlds*; Gwenda Morgan and Peter Rushton, *Rogues, Thieves and the Rule of Law: The Problem of Law Enforcement in the North-East of England*, London: UCL Press, 1998, 85–95.

[32] Arlette Farge, *Délinquance et criminalité: le vol d'aliments à Paris au XVIII siècle*, Paris: Plon, 1974, 179–82.

[33] Ibid. 118–19; Nicole Castan, *les criminels de Languedoc: Les exigences d'ordre et les vices du ressentiment dans une société pré-révolutionnaire (1750–1790)*, Toulouse: Publications de l'Université de Toulouse-Le Mirail, 1980, 290–2.

necessarily isolated individuals. There was much short-distance movement within big cities like London and Paris and many among the poor appear to have had friends and family. In Paris, moreover, there were a few poorer trades each of which was dominated by men from a particular region. The poor knew each other. They had little private life. They rubbed shoulders at work; they met each other in the streets, in cheap lodging houses, and in pubs or *cabarets* over a drink. This could engender solidarity, encouraging companions in hunger and misfortune opportunely to steal growing fruit, fowls, or anything else that came their way. There also must have been loneliness, encouraging the desperate individual to the desperate, opportunist action of a paltry theft. When property disappeared in a crowded tenement, lodging house, or at a workplace, it was easier to suspect the newcomer or stranger who had yet to acquire any sort of reputation among his or her peer group.

Petty theft was the most common kind of crime, and in instances of such crime there appears often to have been little economic and social difference between offenders and victims. The incidence of such crime may also have acted as an irritant, further encouraging the stigmatization of beggars and vagrants. But it was violent crime that particularly concerned people, whether it was highway robbery or murder. While figures are fragmentary and notoriously unreliable, murder appears to have been broadly in long-term decline right across Europe.[34] Moreover, during the eighteenth century there is some evidence to suggest a gradual shift from killings among strangers to killings between intimates in a domestic setting. This, Pieter Spierenburg argues in his micro-study of two murders in eighteenth-century Amsterdam, was part of a long-term shift that occurred between the sixteenth and twentieth centuries from relationships that largely involved performing duties towards a partner to ones that involved the exploration of innermost feelings. This was, he suggests, a 'revolution in love' manifested by expressions of intense longing and desire for another individual coupled with the idea of being with that individual for the whole time.[35] But whatever the changing shape of murder, those convicted for the offence were usually the individuals most likely to be execrated by the crowds at their execution. Yet even a murderer might evoke some sympathy among the crowd. Antoine-François Derues, for example,

[34] Manuel Eisner, 'Modernization, Self-Control and Lethal Violence: The Long-Term Dynamics of European Homicide Rates in Theoretical Perspective', *British Journal of Criminology*, 41 (2001), 618–38; idem, 'Long-Term Historical Trends in Violent Crime', in Michael Tonry, ed., *Crime and Justice: A Review of Research*, 30, Chicago: University of Chicago Press, 2003, 83–142.

[35] Pieter Spierenburg, *Written in Blood: Fatal Attraction in Enlightenment Amsterdam*, Columbus: Ohio State University Press, 2004, 18.

had a small grocery and hardware shop in Paris; he also had big aspirations. Early in 1777 he murdered Madame de Lamotte, a provincial aristocrat, and her son as part of a plan to acquire her property. Possibly because he was young, because he steadfastly refused to admit his guilt even when the evidence was stacked against him, because of the speed of his conviction and execution, because of suspicion of the police and of royal justice, and partly also, perhaps, because he was a small shopkeeper who had killed his social superiors, the Parisian crowd looked on him with a degree of sympathy. So much so, in fact, that the *lieutenant général* of police sanctioned a series of pamphlets and prints designed to convince people of his guilt. At the same time, in keeping with its moves towards demonstrating the correctness of its decisions and detailing the wickedness and responsibility of offenders, the *parlement* of Paris authorized the printing and distribution of the judgment in the case with a particular stress placed on Derues's hypocrisy and vice.[36]

Murder and violence inflicted during a robbery were the most dramatic forms of interpersonal violence during the eighteenth century, but they were not the most common. And much of the interpersonal violence was never pursued in the courts. Attitudes to personal and family honour have never been static but it is common for historians of the eighteenth century to detect, primarily among sections of the elite, an increasing shift away from violence to defend honour. Even so, duels continued to be fought between gentlemen and were often regarded with ambivalence. Killing an opponent in a duel could result in a prosecution for murder; yet fighting a duel was also seen by some as a way for members of a military elite to maintain and demonstrate martial courage and prowess. The beating of wives, children, and servants increasingly came under legal pressure in some countries and in some regions during the eighteenth century. Yet hostility towards male violence directed at women was not the prerogative of districts that might be considered as being more modern or more economically advanced. Working women in Paris enjoyed greater freedom and autonomy than their sisters in, for example, Languedoc. But in eighteenth-century Paris there was less likely to be any public condemnation of a man who violently struck a woman.[37]

---

[36] Annie Duprat, 'L'affaire Derues ou le premier tombeau de l'ancien régime', in Frédéric Chauvaud, ed. *La Justice en images, Sociétés et Représentations*, 18 (2004), 125–34; Pascal Bastien, 'Private Crimes and Public Executions: Discourses on Guilt in the *Arrêts Criminels* of the Eighteenth-Century Parliament of Paris', in Amy Gilman Srebnick and René Lévy, eds., *Crime and Culture: An Historical Perspective*, Aldershot: Ashgate, 2005.

[37] Garrioch, *Neighbourhood and Community*, 85–6; for a broad picture of shifting attitudes to violence see Ruff, *Violence in Early Modern Europe*.

Across Europe interpersonal violence continued to be found in the home, at the workplace, in the pub, and at fairs and village festivities. Sometimes it went to court, though often assaults were pursued at civil law.

There were some forms of offending, labelled as criminal, in which class, economic, and social distinctions were significant. An example can be found in instances where proprietors or manufacturers employed the law of theft against those claiming customary rights of gleaning, the use of common land, or the traditional perquisites of the scraps of cloth, wood, or other materials left over from a production process. But while a bipolar class conflict image suits some instances of economic appropriation and of violence, it can also provide an anachronistic concealment of eighteenth-century workplace complexities. In pre-Revolutionary France, for example, the ideal was that trades were self-regulating with masters—often men employing a small number of journeymen—united in trade corporations and journeymen linked in confraternities. The corporations embraced a single trade in a single town and there were commonly rivalries between them. The *compagnons* in the journeymen confraternities sometimes crossed trade boundaries and they also linked across the country so that when a *compagnon* on the tramp moved from one town to another he could find work through the organization. Masters and journeymen clashed over wages and sometimes over work practices; rival confraternities had savage, sometimes lethal, fights, but they all shared the aspiration of maintaining morality within their trades and honesty among their fellow members.

Poaching also has the image of a crime rooted in economic and class conflict. At times this image was justified, but not always. Restrictions on hunting were extensive for all but the most wealthy landowners during the eighteenth century. Among both tenant farmers and peasants there was considerable hostility to game birds or animals that ate seeds and damaged growing crops but that could not be killed, or even disturbed, by the victims of such damage, since they were legally protected for the pleasure of the land-owning huntsman. Killing such game was, like an arson attack or animal maiming, a means of getting back at a landowner. But poaching could also provide a valuable addition to a family's cooking pot, especially at a time when meat did not often figure in the diet of the poor. Killing game was also something that respectable gentlemen, and even clergy, without the official right to hunt considered was as much their right as that of those marginally above them in the social order. And there were always innkeepers ready to purchase game for their dinner table without asking questions. The latter encouraged entrepreneurial poaching gangs who, only with difficulty and linguistic elasticity, can be classified as social offenders asserting a right to hunt and challenging the rights of the gentry and nobility.

The assumption is often made that urban society was more concerned about petty theft than its rural counterpart and that urban dwellers were beginning to have more moveable property—the target for thieves—as the eighteenth century wore on. Yet it appears also that in London at least it was more difficult to raise a hue and cry at the end of eighteenth century than it had been at the beginning.[38] Durkheim's concept of *anomie* in the city offers one explanation for this, suggesting a greater reluctance to get involved because people no longer knew their neighbours, though, as has been argued above, even migrants were not necessarily isolated strangers in the eighteenth-century city. And there are other, more prosaic explanations, not the least of which was the development of policing, especially in urban areas, that possibly engendered a greater preparedness to hand the pursuit of criminal offenders over to men formally paid for the task. It is to the various responses to crime, and to the kinds of policing systems developing during the eighteenth century, that the focus must now shift.

---

[38] Robert Shoemaker, *The London Mob: Violence and Disorder in Eighteenth-Century England,* London: Hambledon, 2004, 28–36. Shoemaker himself suggests that people were possibly putting greater faith in a more efficient watch.

4

Coping with Crime

WHENEVER individuals are the victims of crime they have to make choices; it was the same during the old regime. It was always possible to take no action and there is every reason to conclude that, in eighteenth-century England for example, the overwhelming majority of criminal activities never resulted in court proceedings even when the offender was known and identifiable.[1] Across Europe, if the victim wanted some sort of retribution or recompense he, and less commonly she, could opt to handle the problem personally or to involve the local community. The alternative of involving the institutions of the law was often a last resort, but the gradual development of police institutions during the eighteenth century probably increased the resort to this option. As in many other instances during the eighteenth century, when seeking models for policing their territories European princes looked to French examples. The English, with their heightened conception of liberty and antipathy towards French absolutism, liked to think that they could avoid the intrusive and military nature of the policing system that they believed they saw across the Channel. This notion pervaded much of the thinking behind police reform in England and then infused the Whig histories of the police. It will be clear from what follows that there were much greater similarities than this traditional perspective allows, and hence the focus of much of this chapter is on the supposed English–French contrast. But the involvement of police suggests, first, that there were police to involve; second, that the police and criminal courts were acknowledged as legitimate bodies; and third, that people had sufficient confidence in such institutions to request their involvement. During the eighteenth century, and beyond, these requirements were often far from being realized.

Members of rural communities in the eighteenth century often appear to have been rather more concerned with restoring equilibrium than with

---

[1] Peter King, *Crime, Justice and Discretion in England 1740–1820*, Oxford: Oxford University Press, 2000, 18–19.

pursuing offenders through courts. Many peasant sayings reflected a profound suspicion of justice as administered by those from outside the community and particularly by lawyers. 'A bad agreement will be better than a good trial' was a popular saying in Languedoc; and until relatively recently Hungarian peasants warned—'Beware of three things: the lawyer, the pharmacy, and the inn; they ruin everybody'.[2] But reluctance to use the official courts was not necessarily because of suspicion of the outsider's justice, there was also the problem of money. A settlement might involve some money payment by an offender to a victim or to a victim's family, but it avoided the financial outlay of a court case, which potentially was much greater; and the chances of recovering money from a case that went to court were often slim. In addition, in some areas the courts were seen as relatively alien institutions. It might be acceptable to take a stranger or a major offence before such a court, but denouncing a neighbour, especially for a minor transgression, could be considered as an inappropriate invitation to an outside body to involve itself in the community's affairs.[3]

Many rural communities also had a different perspective on the world from their urban counterparts, from the educated elites, and particularly from state jurists. They lived in an environment where magic and sorcery still held sway. An unfortunate accident, the death of livestock, even missing articles of property—possibly stolen in reality—might prompt a visit to a local sorcerer or witch, often referred to in England as the 'cunning man' or 'cunning woman'. Accidents, bad luck, and the death of livestock could also be attributed to sorcery, an accusation which could provide the educated magistrate with considerable difficulty when he had to prepare the written case involving, perhaps, a series of fires and animal deaths running over several years.[4] In addition the peasantry were sometimes superstitious about certain practices that the authorities might invoke in pursuing a case. The *monitoire* is the most obvious example. If witnesses had been reluctant to

---

[2] Nicole Castan, *Justice et répression en Languedoc à l'époque des Lumières*, Paris: Flammarion, 1980, 15; Edit Fél and Tamás Hofer, *Proper Peasants: Traditional Life in a Hungarian Village*, Chicago: Aldine Publishing, 1969, 362; see also Judith Devlin, *The Superstitious Mind: French Peasants and the Supernatural in the Nineteenth Century*, New Haven: Yale University Press, 1987, 41, and Eugen Weber, *Peasants into Frenchmen: The Modernization of Rural France, 1870–1914*, Stanford, Calif.: Stanford University Press, 1976, 50.

[3] These issues are pursued in detail by, among others, Castan, *Justice et répression*, ch. 1, and Steven G. Reinhardt, *Justice in the Sarladais, 1770–1790*, Baton Rouge: Louisiana State University Press, 1991, ch. 2 and 3; David J. V. Jones, *Crime in Nineteenth-Century Wales*, Cardiff; University of Wales Press, 1992, 5–9.

[4] Nicole Dyonet, 'Les paroles et les écritures. Fonctionnement et bénéfices de la procédure inquisitoire en France au XVIIIème siècle', *Déviance et société*, 11, 3 (1987), 225–49; 223–36.

come forward in a serious case, then a judge could request the local bishop to issue a document to be read by local *curés* at three consecutive Sunday services. The document, the *monitoire*, required parishioners to reveal what they knew about the offence on pain of excommunication. In some parts of France, fearful for their souls, people came forward. But in other parts, possibly fostered by some *curés* telling their flocks that refusal to obey would mean them being changed into werewolves, the reading of a *monitoire* was believed to bring hailstorms and other misfortunes, and the parishioners vigorously resisted any such reading.[5]

A local offender with a reputation for being tough and violent might be tolerated, at least up to a point. Anyone stupid enough to tangle with him knew what to expect and, as a consequence, was expected to tread warily. For example, in December 1788 the *curé* of Beaugies, near Noyon in the Soissonais, was beaten by one Degrenier, a local innkeeper. Degrenier was regarded by the local community as a passionate and violent individual and someone not to be crossed. He was a heavy drinker. He was suspected of arson. The *curé* had been violently assaulted by Degrenier once before while the *curé* was acting as a local rent collector. On the occasion of the second assault the *curé* appears to have annoyed the innkeeper by reporting him to the excise for selling untaxed drink. The local community seems to have considered that the *curé* had brought the beating on himself. It was no part of a *curé's* formal tasks to act as a rent collector or to report people for excise offences. The *curé* may have felt similarly and did not want to press charges. It was the fiscal attorney of the local seigneur who was keen to institute court proceedings.[6]

There was always the possibility of taking personal responsibility for enforcing justice, and this might be tacitly approved. Degrenier had assaulted the *curé* for denouncing him to the authorities and had been excused by the local community; similarly any victim of a theft or other offence might be excused for beating an offender without recourse to the formal law or the courts. Yet victims and the local community were often less interested in the punishment of the offender than in the restoration of stolen goods. For this reason they often turned to arbitration engineered through the ruling of a local man with some social standing. It might be a priest; but it might also be a

    [5] Timothy Tackett, *Priest and Parish in Eighteenth-Century France: A Social and Political Study of the Curés in a Diocese of the Dauphiné*, Princeton: Princeton University Press, 1977, 213 and note; Reinhardt, *Justice in the Sarladais*, 154 and 254–7.
    [6] Clay Ramsay, *The Ideology of the Great Fear*, Baltimore: Johns Hopkins University Press, 1992, 162.

magistrate or seigneurial official whose standing came through his legal office but who was prepared to resolve problems by an infrajudicial route. Such a route avoided expense, might see goods returned or replaced, and could also bring about a restoration of personal or family honour.[7] In southern Europe especially there were kin and loyalty networks linked into local factions. The leaders of these factions acted to ensure that a high percentage of criminal cases were settled without a judicial verdict. Cantabria, in northern Spain, provides a good example of this kind of activity. It also demonstrates that factional loyalty was expected to go down as well as up, and that the abuse of power by any local leader (*caique*), even when his authority was sanctioned by a nobleman or the state, could lead to resistance and popular attempts to remove him.[8]

Neighbours and community groups were also important in towns and cities. In north Germany a petty offence committed by one journeyman against another could be resolved autonomously and ritually among a trade group. The journeymen assembled to see the victim slap the offender, the men made up, and the whole concluded with a few rounds of drinks. The victim's honour was satisfied and the drinking strengthened community bonds between the journeymen.[9] Often close relationships and knowledge of neighbours in the crowded tenements, courts, and streets meant that thieves were spotted and seized by neighbours and acquaintances; assault victims were sometimes aided similarly.[10] But urban communities appear to have used rather less arbitration than their rural counterparts. This may have been partly because the state's formal justice was a system that functioned according to calculable and rational rules and such rules were increasingly valuable in societies developing national markets and sophisticated methods of business and financial exchange. Embezzlers and forgers could hardly be handled in an informal, infrajudicial manner when examples needed to be made to maintain faith in the changing commercial system. Admittedly there were relatively few such offences and they affected only certain sections of the

---

[7] Benoît Garnot, 'Justice, infrajustice, parajustice et extrajustice dans la France de l'ancien régime', *CHS*, 4, 1 (2000), 103–20; Peter King, 'The Summary Courts and Social Relations in Eighteenth-Century England', *Past and Present*, 183 (2004), 125–72.

[8] Tomás A. Mantecón Movellán, 'Popular Culture and the Arbitration of Disputes: Northern Spain in the Eighteenth Century', in Louis A. Knafla, ed., *Crime, Punishment and Reform in Europe, CJH* 18 (2003), 39–55.

[9] Otto Ulbricht, 'The World of a Beggar around 1775: Johann Gottfried Kästner', *Central European History*, 27, 2 (1994), 153–84; 179–81.

[10] Arlette Farge, *Délinquance et criminalité: le vol d'aliments à Paris au XVIII siècle*, Paris: Plon, 1974, 192–4; David Garrioch, *Neighbourhood and Community in Paris, 1740–1790*, Cambridge: Cambridge University Press, 1986, 19 and 230.

community, but they may have contributed to a greater preparedness to use the law across the board. Moreover, in many big towns there was a greater availability of speedy, cheap, and, sometimes for the poor, free justice for the resolution of petty offences and injuries. The offices of the *commissaires* provided this in Paris; 'trading justices' did so in London. Such justices have received a bad press, not least because of Henry Fielding's portrait, in *Amelia*, of the grasping Justice Thrasher who knew no law and who acted primarily with an eye to his own pocket. But Fielding and his brother were themselves trading justices to the extent that their offices were open regularly and that they worked for fees. The rotation offices, established in London by the Middlesex magistrates in 1763, formalized and better regulated the trading justice system; they provided daily courts meeting from 10 a.m. to 3 p.m. administering justice for rarely more than a few shillings.

Royal justice may also have been becoming rather more favoured in rural areas. Even in states that did not subscribe to equality before the law, royal justice provided the opportunity for individuals to confront their social superiors on equal terms. Moreover in eighteenth-century France cheap and speedy justice was offered through the *prévôtal* courts of the *Maréchaussée*. The evidence suggests that these courts were becoming increasingly popular with relatively poor rural inhabitants as the century progressed.[11] The 'booted justice' of military policemen was not to the taste of many liberal, Enlightenment thinkers. But such thinkers had no problem with the concept of organized police structures, and as the century progressed formal policing institutions began to be established and sanctioned across Europe by enlightened princes and their advisers.

The word 'police'—*politie, Polizei, polizia*—pre-dates the bureaucratic institutions labelled as such during the nineteenth century. The meaning of the word shifted considerably over time. In the sixteenth century in continental Europe it was equated with governance itself and in the German lands the many variants of *Pollicey(ei)* were commonly linked with 'good order'. 'Police' ordinances were passed by princes and municipalities during the seventeenth and eighteenth centuries and were designed broadly to promote the material and secular welfare of the territory and its inhabitants. By the eighteenth century in Germany the word *Polizei* was synonymous with *Wohlfahrt* (welfare) and *Gemeine Nutz* (general welfare). It was a key

---

[11] Iain A. Cameron, *Crime and Repression in the Auvergne and the Guyenne, 1720–1790*, Cambridge: Cambridge University Press, 1981, ch. 4; Jacques Lorgnier, *Maréchaussée, histoire d'une révolution judiciare et administrative*, Paris: L'Harmattan, 1994, i, ch. 17 and ii, ch. 8.

element within Cameralism, the study of government and administration that put major emphasis on those practices that maintained domestic stability and sought to develop fair and efficient fiscal policy. In the German lands especially university professors wrote treatises and delivered lectures on *Polizeiwissenschaft*—which might be translated as 'policy science' but also, given the understanding and broad definition of the period, as 'police science'.[12]

Neither the use of the word police nor the deployment of men whose tasks were the maintenance of order and the pursuit of offenders guaranteed the enforcement of laws and public security. While seventeenth-century German princes issued police ordinances, they often lacked functionaries committed to enforcing them. The problem continued into the eighteenth century. Paul Bernard has described the 'veritable masterpiece of Austro-bureaucracy' that developed in Vienna combining 'the maximum imaginable concentration of administrative agencies with the least possible actual substance'. There was a *Polizei-Hofkommission* reporting directly to central government. It linked also with the provincial government and the wide-ranging *Kommission für Sicherheits-, Armen-, Verpflegs- und Schubsachen* (Commission for Security, Poor Relief, Provisions, and Deportations); given the fears about vagrants it became policy, not just in Vienna, periodically to deport offenders and vagrant aliens from the city. The two commissions liaised through a third body, the *Mittelstelle*, but it was not until 1753 that a body of police officers was created for them to supervise. Moreover the 188 police officers were directly the charge of yet another body, the newly established *Unterkommission aus der Wiener Bürgerschaft*.[13] Many Italian states had police institutions during the seventeenth and eighteenth centuries but, the further away they were from the centre of power so the more unreliable were these *sbirri*. The *sbirri* acquired an unenviable reputation for brutality, for corruption, and for being little better than the bandits they were required to suppress. The situation was not helped by the stigmatization of their trade as 'vile', by poor pay, which was often late, and by the reluctance of many of the nobility to recognize any

[12] Marc Raeff, *The Well-Ordered Police State: Social and Institutional Change through Law in the Germanies and Russia 1600–1800*, New Haven: Yale University Press, 1983; Roland Axtmann, ' "Police" and the Formation of the Modern State: Legal and Ideological Assumptions on State Capacity in the Austrian Lands of the Habsburg Empire, 1500–1800', *German History*, 10, 1 (1992), 39–61; Mark Neocleous, 'Policing and Pin-Making: Adam Smith, Police and Prosperity', *Policing and Society* 8 (1998), 425–49; idem, 'Social Police and the Mechanisms of Prevention: Patrick Colquhoun and the Condition of Poverty', *BJC* 40, 4 (2000), 710–26; 721–3.

[13] Paul P. Bernard, *From the Enlightenment to the Police State: The Public Life of Johann Anton Pergen*, Urbana and Chicago: University of Illinois Press, 1991, 120.

superior jurisdiction. In clashes with the nobility and their hired thugs it was generally the *sbirri* who came off worst.[14]

In eighteenth-century England the word 'police' was scarcely used, at least in general discourse. 'Good Lord!' a Frenchman is alleged to have cried, appalled by the squalid and disorderly state of London streets, 'how can one expect Order among these People, who have not such a Word as *Police* in their Language'.[15] The reason appears to be principally because of the way in which the words *polis* and *politeia* had been translated from Aristotle's *Politics*. The French and the Germans used the word 'police' while the English used 'commonwealth' and 'policy'. But use of a precise word hardly mattered. In the middle of the century Montesquieu could describe England as 'a well-policed nation' (*une nation très bien policée*).[16] Some forty years later a German traveller also noted that 'the English have not a single word in their whole language, to express what we term the *police*; if one however concludes from thence, that the thing itself does not exist among them, he will be grossly deceived.'[17] Towards the end of the century, moreover, reformers were beginning to use the word and were arguing that it would be possible to construct a form of police that was in keeping with the notions of English liberty. Such a form, they insisted, naturally would be different from that developing in absolutist France and seen as a model by many princes elsewhere.

By the mid-eighteenth century in France the word 'police' appears to have been used principally with reference to the internal management of the city. Institutions were established whose head, at least, had the word police in his title—the *lieutenant général de police de Paris* was established in 1667. An ordinance of 1699 established police lieutenants in other French towns. In accordance with old regime practice, these posts were purchased; the individuals who made the purchase were charged with supervising the broad duties then understood by the word police. According to Nicolas Delamare, who was a subordinate officer of the Parisian lieutenant and who published a much celebrated *Traité de la Police* at the beginning of the eighteenth century,

---

[14] There has been little detailed work on the *sbirri* of the old regime, but see, Steven C. Hughes, 'Fear and Loathing in Bologna and Rome: The Papal Police in Perspective', *Journal of Social History*, 21, 1 (1987), 97–116.

[15] Quoted in Leon Radzinowicz, *A History of English Criminal Law, iii. The Reform of the Police*, London: Stevens & Sons, 1956, 1. See also J. M. Beattie, *Policing and Punishment in London 1660–1750: Urban Crime and the Limits of Terror*, Oxford: Oxford University Press, 2001, 77–8.

[16] Montesquieu, *De l'esprit des lois*, bk. 6, ch. 7.

[17] Johann Wilhelm von Archenholz, *A Picture of England: Containing a Description of the Laws, Customs and Manners of England*, Dublin, 1790, 178.

these duties fell into eleven categories: religion; manners and morals (*mœurs*); public health; food and the necessities of life; highways and the freedom and safety of movement along them; security and the maintenance of the public peace; the sciences and the liberal arts; commerce; manufacturing and the mechanical arts; domestic servants, workers, and labourers; the poor. Half a century later the article 'Police' in *L'Encyclopédie* accepted these categories without change. So too did Jean-Charles-Pierre Lenoir, a former *lieutenant général*, when he came to write his memoirs and thoughts on policing whilst in exile during the Revolution.[18]

Delamare's treatise, and the publications of the German theorists, linked with thinking in other countries with absolutist regimes. It is unclear how much of the material published in this area in eighteenth-century Spain was original and how much was essentially translations from the French and German. In 1766 the Spanish monarchy sought to limit the opportunities for robbery in Madrid by prohibiting the wearing of traditional long cloaks and wide-brimmed hats; the former, it was maintained, enabled the concealment of weapons, while the latter facilitated anonymity. The decree was the spark that ignited serious rioting. The riots were suppressed; the Jesuit Order, which was blamed for the trouble, was expelled; and henceforth the king and his ministers were keen to establish a new level of control over the urban space of the city. In 1782 the *Superintendencia General de Policía para Madrid y su Rastro* was established; it was based closely on the Paris model.[19] Others also looked to Paris. In 1742 Frederick the Great sent an official to work with the police of Paris for a year with a view to establishing a similar system, moulded to Prussian conditions, for Berlin. As part of his attempt to bring order and enlightenment to Tuscany, Grand Duke Leopold reorganized the state's police. He separated them from the courts and gave them the kinds of powers deployed by their counterparts in Paris, namely street cleaning, controlling street games, the surveillance of family problems, as well as dealing with crime and more general threats to public tranquillity.[20]

---

[18] MO Fonds anciens, manuscrits 1399–1400, Mémoires de J.C.P. Lenoir, ancien Lieutenant général de police de Paris, écrits en pays étrangers dans les années 1790 et suivantes.

[19] Laura Rodríguez, 'The Riots of 1766 in Madrid', *European Studies Review*, 3, 3 (1973), 223–42; Pedro Fraile, 'Putting Order into the Cities: The Evolution of "Policy Science" in Eighteenth-Century Spain', *Urban History*, 25, 1 (1998), 22–35. For an interesting and important parallel between the policing of space in Madrid and Naples see Brigitte Marin, 'Les polices royales de Madrid et Naples et les divisions du territoire urbain (fin de XVIIIe—début de XIXe siècle)', *Revue d'Histoire Moderne et Contemporaine*, 50, 1 (2003), 81–103.

[20] Mario Sismondi, *Classi povere e strategie del controllo sociale nel Granducato di Toscana (1765–1790)*, Florence: Dipartimento Statistico, Università degli Studi di Firenzi, 1983.

Leopold's mother, the Empress Maria Theresa, wrote to the *lieutenant général* in Paris, Antoine-Gabriel de Sartine, with a request for detailed advice on his organization. Sartine, in turn, instructed one of his subordinates to prepare a report for the empress. The response was forwarded to her officials for consideration. When her elder son, Joseph II, became sole ruler in her place, he set out with his earnest, over-hasty enlightened enthusiasm to outdo the French, and failed.[21]

In the mid-eighteenth century the *lieutenant général de police de Paris* commanded a force of around 3,000 men; the city itself had a population approaching half a million. Roughly half of the lieutenant's men provided deterrent patrols and manned police posts through the city. The other half included around 260 garbage collectors, 220 firefighters, as well as censors, farriers, architects and many other subordinate functionaries. The lieutenant's key subordinates were the 48 *commissaires du Châtelet* and the 20 *inspecteurs de police*. In keeping with the traditional administrative structures of the old regime the *commissaires* were not simply subordinates appointed by the lieutenant. They constituted a corporate company; candidates were expected to have some education in the law, but they had to be approved for election to the post by the rest of the company and their appointment was venal, costing up to 100,000 *livres* by the late eighteenth century. Gradually, as the century progressed, successive lieutenants exerted an increasing authority over the *commissaires* transforming them into rather more of an administrative and functional bureaucracy. But the problem remained that many of the duties that the lieutenant wanted the *commissaires* to perform carried no immediate financial reward, whereas some of the traditional tasks—temporarily sealing the property of a deceased individual, for example,—were ones that brought in fees. The *inspecteurs* did not have the same strong corporate structure. Following an edict of 1740 they were required to have served five years as an officer in the army, but the post of *inspecteur* was also venal, costing as much as 24,000 *livres* by the time of the Revolution.[22]

21 Donald E. Emerson, *Metternich and the Political Police: Security and Subversion in the Hapsburg Monarchy, 1815–1839*, The Hague: Matinus Nijhoff, 1968, 6–17. For a published version of the report see Augustin Gazier, ed. *La police de Paris en 1770, mémoire inédit composé par ordre de G. de Sartine sur la demande de Marie-Thérèse*, Paris, 1879. MO MS 1402, Jean-Charles Lemaire, 'Mémoire sur l'administration de la police' is annotationed and corrected by Lenoir.

22 For this and the following paragraph, see Alan Williams, *The Police of Paris 1718–1789*, Baton Rouge: Louisiana State University Press, 1979, ch. 3; Vincent Milliot, ' "Gouverner les hommes et leur faire du bien": la police de Paris au siècle de Lumières (conceptions, acteurs, practiques)', Dossier en vue de l'obtention de l'Habilitation à diriger des recherches, Université de Paris I—Panthéon-Sorbonne, 64–9 and 155–90.

The *commissaires* were based in specific districts of the city but, together with the *inspecteurs*, they also staffed and ran twenty-five police departments each of which focused on a particular set of affairs ranging from the supervision of various markets to supervision of the book trade, of wet-nurses, of prostitutes, Protestants, and other institutions or individuals. The largest department, staffed by three *inspecteurs* from 1750 to 1776, and by four thereafter until the Revolution, was that concerned with criminal investigation and mendicancy. The *inspecteurs* of this department, which was known as the *bureau de sûreté,* met daily to collate and pass on information to other colleagues, and to discuss important cases. Like the other *inspecteurs,* they relied on informers, sometimes employed on a regular basis, sometimes recruited or pressurized into providing information for specific enquiries. They also established a series of registers listing offenders and suspects that could be used when checking the *maisons garnies* or conducting other investigations.

Many of the cities and towns of provincial France had police lieutenants. These posts were also venal, having been created by Louis XIV as a means of raising additional money for his wars. The number of subordinates available to these lieutenants depended upon what the local authority was prepared to organize and, above all, to pay for. There is evidence of a growing professionalism among the police institutions in the towns and cities of eighteenth-century France. This was especially the case on the north-east frontier where there were significant military garrisons that were often called upon to assist with policing and where the rank and file police patrolmen, generally known as *sergents de ville,* were themselves increasingly militarized but, at the same time, became more assiduous and better disciplined. These improvements appear to have made the inhabitants feel safer. Unlike the English, the urban bourgeois of north-east France and of the territories just across the frontier do not appear to have worried greatly about militarized policemen.[23]

Beyond the towns and cities policing provision was much more uncertain. Big landowners paid retainers and gamekeepers to protect their property and their game. Villages commonly recruited guards to protect the harvest from petty pilferers and bigger thieves. In France, exceptionally, the main roads were patrolled by a centralized, royal constabulary, the *Maréchaussée.* Armed and accoutred like cavalrymen, the *cavaliers* of the *Maréchaussée* were

---

[23] Catherine Denys, *Police et sécurité au XVIIIe siècle dans les villes de la frontière franco-belge,* Paris: L'Harmattan, 2002.

ex-soldiers and the institution had been established originally to police the royal armies. However, from the late seventeenth century their jurisdiction over civilians had increased significantly and, while the *cavaliers* enforced the law, their officers could also act as judges for a range of offences in the *prévôté* courts. The force was small, never quite reaching 4000 men before the Revolution. But in size and general efficiency it was unique in eighteenth-century Europe. Some German states recruited ex-soldiers as *Hatschiere*; these were intended to carry out similar tasks, though they do not appear to have been particularly effective or reliable. German princes also used hussars or other soldiers as police in peacetime. Joseph II had plans for a force similar to the *Maréchaussée* in the Austrian Netherlands, but along with his other reforms, the plans evaporated on his death.[24]

Some gave the *Maréchaussée* a bad press. The Comte de Guibert, one of the leading military thinkers of the late eighteenth century, considered the corps to be inefficient and expensive. He urged that the French take a leaf out of the Prussian book and simply rely upon the army for policing the provinces.[25] But the institution also had its intellectual defenders. As one of these put it, the 'unjust' critics were able to sleep quietly in their beds, 'live peacefully in the bosom of their families, surrounded by their possessions, thanks to the vigil and the constant fatigues' of the *Maréchaussée*.[26]

The *Maréchaussée* was often unpopular with certain social groups when it undertook certain duties. When, for example, it confronted food rioters; when it interfered in rough behaviour at village festivals, protected a priest pronouncing a *monitoire*, or disarmed peasants. The authorities generally wanted peasants disarmed for fear of the use of weapons in riots; the peasantry commonly viewed disarming as an attempt to limit poaching. But, unlike the private police of the tax farms, the *Maréchaussée* was not always a pressure on rural communities. Popular dissatisfaction with the corps was most probably the result of its size and the fact that many districts must rarely have seen a patrol. After all, the *Maréchaussée* provided a degree of protection against brigands, bandits, and unruly soldiers. Its courts provided cheap and speedy, if potentially rough, justice. Recent research has emphasized how the

---

[24] Clive Emsley, *Gendarmes and the State in Nineteenth-Century Europe*, Oxford: Oxford University Press, 1999, chs. 1 and 8.

[25] Pascal Brouillet, 'L'armée et la police des campagnes au XVIIIe siècle', *Revue historique des Armées*, 238 (2005), 4–13. Brouillet points out that there were instances of troops being deployed against large poaching gangs and to disarm the population and urges the need for more research on the use of troops as police in eighteenth-century France.

[26] Anon., *Réflexions sur le corps de la Maréchaussée*, Geneva, 1781, 65.

brigades could be well integrated into the communities in which they were based. Brigades often recruited local men who had served in the army; a *cavalier* was much more useful to both the authorities and a community if he spoke the local dialect or language. Some *cavaliers* took local wives and this also bound them more tightly to the local community. The consequence was that on some occasions, when *cavaliers* were in trouble, local people came to their assistance.[27]

France had another police institution, almost six times the size of the *Maréchaussée*, which also patrolled the whole country. This was the body that enforced the regulations and rights of the *Fermiers généraux*, the private company of wealthy financiers entrusted with the collection of indirect taxes. The *Fermiers* were not a popular body and nor were their police, who became known as *gabelous* after the hated salt tax (*la gabelle*). The *gabelous* appear to have had the same kinds of origins as the *cavaliers* of the *Maréchaussée* and there is evidence that some of them also were reasonably integrated into the communities in which they were based. But there is also evidence of hostility; smuggling and tax evasion had many more friends than brigands, unruly soldiers, and wild beasts. The *cavaliers* were often reluctant to get involved in support of *gabelous* and there was little love between the members of the two institutions.[28] The Royal Tax Farm in France was an exceptional institution but the problem of smuggling was universal. Elsewhere in Europe troops were often deployed to combat the problem. The Kingdom of Savoy even created two special regiments to patrol its frontiers against smugglers.[29]

In the British Isles the officers of Customs and Excise often found themselves required to call upon military or naval assistance in the war with smuggling gangs. But English commentators commonly stressed that theirs was a land of liberty that could not tolerate regular military patrols or any of the other methods of the absolutist princes on continental Europe, and especially those of the French Catholic monarch—the usual military enemy in the eighteenth century. Adam Smith had a particular gloss on this suggesting that the crime problem in Paris was aggravated by the large number of servants dependent on the nobility. 'Nothing tends so much to corrupt

---

[27] Eric Hestault, *La Lieutenance de Maréchaussée de Nantes (1770–1791)*, Maisons Alfort: Service historique de la *Gendarmerie* nationale, 2002, 331–41 and 360–3.

[28] Earl Robisheaux, 'The "Private Army" of the Tax Farms: The Men and the Origins', *Histoire Sociale/Social History*, 12 (1973), 256–69; see also Clive Emsley, 'La Maréchaussée à la fin de l'ancien régime: note sur la composition du corps', *Revue d'histoire moderne et contemporaine*, 32, 4 (1986), 622–44; 636–8.

[29] Emsley, *Gendarmes and the State*, 153.

mankind as dependency, while independency still increases the honesty of the people.' Thus Paris had a large police and many volumes of police ordinances, but 'in Paris scarce a night passes without somebody being killed, while in London, which is a larger city, there are scarce three or four [killings] a year.'[30] It would be interesting to know from where Smith, generally an acute and perceptive critic, got these figures. Sir William Mildmay, whose pamphlet was published in the same year as Smith's lectures (1763), considered that the *Maréchaussée* was an efficient institution but unsuitable for a 'land of liberty, where the injured and oppressed are to seek for no other protection, but that which the law ought only to afford, without flying for aid to a military power.' Perhaps something similar might be developed for England, but it would have to be 'subservient wholly to the civil power'.[31] Henry Fielding noted that the absolutist monarchy in France 'affords much more speedy and efficacious Remedies . . . than can be administered in a free State.'[32] What the English metropolis significantly lacked in comparison with Paris, and other major European cities, was an individual or a commission to supervise the city's policing in the broad eighteenth-century sense. In London such supervision was the responsibility of the scores of local parish vestries and their subordinate officers such as overseers of the poor and parish constables. The parish vestries decided on the provision of night watchmen for their district, and by a succession of private acts of parliament began to improve both the watching and the watchmen of the metropolis during the century.

Eighteenth-century English watchmen have generally received a bad press from police reformers and the traditional histories. The trial records of the Old Bailey, however, suggest that there were some tough and active men in the job, who kept an eye out for offenders, who were a significant presence on the streets after dark, and who knew the law. John Whitaker, for example, a watchman in Hoxton in 1770, testified to seeing 'these three young chaps go by; I thought they were disorderly by their looks. . . . I asked them where they were going?' The three men ran away, but Whitaker and another watchmen caught them and they were later charged with burglary. A dozen years later Robert Grubb, a watchman in Brick Lane, stopped three men carrying a

[30] Adam Smith, *Lectures on Justice, Police, Revenue and Arms*, ed. with intro. by Edwin Cannan, New York: Kelley and Millman, 1956, 155.

[31] Sir William Mildmay, *The Police of France: or, An Account of the Laws and Regulations established in that Kingdom for the Preservation of the Peace and the Preventing of Robberies*, London, 1763, 41.

[32] Henry Fielding, *An Enquiry into the Causes of the Late Increase of Robbers and Related Writings*, ed. Malvin R. Zirker, Oxford: Clarendon Press, 1988, 76

bundle that he regarded as suspicious. He asked them to accompany him to the watch house and promptly was slashed with a cutlass. Seriously wounded, Grubb swung his rattle to call assistance, staggered after his assailants, and saw them arrested before being taken to hospital. When a young woman claiming to have been robbed identified as her attacker a young man who was found by the night watch, the watch sergeant advised her: 'be particular in what you are doing, if you swear to him you will take his life away.'[33] There is no similar archive for yielding information about the policing activities of watchmen outside London, but there is no reason to believe that they were necessarily greatly inferior.

Parish constables, supposedly householders appointed in a variety of ways to their tasks for a limited period—usually a year—seem also to have become more professional as some permanent deputies began to accept a payment to substitute for the chosen men year after year.[34] The constables, as well as assisting the victims of offences, were charged with enforcing the laws on regulatory offences such as 'nuisances', the all-embracing category for those things that upset the common good of the community. Vestries, and especially the powerful municipal corporation of the square mile that constituted the City of London, jealously guarded their independence. There was a general suspicion of centralizing or coordinating structures, especially where the posts were Crown appointments since, at best, this increased royal patronage.[35] Thus it was inconceivable that a post like that of the Parisian *lieutenant général* could have been created for eighteenth-century London. However, central government did begin, tentatively, to involve itself in policing the metropolis by providing a small sum to Henry Fielding, the principal magistrate in Bow Street, to establish preventive patrols on the main roads; and Fielding, together with his brother Sir John, began to develop an effective detective police.

The Fieldings are hailed by traditional police historians in England as fathers of the English police. Yet the kind of police that the Fieldings

[33] http://www.oldbaileyonline.org, respectively at t17700425–23, t17820703–58, and t1779090915–4.

[34] Elaine A. Reynolds, *Before the Bobbies: The Night Watch and Police Reform in Metropolitan London, 1720–1830*, London: Macmillan, 1998; Beattie, *Policing and Punishment*, esp. ch. 3.

[35] Beattie, *Policing and Punishment*, 117, suggests that one reason why the number of constables was not increased in London and financed by taxation was that this 'was more likely to produce anxieties about the power of government than a force of paid watchmen, who commanded no power to intrude and harass'. He supports his case with reference to the concerns about the increase in the number of excise officers and what this meant for the power of the government during the passage of Walpole's Excise Bill in 1733.

sought to develop was actually very different from the Metropolitan Police established by Sir Robert Peel in 1829. Moreover, it is interesting to note some similarities between the Fieldings's *modus operandi* and the system in Paris, and some of the ideas which they, and other eighteenth-century English police reformers, shared with their continental neighbours. Both the similarities and the shared ideas have tended to be obscured by the continuing stress on England's greater 'liberty' and the emphasis on the unique nature of English policing. A major error of traditional English police history has been to separate these men from their Enlightenment roots and to see them, not as thinkers of their time often developing ideas in parallel to men in continental Europe, but rather as heralds of the institution that was to be created in 1829 and as somehow envisaging the kind of institution that was to develop subsequently. This is not to argue that the Fieldings and others had necessarily read the works of the continental police theorists, but they were thinking and writing in the broad intellectual environment of Enlightenment ideas and it would be odd if some European ideas did not filter across the Channel in some form.

Henry Fielding, and later Sir John Fielding, was no *lieutenant général* but his system of working was not unlike that of a *commissaire du Châtelet*. Both the Fieldings and other London trading justices, like the Paris *commissaires*, were based in police offices where they heard and resolved minor disputes and petty offences. The lieutenant appears merely to have made formal validations of the *commissaires'* decisions in his regular court at the Châtelet.[36] The Fieldings had the advantage of not having to submit daily reports to a chief, and not having to have their decisions validated by a superior. However, they recognized the importance of the circulation of information in the pursuit of offenders and stolen property, not unlike the Paris *bureau de sûreté* with its staff of *inspecteurs*. Little is known about precisely how the Paris bureau functioned and how it worked with its *sous-inspecteurs* and informants. Similarly, there has been little serious work on how the Principal Officers of Bow Street worked but, like more modern police officers involved in the detection and apprehension of offenders, they appear to have used informants. They also depended on their knowledge and experience in the job, together with their physical strength and courage.[37] They also functioned

---

[36] Williams, *Police of Paris*, 121.

[37] Patrick Pringle, *The Thief-Takers*, London: Museum Press, 1958, provides a racy, popular account; J. M. Beattie, 'Early Detection: The Bow Street Runners in late eighteenth-century London', in Clive Emsley and Haia Shpayer-Makov, eds., *Police Detectives in History, 1750–1950*,

outside London and, for appropriate remuneration, they claimed to be ready to leave at 15 minutes' notice.[38]

In addition to sharing their continental European counterparts' concerns about the idle poor and the Paris police's recognition of the importance of information in the detection of crimes and the pursuit of offenders, the Fieldings also sought to crystallize the idea of police as respectable crime fighters. In eighteenth-century England the thief-taker was perceived as necessary, but he was also despised and with some justification given the well-publicized and notorious behaviour of first, Jonathan Wild and then, a generation later, the McDaniel gang.[39] The problems were principally the result of the reward system which, even though significantly limited in the second half of the eighteenth century, still provided opportunities for the unscrupulous, entrepreneurial thief-taker.[40] But for Henry Fielding, 'if to do Good to Society be laudable, so is the Office of a Thief-catcher; and if to do the Good at the extreme Hazard of your Life be honourable, then is this Office honourable.'[41] European thief-takers were not singled out for the same sort of odium as those in England, but then the opportunities for 'blood-money' rewards do not appear to have been anything like as significant. The *Maréchaussée*, as noted above, was perceived as providing cheap and speedy justice, even if the presence of the *cavaliers* to break up boisterous and rough behaviour at village fêtes or to seize peasants' guns was not always appreciated. The *cahiers des doléances* at the outset of the Revolution generally

Aldershot: Ashgate, 2006; David John Cox, ' "A Certain Share of Low Cunning": An Analysis of the Work of Bow Street Principal Officers, 1792–1839, with Particular Emphasis on their Provincial Duties', Ph.D., Lancaster University, 2006. The Principal Officers are commonly referred to as 'Runners'. The term 'Bow Street Runner' appears to have been first used at an Old Bailey trial in September 1754. Bow Street personnel did not use the term and considered it to be disparaging.

[38] *Public Advertiser*, 19 Oct. 1754. My thanks to David Cox for this reference.

[39] Gerald Howson, *Thief-Taker General: The Rise and Fall of Jonathan Wild*, London: Hutchinson, 1970; Ruth Paley, 'Thief-Takers in London in the Age of the McDaniel Gang *c.*1745–1754', in Douglas Hay and Francis Snyder, eds., *Policing and Prosecution in Britain 1750–1850*, Oxford: Clarendon Press, 1989. Henry Fielding, of course, contributed to the notoriety of Wild with his novel about the thief-taker, even though this was intended as a satire on the prime minister Sir Robert Walpole. For criticism of the thief-taker see e.g. Blizard, *Desultory Reflections*, 4.

[40] An Act of 1692 was the first to establish a permanent reward: it promised £40, together with the horse, arms, and any legally acquired money belonging to an offender, to any individual involved in the arrest and conviction of robbers on either the highways or urban streets. Similar legislation followed for other types of offence and, from time to time, royal proclamations offered huge additions for a fixed period to combat a particular form of crime. These rewards encouraged some of the less scrupulous thief-takers to organize a prosecution, even to organize an offence so that they could claim the blood money. That the restrictions imposed in the second half of the century did not stamp out abuses was demonstrated with the prosecution of a corrupt Bow Street patrolman, George Vaughan, in 1816 (see below, p. 106).

[41] Fielding, *An Enquiry* 153.

called for more, rather than less of them. The Paris police were used similarly by the populace; and even families of relatively modest means called on the *lieutenant général* to discipline unruly children by means of a *lettre de cachet*. But the *lettre de cachet* and the 'booted justice' of the *Maréchaussée* appeared as arbitrary instruments to Enlightenment thinkers. The spies of the police appeared too involved with shoring up the regime and persecuting its critics; as a consequence the *lieutenant général* became a target for the libels of Grub Street critics—Lenoir was accused, for example, of using his police to kidnap men's wives so as to supply women for the orgies of aristocrats.[42] When the Revolution swept away the old order, the *lieutenant général's* police organization went with it.

[42] Robert Darnton, 'The Memoirs of Lenoir, Lieutenant de Police of Paris, 1774–1785', *English Historical Review*, 85 (1970), 532–59; 535 n. 1.

PART II

THE REVOLUTIONARY ERA

5

The New French System

THE French Revolution provided the opportunity for sweeping away the old structures in France and building anew in accordance with the ideas of the Enlightenment. The liberal, constitutional reformers of the early years of the Revolution expected to be able to construct a uniform, rational system of administration across France. Reforming the criminal law so as to establish equality and impartiality towards victims, the accused, and the convicted was part and parcel of this expectation. Contingency and difficulties unforeseen by ardent holders of the Enlightenment faith, together with political events, conspired to hamper their aspirations towards creating the perfect system. Yet significant reforms and changes were effected, many of which had been prefigured in the thinking and in the more tentative steps taken as the old regime neared its cataclysmic demise. The reforms and changes, promised by the Enlightenment and wrought by the Revolution, provided models and inspiration for princes, their ministers, and criminal law reformers across Europe. Over the three decades following the fall of the Bastille, sometimes with the encouragement of French bayonets but more often without, criminal law reform and penal change were keenly debated and oftentimes implemented.

The Declaration of the Rights of Man and Citizen adopted by the French Assembly on 26 August 1789 made a series of statements central to any criminal law. Liberty was to be determined only by law and law could only prohibit actions injurious to society (articles iv and v). All citizens were equal before the law (article vi). No one was to be arrested, detained, or indicted except in instances determined by the law, and such law had to have been in existence prior to the alleged offence (article vii). No one was to be punished except by use of a punishment determined by the law (article viii) and no one was to be deemed guilty until proven such (article ix). Within a few years of the Declaration the old mixture of courts was replaced with little controversy. Minor offences such as petty thefts and assaults, damage to crops, verbal insults, and so forth, were to be brought before correctional courts presided over by the new justice of the peace (*juge de paix*) sitting with two *assesseurs*. More serious offences were to be heard before judges in criminal courts. There were between three and eight correctional courts and one criminal court in each of the new administrative departments. Changes were made particularly to the form of the correctional courts over the revolutionary decade, but the two-tier system of correctional and criminal courts was to last throughout the nineteenth century and beyond.

The National Assembly appointed two committees to prepare a new code of criminal procedure and a new criminal code. Each had for its *rapporteur* a young former magistrate from the now abolished *parlement* of Paris, respectively Adrien Duport and Louis-Michel Le Pelletier de Saint Fargeau. Duport was particularly keen on the English legal system and the use of the jury. The jury, he maintained, replaced rigid legal proofs and measures of guilt with the common sense of citizens. In spite of opposition from some members of his committee, he succeeded in making juries a central feature of the new criminal procedure. As in England, a grand jury (*jury d'accusation*) was to assess the evidence and decide whether a case should go to trial, while a petty or trial jury (*jury de jugement*) was to determine the case on the oral evidence presented in court. The new code of criminal procedure was established by law on 16 September 1791. The new criminal code followed nine days later.

Le Pelletier was full of Enlightenment idealism:

Everywhere that you find despotism it is noticeable that crimes multiply all the more. And so it must be, because there man is degraded; and it can be said that liberty, like strong vigorous plants, soon purifies of all wicked impurities the happy soil where she has germinated.

In explaining the intentions of his committee he spoke in terms of a humane and simplified code that sought to prevent crime rather than just to punish. Punishment itself, he maintained, should be designed to deter potential offenders but also to rehabilitate those who suffered it. Moreover, it should be in direct relation to the offence committed; thus, fierce and violent offenders should suffer pain while those who committed crimes as a result of their idleness should be punished with hard work. Finally, punishment should be fixed and invariable with no opportunity for a judge to employ any capriciousness. For the same reason the prerogative of the head of state to pardon or commute a sentence was also to be removed. The principal form of punishment for serious offenders was to be prison, though the committee also suggested deportation for life for recidivists after a second term of imprisonment. In keeping with much Enlightenment thinking on punishment, the committee recommended the abolition of both corporal punishment and the death penalty.[1]

While there had been sympathy for reforming the system under the old regime, the proposals of Le Pelletier's committee went much further than many had envisioned before 1789. There were heated exchanges over the proposed abolition of corporal punishment and the death penalty. The former proposal was accepted but, in spite of powerful arguments against the death penalty, not least by the deputy for Arras Maximilien Robespierre, the punishment was maintained for the most serious offences such as murder, treason, and the destruction of public property by arson or the use of explosives. The decision was also made to establish decapitation, the practice previously reserved for nobles, as the sole means of execution. The public executioner in Paris, Charles Henri Sanson, expressed concerns about this. It may have been that he lacked confidence in his skill with a sword—he had botched the execution of the Comte de Lally in 1766—but he drafted a report noting the need for several expensive blades in case damage occurred during multiple executions. He was also worried that, in the case of multiple executions, those who came towards the end of the list might become faint or cringe before the blow and this, he warned, could lead to accidents and errors. As a response the secretary of the Academy of Surgery was charged with developing a machine previously proposed by Dr Joseph Ignace Guillotin, who was himself a member of the assembly and well-known for his courageous stand on behalf of the Third Estate at the outset of the Revolution. Guillotin's intention in advocating the instrument that was subsequently to bear his name was to ease suffering and cruelty on the scaffold with a speedy, mechanical action. The machine was another way to demonstrate the intellectual and social progress manifested by the Revolution. It was first used on a street robber, Nicolas Jacques Pelletier, on 25 April 1792. The Parisian crowd appear to have been unimpressed and some expressed disappointment at the speed of the proceedings. Over the following year, however, the machine, *la Sainte Guillotine*, acquired its frightful image as the 'ensign' of the Jacobin

[1] *Archives Parlementaires de 1787 à 1799*, vol. 26, 23 May 1791, pp. 319–32; quotation at p. 332. Pierre Lascoumes, Pierrette Poncela, and Pierre Lenoël, *Au nom de l'ordre: une histoire politique du code pénale*, Paris: Hachette, 1989, provides a detailed assessment of the origins and development of the Criminal Code of 1791 including a full text of Le Pelletier's speech (pp. 327–53) and of the code itself (pp. 357–70).

Terror.[2] This made excellent propaganda for opponents of the Revolution. Yet the guillotining during the Terror, inflicted on the political, social, and economic enemies of an embattled regime, and the guillotining during its immediate aftermath, when scores were settled and different political enemies were eradicated, were exceptional. They did not set a pattern for the mass execution of criminal offenders, and the annual number of non-political victims remained relatively few and relatively static.

The code drafted by Le Pelletier's committee in 1791 intended that incarceration should be the principal form of punishment. The committee expressed the hope that prison would correct the offender through a mixture of solitude and paid work. A *maison d'arrêt et de justice* was to be established close to each tribunal for those awaiting trial. Those sentenced for misdemeanours (*délits*) were to be imprisoned in *maisons de correction*; those sentenced for felonies (*crimes*) were to be imprisoned in *maisons de force*, and the most serious offenders were to be sent to work in the arsenals, the *bagne*. Over the next two decades a few old prisons were extended and other buildings were converted, especially convents and various other church buildings that had been appropriated by the state. But in spite of the floods of prisoners brought in by various purges and panics during the Revolution, little money was available for prison conversions let alone for a major prison building programme. While the revolutionary period is notorious for the manner in which political, economic, and social suspects were identified, arrested, and often killed by different regimes, there was little change in the understanding of non-political offenders. The same social groups remained suspect; beggars and vagabonds remained high on the list of those stigmatized. In Messidor year VI, for example, Dr Pierre-Jean-Georges Cabanis urged the Council of Five Hundred to develop a common system across the country to link prisons with *hôpitaux* so as to deal with the linked problems of poverty, vagabondage, and crime. 'How could mendacity be declared a crime if public authority, in the name of the nation, had not established sufficient assistance to prevent or to alleviate misery?' He wanted prisons to be 'veritable infirmaries for crime, where this form of malady could be treated with the same surety of method and the same hope of success as other disorders of the spirit'.[3] The revolutionaries had great plans for dealing with the poor but, as with the

---

[2] Daniel Arasse, *The Guillotine and the Terror*, tr. Christopher Miller, London: Allen Lane, 1989; first published as *La guillotine et l'imaginaire de la terreur*, Paris: Flammarion, 1987.

[3] *Conseil des Cinq-Cents, Opinion de Cabanis, Deputé de la Seine, sur la nécessité de réunir en un seul système commun, la législation des prisons et celle des secours publics. Séance de 7 messidor an 6*, pp. 2–3.

plans for prisons, these were severely hampered by a lack of money—a lack that was worsened by the costs of continuous war.

The situation did not improve when revolutionary regimes gave way to the rule of Napoleon. Imperial directives were issued. In 1808 the building of *maisons centrales* was ordered; these institutions were to provide work facilities for all inmates. Two years later instructions were issued that all prisons should be brought up to a basic standard. On this occasion money was set aside for the building of central prisons and, within a decade, eight new prisons were constructed. A division was also made between institutions that were to hold those given short-term sentences of up to a year and institutions that were to hold those with longer sentences. The former were to be the responsibility of the departments in which they were situated and the latter were to be directed by central government. This division was to continue until the close of the Second World War, but it was the only significant long-lasting change in the prison system to emerge from the Napoleonic regime.[4] Changes in the criminal law, however, were a different matter.

The fears and pressures of the revolutionary decade prompted some backtracking on the legal rights enshrined in the Declaration of the Rights of Man and Citizen and in the codes of 1791. It has been popular among some historians to see the violence of the Terror as the logical outcome of pre-revolutionary thought and as inherent in the Revolution from the beginning. In a similar manner, and following Foucault, it has been popular recently to dismiss the humanitarian discourse of the Enlightenment as largely irrelevant in the moves towards the imposition of greater control and of increased social discipline. Yet a careful assessment of the way that political justice functioned in 1789–90 suggests that the authorities in Paris were trying to act with restraint and humanity consistent with the liberal and humanitarian ideals of the Enlightenment. There were some signs of unwillingness to tolerate opposition, but there is no reason to dismiss the idealism and professed humanitarianism of the revolutionaries in the early stages of the upheaval simply because they run counter to a broad theoretical perspective that privileges a perspective of control.[5]

The Law of Suspects of 17 September 1793 was a notable act backtracking on the new rights promised in 1789. It was passed in the aftermath of

---

[4] Patricia O'Brien, *The Promise of Punishment: Prisons in Nineteenth-Century France*, Princeton: Princeton University Press, 1982, 22.

[5] Barry M. Shapiro, *Revolutionary Justice in Paris 1789–1790*, Cambridge: Cambridge University Press, 1993.

the Parisian Sections' march on the Convention demanding that 'terror' be made 'the order of the day'. It authorized local surveillance committees to draw up lists of people to be arrested, including, amongst the usual political suspects, those who could not show that they had a job. Individuals who idled were seen as much as a threat to, and drain upon, the Republic by the radical *sans-culotte* populace as they were by the respectable deputies in their knee-breeches and stockings. Napoleon wanted both a tougher and a more pragmatic legal system than that established in 1791. He restored the head of state's prerogative of clemency when he became consul for life in 1802. Thereafter he instructed the preparation of a new code of criminal procedure and a new criminal code as part of his legal reorganization of France and its empire. The Code of Criminal Procedure (1808) reintroduced some of the old regime's practices in the form of initial, written assessments of a case prepared by a *juge d'instruction* without the accused knowing much of the charges against him. At the same time the *jury d'accusation* was abolished and only with difficulty was Napoleon persuaded to allow the trial jury to continue for serious cases. Preventive detention was formally established. This is best known for having been used against Napoleon's political opponents but it also had a much wider use. For some years the new Prefect of Police in Paris had been following the tradition of the old regime by imprisoning petty offenders and others, often at the behest of their distraught families, and for what he interpreted as the good of society. In Fructidor Year XII, for example, the prefect was faced with the problem of 16-year-old Nicolas Brunet, an apprentice roofer and a known thief with a string of convictions, and 19-year-old Jean-Nicolas Laventurier, also a roofer, who had been arrested on several occasions for theft but never convicted. Brunet had just been arrested for attacking and robbing a dealer in second-hand clothes; a victim who had had his watch stolen had identified Laventurier as the thief. In neither case, however, did the prefect think that there was sufficient evidence to get a conviction before a tribunal. He therefore proposed to the minister of police that both Brunet and Laventurier be imprisoned for three months; the minister approved the suggestion.[6] Just under three years later, in July 1806, there was the problem of 21-year-old Marguerite Besnard, who had been surprised in the act of stealing from a wine-merchant's till. Unfortunately the wine merchant's wife had acted before Besnard had taken any money and there was no sworn complaint to lay before a tribunal. Irrespective of

---

[6] AN F⁷ 3119, 7 fructidor, Year XII.

the suspicion of theft, the prefect was worried that alone and without means of existence in Paris, Besnard would become a prostitute and he therefore proposed to send her back to the Calvados, her department of origin, to a village close to her parents.[7] Some parents were even prepared to apply to the prefect to have unruly children held under preventive detention or, if a son was a little older, to have him sent into the army.[8]

The Criminal Code of 1810 coincided with the regime's attempts to bring prisons up to a basic standard and still saw prison as a key component in the broad pattern of punishment. But the new code restored some of the more brutal elements of punishment such as branding and mutilation—henceforth a parricide was to have his hand lopped off before being guillotined. The Comte de Treilhard, another veteran of the *parlement* of Paris, introduced the new Criminal Code to the legislature, suggesting that the assembly in 1791 had erred a little too far on seeing goodness in people.

The Constituent Assembly liberated our penal legislation from many tendencies against which humanity had long protested. . . .

This was already a great step towards perfection; but this celebrated assembly, that distinguished itself with so many useful ideas, that destroyed so many abuses, that had, as no one can deny, such a purity of intentions, did not always protect itself against its enthusiasm for the good. The torch of experience, that it lacked, has led us to appreciate useful improvements required by the Code of 1791.[9]

Criminal justice under Napoleon thus took a step back towards some of the crueller elements of the old regime. Overall it became more personalized and contingent; and, depending on an observer's perspective on the Napoleonic regime, justice became 'more arbitrary or more pragmatically flexible'.[10]

But while, in theory, the sense of the criminal law after 1791 was rigid but liberal, and while, under Napoleon, it became more flexible and pragmatic, if much more harsh, the ways in which the law was administered and interpreted on the ground could vary enormously. There is often an assumption that the creation of new legislation meant, automatically, that such legislation was understood and enforced uniformly across a nation state or an empire. In fact the way in which information about the law, about new rights and

    7 AN F[7] 3124, 16 July 1806.
    8 AN F[7] 3119, 30 thermidor, Year XII; F[7] 3129, 16 Sept. 1808; F[7] 3139, 18 June 1812.
    9 *Le Moniteur*, 7 February 1810.
    10 Isser Woloch, *Napoleon and his Collaborators: The Making of a Dictatorship*, New York: W. W. Norton, 2001, 191. Lascombes, Poncela and Lenoël, *Au nom de l'ordre*, stress that, while the Code of 1810 is normally taken as a point of reference for French Criminal Law it was, in essence, only a reform of the Code of 1791. They reproduce the code on pp. 371–94.

liberties spread through the countryside of revolutionary France has rarely been considered. The culture of most rural inhabitants was an oral one and most French rural dwellers spoke a patois or even a language different from French. Across France in the summer and autumn of 1789 there were long sessions after Sunday mass in which the new revolutionary decrees were read out to the congregations. While the listeners were used to oral exposition, it remains questionable as to how much they absorbed and understood.[11] Parish priests, and perhaps even some gendarmes, provided conduits for making the law public, though such men may not always have had the literacy or knowledge to do this without mistakes. Similarly there were private intermediaries and lawyers, sometimes with personal axes to grind or an interest at stake, who also provided explanations and interpretations of the law for those who wanted to know, or who would listen.

The announcement of legal change and of the creation of new laws based on rationality was not going to change peasant attitudes overnight. The creation of the new, local justices of the peace in 1790 had an impact on the countryside, but this impact was slow and varied rather than sudden and uniform. These men, locally appointed, provided speedy justice in the name of the state. They were authorized to deal with a range of petty offences including verbal and physical assault, petty theft, vandalism, begging, and vagrancy. Over the long term, the justices probably helped to legitimize and to further the acceptance of the state and its law in the countryside.[12] But for a long time peasants also maintained their own view of the world that made perfect sense to them and did not necessarily conform to the rational beliefs of enlightened jurists and legislators. There may have been an insistence that the new law was impartial, yet it might not have appeared that way within rural communities. The law, as ever, depended upon individuals coming forward to give information. If individuals were too suspicious of the state and its agents or too frightened to come forward in this way, then either no case could be made or else agents of the state could become involved in a way which might suggest that they were taking sides in a community conflict. A French justice of the peace outlined such a problem in the Year IV: 'A proprietor sees an animal on his land and seizes it; there is no witness. The owner of the animal accuses the proprietor of theft; sometimes they come to

[11] Clay Ramsay, *The Ideology of the Great Fear: The Soissonais in 1789*, Baltimore: Johns Hopkins University Press, 1992, 173–6.

[12] Anthony Crubaugh, *Balancing the Scales of Justice: Local Courts and Rural society in Southwest France, 1750–1800*, University Park: Pennsylvania State University Press, 2001.

blows. It would surely be embarrassing for the agent of the state to render justice in this instance.'[13] In addition, the high-flown rhetoric of members of the national assemblies about rights and liberties could take on a very different meaning in the context of the peasant community. The peasants had, after all, wrestled with seigneurs and their agents over feudal dues for at least a hundred years before the Revolution. In the Year VII a farmer protested that peasant offenders were now filled with the idea of their rights to do whatever they wished with the lands appropriated from the church, the monarchy, and *émigrés*. '[The peasant] sees himself as the sole proprietor of the *biens nationaux* that are within his reach, and he doesn't doubt that he can ravage at will. He has learned to covert particular properties; in his opinion some are too extensive while others are in the hands of people he can despoil.'[14] No doubt this farmer had his own agenda and quite possibly was overstating his problems. But similar examples of peasant interpretations of new rights were to recur far beyond the frontiers of France during the nineteenth century when revolutionaries or new regimes made declarations about new laws and new liberties.[15]

Nor were rural communities readily convinced by the rationality of the jurist's law. Indeed, in some instances in the eyes of many peasants the law could seem quite irrational, at least in their terms. A village community might know who had committed an offence but then find that the state's functionaries refused to proceed with a trial on the grounds of insufficient evidence. In cases of witchcraft where a victim or victims consulted a counter-sorcerer and believed that their subsequent actions had led to the death of their tormentor, the state's law might respond in two distinct ways. On the one hand the state's functionaries could refuse to prosecute on the grounds that a case could not be based on what the law considered to be an

[13] Octave Festy, *Les délits ruraux et leur repression sous la Révolution et le Consulat*, Paris: Éditions Marcel Rivière, 1956, 44 n. 1.

[14] Ibid. 22.

[15] Peasants in Valencia, for example, took the declaration by the liberal Cortes of August 1811 abolishing *seigneuries* to mean that all territorial and jurisdictional privileges had been abolished. Adrian Schubert, *A Social History of Modern Spain*, London: Unwin Hyman, 1990, 92 and 97. In 1908 Edith Durham met Albanians who declared that: 'If it is true that Konstitutzioon means that all the land is free, [prisons] will not be wanted anymore.' Moreover, they were not prepared to support the 'Konstitutzioon' unless it was wealthy and suited them, at which point they would be prepared to pay 'a little tax'. Edith Durham, *High Albania: A Victorian Traveller's Balkan Odyssey*, London: Phoenix Press, 2000, 327–8 (1st edn., London: Edward Arnold, 1909). Irish land claimants were incensed when tribunals established by the Dáil Éireann in 1920, as alternatives to British courts, made decisions in favour of existing landowners. In consequence, they declared the new system to be 'worse than the British'. Heather Laird, *Subversive Law in Ireland 1879–1920: From 'Unwritten Law' to the Dáil Courts*, Dublin: Four Courts Press, 2005, 125–7.

illogical superstitious premise. On the other hand a prosecution might be conducted. In the latter instances a severe sentence could prompt protests that the convicted person had only meant to frighten a tormentor. A lenient sentence, imposed on the grounds that the perpetrator was ignorant, foolish, and superstitious, in turn was seen as illogical. Peasants, after all, knew the seriousness of witchcraft. It might be foolish, even illogical, in the way that it was read by some policemen and all lawyers, and in the way that it was translated by these functionaries into the language of the law. But it was not illogical superstition by those caught in the perception of the peasant community.[16] In 1845 the frustrated president of the assizes in Pyrénées-Orientales wrote to the Ministry of Justice to explain the recent acquittal of a man accused of murdering an old woman. The man's family had been struck down by a mortal sickness.

It is believed in this region that to compel a witch to remove a spell that she has cast you must beat her with a sack full of sand, and if you put a piece of silver in the bottom of the sack this will prevent the witch from remembering the name or the face of her attacker. . . . The foreman of the jury, in giving his report of the acquittal verdict exclaimed: 'Well, that's one witch less!'[17]

Beyond the webs of sorcery and witchcraft some communities challenged the new law and legal structures in other ways. The jury was the clearest example. Many of the men selected for jury service preferred to use local knowledge of the victim and of the accused and to follow instincts of community solidarity and preservation rather than reaching a verdict based on evidence presented in court. Moreover, as one official noted from distant Roussillon: 'Every means is employed to influence the jury or make it sympathetic. The accused are seconded by immoral men who, in many instances, don't hesitate to use intimidation.'[18] This problem became particularly acute in the aftermath of the Terror as individuals and communities sought to settle old scores and the juries hearing cases could be cheered or menaced from the public galleries.

---

[16] Judith Devlin, *The Superstitious Mind: French Peasants and the Supernatural in the Nineteenth Century*, New Haven: Yale University Press, 1987, 116. See also Jeanne Favret-Saada, *Deadly Words: Witchcraft in the Bocage*, Cambridge: Cambridge University Press, 1980, 65. Favret-Saada did anthropological work in north-west France between 1969 and 1975. Only when she was 'caught' in the web of sorcerers was she made party to local perceptions and did she hear the local words for these individuals.

[17] Quoted in Elisabeth Claverie, 'De la difficulté de faire un citoyen: les "acquittements scandaleux" du jury dans la France provinciale du début du XIXe siècle', *Études rurales*, 95–6 (1984) 143–66; 157.

[18] Quoted in Michel Brunet, *Le Roussillon: une société contre l'état (1780–1820)*, Perpignan: Llibres del Trabucaire, 1990, 512.

But the problem of wilful juries did not only involve political animosities generated by the experience of revolution. In Year V Jean-Claude Levan, a pedlar of no fixed abode, and his wife were arrested while wearing and carrying goods that had been reported stolen. At their trial in the Côte d'Or, however, the jury found them not guilty and went so far as to declare that no crime had been committed.[19] This was probably a particularly extreme case but, as a verdict against strong evidence, it was not unique. The 1808 Code of Criminal Procedure kept the jury trial for felonies but it raised considerably the requirements of eligibility for service with the intention of recruiting men of greater property who were expected to be more dependable. The better-off, however, often successfully avoided the burden of jury service, and even under the new restrictions the pool of jurors could still include rural dwellers who, while they had property, had little education and an imperfect understanding of French; many still generally conversed in the local patois. Jurors also continued to bring to the courtroom local knowledge that they had no intention of rejecting when the logic of the legal evidence pointed to a conclusion that did not conform to it. Well into the nineteenth century juries, particularly those in overwhelmingly rural areas, continued to convict and to acquit against the evidence. Sometimes they did so when a long period had elapsed between the offence and the prosecution, especially if the accused was shown to have lived a good life since the offence, even when the offence was homicide. Juries commonly showed a greater generosity towards offenders against the person than offenders against property, and more sympathy towards men of substance and local influence. Moreover, while regimes constantly changed the regulations to ensure juries that might be assumed more likely to convict those charged with political offences and with publishing radical newspapers and tracts, for most of the time jurors appear to have been singularly unwilling to find such offenders guilty.[20]

---

[19] Robert B. Allen, 'The Criminal Court of the Côte-d'Or, 1792–1811', Ph.D., Columbia University, 1991, 276.

[20] For the jury during the Revolutionary and Napoleonic period see Allen, 'The Criminal Court', and Isser Woloch, *The New Regime: Transformations of the French Civic Order, 1789–1820s*, New York: W W. Norton, 1994, ch. 12. For the jury of the Restoration, the July Monarchy, and beyond see James M. Donovan, 'Justice Unblind: The Juries and the Criminal Classes in France, 1825–1914', *Journal of Social History*, 15, 1 (1981), 89–107; Claverie, 'De la difficulté de faire un citoyen'; and Yves Porcher, '"Des assises de grâce?" Le jury de la cour d'assises de la Lozère au XIXe siècle', *Études rurales*, 95 (1984), 167–80; François Ploux, *Guerres paysannes en Quercy: violences, conciliations et répression pénale dans les campagnes du Lot (1810–1860)*, Paris: La Boutique d'histoire, 2002, 312, 314–16, and 329–53. For the changing regulations and for the reluctance of juries to convict political offenders see James M. Donovan, 'The Changing Composition of Juries in France, 1791–1913', *Proceedings of the Western Society for French History*, 23 (1996), 256–72.

Beyond the frontiers of Revolutionary France old regime jurists continued to refine the traditional ideas. In Prussia, for example, the legal scholars Cristoph Stübel and Karl von Grolmann had expounded the theory of behavioural prevention (*Spezialpräventionstheorie*) that justified the state's right to hold in indefinite detention any offenders considered to be of a danger to society. The *Allgemeines Landrecht* promulgated for Prussia in 1794 incorporated this theory by providing for the indefinite detention of thieves and recidivists until they could prove their reformation and how they would make an honest living when released. This was alleviated somewhat by an order for the punishment of theft in 1799 and the Criminal Ordinance of 1805 that allowed indefinite detention until an offender was deemed rehabilitated.[21] But in many parts of Europe both the new ideas and the French legal codes themselves were carried and established first by the armies of the Revolution and then by those of Napoleon.

Those areas incorporated into France had the new legislation imposed upon them. In Belgium, Piedmont, and the Rhineland the experience of the legislation lasted for many years and left a powerful legacy. Many favoured continuing with the French system after Napoleon's fall partly because it seemed to function better than the alternative, partly because people had become used to it and resented further change, especially when this was foisted on them by other outsiders. Piedmont was incorporated into France in 1802; twelve years later, when Victor Emmanuel I of Savoy was restored to his throne, he set out also to restore the old legal structures. The French courts were abolished and the judges who had collaborated were dismissed; the presentation of evidence in open court was replaced by the old inquisitorial methods. But Victor Emmanuel's actions generated concerns among many of those responsible for the administration of justice, while the corruption that seeped back into the system was disliked by those who had to use it. In 1822 the first steps were taken to re-establish French court practices though it was not until 1848 that a Piedmontese Code of Criminal Procedure on the French model was reintroduced.[22] Piedmont remained wary of the jury trial, however, and in 1848, when, very tentatively, it

21 Richard F. Wetzell, 'Criminal Law Reform in Imperial Germany', Ph.D., Stanford University, 1991, 17–19.
22 Michael Broers, *Napoleonic Imperialism and the Savoyard Monarchy, 1773–1821: State Building in Piedmont*, Lewiston, NY: Edwin Mellen Press, 1997, 504–6; Ettore Dezza, 'L'organization judiciaire et la procédure pénale en Italie de 1796 à 1859', in Xavier Rousseaux, Marie-Sylvie Dupont-Bouchat, and Claude Vael, eds., *Révolutions et justice pénale en Europe: modèles français et traditions nationales (1780–1830)*, Paris: L'Harmattan, 1999, 137–8.

was introduced for the first time, the jury was restricted to trials involving the press.

Belgium, liberated from Habsburg control, was incorporated into the French Republic and made subject to French laws from the end of 1795. On the final defeat of Napoleon, however, it was annexed to the Kingdom of the Netherlands and subject to Dutch law. The Netherlands itself had experienced a succession of legal changes under French influence over the revolutionary and Napoleonic period. A committee had been appointed in 1798 to consider a new code for the then Batavian Republic but it was six years before any legislative change occurred. As the Kingdom of Holland, with Napoleon's brother Louis as king, it received yet another new code in 1809. In the following year Louis was forced to abdicate and his kingdom was annexed to France with the Code Napoleon imposed from 1811. The new code was unpopular, partly perhaps because of a poor translation into Dutch but also, probably, because of a general resentment at Napoleon's behaviour and, worst of all, by his imposition of conscription. It is tempting to wonder just how far French legal procedures were followed, particularly in some of the more remote areas of departments such as Bouches-de-l'Yssel and Frise. In 1814, after he had assumed the title of king, William, Prince of Orange, decided to keep most of the French criminal code, but he abolished the jury, reintroduced whipping as a punishment, and replaced the guillotine with hanging. A new Dutch Code was hammered out over the next decade that kept these changes, but once the Belgians won their independence in 1830 their Francophile elite looked back to, and restored, French practices such as the jury.[23]

The left bank of the Rhine had a rather similar experience to Belgium. It was occupied by French troops in the 1790s and its fifty-odd territorial entities were incorporated into the Republic and then the empire. When the Rhineland was handed to Prussia on the fall of Napoleon, the influential inhabitants who for nearly twenty years had prospered under French rule vigorously resisted the attempts by their new political masters to impose the *Allgemeines Landrecht* of 1794. The Rhinelanders appear particularly to have favoured the procedural system of the French. Court proceedings were oral and in public and the freedom from arbitrary decisions seemed guaranteed through trial by jury and a judiciary independent of the administration.

---

[23] Fred Stevens, ' "Il y aura un code pour tout le royaume": la codification du droit pénal dans le territoire de la Belgique et les Pays-Bas (1781–1835)', in Rousseaux, Dupont-Bouchat, and Vael, eds., *Révolutions et justice pénale*.

Rhenish judges were reputed to have used the law to stand up to Napoleon himself, and the politically active elements of the population appear to have seen the French code as a constitutional bulwark against the authorities in Berlin. The problem for the Prussians was compounded by the fact that the legal profession in the Rhineland had all been trained in French law and were unfamiliar with the Prussian system. Reluctantly the government in Berlin agreed that the new provinces in the west be allowed to keep the Napoleonic Code until a revision of the French and Prussian systems could be made. The King of Prussia was further surprised when his law commissioners concluded that the legal principles of the French system were, in many respects, superior. About 40 per cent of judges from the eastern provinces of Prussia served in the west at some time between Waterloo and the Revolution of 1848. Most appear to have returned to the east impressed by Rhenish legal practices and, contrary to what the king and his ministers had expected, the French code was to have a significant impact on the whole of Prussia. In 1849 Louis Simons, a Rhenish-born lawyer, became minister of justice in Berlin and fed elements of his French training into the revised legal code promulgated for Prussia in 1851.[24]

Belgians, Piedmontese, and Rhinelanders had little option in accepting French laws as part of French rule. The fact that many of the elite in Belgium and the Rhineland appear to have preferred it to the replacements offered after 1815 may have something to do with a desire to assert regional independence as much as any belief in the superiority of the French criminal justice system. Yet that system, for all Napoleon's toughening up of some of the liberal elements established in 1791, also continued to reflect many of the Enlightenment's aspirations for criminal procedure and punishment. Napoleonic patronage and the example of the new French administrative system, a system which appeared much more successful than old regime models, gave some other princes the encouragement that they needed to carry through reforms that were but dreamt of before 1789. In Bavaria, for example, Maximilian I Joseph, who owed his crown and his greatly extended kingdom to Napoleon's reorganization of Germany, ordered the preparation of a new legal code as one of several enlightened reforms that he and his principal minister, Count Montgelas, introduced. The man entrusted with

---

[24] Michael Rowe, *From Reich to State:The Rhineland in the Revolutionary Age, 1780–1830*, Cambridge: Cambridge University Press, 2003, 107–8 and 259–63; Jörg Engelbrecht, 'The French model and German society; the impact of the *Code penal* on the Rhineland', in Rousseaux, Dupont-Bouchat, and Vael, eds., *Révolutions et justice pénale*.

the preparation of the code was the young Prussian-born jurist Paul Anselm von Feuerbach, who had made his name with a series of legal writings at the turn of the century. Feuerbach was influenced by the reforming ideas of Beccaria and by the philosophy of Immanuel Kant. He was sceptical of ideas that suggested the perfectibility of any laws made by human beings and critical of vindictive punishment. He agreed with Kant that the law and ethics were separate, that moral behaviour was the result of choice, and that the state had no role to play in using the law to enforce morality. Crimes, however, were distinct from moral behaviour. From Beccaria he developed the idea of the principal purpose of criminal law being the deterrence of crime. Anyone guilty of a crime should be sure to get the same, predictable and fixed, punishment, regardless of rank. In this he challenged the *Spezialpräventionstheorie* of Stübel and von Grolmann. The new Bavarian Code, promulgated in 1813, was the first German legal code to deploy the new lines of thinking. It constituted a significant step away from the absolutist state and towards the *Rechtsstaat*, the state in which there was no crime and no punishment without the law and in which all functionaries of the state were equally subject to the law. The code formally abolished torture but it maintained the death penalty and the inquisitorial practices of the old regime; and also continued to require the deliberate confession of the accused either before two witnesses or the presiding judge. Roughly one-eighth of the 482 articles concerned the examination of the accused, and for at least two decades the courts and legal minds in Bavaria sought alternatives to ensure an open confession. Feuerbach believed that confessions eventually came through the offender's remorse and inability to withstand the pressure exerted by a judge in full possession of the facts.[25] He remained opposed to the introduction of the jury which he saw as introducing too many elements of unpredictability and discretion. While the Rhineland (under Prussia) and Belgium (once independent) maintained the jury system, Bavaria did not establish juries until the revolution of 1848. Other German states were similarly hesitant and similarly yielded to demands for juries only during the mid-century upheaval: Hesse-Darmstadt in 1848; Baden, Nassau, Prussia, and Württemberg in the following year. Other states established juries over a lengthy period in the second half of the century: Austria (1850–3); Piedmont/Italy (1859–65); Russia (1864); Spain (1869–75). The Bavarian Code struck a chord with princes, rulers,

---

[25] Wetzell. 'Criminal Law Reform', 19–23; Nassau Senior, 'Penal Jurisprudence of Germany: A Review of P. J. A. von Feuerbach's *Merkwürdige Criminal-Rechtsfalle*', *Edinburgh Review*, 82 (1845), 318–66.

and jurists elsewhere. The King of Sweden ordered it translated into Swedish. Three German states made it the basis of their own new codes: Saxe-Weimar, Württemberg, and the Grand Duchy of Oldenburg. It was used similarly in several Swiss cantons, but the Swiss also provide an example of this general pattern of penal reform going into reverse.

In Switzerland towards the end of the eighteenth century the kind of ideas popularized by Beccaria had also made an impact. The short-lived Helvetic Republic introduced a raft of penal reforms along Enlightenment lines. When the republic collapsed in 1803, however, some of the cantons reintroduced the *Carolina*. Zurich went so far as to re-establish a system that depended upon tradition and the discretion of judges who had no legal training. The return to the *Carolina*, moreover, implied a return to, and the sanction of, the use of torture to extract confessions from suspects; however, in practice torture does not appear to have been used.[26]

In the midst of the National Assembly's debates on law reform, and while the question of prison reform was under discussion, Jeremy Bentham sent to France his proposal for a circular prison in which convicts in their cells could be observed at all times by a keeper situated in the central well—the celebrated Panopticon. His letter to Brissot about the project contained the oft-quoted lines about 'a mill for grinding rogues honest, and idle men industrious'. The assembly appears to have thought that Bentham and his brother, a military engineer responsible for much of the design, were offering to establish and manage the institution without reward. The Benthams were not that altruistic and returned to pressing the project on the British government with, ultimately, a similar lack of success. The model continued to fascinate some penal reformers, as it has done historians. The Spanish Cortes established in the wake of the rebellion of 1820 planned to introduce it into Spain; but the liberals' rapid overthrow meant an end to their plans.[27] In the 1820s the Genevan-born Enlightenment thinker Étienne Dumont, who had become an intimate of Bentham and who had made a free translation of his penal work, oversaw the building of a Panopticon-style prison for Geneva. But while Bentham had proposed a full circle for the building with a supervisor based at the centre, Dumont's prison was only a semicircle. Moreover it was publicly managed rather than being contracted to a private

---

[26] Regula Ludi, *Die Fabrikation des Verbrechens: Zur Geschichte der modernen Kriminalpolitik, 1750–1850*, Tübingen: Bibliotheca Academica, 1999, esp. 325–6.

[27] Janet Semple, *Bentham's Prison: A Study of the Panopticon Penitentiary*, Oxford: Clarendon Press, 1993, 99–110 and 312. Semple also provides (pp. 11–14) an important corrective to the way that Foucault understood Bentham's project.

entrepreneur. Indeed, for an institution that was never built in Europe and when it was built, in Pittsburgh in the 1820s, that turned out to be riddled with problems, the Panopticon has acquired an amazing centrality in the work of historians of the prison.[28] The cold, supervisory mechanics might appeal to those analysts who find oppression as a key element in the new form of society emerging with what Eric Hobsbawm called 'the dual revolution', but the system did not find such favour with the men of power and authority in that society that they all decided to find the necessary money and to rush out and build it.

In Britain the same, or similar, ideas of legal and penal reform were in circulation but the different political context led to a rather different set of outcomes. The French assemblies were filled with men enthusiastic for reform. Napoleon's regime may have been repressive but several of his collaborators from the Brumaire coup maintained a brake on some of his more authoritarian aspirations and ensured the continuation of a liberal agenda.[29] The Bourbons made no attempt to restore the legal system of the old regime, indeed it was in the interests of the restored monarchy to maintain the new codes and systems since these ensured that the royal authority was now the sole legal authority. The British parliament had its liberal, penal reformers in the shape of men like Sir Samuel Romilly and Sir James Mackintosh. They had earnest and dedicated extramural collaborators particularly among the Evangelical and Quaker communities with men and women such as William Allen, Thomas Fowell Buxton, Elizabeth Fry, and Samuel Hoare. Parliament was prepared to countenance piecemeal change such as the abolition of the death penalty for picking pockets in 1808. But parliament was essentially a conservative body. In a narrow sense this conservatism was manifested by the House of Lords' rejection, five times in eight years, of a bill to remove the capital sanction from the offence of stealing from a shop.[30] In a broader sense such conservatism was reflected in both the continuance of eighteenth-century notions of the freeborn Englishman and the continuing pride in the long traditions of Habeas Corpus and trial by jury. The majority agreed with Edmund Burke, at least implicitly, that society was organic and it looked with horror at the chaos caused in France by attempts at root and branch reform.

---

[28] Robert Roth, *Pratiques pénitentiaires et théorie sociale: l'exemple de la prison de Genève (1825–1862)*, Geneva: Droz, 1981.

[29] Woloch, *Napoleon and his Collaborators*.

[30] Clive Emsley, *Crime and Society in England, 1750–1900*, 3rd edn., London: Longman, 2004, 272–3.

John Howard's work had encouraged parliament to pass enabling legislation for the building or improvement of local gaols and to talk about national convict prisons. It was this that had encouraged Bentham into offering his Panopticon plans, and his services as the entrepreneurial gaoler, to Pitt's government. Links that had developed between individual penal reformers in Britain and the American colonies had continued after the War of Independence and were strengthened by a formal link between the Philadelphia Society for Alleviating the Miseries of Public Prisons and the British Society for Diffusing Information upon the Punishment of Death. These societies saw it as their role to educate opinion and thus foster reform; they exchanged ideas and also published each others' works. The British association extended its remit by merging, in 1816, with the Society for Investigating the Cause and Increase of Juvenile Delinquency and becoming the London Society for the Improvement of Penal Discipline.[31] Significant change in imprisonment came, however, less through legislation and more because of changing practice in the courts. At the beginning of the nineteenth century many members of the judiciary were concerned about the sentencing options available to them, particularly when it came to dealing with juveniles. No formal system existed whereby such offenders could be sent to reformatory institutions, as many judges appear to have wished. As a consequence judges at the Old Bailey and some magistrates began making their own penal policy by using what was known as the 'respited judgment'. A nominal fine was recorded against a convicted juvenile's name and he or she was then sent to an institution, established and run by a philanthropic organization, where, it was hoped, he or she would be reformed. Initially the courts used the small Philanthropic Society and then, once it was opened in 1806, the London Refuge of the Destitute as the institutions for receiving these offenders. At these refuges, even though technically inmates were free to leave, in practice the juveniles sent from the courts were incarcerated and required to work through a two-year training programme. In 1816 the government tacitly recognized what was going on by awarding the London Refuge a substantial grant to continue the practice even though it remained without formal legal sanction.[32]

The development of this juvenile reformatory system took place in the economic and social context of a rapidly expanding metropolis, a war of

---

[31] Cindy C. Burgoyne, ' "Imprisonment the Best Punishment": The Transatlantic Exchange and Communication of Ideas in the Field of Penology, 1750–1820', Ph.D., University of Sunderland, 1997, esp. ch. 5.

[32] Peter King, *Remaking Justice from the Margins: The Courts, the Law and Patterns of Lawbreaking, 1750–1840*, Cambridge: Cambridge University Press, 2006, ch. 4.

unprecedented scale and duration, and amidst concerns about growing juvenile delinquency. Unlike many, and probably most, such developments, it did not involve debates among legislators. But debates among legislators about crime and legal reform are never conducted in an economic, political, and social vacuum. The French Revolution provided opportunities for the implementation of some Enlightenment aspirations. But the tensions and conflicts generated by the fevered atmosphere of revolution and its aftermath meant that many of the liberal ideas espoused in 1789 for equality and penal reform were obscured or remoulded in the light of subsequent violent events and political fears. In addition, the wars that followed the Revolution contributed, if not to a demonstrable increase in criminal behaviour, then at least to heightened anxieties about such. These anxieties contributed to calls for improvements in policing structures while the wars, and new systems of government and administration that emerged from the wars, provided opportunities for developing models that contemporaries believed to be more efficient and effective.

6

Crime and Police in Revolution and War

THE new French legal system was established, developed, and exported in a particularly turbulent period. Crowd action in the early stages of the Revolution was fostered and aggravated by food shortages, high prices, and the fear of brigands. The three decades following 1789 witnessed serious harvest deficiencies that led to popular disorder in markets and probably contributed to some petty theft. Moreover, as French revolutionaries closed convents, so the opportunities for the homeless and impoverished to find relief at the hands of the church were considerably diminished, again with the potential for driving the desperate to petty theft. Writing in 1806 Lenoir, the former *lieutenant général de Police*, drew attention to the problem and included the end of the old system of police together with the end of regular church charity as a contributory element in an apparent increase in vagrancy. The money for relief made available by the government, he believed, was woefully insufficient. Lenoir was hardly an unbiased commentator, but his basic argument was sound.[1] Again the focus of this chapter is France and England. Again this is justified by the contrasting models of policing that were identified at the time and that were taken up by the early historians of policing and perceived as immutable—a supposedly centralized and militarized system in France, a supposedly decentralized and unarmed, civilian system in England.

The incessant wars of the period 1792 to 1815 contributed to a rise in banditry in many areas and in a variety of ways. In Brabant and Piedmont the chaos brought about by war encouraged an upsurge in banditry, though in both regions the problem was eventually brought under control by the French. The breakdown of law and order during the Directory and the counter-revolutionary insurrection in the west fostered banditry in France. *La bande d'Orgères*, whose members murdered, raped, and robbed households, farms, and travellers on the highways, appears to have been a continuation of Hulin's band in the Beauce but reinvigorated by the

---

[1] MO Fonds anciens, manuscrit 1400, Mémoires de J.C.P. Lenoir, fo. 702.

flotsam of war and the chaos of revolution.[2] Economic upheaval aggravated by war contributed to a wave of brigandage in the mountainous regions between Baden, Franconia, and Hessen. In the seasons of fairs and markets particularly, between March and April and again in September, armed robberies and small-scale thefts occurred on the main roads running into the principal cities of Aschaffenburg, Frankfurt, and Mannheim. Here, once again, the boundaries and jealousies of different jurisdictions made pursuit and prosecution difficult.[3]

The demands of conscription led many young men to take to the forests and to swell bandit gangs. Deserters and stragglers from the different armies that crossed and recrossed much of Europe in the quarter-century of conflict also drifted into brigandage and other forms of robbery and violence. Three reports from the daily police bulletins of mid-July 1812 are illustrative of the problem across Napoleon's empire:

10 July, Tuscany—the night of 26 June 5 Neapolitan deserters broke in to a property in Palazzuolo (Arno); they tied up the owner and his son and carried off all that they could find.

14 July, Haute-Saône—the night of 6 July, 12 unknown individuals passed by close to Lure, firing a shot as they went down the mountain and headed towards the department of Doubs; they were deserters, born in Piedmont or Italy, travelling from the north.

15 July, Ille-et-Vilaine—the night of 6 July, 4 brigands demanded asylum of a farmer in the village of Landéan, claiming to be deserters; when the farmer refused they broke into his house; the farmer and his family fled; the brigands pillaged the surroundings for 2 hours.[4]

In Spain and Italy the wars saw guerrilla bands organized against the French, sometimes funded by British gold. Some of these bands became integrated with the armies, but more often, it appears, they were as dangerous to civilians as they were to the purported enemy. Historians of the brigands

---

[2] Michael Broers, *Napoleonic Imperialism and the Savoyard Monarchy, 1773–1821: State Building in Piedmont*, Lewiston, NY: Edwin Mellen Press, 1997, 329–49; Florike Egmond, *Underworlds: Organized Crime in the Netherlands 1650–1800*, Cambridge: Polity Press, 1993, 167–75; Richard Cobb, *Reactions to the French Revolution*, Oxford: Oxford University Press, 1972, ch. 5, esp. p. 193 and p. 289 n.o; and see also idem, *Paris and its Provinces, 1792–1802*, Oxford: Oxford University Press, 1975, ch. 5.

[3] Wolfgang Seidenspinner, 'Wirtschaftliche, Krisensituation und Bandenkriminalität. Das Beispiel des Spessart-Odenwald Bande (1802–1811)', in Gherardo Ortalli, ed., *Bande armate, banditi, banditismo e repressione di giustizia negli stati europei di antico regime*, Rome: Jouvence, 1986.

[4] Nicole Gotteri, ed., *La Police Secrète du Premier Empire: bulletins quotidiens addressés par Savary à l'Empereur de juillet à décembre 1812*, Paris: Honoré Champion, 2001, v. 40, 48, and 53.

fighting the Napoleonic armies in central and southern Italy have drawn conclusions about some of these brigands that are not greatly dissimilar from the conclusions drawn by the French who fought them.[5] A Spanish artillery officer, writing in 1811, considered that the guerrillas fighting on his side should be 'exterminated':

If some of them have brought benefits, the damage that others have wrought is one thousand times greater . . . Those who believe these bands . . . to be very useful are many, but if they meditate on the desertion from the enemy that has not occurred for fear of being murdered . . . the burnings and other disasters suffered by the villages . . . the many highwaymen and bandits who carry out their crimes under this pretext, and finally the manner in which their disorder and independence have caused all kinds of evil, they will understand how far the disadvantages outweigh the benefits.

One of the guerrilla leaders, Fransisco Espoz y Mina, reported that the bands in Navarre were in an appalling state before he established a semblance of order among them. Admittedly, like the artillery officer, he was hardly an unbiased observer, but it was significant that he found among these guerrillas not only Navarrese known for criminal behaviour and for escaping from prison, but also numbers of deserters from the imperial army of French, Swiss, Polish, Italian, and German origins.[6]

Napoleon's attempt to put Britain in a state of blockade also fostered an enormous growth in smuggling. This became a problem, not just in the traditional bandit-smuggler areas like the mountains of Piedmont but along the entire North Sea coast of the empire and also inland wherever it was possible to profit from bypassing customs duties. In January 1810, for example, there were reports from Holland and Belgium of floods of contraband with gangs of up to 200 men involved in the trafficking. Towards the close of the following year the police reported that, around Dunkirk, the principal resource of the workforce was smuggling. 'If this should be ended there would be a large number of indigents among them.' There were similar reports from north Germany where military occupation and imperial economic policy wrecked the Hanseatic ports and where the marshlands were

    [5] Milton Finley, *The Most Monstrous of Wars: Napoleonic Guerrilla War in Southern Italy, 1806–1811*, Columbia: University of South Carolina Press, 1994; Alexander Grab, 'State Power, Brigandage and Rural Resistance in Napoleonic Italy', *European History Quarterly*, 25, 1 (1995), 39–70.
    [6] Charles J. Esdaile, *Fighting Napoleon: Guerrillas, Bandits and Adventurers in Spain, 1808–1814*, New Haven: Yale University Press, 2004, quotations at 117 and 147.

full of draft-dodgers and poor people for whom smuggling seemed the only means of survival. [7]

But if war fostered banditry, the new state structures that Napoleon imposed on the western part of the old German Empire and that were maintained after his final defeat also provided the ideas and the means to check it. The creation of bigger states reduced the number of jurisdictions that bandits could cross and recross to avoid capture. More efficient state bureaucracies and treasuries, modelled on those of the French Empire, enabled the recruitment and maintenance of more efficient police. These police were also based on French models and were continued after the wars because of their apparent efficiency.

War, banditry, and trafficking in contraband were far from the minds of the liberal, constitutional monarchists who dominated the French National Assembly at the outset of the French Revolution. The revolutionaries' faith in humanity, the rights of man, rational argument and elective processes encouraged them in the belief that policing could be devolved to local administration. In Paris the *commissaires du Châtelet* became *commissaires de police*, and they were elected by the male citizens of their *quartier* for a term of two years. Similar posts under similar terms were established for provincial cities and towns. The *Maréchaussée* was reformed, expanded into the *Gendarmerie nationale* and, for a brief period, all appointments to the corps were the responsibility of the new local departmental administrations. The *inspecteurs* in Paris were replaced by *officiers de paix*, appointed by the municipality and responsible to the city mayor's police lieutenant. The twenty-four *officiers de paix* had authority throughout the city, and their role was seen as preventive. They were to be 'the protective shield of the metropolis' (*le bouclier de la sûreté de la Métropole*). They were expected to be paragons of revolutionary virtue showing respect for the law, liberty, and the rights of the individual, and it was expected that 'the fear of their presence [would] suffice to prevent the greater part of. . . disorders and offences.'[8]

Faith in humanity, unfortunately, did not mean faith in all social groups. The revolutionaries, like their predecessors, readily assumed that there were clear distinctions between those incapable of work, those temporarily out of

[7] Ernest d'Hauterive, ed., *La Police Secrète du Premier Empire: bulletins quotidiens adressés par Fouché à l'Empereur*, NS 5. *1809–1810*, Paris: Clavreuil, 1964, 302; Gotteri, ed., *La Police Secrète . . . juillet à décembre 1811*, iii. 362; Burghart Schmidt, 'Die Französische Polizei in Nord-deutschland: Die Berichte des Generalpolizeidirektors D'Aubignosc aus den Jahren 1811–1814', *Francia*, 26, 2 (1999), 99–114.

[8] J. Charron, *Des Officiers de Paix et de la Police Correctionelle*, Paris, 1792, 7–9.

work and those wilfully idle. Le Pelletier considered that need, 'the child of idleness', was the most common cause of crime. The prisons proposed by his committee were to encourage the offender to appreciate the value of work.[9] The National Convention's committee on welfare took a similar line. The able-bodied poor were to be offered subsistence through work.[10] Even before the closing of the church charities and the problem of growing numbers of deserters and draft-dodgers, the pamphlets of police reformers were expressing the old concerns about beggars and vagabonds, and the corrupting power of idleness among the labouring classes. Individuals that 'wallowed in idleness and did not blush from living at the expense of their fellow citizens' were identified once again as the problem.[11] An improved police together with a system of enforced registration were advocated, once again, as remedies, often by people, like Citizen Deroz of the Val-de-Grâce district of Paris, who had made such proposals under the old regime and who dusted them off and polished them up in the early years of the Revolution.[12]

These traditional anxieties, however, were rapidly eclipsed by the fear of counter-revolution, of political subversives, spies, and traitors. Then, as France emerged from the Terror, it was plunged into the plots, coups and counter-coups of the Directory. While Dr Cabanis was urging a common system linking prisons and *hôpitaux*, others called for fierce laws against offenders and for a thoroughgoing reorganization of the police and the *Gendarmerie* to meet the variety of internal threats.[13] Most people of property appear to have welcomed the strong hand that Citizen General Bonaparte promised following the coup of Brumaire. It is significant, however, that in the aftermath of the Revolution the strong hand sought at least the veneer of consent. One week after his appointment to head the new centralized police of Paris, Prefect Dubois addressed his fellow citizens promising a police that would be 'tough but humane' (*sévérité mais humanité*). 'Everything that has at some stage been the subject of your complaints will henceforth be the

---

[9] *Archives Parlémentaires de 1787 à 1799*, vol. 26, 23 May 1791, 323.

[10] Alan Forrest, *The French Revolution and the Poor*, Oxford: Basil Blackwell, 1981, 28; Isser Woloch, *The New Regime: Transformations of the French Civic Order, 1789–1820s*, New York: W. W. Norton, 1994, 247.

[11] Anon., *Plan de police, pour la sûreté et la tranquillité des habitans de la capitale*, Paris, 1790(?), 2–3.

[12] Le Sieur Deroz, *Sûreté publique, ou moyens simples de réformer et prévenir les désordres occasionnés par les vagabonds et gens sans aveu*, Paris, 1787; Citoyen Deroz, *Plan d'organization pour l'établissement d'un bureau de sûreté dans la capitale*, Paris, 1791(?); idem, *Observations importantes sur l'organization du bureau de sûreté*, Paris, 1791(?); see also, anon., *À monsieur le maire de Paris, et aux vrais patriotes, amis de l'ordre et des bonnes mœurs*, Paris, 1790.

[13] Vandermaesen, *La nouvelle police devoilée, ou les abus du government français*, Paris, 1798(?).

object of my care. . . . My eye will penetrate the hidden most recesses of the criminal soul but my ear will be open to the cries of innocence and even to the groans of repentance.'[14] An eye was also to be kept on people travelling the roads. The passbook for working men on the move that had been introduced towards the end of the old regime had fallen into disuse during the Revolution. In 1803 the Consulate brought in a more stringent system. The new *livret* was to be issued by the police or by municipal authorities to all male wage-earners in construction yards, factories, and workshops. It contained a physical description of the holder. When a man took a job he had to surrender the book to his new employer and, in theory at least, he could not get a job without such a book. The *livret*, in addition to reinforcing the worker's subordinate position, restricted movement and enabled the police easily to check up on travellers. Without an up-to-date *livret* any working man found on the roads could be apprehended by the police as a vagabond and was liable to a prison sentence. In addition, the Napoleonic police maintained their predecessors' surveillance of who was living in the *maisons garnies* and required also that all innkeepers and hoteliers keep up-to-date details of who was staying under their roofs.

In the eyes of many contemporaries and also of subsequent historians, the police in the France of Napoleon became strictly centralized and uniform. Yet the broad and varied tasks of policing were never brought together in a single institution and there could be rivalries and sharp divisions within the organizations responsible for carrying out different tasks in different administrative and geographical areas. These divisions were at their sharpest in what has been termed the 'duel' between Joseph Fouché, Minister of Police, and Marshal Moncey, Inspector General of the *Gendarmerie*.[15] From a distance the police in Paris may have appeared centralized and militarized, but the *Gendarmerie* company, established in the city in the wake of General Malet's failed coup in 1812, jealously guarded its independence and its military nature. The Prefect of Police might request the assistance of the gendarmes; he could not simply order it. His *commissaires* and *officiers* might carry out investigations, but it was not until 1809 that a separate detective department was established and, given the origin of its members (they were all ex-convicts), the prefect was not prepared to have it under the roof of the

---

[14] Quoted in full in Jean Rigotard, *La Police parisienne de Napoléon: la préfecture de police*, Paris: Tallandier, 1990, 45–6.

[15] Aurélien Lignereux, *Gendarmes et policiers dans la France de Napoléon: le duel Moncey–Fouché*, Maisons-Alfort: Études, Service historique de la *Gendarmerie* nationale, 2002.

Prefecture. This detective department was, moreover, funded out of secret money.

The *commissaires* in provincial France became centrally appointed under Napoleon, but both their remuneration and the number of men employed in the towns as their subordinates still depended on the local municipality and its financial discretion.[16] In 1791 the National Assembly authorized rural communes to appoint watchmen, the *gardes-champêtres*, to protect property and crops. Like the *commissaires*, these *gardes* were dependent on local inclination for appointment and payment. Some of them may have been efficient and courageous, but the overall impression reflected in contemporary correspondence and debate was that they were commonly the creatures of local mayors, underpaid, unreliable, and open to corruption.[17]

Much historical work on Napoleon's police has generally focused on their role in maintaining the regime and on what is commonly described as *haute police*. Unquestionably this role was important in the eyes of Napoleon and of the two men who served him successively as minister of police, Joseph Fouché and General Anne-Jean-Marie-René Savary. But the concept of police did not change significantly in France during the Revolutionary and Napoleonic periods and it continued to encompass a wide variety of functions. The *Gendarmerie nationale* was much bigger than its predecessor. This increased size and its better-quality personnel made it more effective in dealing with popular disorder and with various forms of crime and banditry. But it was also expected to keep an eye on public opinion and on the state of the markets, and to send in monthly reports on these matters.[18] Under Napoleon and his successors the *commissaires* in the towns were expected to make similar reports, thus providing central government with a new, regular, and significant perspective on its citizens and with the potential for more and better information on events and attitudes in the provinces. It is difficult to measure how much more effective than their predecessors the *commissaires de police* of early nineteenth-century Paris were. They still carried out a range of duties little different from those undertaken by the *commissaires du Châtelet*. There were stories of corruption, of offices not being open when they should

---

[16] John M. Merriman, *Police Stories: Building the French State, 1815–1851*, New York: Oxford University Press, 2006.

[17] Isser Woloch, *The New Regime: Transformations of the French Civic Order, 1789–1820s*, New York: W. W. Norton, 1994, 156–63; Fabien Gaveau, 'L'ordre aux champs. Histoire des gardes champêtres en France de la Révolution à la Troisième République: Pour une autre histoire de l'État', Doctorat, University of Dijon, 3 vols., 2005; vol. i covers the period 1791–1810.

[18] Emsley, *Gendarmes and the State*, chs. 3 and 4.

have been, and so forth. But the *commissaire* no longer purchased his office; he was a state servant who could more easily be promoted or dismissed according to his qualities and performance in the job, though this did not, of course, eradicate favouritism or nepotism.[19]

French bayonets and Napoleonic administration imposed similar structures of bureaucratic repression and more effective, permanent policing across much of Europe. In areas incorporated into the French Empire, such as Belgium, the Rhineland, and Piedmont, the entire system of *commissaires* and gendarmes was established. Many of the states that were occupied by Napoleon or which were created as a result of his diplomacy and drawn tightly in to his sphere of influence established *gendarmeries* and continued to maintain these for internal security after the Congress of Vienna. In the areas incorporated into the empire especially, the new policing structures inflicted severe blows on gangs of bandits and smugglers in spite of the lease of life that the military upheavals had initially provided. The best-known, and probably the most successful campaign against bandits during the Napoleonic period was that in the Rhineland directed by Anton Kiel.[20] The old regime in Germany had allowed a variety of officials to issue passports to enable local people to travel; venal officials in tiny statelets were popular with any individuals working on the fringes of legality who sought some form of documentation to justify their movements. The French set out to restrict the issuing of all passports. A degree of fraud and corruption remained, but it appears to have been on a greatly reduced scale. The rational bureaucratic structure first deployed by the French encouraged police administrations to print and exchange among themselves detailed descriptions of criminal offenders. Initially this documentation was sometimes also sold to others for entertainment value and even police officials could be expected to pay for receipt. But from 1819 such information in Prussia was publicly financed. In the early 1820s in Baden a crackdown was mounted against bandits based on the prompt, if often rough, justice meted out by the French courts in the Rhineland twenty years earlier.[21]

North Germany was occupied by the French for a much shorter time than the Rhineland but one British traveller at least was struck by the legacy of

---

[19] Clive Emsley, 'Policing the Streets of Early Nineteenth-Century Paris', *French History*, 1, 2 (1987), 257–82.

[20] Norbert Finzsch, 'Räuber und Gendarme im Rheinland: Das Bandenwesen in den vier rheinischen Départements vor und während der Zeit der französischen Verwaltung (1794–1814)', *Francia*, 15 (1987), 435–71; for Kiel, see pp. 450–60.

[21] Carsten Küther, *Räuber und Gauner in Deutschland: Das organisierte Bandenwesen im 18. und frühen 19. Jahrhundert*, Göttingen: Vandenhoeck und Ruprecht, 1976, 134–44.

Napoleonic policing when he visited Prussia and Hanover a few years after Waterloo. In both states Thomas Hodgskin found the proprietors of the inns where he lodged requiring his passport and liaising with the local police about his presence. Policing also appeared more efficient and widespread.

Prior to the occupation of [Hanover] by the French, the police of the towns, which included the regulations of the market, fixing prices, giving passports, apprehending vagrants, and determining a great variety of small cases, and punishing a great many small offences, was exercised by the magistrates of the towns. It is now, however, regulated by three commissioners appointed by the crown, who have subordinate officers, with a regular corps of Gens d'armes. It is one of the new establishments, by which the expenses of government, and its influence, are very much increased.

Hodgskin correctly perceived that 'power is leaving the nobles, and concentrating itself in the hands of the sovereign.'[22]

Fears generated by the French Revolution encouraged developments in *haute police* both in France and in areas that were never occupied and remained generally hostile to the advance of the Napoleonic empire. The turmoil and bloodshed of the revolutionary period and the legacy of potential threats to subsequent regimes meant that no French government could seriously have been expected to ignore this kind of policing. In Paris the prefect's *commissaires* and *officiers* all carried out *haute police* duties. So too, in the provinces, did *commissaires* and gendarmes, and while this infuriated liberals and opponents of the different regimes and has both appalled and fascinated historians, it was never the major function of these police. In the Habsburg lands before the Revolution the concept of *Polizei* had been refined significantly by Joseph von Sonnenfels, Professor of Political Science at the University of Vienna and a Councillor of the Court of Chancellery. Sonnenfels urged that police should be an instrument in the hands of the prince to ensure the public security of the state; as such it would protect citizens but it would also protect the state by augmenting the powers of the prince over those of the Estates and local power-holders. Sonnenfels intensely disliked secret police organizations and was keen that every citizen be aware of his rights and of the precise powers of any government functionary. In 1791 the Emperor Leopold invited him to draw up a plan for a reform of the Viennese police. Unfortunately war with Revolutionary France and the fear of Jacobin insurrection within the Habsburg empire led to the collapse of Sonnenfels's experiment—possibly

---

[22] Thomas Hodgskin, *Travels in the North of Germany*, 2 vols., Edinburgh, 1820, quotations at i. 403 and ii. 6.

already doomed because of its cost. The war and the fears also brought about the resurgence of an emphasis on *haute police* and the imposition of a vigorous supervisory policing structure directed by Johann Anton, Count von Pergen.[23] Nor was there any let-up after the fall of Napoleon. The fear of different forms of liberal and Jacobin thought ensured the continuing presence of political police across Europe. Friedrich von Gentz, an adviser to the Austrian Chancellor Prince Metternich, expressed very clearly the three freedoms that he considered should be preserved within Restoration Europe: 'first freedom (that is, security) for the life of the state, then freedom for the church, then freedom for all who can use it'.[24]

The British liked to maintain their claim to difference yet, at the close of the eighteenth century, there were moral entrepreneurs in Britain pressing for police reform. The government took a few modest steps in this direction, though never enough to satisfy those who insisted that they had identified both serious problems and the necessary solutions. Patrick Colquhoun's *Treatise on the Police of the Metropolis*, first published in 1796, ran through three editions in its first year and a total of seven editions in ten years. Colquhoun may, as Sir Leon Radzinowicz suggested, have been the first major writer in England to use the word 'police' in a relatively modern sense. But he also employed it in the very general and traditional continental European sense to include a range of supervisory activities within the city and not simply with reference to the prevention and detection of crime.[25] In the *Treatise* Colquhoun revealed himself as a man of the Enlightenment, but also, perhaps, as a Scottish rather than an English gentleman. Police institutions in the big Scottish cities were developing along lines much closer to those in continental Europe than in London.[26] But there was a theoretical

[23] Roland Axtmann, ' "Police" and the Formation of the Modern State: Legal and Ideological Assumptions on State Capacity in the Austrian Lands of the Habsburg Empire, 1500–1800', *German History*, 10, 1 (1992), 39–61; 46–8; Ernst Wangermann, *From Joseph II to the Jacobin Trials*, Oxford: Oxford University Press, 1969, 21–3 and 95–6.

[24] Donald E. Emerson, *Metternich and the Political Police: Security and Subversion in the Hapsburg Monarchy (1815–1830)*, The Hague: Martinus Nijhoff, 1968, 36.

[25] Leon Radzinowicz, *A History of English Criminal Law*, iii. *The Reform of Police*, London: Stevens & Sons, 1956, 247; Elaine A. Reynolds, *Before the Bobbies: The Night Watch and Police Reform in Metropolitan London, 1720–1830*, London: Macmillan, 1998, 89–90. For an excellent reappraisal of Colquhoun's work, emphasizing his broad understanding of 'police' and 'prevention' see Mark Neocleous, 'Social Police and the Mechanisms of Prevention: Patrick Colquhoun and the Condition of Poverty', *BJC* 40, 4 (2000), 710–26.

[26] John McGowan, 'The Emergence of a Modern Civil Police in Scotland: A Case Study of the Police and Systems of Policing of Edinburghshire, 1800–1833', Ph.D., Open University, 1996; David G. Barrie, 'Britain's Oldest Police? A History of Policing in Glasgow 1779–1846', Ph.D., University of Strathclyde, 2001.

focus in Colquhoun's perceptions, similar to that of Henry Fielding, and this helped to shape much of his argument. Colquhoun also published (in 1806) a *Treatise on Indigence* and, in the words of Victor Bailey, he 'found difficulty in distinguishing and demarcating the active delinquent from the poor who were indigent through "culpable causes" '.[27] Like Fielding, and like others across continental Europe, he condemned the poor's love of luxury and their general immorality. Similarly he differentiated between those members of the poor who would work, those who could not work, and those who refused to work; and he also singled out vagabonds and beggars as significant criminal offenders. His remedy was to establish a vigorous surveillance of the criminal and indigent poor, of those institutions such as pawnbrokers' shops which could so easily be fronts for receivers, and of common lodging houses where, Colquhoun believed, the suspect poor dwelt and where they were encouraged into offending.

Colquhoun had been appointed as one of the first stipendiary magistrates under the Middlesex Justices Act of 1792. This legislation created seven police offices situated across the metropolis, on the lines of that in Bow Street. The offices provided improved, speedy justice for the victims of petty offences and a greater facility for the detection and pursuit of offenders. Each office contained three stipendiaries and half a dozen or more constables; and these latter were given new powers to apprehend reputed thieves and suspect individuals. The constables appear to have functioned as detective police much like the better-known Principal Officers of Bow Street, but a detailed historical assessment of their activities and efficiency is still awaited. Suspicion of thief-takers continued and was shown to have some substance when, in 1816, George Vaughan, a respectable and apparently successful member of the Bow Street patrol, and other officers were convicted of setting up individuals to commit offences and then claiming the reward money for their arrest and conviction. It may have been these revelations which prompted a correspondent of the *Gentleman's Magazine* to criticize Colquhoun's 'system of espionage, which was to have, for its main spring, ample rewards'.[28] In several instances, generally connected with the security of the state, the stipendiaries themselves took on delicate detective tasks for

[27] Victor Bailey, 'The Fabrication of Deviance: "Dangerous Classes" and "Criminal Classes" in Victorian England', in John Rule and Robert Malcolmson, eds. *Protest and Survival: Essays for E. P. Thompson*, London: Merlin Press, 1993, 226.

[28] *Gentlemen's Magazine*, 88 (Sept. 1818), 219. For the 1816 prosecutions see Leon Radzinowicz, *A History of English Criminal Law*, ii. *The Enforcement of the Law*, London: Stevens & Sons, 1956, 333–7 and 343–5.

central government; most notable here was William Wickham, who ran the government's secret war against Revolutionary and Napoleonic France.[29] As with the Fieldings, this puts the stipendiary magistrates much closer to the Parisian *commissaires de police* and *officiers de paix* than the conventional English Whig police histories would allow. It also raises the spectre of un-English *haute police* in ways unacknowledged in those histories. But, as with the *commissaires* and *officiers de paix* in Paris, such secret service activities never constituted the major task of the magistrates and constables in the London police offices.

These constables and magistrates in the metropolis acted alongside the parish watchmen. The watches continued to be composed of respectable, fit men who knew their beats and were quite able to, and often fully prepared to, confront and apprehend offenders and suspects. In addition there were the armed patrols of Bow Street, both mounted and on foot, which had been successfully revived towards the end of the century by Sir Sampson Wright, formerly an assistant justice to the Fieldings; eventually these 'patroles' numbered roughly 200 men. Colquhoun himself had been instrumental in organizing the armed river police initially established to protect merchant ships moored in the Thames. The City proper also had its own constables, patrolmen, and parish police. London at the end of the eighteenth and beginning of the nineteenth centuries did not lack police, but its police lacked central direction.

At the end of the Revolutionary and Napoleonic wars there was a general feeling among sections of the ruling elite in England that the policing of London could be improved; there were also growing concerns about crime. This is not to say that such feelings and concerns were clearly defined. Nor is it to say that there were new, growing, and serious problems with crime and public order, as the police reformers and the traditional Whig historians of the English police argued. It is simply to emphasize that there was a perception of such problems. Between 1812 and 1828 a succession of parliamentary committees reported on the state of police in the metropolis. The English ruling elite now appeared comfortable with the word 'police', but still worried about the French model—'a system of espionage' as Sir Robert Peel implied to the Commons in June 1822.[30] However seven years later Peel succeeded in

---

[29] Clive Emsley, 'The Home Office and its Sources of Information and Investigation 1781–1801', *English Historical Review*, 94 (1979), 532–61; Elizabeth Sparrow, *Secret Service: British Agents in France 1792–1815*, Woodbridge: Boydell Press, 1999, ch. 2.

[30] *Parliamentary Debates*, vii, col. 803, 4 June 1822.

squaring the circle by creating the Metropolitan Police with an institutional structure that promised to reject things French.

Nineteenth-century police reformers and the Whig historians of the police referred to the Metropolitan Police as the New Police, and they stressed that Peel went out of his way to ensure that the police uniform did not make the new institution appear military. What recent research has begun to stress, however, is that in many respects the new police were doing what the old parish watches had done, except for twenty-four hours a day rather than simply after dark. In some instances large numbers of the parish watch personnel transferred directly into the Metropolitan Police. Furthermore, while some of the poorer parishes, which had been unable to afford large numbers of fit, active watchmen, had better preventive patrols under the new system, some of the wealthier parishes protested that they now had fewer police constables than they had previously had watchmen.[31] Above all, Peel's new policemen were not thief-takers; detective provision remained the task of the constables of Bow Street and the other police offices, until these were closed in 1839. The task of the new policeman was the 'prevention of crime' which was to be achieved, first, by his regular patrolling of a beat and his intimate knowledge of the people and places on that beat, and secondly by the wide legal authority that he possessed.

'Crime', according to the instructions drawn up for the police constables, particularly encompassed felonies such as burglary and picking pockets. The new policeman could arrest anyone whom he caught in the act of committing a felony or anyone about whom he had 'reasonable suspicion'; and while not singled out in his instructions as the perpetrators of crime, the new policeman also had considerable powers to arrest 'vagrants'.[32] These powers came from the Vagrancy Act of 1824 which had consolidated earlier legislation, and which enabled a variety of individuals—prostitutes, beggars, tramps sleeping rough, and 'all loose idle and disorderly persons'—to be drawn under its conditions at a police officer's discretion. Yet in this respect the instructions largely echoed the powers of watchmen set out in the Westminster Night Watch Act passed half a century earlier.[33] The instructions of 1829 gave

[31] Reynolds, *Before the Bobbies*, 153; Ruth Paley, '"An Imperfect, Inadequate and Wretched System?": Policing London before Peel', *CJH* 10 (1989), 95–130; 114–15.

[32] The 'New Police Instructions' were printed in full over four and a half columns of *The Times*, 25 Sept. 1829.

[33] The act of 1774 'authorized and impowered' the watchman 'to arrest and apprehend all Night Walkers, Malefactors, Rogues, Vagabonds and other loose idle and disorderly Persons, whom he shall find disturbing the public Peace, or that he shall have Cause to suspect of any evil Designs.'

the new uniformed policemen discretion to arrest, or for a possible future summons to take the name and address of those involved in a variety of street nuisances, gaming, careless driving, and keeping pubs, tea and coffee shops open after the regulatory hours. These were tasks that old parochial constables had possessed; they were also powers enjoyed by the police of Paris, both before and after the Revolution.

The prevention of crime by regular patrolling was neither cerebral nor skilled. Peel and his associates in the formation of the Metropolitan Police believed that the task was one that could be performed by working-class men, supervised by working-class men. This resulted in a meritocratic structure for the new institution. Every man, with the exception of the commissioner(s) and the initial appointments to the rank of sergeant, inspector, and superintendent, began his police career on preventive patrol. Whether in the long term this was beneficial or detrimental to English policing, especially following the development of departments concerned with detection, is a matter for debate; though it is unlikely that such a debate would produce a conclusion that all would accept. In the late nineteenth and throughout the twentieth centuries the meritocratic structure was jealously guarded by the rank and file, and this constituted a significant and distinctive element of the English police.

The stress on the prevention of crime, which became something of an obsession for the police forces of Victorian England, and the requirement that the police officer know his district intimately were not new, nor were they specifically English. Beccaria, for example, had stressed the importance and value of the prevention of crimes.[34] At least one supporter of the institution established in London in 1829 argued that its *modus operandi* was 'the only way worthy the character of Englishmen' since it was 'open and manly, not sneaking and cowardly'.[35] But, as noted above, when the *officiers de paix* were created in Paris it was expected that 'the fear of their presence' would have a significant impact on offending. Similarly General Louis Wirion expected gendarmes to have an intimate knowledge of the districts in which they served.[36] The rejection of thief-taking and detective work by the police,

Quoted in Elaine A. Reynolds, 'Sir John Fielding, Sir Charles Whitworth, and the Westminster Night Watch Act, 1770–1775', Louis A. Knafla, ed. *Policing and War in Europe CJH* 16 (2002), 1–19; quotation at p. 9.

[34] Cesare Beccaria, *An Essay on Crimes and Punishments . . . with a Commentary by M. de Voltaire*, new corrected edn., Edinburgh, 1778, ch. 41, *passim*.

[35] Anon., 'The New Police', *New Monthly Magazine*, 26 (1829), 426–32; 428.

[36] Charron, *Des Officiers de Paix*, 8; Emsley, *Gendarmes and the State* 58–9.

moreover, ran counter to the ideas and efforts of the Fieldings and of Colquhoun, and was not necessarily for the good of policing. 'A man in uniform will hardly ever take a thief' explained Superintendent Andrew McLean to a parliamentary committee some five years after the new police were created. In the same forum, the commissioners of the Metropolitan Police reported an assessment that three-quarters of the 'beggars and felons' apprehended were taken by officers 'in plain clothes'.[37] The centralized system directly confronted the traditional worries about central government in Hanoverian England, yet the opposition to the role of central government in the appointment of the new police commissioners and, indirectly, their subordinates, was muted. Indeed the issue was glossed over in rather the same way that a uniformed, hierarchical institution in which the men were strictly drilled and disciplined could be defined as 'non-military' simply because they did not wear helmets or shakos, did not wear red coats, and did not, as a rule, carry firearms or edged weapons.[38] Peel informed the Commons that the centralization of the new police was rational, logical, and would achieve efficiency. 'The chief requisites of an efficient police', he declared, 'were unity of design and responsibility of its agents—both of which were not only not ensured by the present parochial watch-house system, but were actually prevented by it.'[39] By September 1830 Peel's new force consisted of 3,000 men, twice the size of the *lieutenant général's* deterrent patrol in eighteenth-century Paris; but then Metropolitan London was twice the size of Paris and growing fast.

In Paris in 1829 there were roughly 1,500 gendarmes, always in uniform. There were also 48 *commissaires*, 24 *officiers de paix*, 140 *inspecteurs*, and a number of auxiliary *inspecteurs*, none of whom wore any uniform. In 1829, however, uniformed civilian police—as opposed to the military gendarmes—known as *sergents de ville* were introduced on to the streets of Paris by the Prefect. The Parisians were no longer addressed fraternally by the Prefect, as in the early days of the Consulate, but the Paris police were informed by their immediate superior that their tasks were paternal, and orders were given for their behaviour very similar to that required of the Metropolitan Police in London. *Commissaire* Thouret, appointed to command

---

[37] *Parliamentary Papers*, 1833, xiii. 627, *Report from the Select Committee on the Petition of Sir Frederick Young, and others . . . complaining that Policemen are employed as Spies*, qq. 1127 and 1759.

[38] However, one of the early supporters of Peel's new police did acknowledge that they were 'necessarily more military than civil.' Anon., 'Principles of Police and their Application to the Metropolis', *Fraser's Magazine*, 16 (1837), 169–78; 170.

[39] *Parliamentary Debates*, xxi, col. 872, 15 April 1829.

the municipal police in 1828, told his subordinates: 'The essential object of our municipal police is the safety of the inhabitants of Paris. . . . Saftey by day and night, free traffic movement, clean streets, the supervision of and precautions against accident, the maintenance of public order in public places, the seeking out of offences and their perpetrators.'[40] Almost exactly a year later, in his first order of the day to the new *sergents de ville*, he instructed them that 'the success of this institution is assured if the *sergents de ville* are distinguished by a good turnout, good conduct, honest and moderate language and proceedings with the public.'[41] The creation of the *sergents* appears to have been partly a public relations exercise and partly an attempt to ensure better behaviour by better controlled police officers. During the Restoration, and especially in the 1820s, the Paris Police had been greatly criticized for aggressive *haute police* activity specifically in the sense of political surveillance and the repression of those considered critical of or hostile towards the restored monarchy. The situation was worsened by revelations of corruption among the ex-convicts who made up the detective bureau and by the sensational memoirs of their chief, Eugène-François Vidocq.[42] The *sergents de ville* were to show a uniformed presence, unarmed apart from a baton during the day and a sabre at night, to which people in distress or trouble could turn. The uniform was also intended to ensure that the police officers endeavoured to re-establish order during a disturbance, rather than disappearing anonymously into the crowd, and that they kept out of bars and generally manifested good habits. In the aftermath of the July Revolution there was a conscious effort to improve the detective police. The ex-convicts were all removed, and from then on the *Sûreté* was staffed by professional police officers only. The major contrast with London in policing provision by the middle of the nineteenth century was the smallness of the civilian deterrent patrol in Paris. On the eve of the Revolution of 1848 the *sergents de ville* numbered just over 300.

The structures established in the capital cities of London and Paris were not replicated in the provinces. The traditional Whig view of English police

[40] Quoted in Jean Tulard, *Paris et son administration 1800–1830*, Paris: Ville de Paris Commission des Travaux Historiques, 1976, 436–37. Thouret had served as *commissaire* in the *quartier* Faubourg Montmartre from 1823/4 to 1827/8.

[41] Quoted in Alfred Rey and Louis Féron, *Histoire du Corps des Gardiens de la Paix*, Paris, 1896, 88.

[42] See e.g. Louis Guyon, *Biographie des Commissaires de Police et des Officiers de Paix de la Ville de Paris*, Paris, 1826, and Froment [former *chef de Brigade du Cabinet particulier du Préfet*], *La Police Devoilée, depuis la Restauration, et notamment sous Messieurs Franchet et Delavau, et sous Vidocq, chef de la police de Sûreté*, 2nd. edn., 3 vols., Paris, 1830. And see below, pp. 146.

development was that the example of the Metropolitan Police pointed to the need for, and provided the model for, police institutions outside London. In fact police development in the English boroughs and counties was already being debated and was progressing before 1829. The wave of public police legislation from the mid-1830s to the mid-1850s established the framework for police institutions responsible, in varying degrees, to the traditional organs of local government.[43] As a result the members of some provincial police forces, especially in the smaller boroughs, carried out a wide variety of administrative and ceremonial functions in addition to their widely proclaimed first duty of the prevention of crime. Yet it is worth stressing that one of these additional tasks, the supervision of lodging houses and, in some instances, even the administration of poor relief itself continued the assumption that the poor, especially the poor who were on the move, were the principal perpetrators of crime. Only the appointment of the chief constables of counties needed the approval of central government, in the shape of the home secretary. But the provision, in 1856, of a Treasury grant for efficiency, together with the creation of Inspectors of Constabulary to assess that efficiency and to make annual reports to parliament, was a significant step towards uniformity and involvement by central government bureaucracy in national policing.

In France the *Gendarmerie* was a national body, but its fortunes varied from regime to regime. The *commissaires* may have been formally appointed from Paris, but their professionalization and their understanding of themselves as a national body developed only gradually over the course of the century. They also remained in an awkward position. They were officials appointed by the state and responsible to the local prefect but, at the same time, they served the municipality that paid their salary and they answered to the local mayor. There was no uniformity in the ranks of the municipal police below the *commissaires*, and no national inspection system like that established in the British Isles in the mid-1850s. The rural *gardes-champêtres* were periodically inspected by the *Gendarmerie*, and were generally condemned as inefficient and ineffective. Much of the criticism and condemnation was probably unfair and was similar to that of the reformers and moral entrepreneurs in Britain who condemned the old system of policing. Central proposals for reorganizing and improving the *gardes* failed, partly through cost and partly also because pursuing the proposals threatened to open up much wider

---

[43] David Philips and Robert G. Storch, *Policing Provincial England 1829–1856: The Politics of Reform*, London: Leicester University Press, 1999.

debates concerning the relationship between state and society.[44] The range of police tasks remained wide, and the surveillance of the poor and of people on the move remained significant. The requirement that every worker carry and up-to-date *livret*, declaring his trade and outlining his work-history, and the requirement that inns, hotels, and lodging houses provide details of their visitors to the local *commissaires* ensured that this sort of surveillance was much more bureaucratic, uniform, and significant than any such in England. Thanks to a combination of old regime legacies and the impact of the French Revolution and Napoleon, these practices were common across continental Europe in the early nineteenth century. There is plenty of evidence to suggest, however, that it was never particularly difficult for a determined individual either to acquire forgeries or to hoodwink the police over passports and workers' travel documents.[45] In the end it must remain an open question as to whether all of this had any greater effect on levels of offending or prevention than the more relaxed practices in England. But whatever the systems were that they had in force, everywhere in Europe in the early nineteenth century men began to measure and to take note of what were seen as the problems of crime and the criminal classes.

[44] Fabien Gaveau, 'De la sûreté des campagnes. Police rurale et demandes d'ordre en France dans la première moitié du XIXe siècle', *CHS* 4, 2 (2000), 53–76.

[45] Richard J. Evans, *Tales from the German Underworld*, New Haven, and London: Yale University Press, 1998, 154–5.

PART III

THE DISCOVERY OF THE CRIMINAL CLASSES

7

Measuring a Problem

THE early nineteenth century was a golden age of faith in social statistics. The statistics of crime were a key element in revealing what was understood as the moral health of a country and its people. On the more mundane level they were also believed to show the scale of the problem and the effectiveness of the institutions established to deal with it. It was supposed, in consequence, that their collection would provide an empirical base that would enable governments and legislators better to debate policy. In a manner unplanned for, however, the collection of statistics also contributed to concerns about crime. People may have worried about brigands, criminal gangs, and vagabonds in the eighteenth century, but national figures gave a measurable scale and substance to the problem and to the fears. They also led to the developments of some early criminological theory. In particular, as crime and criminals began to be measurable phenomena so criminal offenders were gradually separated from the poor and labelled separately as the dangerous and the criminal classes.

There had been some interest in collecting statistics about the activities of different courts during the old regime. Prussia began collecting various judicial statistics from 1716, increasingly refining the process over the next hundred years. In France the Ordinance of 1670 required regular statistics from the courts, though renewed calls for this information during the early eighteenth century suggest that it was not always forthcoming. Shortly before the Revolution some individuals began trying to analyse such information as they could collect so as to draw broad conclusions about crime and morality in France. Various regimes during the decade of the Revolution required the collection of different criminal statistics, but this was as much to assess the work of magistrates and the various courts as it was to assess the scale of offending.[1] The real boost to the collection of statistics came during the First

---

[1] Emmanuel Berger, 'Les origines de la statistique judiciaire sous la révolution', *CHS* 18, 1 (2004), 65–91. For an attempt at statistical analysis made towards the end of the old regime for

Empire. Napoleon wanted facts—facts about agriculture, the economy in general, the population, and what the population was thinking and doing. The various police institutions were one source for such information, particularly with reference to the movement of people and to popular opinion. The Prefect of Police in Paris collected and listed daily statistics of the numbers of individuals entering the city, the numbers of crimes committed, the numbers of individuals arrested, the numbers of interrogations and of persons held in the various prisons. Particularly shocking and major incidents were noted in some detail in his daily reports under the heading *événements*. Initially the reports were all handwritten, but towards the end of the empire all of the information was entered in the appropriate spaces on specially printed forms. The *Gendarmerie* companies prepared monthly reports listing similar information, as well as the agricultural situation in their department, the state of public opinion, and the number of patrols that each company's brigades had made. The collection of this information long outlived the fall of the empire.

The Enlightenment interest in social facts, often statistical facts, was also to be found in Britain, particularly during the years of war against the French Revolution and Napoleon. The needs of war prompted the government to enquire into the size of the population and the state of agriculture. The gloomy conclusions of Thomas Malthus, that relied on a mathematical equation and that had followed a succession of bad wartime harvests, were another spur to extending this knowledge. Statistics were also deployed in the continuing debates about crime and policing. Patrick Colquhoun laced his discussion of the police of the metropolis with statistics. In some instances he carefully cited his sources and warned about problems of accuracy as, for example, with the note to his summary of what happened to the individuals held in the eight gaols of the metropolis in the year ending October 1795. 'Although the author has been at infinite pains to render this Summary as exact as possible yet, from the different modes adopted in keeping the accounts of prisons, he is not thoroughly satisfied in his own mind that the view he has given here

the Paris region see Jean Lecuir, 'Criminalité et moralité: Montyon, statisticien du Parlement de Paris', *Revue d'histoire moderne et contemporaine*, 21, 3 (1974), 445–93; for a general introduction see *La statistique judiciaire: son histoire et ses usages scientifiques*, special issue of *Déviance et Société*, 22, 2 (1998). The most detailed assessment of the development of criminal statistics in the early nineteenth century is Axel Tixon, 'Le pouvoir des nombres. Une histoire de la production et de l'exploitation des statistiques judiciaires belges (1795–1870)', Doctorat en histoire, Université de Louvain-la-Neuve, 2001. Whatever the title says, this thesis ranges far beyond the frontiers of Belgium.

is accurate, to a point.'[2] Elsewhere, however, he was singularly cavalier about statistics even when he used them to make key points about the number and categories of criminal offenders. Perhaps the most notable instance of this is his bald statement that the number of women in the metropolis living wholly or partly by prostitution was 50,000. Even though he spelled out some of his reasoning, the validity of this figure, and of many other of his numerical assessments, remains highly dubious.[3] In 1805, stimulated by the desire to have detailed information for debates about the death penalty, the Home Office directed the clerks of courts and assize circuits to send in details of committals for trial on indictment, and the number of capital sentences passed and carried out. The statistics began to be published annually, if sometimes irregularly, from 1810 though without any introductory analysis. These bald statistics were hardly sophisticated; nevertheless the information was deployed in debates on both the death penalty and changes in policing. Gradually greater clarity was introduced together with an expansion in the material collected. By the mid-1830s the criminal statistics had become standardized into six main types of offence: offences against the person; offences against property with violence; offences against property without violence; malicious offences against property; offences against the currency; and miscellaneous offences. Twenty years later there was a further, tripartite division into indictable offences known to the police, the numbers committed for trial both on indictment and summarily, and the numbers convicted and sentenced. Also from the 1850s the police were required to enumerate the number of 'known thieves and depredators' in their respective districts; the problem here was that, until the end of the century, no clear guidance was given on precisely who should be included in this category.

The collection of statistics from the Prefect in Paris and the *Gendarmerie* companies continued in France during the Restoration. The national details of crime that began to be collected in France during the 1820s, however, known as the *Compte général de l'administration de la justice criminelle*, marked a step change and had a major impact across Europe. The reason for the *Compte général* was expressly stated as being to 'enlighten justice' and because 'Exact knowledge of the facts is one of the prime needs in our form of government. Such knowledge makes for enlightened deliberations,

---

[2] Patrick Colquhoun, *A Treatise on the Police of the Metropolis*, 7th edn., London, 1806; repr. Montclair, NJ: Patterson Smith, 1969, 431. For his table of prostitutes see p. 340.
[3] David Philips, 'Three "Moral Entrepreneurs" and the creation of a "Criminal Class" in England, c.1790–1840', *CHS* 7, 1 (2003), 79–107; 83–5.

which it simplifies and places on a solid foundation by substituting the
sure and positive guidance of experience for theoretical vagueness.'[4] While
the *Compte* continued to increase and develop its categories throughout the
nineteenth century, the broad framework was settled within a decade. It
gave details of defendants charged with crimes by age and sex (from 1826);
it listed their civil status, place of birth, residence, and level of education
(from 1828); their occupation according to a nine-class division (from 1829);
whether their residence was urban or rural (from 1830); whether they were
wage-earners, self-employed, or unemployed (from 1831). Criminal lawyers
across Europe and beyond praised the form and content of the *Compte* and
the format was copied in Austria, Belgium, Sweden, and several German
states, notably Baden. The wealth of raw material was seen as a rich mine
by social statisticians, notably the French lawyer André-Michel Guerry and
the Belgian academic Adolphe Quetelet. Working separately, Guerry and
Quetelet were both struck by the regularity and uniformity of the statistics
year in and year out with regard to offences, offenders, regions, and seasons.
'Each year', noted Guerry, 'sees reproduced the same number of crimes in the
same pattern, in the same regions; each category of crime has its particular
and unchanging distribution by sex, by age, by season.'[5]

At the same time as the French statistics began to be published Quetelet had
begun exploring local evidence from the Belgian provinces of the Kingdom
of the Netherlands. He considered that the collection and publication of
such statistics by governments was a welcome step since he believed that the
analyses and interpretations of men like himself would help to establish the
laws that governed humankind. Knowledge of these laws, in turn, would
enable progress since man 'possesses a moral power capable of modifying the
laws which affect him'.[6] In the new Kingdom of Belgium created after the
Revolution of 1830 the statistical evidence welcomed by Quetelet as a means
of improving society began to be used by politicians for the reasons that the

---

[4] Quoted in Michelle Perrot, 'Delinquency and the Penitentiary System in Nineteenth-Century France', in Robert Forster and Orest A. Ranum, eds., *Deviants and the Abandoned in French Society*, Baltimore: Johns Hopkins University Press, 1978, 217–18. The 1880 edition of the *Compte* included a general assessment of crime for the period since 1826. This has been reissued with an important introduction, Michelle Perrot and Philippe Robert, eds., *Compte général de l'administration de la justice criminelle en France pendant l'année 1880 et rapport relatif aux années 1826 à 1880*, Geneva: Slatkine Reprints, 1989.

[5] André-Michel Guerry, *Essai sur la statistique morale de la France*, Paris, 1833, 9.

[6] Adolph Quetelet, *A Treatise on Man and the Development of his Faculties*, Edinburgh, 1842, 96. This was the first English translation of *Sur l'homme et le développement de ses facultés*, first published in 1835.

British had begun their collection of criminal statistics in the first place. The information provided members of the Belgian parliament with detail that could fortify the arguments both for and against capital punishment. It was also used to highlight the problem of recidivism. But such political use of the figures on different sides of the debates did not diminish the enthusiasm of those for whom the regularity and uniformity of the criminal statistics appeared to prove the existence of detectable and measurable laws that shaped societies.

Comparing the statistical information of Belgium with that of France and with other statistics drawn from the Austrian Empire and several German states, Quetelet drew a series of general conclusions, some of which would not seem out of place in modern assessments of criminality. Crime, the evidence suggested, was generally committed by young men; property crime was more common in the winter months; and alcohol consumption appeared to have an impact on levels of violent crime. But with other conclusions he reflected the thought of his time. The French statistics revealed significant regional differences and this he put down to France being peopled by three races: Celtic, German, and Pelasgian. The Celtic people appeared the most moral; the regions where they were dominant showed relatively low levels of violence against the person. The 'Germans' lived in greater concentrations of people and were surrounded by more property which provided opportunities for much crime. The Germans were also inclined to consume more strong drink and this, in turn, encouraged excess and some violence. The Pelasgian peoples of the south and the Mediterranean were particularly prone to inter-personal violence, and here Quetelet stressed the violence of Corsica.

The Corsicans, indeed, impelled by cruel prejudices and warmly embracing feelings of revenge, which are frequently transmitted from generation to generation, almost make a virtue of homicide, and commit the crime to excess. Offences against property are not frequent, and yet their number exceeds the average of France. We cannot attribute this state of things to want of instruction, since the number of accused who could neither read nor write was comparatively less than in France.[7]

While Quetelet insisted that knowledge would enable people to modify the laws of humankind, the regularity and uniformity of the statistics as he delineated them contributed to a sharp controversy, especially in Germany, over free will and social determinism. If, as Quetelet concluded, the statistics made it possible to predict the number and types of crimes that would

[7] Ibid. 87.

be committed in any year in any society, and if each society was itself responsible for generating those crimes, then how might different societies, and humankind in general, break out of the cycle? The conservative Lutheran theologian Alexander von Oettingen and the economist and social reformer Adolph Wagner, both briefly at the Russo-German university in Dorpat, became major antagonists on opposite sides of this debate during the 1860s.

The statistics enabled what appeared to be more accurate assessments to be made of traditional problems; they also facilitated the making of links between various social and economic phenomena. In Belgium, for example, the economist and philanthropist Éduard Ducpétiaux used statistics from England and France to urge the ineffectiveness of the death penalty. A generation later Knut Olivecrona, a conservative professor of law but fervent abolitionist, deployed an even wider range of statistics to make a similar case in Sweden. Ducpétiaux went on to set crime and education statistics alongside each other in an attempt to demonstrate that the availability of public instruction in the United States, the Netherlands, and Scotland contributed to their lower levels of crime in comparison with France and England.[8] The relationship between crime and levels of education became a popular area for statistical analyses by others, especially those interested in educational reform and its spread across social classes. As Joseph Fletcher, a barrister and honorary secretary of the Statistical Society of London, put it: 'the figures . . . bear conclusive evidence to the fact of the immediate alliance of all the moral evils of which we can yet obtain statistical cognizance with *ignorance.*'[9] Even when Guerry and two collaborators showed that, statistically at least, the relationship between crime and education was the opposite to that which the reformers maintained, the reformers did not lose heart. If Guerry's calculations suggested that crime was more apparent in areas where there was more extensive educational provision, then this served merely as a warning about drawing hasty and false conclusions and demonstrated to men like Ducpétiaux and Fletcher the need for more careful and thoughtful analysis.[10] Other phenomena, in addition to education statistics, were also

    8 Éduard Ducpétiaux, *De la mission de la justice humaine et de l'injustice de la peine de mort*, Brussels, 1827; idem, *De la justice de prévoyance, et particulièrement de l'influence de la misère et de l'aisance, de l'ignorance et de l'instruction sur le nombre de crimes*, Brussels, 1827; Martin Bergman, 'The Swede in Nineteenth-Century Capital Punishment Abolition: Knut Olivecrona and his *Om dödsstraffet*', Paper presented at the ESSH Conference, Amsterdam, March 2006.

    9 Joseph Fletcher, 'Moral and Educational Statistics of England and Wales', *Journal of the Statistical Society*, 10 (1847), 193–233; 221.

    10 Theodor M. Porter, *The Rise of Statistical Thinking, 1820–1900*, Princeton: Princeton University Press, 1986, 173–4.

deployed enthusiastically by social investigators alongside the statistics of crime.

Georg von Mayr has some claim to being the father of the statistical movement in Germany. In the mid-1860s he was appointed to the Bavarian Statistical Bureau where he acted as an assistant to Professor Friedrich von Hermann, his future father-in-law. Mayr rapidly outshone Hermann. His first book, published in 1865, was an analysis of the statistics of beggars and vagrants in Bavaria since the beginning of the nineteenth century but focusing particularly on the period from the mid-1830s.[11] He followed this with an investigation of crime based on the Bavarian police statistics from 1835 to 1861.[12] Many of Mayr's conclusions, like those of Quetelet, would not seem out of place in a modern statistical analysis of crime. His figures showed property crime to be significantly greater than physical assaults against the person and that men were five times more likely to commit offences than women. Particularly significant, however, was his economic analysis and the way in which he sought to demonstrate the extent to which the statistics of crime were subject to changing economic and social conditions. He set his crime figures alongside price fluctuations and showed a link between offending and high prices, especially high prices for grain. Some of his other comparisons were less convincing. It was one thing to suggest that wood theft could be related to varying winter temperatures, but from here he sought also to correlate regional fluctuations with the size of forests, the kinds of forests, and the prices for different kinds of wood. Other conclusions demonstrated somewhat simplistic reductionist assumptions about the impact of crime on the economy. Victims of assault might be unable to work; if the number of individuals assaulted in Bavaria east of the Rhine were off work for eight days in the 26 years of his study, then the kingdom had lost 450,000 working days. Victims of theft would make better use of the property taken than the thief, either feeding their family, or investing in more land or livestock and thus improving personal and national living conditions. Since the thief would not do this, then the value of property, and especially of money stolen, was destroyed. A generation after Mayr's work, Wilhelm Starke, an official in the

---

[11] Georg von Mayr, *Statistik der Bettler und Vaganten im Königreiche Bayern*, Munich, 1865. There were no statistics available between 1816 and 1835. Mayr assumed (p. 3) that the numbers of beggars and vagabonds increased considerably from around 1815 and that the authorities did not wish to publish the figures. Mayr (1841–1925) was Professor of Political Economy, Public Finance, and Statistics at the University of Munich and Director of the Royal Bavarian Statistical Office. In 1890 he founded the journal *Allgemeines Statistisches Archiv*, and he became chairman of the *Deutsche Statistische Gesellschaft* when it was first established in 1911.

[12] Georg von Mayr, *Statistik der gerichtlichen Polizei im Königreiche Bayern*, Munich, 1867.

Prussian Ministry of Justice, set out to assess the statistics of crime in Prussia. His work reinforced trends described by others, such as the preponderance of young males among offenders. But he also detected other patterns. The incidence of petty offences appeared to have declined in both Prussia and France during the Franco-Prussian War of 1870–1. This he attributed to the employment in the army of 'a large contingent of young and strong men, a significant part of which was drawn from the lower echelons of urban society'. He was also led to conclude that urbanization and industrialization were not obviously contributing to an increase in offending by the working class.[13]

The individuals who sought to work with the statistics of crime on a sophisticated level rapidly became aware of the pitfalls of the material. In Germany as early as the 1830s questions were posed about how far increased activity by police and other functionaries of criminal justice led to increased awareness and, possibly also, increased statistics of crime.[14] In England in the 1860s, for example, it was noted that the lack of a precise definition of 'known thieves' meant that the statistics collected by different police forces could not be compared and were largely meaningless. Similarly, different ways of collecting statistics on street robbery made Manchester appear infinitely more dangerous than Liverpool.[15] Recognizing that in Bavaria conviction rates were only between 40 and 50 per cent, Mayr based his work on police statistics, including cases where the accused was acquitted. He stated his assumption to be that, providing the law and the enforcing institutions did not change, there was a constant relationship between the number of reported and detected offences and the number of criminals.[16] Quetelet himself noted the problem of what contemporary criminologists today call the 'dark figure', that is, the unknown gap between the number of crimes actually committed and the number known by being reported to, and listed by the authorities. '[O]ur observations can only refer to *a certain number of known and tried offences, out of the unknown sum total of crimes committed*', declared Quetelet.

---

[13] Wilhelm Starke, *Verbrechen und Verbrecher in Preussen, 1854–1878: Eine kulturgeschichtliche Studie*, Berlin, 1884, quotation at p. 61. With reference to the latter point Eric Johnson notes that Starke was dealing primarily with major offences in this discussion and it is possible that there was an increase in lesser offending. Moreover, the period Starke discusses was before the major industrial advances in nineteenth-century Germany. Eric A. Johnson, *Urbanization and Crime: Germany 1871–1914*, Cambridge: Cambridge University Press, 1995, 211.

[14] Herbert Reinke, 'Une "bonne" statistique pour la lutte contre la criminalité? Observations sur les origines de la statistique criminelle en Allemagne au XIXe et au début du XXe siècle', *Déviance et Société*, 22, 2 (1998), 113–25; 116–17.

[15] Clive Emsley, *Crime and Society in England 1750–1900*, 3rd edn., London: Longman, 2004, 23 and 27.

[16] Mayr, *Statistik der gerichtlichen Polizei*, 1–4 and 76.

Nevertheless, he believed that the ratio between known and unknown crimes was 'invariably the same'.[17] At the International Statistical Congress held in Brussels in 1853 Quetelet also urged debates on the comparison of statistics between countries and the conference organizers suggested various categories that might be adopted to facilitate cross-national comparisons. At a subsequent congress in St Petersburg in 1872 von Mayr produced a template with a similar aim in mind.[18] But enormous difficulties remained, not the least of which being the fact that different states had different definitions and different categories of crimes that were not always compatible and capable of cross-national comparison.

Whatever the awareness of the problems, however, the temptation to use the statistics in a positivist fashion as a reflection of absolute categories of crime and criminals remained strong. Later in the century several of the founders of the new science of criminology fell into the trap. The Italian Positivist Enrico Ferri declared that: 'Criminal statistics tell us this and nothing more:—In such a year there was more or less crime than in other years.' But he also noted that an increase in police, a change in the scarcity or abundance of cereals, or in the pattern of the trade cycle, changes in the amount of moveable property, and in the extent of alcohol abuse could all have an impact on the figures.[19] How far, and with what caveats, historians might use crime statistics has also generated considerable controversy. Since, however, most of the broad conclusions about the pattern of crime since the late eighteenth century ultimately depend on them, a brief digression from the broad chronological trajectory is necessary here.

For the period before the official collection of crime statistics historians have constructed their own figures, usually from various court records. The argument has been made, similar to that of Mayr, that it is reasonable to assume that there was a relatively constant relation, year on year, between offences committed and decisions to prosecute.[20] This has been seriously challenged in the English context, however, by the contention that in times of dearth, when the propertied were conceivably more anxious about the likelihood of theft, there was probably a greater inclination to pursue relatively small thefts and to make an official example of an offender so as to deter

[17] Quetelet, *Treatise on Man*, 82.   [18] Tixhon, 'Le pouvoir des nombres', part 3, ch. 3.
[19] Enrico Ferri, *Criminal Sociology*, Boston: Little, Brown, 1917 (repr. New York: Agathon Press, 1967), 173 and 208.
[20] J. M. Beattie, 'Judicial Records and the Measurement of Crime in Eighteenth-Century England', in Louis A.Knafla, ed., *Crime and Criminal Justice in Europe and Canada*, Waterloo, Ontario: Wilfred Laurier University Press, 1981, 138, for a particularly good statement of this.

others. Thus, while high prices and food shortages may have encouraged theft, they may also have fostered a greater sensitivity to theft and, in consequence, an increase in reporting and the use of the criminal justice system.[21]

Statistics for violence against the person are even more problematic. The understanding of male honour was shifting during the eighteenth century. Arguably this led to a general decline in physical confrontations, especially of the sort that were seen as personal matters and no concern of the law. But within many communities, especially in rural areas and also in teeming urban districts with a largely unskilled working class and where physical toughness was the currency by which a man won respect and social standing, violence remained a significant part of life. Violence in such communities was rarely reported to the authorities. Towards the end of 1833 the mayor of Teyssieu in south-west France explained to the local *procureur du roi* that, in his opinion: 'The men of this region have reprehensible customs; they exchange words with one another; they get involved in disputes, in quarrels that usually end with blows and injuries, and then with a financial arrangement that washes away all the injuries of the wounded.'[22] Nor was the exaltation of male toughness, physicality, and courage confined to traditional or rough working-class communities, as is demonstrated by, amongst other things, the cult of the duellist in nineteenth-century German universities. But while male and family honour may have restricted the reporting of many violent incidents, it was less easy to explain away a dead body bearing marks of violence. In a series of stimulating and provocative essays Manuel Eisner has drawn together the statistics of homicide across a range of Western countries and has exposed a common pattern. While some countries and regions have experienced much higher ratios of homicide, it is possible to detect an overall pattern of decline from the late medieval and early modern periods with an upward movement beginning again in the mid-twentieth century. The problem remains to explain the pattern and there are several alternatives available, not mutually exclusive, but not provable either. There is Elias's indication of a greater sensitization to violence developing from the early modern period. There is the argument that a greater degree of social discipline was increasingly imposed, not least by extended bureaucratic state structures. Equally there is the perceived rise of a moral individualism

---

[21] Emsley, *Crime and Society*, 24–5 and 31.

[22] Quoted in François Ploux, *Guerres paysannes en Quercy: violences, conciliations et répression pénale dans les campagnes du Lot (1810–1860)*, Paris: La Boutique d'histoire, 2002, 9.

that separated individuals from collective bonds and emotions.[23] It would be folly to opt for one of these alternatives in preference to the others and thus to deny the interplay between shifting personal attitudes and sensibilities and new forms of social discipline. And while it may appear prosaic to suggest that there was a decline in homicide and probably also in other forms of inter-personal violence because of greater personal restraint and greater external pressures, this seems also to be a reasonable assumption.

Few, if any, contemporary historians set out to use the official criminal statistics that date from the early nineteenth century with the faith that many contemporaries showed. Recognizing the dangers and pitfalls, however, they also recognize that such statistics are one of the few sources for gauging long-term patterns in crime. Howard Zehr made a sophisticated comparative study of statistics from France and Germany concluding that crime was more frequent in 1913 than it had been in 1830. This was particularly the case with offences against property; crimes of violence, especially serious violence, appeared generally to have been in decline. Drawing on Durkheim's conclusions that crime was normal within a healthy society and involved behaviour not greatly different from legal activity, Zehr took the statistics as indicative of broader shifts within the two societies. Theft was another response to changing expectations and new economic values. Violent criminality, on the other hand, was more traditional, a reflection of frustration and tension, even a form of social conflict. Zehr's changing pattern of crime echoed the *violence au vol* shift that French historians had deployed earlier in assessing change over a much longer period. He constructed a formula, the Theft–Violence Ratio, to explore the shift from interpersonal to property crime, but the problem was that his statistics for French rural departments did not fit easily with the formula. He solved the problem by stressing the fact that traditional rural societies had a greater toleration of inter-personal violence and by including incidents of popular disorder in with his statistics. In Zehr's understanding, crime modernized along with society in general.[24] But subsequent findings, using the same material, have been rather more sceptical.

---

23 Manuel Eisner, 'Modernization, Self-Control and Lethal Violence: The Long-Term Dynamics of European Homicide Rates in Theoretical Perspective', *British Journal of Criminology*, 41, 4 (2001), 618–38; idem, 'Long-Term Historical Trends in Violent Crime', in Michael Tonry, ed., *Crime and Justice: A Review of Research, 30*, Chicago: University of Chicago, 2003, 83–142.

24 Howard Zehr, *Crime and the Development of Modern Society: Patterns of Criminality in Nineteenth-Century Germany and France*, London: Croom Helm, 1976.

A study of the rural Breton department of Morbihan did not find any significant shift from inter-personal violence to property crime. The conclusion here was that the very gradual socio-economic change in the region enabled it to absorb possible disruption, particularly in contrast to the department of Seine-Inférieure which experienced rapid industrialization and urbanization.[25] A much more serious and sustained critique has been made of the German side of Zehr's work, however. Eric Johnson has combined the Imperial German statistics, available from 1882, and coroners' records with the range of Bavarian and Prussian material deployed by Mayr and Starke. In some respects his conclusions coincide with Zehr's; most notably, his evidence suggests that theft increased in urban areas. But Johnson's evidence also suggests that theft significantly decreased in rural regions. Moreover, Johnson's statistics force the conclusion that there was an increase in violent crime from about 1830 to 1870 and again after 1890. The only consistent change that he can find in the second half of the nineteenth century is an increase in prosecutions for political offences.[26] The notion of a modernizing shift from violence to theft is a comforting one, yet the broad patterns of the statistics are confusing and overall shifts are not as easy to measure as has been hoped or supposed.

Murder is commonly taken as a measure of the extent of violence in a society. Anne Parrella has assessed the pattern of murder in the department of Nord for roughly the same period as Zehr's work. Murder was already infrequent in the department at the beginning of the nineteenth century, and the figures there were amongst the lowest for the whole of France. Nevertheless, starting from the figures and moving into the details of specific cases, Parrella was able to detect a significant shift from what she considers to have been a pre-modern pattern of killing, with a large percentage of victims being virtual strangers to their assailants, to a modern pattern that involved intimates and family members. These changes were apparent by the 1870s. Overall the behaviour in cabarets had become more restrained and deaths resulting from violence exploding out of general, drink-fuelled rowdiness, gave way to deaths resulting from quarrels between men who knew each other and argued, for example, over the courting of a young woman. At the same time, killing within the family shifted from 'a mercenary crime between relatives to an emotionally motivated crime between couples'.

[25] Cynthia Story Bisson, 'Crime and the Transition to Modernity in Nineteenth-Century France', Ph.D., Ohio State University, 1989.

[26] Johnson, *Urbanization and Crime*, ch. 3.

Home-centred production had given way to men, particularly, leaving home in the morning for factory-based labour and murder in the family increasingly involved individuals in big cities and from non-propertied groups.[27] Parrella's statistical conclusions about the shift from killing among strangers to killing between intimates parallels the conclusions drawn by Pieter Spierenburg from his micro-histories in eighteenth-century Amsterdam. Both Spierenburg and Parrella adopted a narrow focus compared with that of Zehr, but the idea of emotional violence as a product of a new sensibility or of shifting work patterns and the modernization of France run at a sharp tangent to the thrust of his conclusions.

The crime statistics for England and Wales show an overall decline in both theft and violence from the mid-nineteenth to the beginning of the twentieth century; after the First World War there was a gradual but steady increase. The nineteenth-century decline was perceived by contemporaries as 'the English miracle'. The most sustained assessment of the decline, by V. A. C. Gatrell, stresses at the outset how contemporaries noted the decline as a fact and then develops explanations for it. The decline in violence, Gatrell suggests, is rooted in the broad impact of education, environmental reform, and religion. The decline in theft is probably to be found in the broad economic improvements of the second half of the nineteenth century, increased supervision of the casual poor, and the deterrent effect and improved efficiency of the police and the courts.[28] The Swedish statistics suggest a long-term decline in violence with little or no movement in property offences during the nineteenth and early twentieth centuries. In Finland, however, during the nineteenth century the most economically prosperous of the provinces, Southern Ostrobothnia, suffered the so-called era of the knife-fighters (*puukkojunkkarit*), with an astonishingly high level of violent killings.[29] The English, Swedish and Finnish statistics have not been used to explore change in quite the way

[27] Anne Parrella, 'Industrialization and Murder: Northern France 1815–1914', *Journal of Interdisciplinary History*, 22, 4 (1992), 627–54; 647.

[28] V. A. C. Gatrell, 'The Decline of Theft and Violence in Victorian and Edwardian England', in V. A. C. Gatrell, Bruce Lenman, and Geoffrey Parker, eds., *Crime and the Law: The Social History of Crime in Western Europe since 1500*, London: Europa, 1980.

[29] Jan Sundin, 'Current Trends in the History of Crime and Criminal Justice: Some Conclusions with Special Reference to the Swedish Experience', *Historical Social Research/Historische Sozialforschung*, 15, 4 (1990), 184–96; Heikki Ylikangas, *The Knife Fighters: Violent Crime in Southern Ostrobothnia, 1790–1825*, Helsinki: Academia Scientiarum Fennica, 1998.

that Zehr has used the French and German data, but they suggest further problems about trying to draw comparisons and broad, cross-cultural conclusions.

While focused specifically on the English data, an even more challenging critique has been levelled at the overall usefulness of criminal statistics. Contemporaries and historians may have thought that the figures, though not revealing actual levels, nevertheless reflected the broad pattern of crime. But did they in fact only represent the amount of crime for which various governments were prepared to finance investigation and prosecution? Howard Taylor has argued that in England and Wales even the number of murders (crimes that criminologists have usually argued bear a closer relation to the statistics than any other because of the difficulties in disposing of a body, the evidence of the crime) was limited in the statistics by the amount that the Treasury was prepared to allow for criminal justice. His arguments have not gone unchallenged, not least because there appears to be evidence neither for any Treasury directives making limitations in this way nor for central government seeking to suppress the rates of criminal investigation or prosecution. Nevertheless, it is true to say that a very large number of dead babies were not investigated in Victorian Britain because of the restrictions on coroners' finances as well as a general lack of professionalism among many who held the post. Abortion presents a similar problem and, by the close of the nineteenth century at least, abortionists were deploying a variety of subterfuges to cover their tracks, even to the point of placing euphemistic advertisements in the press.[30]

In addition to the missing figures of child murder and abortion there were other offences which never appeared on the criminal statistics. Alongside the French Criminal Code the Rhenish provinces of Prussia had also acquired the French Civil Code when part of the Napoleonic Empire. Women used the code to demand respect in a more egalitarian companionate marriage and to challenge a husband's 'right' to beat his wife. It appears that there was an increase in domestic violence by men in many rural communities in Germany during the early nineteenth century. This, it has been suggested, was generated by a shifting economic structure that began to undermine male

    [30] Howard Taylor, 'Rationing Crime: The Political Economy of the Criminal Statistics since the 1850s', *Economic History Review*, 51 (1998), 569–90; Robert Morris, '"Lies, Damned Lies and Criminal Statistics": Reinterpreting the Criminal Statistics of England and Wales', *CHS* 5, 1 (2001), 111–27; Clive Emsley, *Hard Men: The English and Violence since c.1750*, London: Hambledon, 2005, 71–3; James M. Donovan, 'Abortion, the Law, and the Juries in France, 1825–1923', *CJH* 9 (1988), 157–88; 160–1.

dominance within the household and, consequently, within the marriage. The increase was fuelled further by the economic crisis of the 1840s and possibly also by new patterns of sociability that focused on the availability of strong drink in the male world of the tavern. German women victims responded by going to civil law and seeking a divorce.[31] Changes in the economy appear to have fostered a similar pattern of domestic violence in England. But in England the response tended to be different from that in Germany, taking one of two directions. The traditional, folkloric form of charivari, which again would have kept such domestic assaults out of the criminal statistics, remained a popular, extra-judicial way of dealing with domestic violence by ridiculing and humiliating the offender. And in England also, the criminal courts were used, possibly increasingly, since new attitudes among magistrates and judges, though not always among juries, were leading to much stricter sentences being imposed from the bench.[32]

The niceties of which offences appeared in the criminal statistics, which did not, and why, did not bother some of those contemporaries who sought to use them. Police chiefs and police reformers, and some individuals within both central and local government, saw immense value in the figures for boosting or maintaining police numbers and budgets. The police used the statistics to show their efficiency. The daily reports of the Paris Prefect have already been mentioned. They listed the numbers entered in the registers of the *maisons garnies* as well as all of those apprehended by different patrols, all carefully categorized by offence—vagabond, prostitute, night-time prowler or known prowler (*rodeur de nuit* or *rodeur connu*), and so forth. The reports from the *Gendarmerie* companies were similar and during the Restoration they began carefully categorizing all of their patrols as ordinary circuits of their districts, as service at fairs or at markets, as physical support for the civil power, as the serving of warrants, and so on.[33] The advocates of police improvement could set police costs alongside the costs of property stolen. Offences that were tabulated as the result of unsecured doors or windows, or in which the victim was drunk or consorting with a prostitute, was a way of diverting attention from the total crime figure and spreading some

---

[31] Lynn Abrams, 'Companionship and Conflict: The Negotiation of Marriage Relations in the Nineteenth Century', in Lynn Abrams and Elizabeth Harvey, eds., *Gender Relations in German History: Power, Agency and Experience from the Sixteenth to the Twentieth Century*, London: UCL Press, 1996.

[32] Emsley, *Hard Men*, 60–4; Martin J. Wiener, *Men of Blood: Violence, Manliness and Criminal Justice in Victorian England*, Cambridge: Cambridge University Press, 2004.

[33] Clive Emsley, *Gendarmes and the State in Nineteenth-Century Europe*, Oxford: Oxford University Press, 1999, 95–6.

of the culpability to foolish victims. Moreover, faith in the value of social statistics encouraged the idea that, by identifying and enumerating the scale and structure of any problem, that problem became potentially manageable. At the same time, by identifying and enumerating the measures deployed against a problem, it appeared that those responsible for dealing with it were, in reality, dealing with it.[34]

But critics of the police and criminal justice system could also use the statistics. In the towns of provincial France some mayors and their councils queried why they had to pay for one or more *commissaires* when their municipalities appeared relatively free of crime.[35] In the early 1840s ratepayers in the English counties that had established rural constabularies posed similar questions and in Bedfordshire there was even a proposal to remove the new police from part of the county as an experiment to assess empirically whether or not they were having any impact.[36] A quarter of a century later the new Inspectors of Constabulary could raise questions about police effectiveness by looking at the crime statistics. First, Lieutenant General William Cartwright who was responsible for inspecting police in the east, the midlands and the north of England, expressed concerns about the lack of clear directives on how to collect the information. The table that represented indictable offences reported, he explained, 'is a most important return to prove the efficiency of a force as to prevention and detection of crime, it is highly desirable that it should be made upon the same system by all forces, both county and borough, which it is quite clear is not the case at present.' But second, even with the statistics that were available, it was possible to pick up some potential local problems. 'The large amount of crime reported and the few committals led me to refer the returns to the Town Clerk [of Nottingham] for his inspection, and they have been reported as correct.' Further on in Cartwright's report the police of the city of Oxford also came in for criticism based on the statistics. They had increased the number of indictable offences collected and their detection rate was 'a fair average' but there were no statistics to suggest

[34] Chris A. Williams, 'Les catégorisations policières à Sheffield, au milieu du XIXe siècle', *Revue d'histoire moderne et contemporaine*, 50, 1 (2003), 104–25; 122–5.

[35] John M. Merriman, *Police Stories: Building the French State, 1815–1851*, New York: Oxford University Press, 2006, ch. 7.

[36] Clive Emsley, *The English Police: A Political and Social History*, 2nd. edn., London: Longman, 1996, 45–46; idem, 'The Bedfordshire Police 1840–1856: A Case Study in the Working of the Rural Constabulary Act', *Midland History*, 7 (1982), 73–92; 88.

that they were taking any of the normal procedures against pubs and beer houses.[37]

There was another downside. National crime statistics gave substance to the idea that crime was a national problem. Quetelet may have been keen to provide humankind with information that would allow it to break the cycle of crime but, while most national statistics showed a steady rise in the first half of the nineteenth century, no one appeared to be reading any messages that would, in fact, break the cycle. Memories of the French Revolution of the 1790s and continuing outbreaks of economic, political, and social disorder aggravated the concerns of property owners and tempted them to equate criminals with dangerous, lower-class revolutionaries. Less than three weeks after *les trois glorieuses* that toppled Charles X and brought Louis Philippe to the throne the new Prefect of Police in Paris, who owed his appointment to the Revolution and the new regime, could write: 'It seems probable that most of the individuals who take part in these riots are tricksters and vagabonds who are only motivated by the desire for plunder and theft. Perhaps some among them are paid by the enemies of government to excite the population into troubling the public peace.'[38] In the spring of 1848, as revolutionary ferment spread across Europe, the chairman of the Dutch Prison Society expressed his concerns that 'released prisoners could play a pernicious role and could threaten and endanger the tranquillity, possessions, health,—yes the very lives of many in municipality and town.' The recent revolution in Paris, he believed, had drawn significantly on 30,000 to 40,000 released prisoners 'assisted by their wives, concubines and children [who] have formed a strong army that, having nothing to lose, had no thought of respect or fear whatsoever.'[39] A few year later Arnould Bonneville de Marsagny, a leading penal theorist of the French Second Empire, could confidently state that the 'moral anarchy' of 1848 was a direct result of the amelioration of the treatment of convicts that had begun in 1832 under Louis Philippe's monarchy.[40]

[37] *Parliamentary Papers*, 1867 xxxvi. 417, pp. 8–9, 34, and 36–7.
[38] Quoted in Jean Tulard, *La Préfecture de Police sous la Monarchie de Juillet*, Paris: Imprimerie Municipale, 1964, 84.
[39] Quoted in Chris G. T. M. Leonards, 'Priceless Children? Penitentiary Congresses Debating Childhood: A Quest for Social Order in Europe, 1846–1895', in Clive Emsley, Eric Johnson, and Pieter Spierenburg, eds., *Social Control in Europe, 1800–2000*, Columbus: Ohio State University Press, 2004, 125.
[40] Thomas Duesterberg, 'The Politics of Criminal Justice Reform: Nineteenth-Century France', in James A. Inciardi and Charles E. Faugel, eds., *History and Crime: Implications for Criminal Justice Policy*, London: Sage, 1980, 139.

The new science of statistics had promised much and, as the international congresses that met from 1853 testify in themselves, faith in that promise was not dead in the third quarter of the nineteenth century. But the statistics of crime, indicating as they did national and apparently increasing problems, served to undermine many liberal aspirations. So too did popular assumptions among the propertied classes that criminals, rioters, and radical barricade fighters were one and the same, and that these made up an identifiable criminal and dangerous class that constituted a serious and increasing threat to their way of life.

8

Danger in the City: Danger in the Countryside

DURING the early nineteenth century statistics were deployed especially to underpin theories about urban living. Quetelet, for example, argued in his *Recherches sur le penchant au crime aux différents âges* (1830) that crime statistics were the crucial measure for the condition of urban life. Crime statistics seemed to express the unhealthy state of the city better than anything else. In the words of the historian Louis Chevalier they showed 'the pathological nature of urban living'.[1] The statistics also fed into the work of social investigators, like Louis-René Villermé best known for his work on industrial workers, and of moral entrepreneurs, like Edwin Chadwick who sought to bring reform based on utilitarian ideas to Britain's expanding urban environment.

Big cities were not new and nor were fears about the unruly, possibly violent and criminal, behaviour of social groups within them. The overwhelming majority of people in Europe in the first half of the nineteenth century did not live in cities or big towns, and certainly not in the new kind of bleak, grimy industrial cities such as Manchester and its near neighbours or the manufacturing conurbation that grew up around the ancient city of Lille. It seems, however, that such cities gave a new shape and urgency to traditional concerns about the poor that went back generations. To be idle and work-shy, as the deviant poor were traditionally labelled, appeared an even greater offence in an economy and a society that was increasingly seen as dependent upon the product of disciplined labour. At the same time there was a growing demand for a greater level of decorum in the public space of cities and towns. Moreover, many municipalities had begun to invest in the widening of their streets, the tidying of butchers' shambles, and the creation of spaces for restrained and sober public leisure. The emerging middle classes,

---

[1] Louis Chevalier, *Labouring Classes and Dangerous Classes in Paris during the First Half of the Nineteenth Century*, tr. Frank Jellinek, London: Routledge and Kegan Paul, 1973, 10; first published as *Classes laborieuses et classes dangereuses à Paris pendant la première moitié du XIX siècle*, Paris: Plon, 1958.

from the poor but respectable clerk to the merchant prince, had no wish to see their new and elegant public spaces invaded by the dirty, dishevelled urban poor who, increasingly confined to their own districts, appeared as a threatening tribe of alien people. These middle classes also began to contrast their refinement, their rationality, and their self-restraint with what they interpreted as the 'uncivilized' behaviour of the working class. This led to the construction of violence as a social problem by the respectable classes who looked with growing disparagement on communities that continued to legitimate traditional forms of physical confrontation both to solve problems and to maintain an individual's public standing. The argument for this development has been made with particular force for the English experience but it would seem also to have relevance for other national experiences in the early nineteenth century.[2]

There continued to be dangerous groups in the countryside and in societies that did not stand out as being increasingly urban. An oral tradition and the novels and operas of Romantics kept the image of the noble bandit alive, though the seizure of foreign travellers leading, towards the end of the century especially, to the occasional international incident for Mediterranean governments demonstrated a more prosaic, brutal, and violent original. Political instability, factional squabbling between local elites who recruited strong-arm men to protect their property and to attack that of their rivals, and poor road communications all contributed to young men drifting in and out of banditry across Spain, and particularly in Andalusia. Many of the Carlist guerrilla bands of the middle years of the century conducted themselves like bandits, much like many of the guerrilla bands that fought Napoleon.[3] The early statisticians noted particularly the violence of the Mediterranean lands and of Corsica and Sicily. The majority of the Sicilian population lived in large, overcrowded agro-towns rather than in the countryside. The island's economy was overwhelmingly agrarian but after an exploration on horseback early in 1876 Leopoldo Franchetti was moved to write of an indigenous 'violence industry' and to present Sicily as a society in which force had replaced economic activity and which was, in consequence, the antithesis of

  [2] John Carter Wood, *Violence and Crime in Nineteenth-Century England: The Shadow of our Refinement*, London: Routledge, 2004.
  [3] Martin Blinkhorn, 'Rioters, Bandits and Rebels in Spain, 1840–1860', in G. Massa, ed., *Paese Mediterranei e America Latina*, Rome: Quaderni del Centro di Studi Americanisti in Italia, 1982; Henk Driessen, 'The "Noble Bandit" and the Bandits of the Nobles: Brigandage and Local Community in Nineteenth-Century Andalusia', *Archives européenes de sociologie*, 24 (1983), 96–114.

liberal legality. Local men of power and influence, ranging from lawyers and farmers down through estate wardens and managers to bandits and cattle rustlers, filled the vacuum left by the end of the Bourbon monarchy and its variant of feudalism. Protection rackets developed that extorted money from local businesses. The 'violence industry', however, had almost certainly pre-dated the end of the Bourbons; and unification with Italy did nothing to staunch the flow of blood and to alleviate the climate of fear. Indeed, with unification and the ensuing Brigands' War that ravaged the south during the 1860s, Italian intellectuals began to identify the *Mezzogiorno* as a problem region and the home of Italy's own dangerous classes. Italy had a long history of civilized urban culture; and it is at least arguable that there was a greater cohesion among the different urban social classes, even in the more economically dynamic and prosperous cities of the north, than there was among those in rural regions. Generally speaking in Italy, it was the peasants of the south, and of the islands of Sardinia and Sicily, that were stigmatized as primitive, savage, and especially dangerous.[4]

Vendetta thrived in Sicily and elsewhere along the Mediterranean coast and into the Balkans. Vendetta was not lawlessness, though that was how state jurists usually portrayed it; rather it was a system of paying back by the men of one family for the murder of the member of another family or clan. Everywhere it was circumscribed by strict rules of who might be killed and in what circumstances; generally speaking the killing of women and children was prohibited.[5] The French authorities in Corsica had problems with vendetta throughout the nineteenth century and it was something that was quite different from the behaviour of peasants on the mainland. The peasants of the poorer areas of metropolitan France were never stigmatized quite like the Corsicans, or like the peasants of southern Italy and Sicily, but they could still be looked on with fear and suspicion. French peasants could be violent. When new legislation in the early nineteenth century reduced their rights

---

[4] John Dickie, *Darkest Italy: The Nation and Stereotypes of the Mezzogiorno, 1860–1900*, London: Palgrave, 1999.

[5] Writing of Albanians in the early twentieth century Edith Durham noted: 'Blood-vengeance, slaying a man according to the laws of honour, must not be confused with murder. Murder starts a blood feud. In blood-vengeance the rules of the game are strictly observed. A man may not be shot for vengeance when he is with a woman nor with a child, nor when he is in company, nor when *besa* (oath of peace) has been given. The two parties may swear such an oath for a few weeks if they choose, for business purposes.' Edith Durham, *High Albania:A Victorian Traveller's Balkan Odyssey*, London: Phoenix Press, 2000, 35 (1st edn. London: Edward Arnold, 1909). For vendetta in Corsica, see Stephen Wilson, *Feuding, Conflict and Banditry in Nineteenth-Century Corsica*, Cambridge: Cambridge University Press, 1988.

to take wood from forests, for example, they embarked on violent protest. The trouble was most marked in the Pyrenees where, in the late 1820s and early 1830s, *la guerre des demoiselles* was fought. But the anger also spluttered into occasional violence elsewhere and especially during the revolutionary years of 1830 and 1848. Wood, after all, was a necessity for poor peasants. 'Ah monsieur,' wrote one Pyrenean, 'those who take wood from the forests are the most unfortunate who deserve pity; to be surrounded by immense forests where trees are allowed to rot, without use, and to see children, poor children shivering with cold! It's impossible to resist temptation.' But not all forest theft was committed out of dire necessity to keep warm, to cook, or to repair homes or other artefacts. Often it seems that it was possible to sell it to local timber merchants who asked no questions. And what brought this kind of offending to an end, in France at least, was as much a general exodus from the contested mountainous, forested regions as any legislation and its enforcement.[6]

In Germany wood theft was also tied in with ideas of traditional rights and the belief that the poor peasant had a right to the necessities of life. It was a debate in the Rhenish Assembly over legislation to deal with wood theft that prompted some of Karl Marx's earliest polemics and helped shape his socio-economic theories. In the *Rheinische Zeitung* of 25 October 1842 he mocked the idea that fallen wood could be considered as property. 'The owner possesses the tree only, but the tree no longer possesses the branches.' He urged support for the customary rights of the poor and argued that the customary rights of the nobility were, in contrast, contrary to law. Four years later one of his collaborators, Ernst Dronke, published a novel called *Die Maikönigin* (The May Queen) in which a poor old woman is apprehended by a rural policeman for taking fallen wood to heat the cottage for her sick male partner.[7] The development of this forest legislation has been described as a new means of control developed by a new bourgeoisie. A detailed study of wood theft in the district of Minden in Westphalia during the early nineteenth century, however, has shown that peasant proprietors, rather than the gentry, were among the most uncompromising when it came to dealing with the landless labourers who were the most common offenders. The

---

[6] Jean-François Soulet, *Les Pyrénées au XIXe siècle*, 2 vols., Toulouse: Eché, 1987, ii. 502–8; 505; Peter Sahlins, *Forest Rights: The War of the Demoiselles in Nineteenth-Century France*, Cambridge, Mass.: Harvard University Press, 1994; Marie-Renée Santucci, *Délinquence et répression au XIX e siècle: l'exemple de l'Hérault*, Paris: Economica, 1986, 168–82.

[7] Pierre Lascoumes and Hartwig Zander, *Marx: du 'vol du bois' à la critique du droit*, Paris: Presses Universitaires de France,1984, 136 and 93–4.

peasant proprietors appealed to the state's laws, but they also invoked more traditional forms of community justice that involved little in the way of a hearing and often considerable violence.[8]

Thieves who took wood and livestock could be part of organized gangs. So too could poachers. But like those who pilfered growing crops they could also be unfortunate individuals driven to such action by desperation. Such was the case in rural England where, for example, one old Suffolk woman told a local vicar: 'Why, sir, we never think anything about taking a few turnips from the field or sticks from the hedges; it is God makes them grow not the farmers.' Other forms of crime in the English countryside were linked with protest over game preservation, low wages, Poor Law reform, unemployment, the recruitment of cheap Irish labour, and the introduction of machinery. For many years after the Captain Swing disorders of 1830 to 1831 a few angry, usually young labourers kept up a campaign against particular landowners and farmers by poaching, animal maiming and, above all, by arson attacks. Their efforts elicited at least tacit support from many in the rural community and probably they contributed to some of the attempts to improve the lot of the rural worker and to revivify notions of paternalism and community leadership among many landowners.[9] Elsewhere too arson was commonly a crime committed by an individual as revenge on his or her own behalf, or on behalf of a community.[10]

Across Europe the kind of economic dislocation of the eighteenth century that pushed rural dwellers into poverty, on to the roads, and occasionally into criminal behaviour was repeated periodically in the generation following Waterloo and especially during the 1840s. Sometimes the wanderers were threatening. It was reported from an Aragonese market town in February 1847, for example, that large gangs of labourers were roaming the streets after

[8] Josef Mooser, 'Property and Wood Theft: Agrarian Capitalism and Social Conflict in Rural Society, 1800–1850', in Robert G. Moeller, ed., *Peasants and Lords in Modern Germany*, London: Allen and Unwin, 1987. For the prosecution of wood theft as a means of social control, see Dirk Blasius, *Kriminalität und Alltag: Zur Konfliktgeschichte des Alltagslebens im 19. Jahrhundert*, Göttingen: Vandenhoeck und Rupprecht, 1978.

[9] John E. Archer, *'By a Flash and a Scare': Arson, Animal Maiming, and Poaching in East Anglia, 1815–1870*, Oxford: Clarendon Press, 1990, quotation at pp. 15–16; see also Barry Reay, *The Last Rising of the Agricultural Labourer: Rural Life and Protest in Nineteenth-Century England*, Oxford: Oxford University Press, 1990; and Timothy Shakesheff, *Rural Conflict, Crime and Protest: Herefordshire, 1800–1860*, Woodbridge: Boydell Press, 2003.

[10] Elisabeth Claverie and Pierre Lamaison, *L'impossible marriage: violence et parenté en Gévaudan, 17e, 18e, et 19e siècles*, Paris: Hachette, 1982, 262–3; Regina Schulte, *The Village in Court: Arson, Infanticide, and Poaching in the Court Records of Upper Bavaria, 1848–1914*, Cambridge: Cambridge University Press, 1994, 25–57.

dark demanding 'alms' and adding that if they did not have work they would form a Carlist guerrilla band.[11] Very occasionally the wanderers appeared to be well-prepared bands of thieves. In October 1833, for example, a band of vagabonds was arrested at an annual fair in the Haute-Loire. They had passports that described them as merchants; they also had road maps and guides to the times and dates of fairs across the whole of France.[12] More often, however, the vagabonds were desperate and pathetic. Landowners in the Papal States made regular complaints about the problem, though they appear rarely to have prosecuted offending day labourers, possibly out of feelings of sympathy and charity, possibly through fear of reprisal. When the violent behaviour of a gang of brigands around Fillotrano in the Marche suggested that the situation was getting seriously out of hand, the authorities responded with the arrest of sixty-nine suspects. The suspects were implicated in fifty-three separate incidents, many of which carried the death penalty. With the arrests the panic came to an end. But while the authorities had acted with speed and determination to suppress the threat, the machinery of Papal justice was still wedded to the long-drawn-out inquisitorial process, and the legal proceedings dragged on for a decade.[13]

In Germany, as in the previous century, thousands could be seen on the roads. Journeymen on the tramp were required to carry a *Wanderbuch*, a passport akin to the French worker's *livret*, that was issued in a man's state of origin. It carried details of his employment and conduct; it had to be shown when he crossed a frontier and was surrendered to the local police for as long as he worked in a town. But the documents were easy to forge, while the police were thin on the ground and often had poor literacy skills. In addition in some states the police were paid a reward for each vagabond that they apprehended; this encouraged corrupt police officials to apprehend and blackmail some of those travellers that had a little money in their pockets.[14] The opportunities for fraud and deception were great on both sides and made any statistics of vagabonds highly suspect. Nevertheless the concerns about the vagrant criminal together with fears about increasing poverty were considerable. In the middle of the 1840s the Brockhaus *Real-Enzyclopädia* noted a new word

---

[11] Blinkhorn, 'Rioters, Bandits and Rebels', 278.

[12] John M. Merriman, *Police Stories: Building the French State, 1815–1851*, New York: Oxford University Press, 2006, 129.

[13] Isabella Rosoni, *Criminalità e giustizia penale nello Stato Pontifico del secolo XIX. Un caso di banditismo rurale*, Milan: Giuffrè, 1988.

[14] Andreas Fahrmeir, *Citizens and Aliens: Foreigners and the Law in Britain and the German States, 1789–1870*, New York and Oxford: Berghahn Books, 2000, 116–21.

in German—*Pauperismus.* Contemporaries perceived there to be a structural crisis in the economy that required an ever-increasing number of individuals to labour in the most intensive fashion merely to exist. Some found refuge in emigration, others found solace in strong drink that became much cheaper as producers switched from grain to potatoes to produce *Schnaps*.[15] As well as solace and a thirst quencher on and off the job, the drink provided a significant food substitute. But the male sociability that accompanied heavy drinking also appeared to generate violence and thus to have an impact on the crime statistics.

Although small towns and rural communities were far from quiescent and never crime free, early nineteenth-century folklorists were 'discovering' peasants and were describing them as the preservers of an earlier, and consequently more pure, national tradition. This was especially the case in Germany where, in the work of men like the conservative social theorist Wilhelm Heinrich Riehl, the peasant acquired a moral image, and the virtues of goodness, humility, loyalty, piety, and natural wisdom were perceived in his frugal life and noble labour.[16] This kind of image seeped into popular literature and provided an important conservative alternative to the anxieties about the city and the problems generated by the changing structure of the economy. The English did not have a Riehl; nevertheless a romantic image was constructed of the countryside peopled by solid yeomen and healthy, deferential peasants. It was a comforting image that provided a stable, steady, and traditional heart for the countryside and a contrast to the new, hectic, industrial city. There was plenty of evidence to contradict the rural idyll. As one commentator put it in the middle of the century: 'Of late years it has become known that this picture is one which rather accommodates itself to the desires of the mind than to the state of the case.'[17] Nevertheless the rural idyll continued to be evoked well into the twentieth century.

Quetelet's statistical analyses led him, and others, to the conclusion that there was a significant difference between the average man and the man who had a tendency towards criminal behaviour. The former chose between the extremes of deficiency and excess, and was rational, sensible, and temperate

[15] James S. Roberts, *Drink, Temperance and the Working Class in Nineteenth-Century Germany*, Boston: Allen and Unwin, 1984, 13–18.

[16] Wilhelm Heinrich Riehl, *Die bürgerliche Gesellschaft*, Stuttgart, 1851; idem, *Naturgeschichte des Volkes als Grundlage einer deutschen Social-Politik*, Stuttgart, 1857; see also the edited and translated version of the latter by David J. Diephouse, *The Natural History of the German People*, Lewiston, NY: Edwin Mellen Press, 1990.

[17] William Johnston, *England as it is, Political, Social, and Industrial in the Middle of the Nineteenth Century*, 2 vols., London: John Murray, 1851, i. 178.

in habits. Quetelet commonly contrasted this average man with vagabonds, vagrants, Gypsies, members of the inferior classes, those with a low moral character or from an inferior moral stock.[18] The term 'the dangerous classes' came into popular use to describe these latter during the 1840s following its use in the title of a book and a use that rooted these classes in urban society. Honoré Frégier, a senior official in the Prefecture of the Seine, published his two-volume *Des classes dangereuses de la population dans les grandes villes et des moyens de les rendre meilleures* in 1840. Frégier acknowledged that there were corrupt and depraved individuals among the wealthy but these were not dangerous.

The poor and depraved classes have always been and will always be the most productive nursery of all kinds of malefactor. It is these who are most particularly categorized under the heading of *dangerous classes*. Even where vice is not accompanied by perversity, once it is unified with poverty in the same individual it becomes an object of which society should be afraid; it is dangerous. Social danger increases and becomes more and more serious as soon as the poor spoil their condition through vice and, which is worse, through idleness. The moment that a poor man, yielding to wicked passions, ceases to work, he becomes an enemy of society because he is ignoring the supreme law that requires work.[19]

Frégier's book was not widely translated, but the concept of the dangerous classes and the juxtaposition of honest, average men with inferior, vagrant types were deployed by commentators elsewhere. In Britain the Sheriff of Lanarkshire, the energetic Sir Archibald Alison, was using the term 'dangerous classes' four years after Frégier's book was first published. Alison linked these classes with 'destitution, profligacy, sensuality and crime', strikes, and periodic insurrection.[20] In a series of official and semi-official publications and journalistic pieces, Edwin Chadwick, the leading Benthamite reformer, took a similar line and asserted that offenders were brought to crime by their own decisions and their own faults. Bad company, drink, gambling, and idleness were contributory factors that tempted individuals to seek to profit from depredations rather than living by honest, paid labour. The dangerous classes were centred in the big cities, especially London, but they also tramped the countryside, looking for opportunities for plunder at,

[18] Piers Beirne, 'Adolphe Quetelet and the Origins of Positivist Criminology', *American Journal of Sociology*, 92 (1987), 1140–69.

[19] Honoré Frégier, *Des classes dangereuses de la population dans les grandes villes et des moyens de les rendre meilleures*, 2 vols., Paris, 1840, i. 7.

[20] [Archibald Alison], 'Causes of the Increase of Crime', *Blackwood's Edinburgh Magazine*, 56 (1844), 1–14; quotation at p. 2.

for example, fairs and races. They found shelter in low, unlicensed lodging houses. Chadwick's arguments were forcefully seconded by William Augustus Miles, a man who used his claim to being the illegitimate son of a royal prince to win patronage and who served as an assistant to Chadwick on the Royal Commission inquiring into the need for a rural constabulary.[21] Henry Mayhew, a journalist who had visited Paris and who was familiar with the work of French social commentators, also claimed to be an expert on crime and criminals before a parliamentary inquiry. But Mayhew's work was directed far beyond government and administrative circles. Above all, he had an impact on the thinking of the respectable classes of Victorian Britain with his extensive study of the London poor, the fourth volume of which revived Fielding's differentiation between those who could not work, those unable to find work, and those who would not work. Mayhew, like Chadwick, saw criminality as rooted in the offender's dislike of steady labour, though he also considered that this could be aggravated by poor parents and tyrannical masters who failed to inculcate a love of work among those whose station in life it was to labour.[22]

A decade after Mayhew's final volume Giovanni Bolis, a police official and subsequently (1879–83) director of the Italian Public Security Police, took up Frégier's formulation with a massive study of the police and the dangerous classes (*classi pericolose*) across Europe, but with particular reference to Italy. Like Mayhew, and others, he emphasized the importance within the category of those who would not work and who preferred a life of idleness and vagabondage to honest labour.

The dangerous classes of society are formed by all those individuals who, not having the necessary means of subsistence, live idly and as vagrants, drawing upon the resources of other citizens. As they disregard the supreme human law, that is the law of labour, they represent a permanent danger to the social order. This danger becomes all the more serious when their idleness is connected to their perverse instincts.

Bolis was also highly critical of those men who preferred to spend their wages on personal pleasure rather than on their suffering families, and of prostitutes, the female representatives of the dangerous class.[23]

---

[21] David Philips, 'Three "Moral Entrepreneurs" and the Creation of a "Criminal Class" in England, *c*.1790–1840', *CHS* 7, 1 (2003), 79–107.

[22] David Englander, 'Henry Mayhew and the Criminal Classes of Victorian England', in Louis A. Knafla, ed., *Crime, Gender and Sexuality in Criminal Prosecutions, CJH* 17 (2002), 87–108.

[23] Giovanni Bolis, *La polizia in Italia, e in altri stati d'Europa, e le classi pericolose della società,* Bologna: Zanichelli, 1871; quotation at pp. 459–60. Bolis's references to England were drawn, not from Mayhew's work directly, but primarily from Léon Faucher, *Études sur l'Angleterre.*

In Germany Frégier's concept does not appear to have been translated and used as it was in Britain and Italy; the Germans appear to have stuck to their own word *Gauner* to describe the persistent criminal offender who was commonly assumed to exist in a kind of counter-society. But, even without the application of a new descriptive phrase, Georg von Mayr's statistics showed significantly greater numbers of beggars and vagrants in the towns of Bavaria than in the surrounding countryside.[24] In Berlin there was manifest nervousness over the growth of the working class, over poverty and vagrancy. The police role was significantly expanded with regard to the supervision of the poor and a stereotypical image emerged of immigrants entering the city as artisans, starting families that they could not support, and then abandoning them to poor relief.[25] The issues were taken up in, for example, Bettina von Arnim's *Dies Buch gehört dem König* (1843). This purported to be a series of dialogues with Frau Rat Goether discussing, among other things, capital punishment and how education might be deployed as a safeguard against poverty and crime. The book's appendix contained observations, purported to have been written by a Swiss student, on the Berlin slum district of 'Vogtland', so called because of its large population of poor immigrant Saxons.[26]

Using texts from the late eighteenth and first half of the nineteenth centuries, Peter Becker has described how crime in Germany was perceived to be the result of moral weakness and how the criminal was responsible for his own downfall. Imbued with the thought of the German Enlightenment and particularly Kantian philosophy, the theorists of crime in Germany believed that evil occurred when men failed to resist temptation. While ideas of evil and temptation smacked of traditional religious thinking and also drew upon it, this was a secular ideology. Man was considered to be a rational being and anyone committing evil or criminal actions was behaving in an egotistical fashion rejecting moral imperatives for hedonistic reasons. In Kantian terms he had the wrong cast of mind or ethos (*Gesinnung*). He was spurning the moral foundations of society by which the proper citizen used his civic freedom to pursue productivity and education. He was also threatening that society by abusing and thus engendering distrust in its social and economic

---

[24] Georg von Mayr, *Statistik der Bettler und Vaganten im Königreiche Bayern*, Munich, 1865, 69.
[25] Dietlind Hüchtker, 'Strategies and Tactics: The Politics of Subsistence in Berlin, 1770–1850', *International Review of Social History*, 49, 3 (2004), 435–53; 450–1.
[26] Donald G. Rohr, *The Origins of Social Liberalism in Germany*, Chicago: University of Chicago Press, 1963, 54–5.

exchange.[27] From here it was but a small intellectual leap to link the criminal with the revolutionary.

Sir Archibald Alison was not alone in linking the concept of the dangerous classes with insurrection. Many others manifested a fear of sinister individuals lurking in the slums of burgeoning towns and cities waiting for the opportunities that riot and revolution would bring for looting and mayhem. Such fears were not new. In England they seem to have been emerging in the eighteenth century even before the Gordon Riots of 1780 appeared to give them a terrible substance.[28] Further substance came, across the length and breadth of Europe, with the reports of the violent *journées* of the French Revolution when prisoners were massacred and respectable politicians, even within the nation's assembly, were killed by crowds and had their heads paraded on pikes. The recurrence of revolution after the fall of Napoleon, in Spain and Italy in the early 1820s, across Europe in 1830 and again in 1848, aggravated these anxieties. So too did the massive manifestations of economic unrest involving industrial groups such as the English Luddites in the second decade of the century, the silk weavers of Lyons in 1831 and 1834, and the Silesian weavers in 1844. The fears were not constant and never maintained a permanently high level but they recurred at sufficiently close and regular intervals to ensure that they were never entirely forgotten. Moreover, popular, often sensational, journalism and literature played on them for profit. The sensationalism that had been apparent in sections of the English newspaper press during the eighteenth century spread across the Channel. The *Procureur Général* attributed a panic about night-time robberies in Paris in the closing months of 1826 to newspapers and he suspected that some of the stories in the press had been fabricated.[29] But, panics apart, respectable and not-so-respectable readers found vicarious thrills in articles and books that took their readers into the depths of the cities and the sinister realms of the dangerous classes. Moreover, these books were not simply the official, semi-official, and propagandist publications of men like Chadwick or the observational accounts of men like Frégier and Mayhew. A large number of them were written by individuals who claimed a first-hand experience of crime and criminals.

[27] Peter Becker, *Verderbnis und Entartung: eine Geschichte der Kriminologie des 19. Jahrhunderts als Diskurs und Praxis*, Göttingen: Vandenhoeck und Ruprecht, 2002, esp. ch. 2.

[28] Nicholas Rogers, *Crowds, Culture and Politics in Georgian Britain*, Oxford: Clarendon Press, 1998, ch. 5, esp. pp. 170–2.

[29] AN BB[18]1145, Rapport du procureur générale sur les crimes d'attaques et de vols nocturnes commis à Paris pendant les trois derniers mois de 1826.

From the late 1820s a wide range of literature began to appear on criminality and policing. In 1828 the French reading public was both shocked and thrilled by the publication of the first volume of the memoirs of Eugène-François Vidocq. Vidocq was the former convict who, for nearly twenty years, had organized the criminal investigation department of the Paris Prefecture. Most of the volume, and of its successors, was ghosted and enhanced at the behest of the publisher who was more concerned with the sales of a sensational book than with any respect for truth. Guessing that he was on to a good thing, the publisher paid Vidocq 20,000 francs for the manuscript. Vidocq was so dissatisfied with the rewriting that he refused to sign off the fourth volume. Yet the story of Vidocq's colourful origins and of his move into a successful police career was essentially correct. Moreover, his experiences with his publisher did not discourage him from acting as an adviser to novelists keen to tap into his experience. Nor did it discourage him from publishing other books. *Les voleurs: physiologie de leurs mœurs et de leur langage*, published in 1836 and again using a ghost writer, claimed to provide honest men with an accurate picture of thieves 'with their vices and their qualities.'[30]

Much of *Les voleurs* focused on the language of thieves. According to Vidocq, they even had their own Ten Commandments, largely phrased in argot:

1

Un seul sentiment t'animera
Celui de grincher gourdement

2

Journe et sorgue tu poisseras
Boucart et baïte chenument

(1   A single sentiment will motivate you | To steal much; 2   Day and night you will steal | Adroitly in both shop and home)

In Germany criminal argot took up the fourth volume of *Das deutsche Gaunerthum in seiner social-politischen, literarischen und linguistischen Ausbildung zu seinem heutigen Bestande*, written some twenty years later by Friedrich Christian Benedikt Avé-Lallement, a police official in Lübeck.

---

[30] Eugène-François Vidocq, *Les voleurs: physiologie de leurs mœurs et de leur langage*, Paris, 1837, p. viii. For Vidocq's career see e.g. Eric Perrin, *Vidocq: Roi des voleurs, roi des policiers*, Paris: Perrin, 1995; James Morton, *The First Detective: The Life and Revolutionary Times of Vidocq*, London: Ebury Press, 2005. For Vidocq's relations with the publisher of his memoirs see Dominique Kalifa, *Crime et culture*, Paris: Perrin, 2005, 72–3.

Avé-Lallement's work purported to trace the development of criminality in Germany from the Middle Ages. His origins were not as sinister as those of Vidocq; his police experience gave his writing authority; but his conclusions constructed an image of criminality that suited and enhanced his readers' prejudices. He emphasized that Germany was a Christian land and he described criminal offending as having developed disproportionately among groups who did not share the Christian values of morality and honesty. Outcast elements such as the men who worked in the dishonourable trades of knackers and skinners were significant here and so too, he argued, were Gypsies and Jews. He emphasized how much the language of these two latter groups contributed to the argot of German criminals. Yet Avé-Lallement also rejected the notion, put forward a few years earlier by the Prussian legal official A. F. Thiele, that there was an organized Jewish criminal underworld threatening respectable, bourgeois society.[31] Thiele's book also, like so many others, made much of the argot of a criminal underworld and contained over 100 pages of dictionary with nearly 3,000 Jewish 'criminal' words.

The fascination with criminal argot was not new to the nineteenth century and books on such cant went back to the early modern period.[32] But the emphasis on criminal language was another way of emphasizing the separateness of the criminal classes from ordinary society. Indeed Henry Mayhew and his collaborator, John Binny, insisted that there was a distinction to be made between the argot of thieves, which they considered to be drawn from medieval Latin, that of beggars (or 'cadgers') which they described as a rhyming slang, and that of the costermongers which was formed by pronouncing words as if they were spelt backwards.[33] A generation later Cesare Lombroso argued that thieves' language was atavistic, that it resembled the language of savages, and that it was similar wherever a person travelled.[34] Whether criminals across Europe did employ their own forms of language as part of a separate, infamous subsection of society as a whole, must remain an

[31] Daniel Vyleta, 'Jewish Crimes and Misdemeanours: In Search of Jewish Criminality (Germany and Austria, 1890–1914)', *European History Quarterly*, 35, 2 (2005), 299–325; 301–2.

[32] For cant in Elizabethan England, see e.g. A. V. Judges, ed., The Elizabethan Underworld: A Collection of Tudor and Early Stuart Tracts, London: Routledge and Kegan Paul, 1965, esp. the glossary (522–32).

[33] Henry Mayhew and John Binny, The Criminal Prisons of London and Scenes of Prison Life, London, 1862, 5–6.

[34] Peter Becker, 'The Criminologists' Gaze at the Underworld: Toward an Anthology of Criminological Writing', in Peter Becker and Richard Wetzell, eds., Criminals and their Scientists: The History of Criminology in International Perspective, New York: Cambridge University Press, 2006, 123.

open question. Migrants and specific outcast groups would have used dialects and patois, though whether such languages were specifically developed for criminal purposes is, at least, debatable. In the early modern Netherlands, for example, it appears that some groups who engaged in criminality 'turned dialects and professional idioms they were already using outside the context of illegality into an asset in the business of crime'.[35] It has also been suggested that Henry Mayhew took the slang for a particular kind of theft and gave it greater currency by creating categories of professional thieves who specialized exclusively in that particular offence. Thus, to give one example, 'sawney hunting' became the craft of 'Sawney-Hunters . . . who go purloining bacon from cheesemongers' shop-doors'.[36] At the very end of the century Émile Nougier, a man with a string of convictions for robbery and awaiting execution for murder, wrote a personal memoir for the French criminologist Alexandre Lacassagne. Together with the memoir he wrote fifty pages on criminal argot. In these latter pages he maintained that at most one in ten of the 10,000 words in a dictionary of argot were correctly explained and that this book was, in essence, an incomplete collection of words in colloquial French usage.[37]

All of this literature helped to develop the image of criminal society as a kind of counter-society at war with everything that the respectable bourgeois held dear. It brought together all of the fears for the safety of life, property, and family and identified a common threat to all of these in the individual criminal and his social class. Nor was this construction something created by those gazing on the problem from outside. One of the most startling representations of the criminal as an individual at war with society was that given by a young, self-publicizing murderer and thief, Pierre-François Lacenaire. Born into a respectable family in Lyons in 1803, Lacenaire had received a good education. But when his father's finances were hit by the problems of the Lyons silk industry, Lacenaire was forced to find work. He drifted through a variety of jobs, failing in each one, before opting for a life on the margins of society. He enlisted in, and deserted from, the army twice before taking to crime. He was already writing poetry while engaged on his

[35] Florike Egmond, *Underworlds: Organized Crime in the Netherlands, 1650–1800*, Cambridge: Polity Press, 1993, 16.

[36] Clive Emsley, *Crime and Society in England*, 1750–1900, 3rd edn., London: Pearson-Longman, 2004, 72.

[37] Philippe Artières, 'What Criminals Think about Criminology: French Criminals and Criminological Knowledge at the End of the Nineteenth Century', in Beker and Wetzell, eds., *Criminals and their Scientists*, 374.

short, but brutal and bloody, spree of offending. In 1833 he wrote a fanciful poetic petition to Louis Philippe:

> Sire de grâce, écoutes-moi:
> Je viens de sortir des galères,
> Je suis voleur, vous êtes roi;
> Agissons ensemble en bons frères,
> Les gens de bien me font horreur,
> J'ai le cœur dur et l'âme vile.
> Je suis sans pitié, sans honneur.
> Ah! Faites-moi sergent de ville.

(Lord of mercy, hear me: | I have just left the galleys, | I'm a thief, you're a king | Let's debate things like good brothers, | Men of property give me the horrors, | I have a hard heart and an evil mind. | I am pitiless, without honour | Ah! make me a police officer.

Arrested, condemned, and awaiting execution he played at being a celebrity, entertaining visitors in his cell and writing his memoirs. The *Gazette des Tribunaux* appears to have tried to undermine his glamour by describing him as a pitiable, terrified figure at the moment when he had to mount the scaffold. Louis Canler, however, the detective responsible for his arrest and who stood close to the guillotine during the execution, portrayed him as fearless at his death. While the publication of his memoirs provoked outrage and even alarm, to some, particularly among literary circles, Lacenaire remained a romantic anti-hero and they spoke of him, as he himself had wished, as an artist of crime.[38] Hippolyte Raynal was less violent than Lacenaire; his offences were vagabondage followed by theft. But Raynal also became a literary star with his *Malheur et poésie*, published in 1834, and his autobiographical novel *Sous les verroux*, published two years later. The novel picked up on and embroidered the popular trope of the prison as a school of crime. Louis Philippe and his queen were reported to have been among the admirers who visited Raynal in prison.[39]

But while Lacenaire's and Raynal's notoriety as criminals helped their literary aspirations, some of the most successful novelists of the period found

[38] Anne-Emmanuelle Demartini, *L'affaire Lacenaire*, Paris: Aubier, 2001; Louis Canler, *Mémoires de Canler: ancien chef du service de Sûreté*, ed. Jacques Brenner, Paris: Mercure de France, 1967, ch. 38. The first edition was published in 1862, but was promptly seized by Napoleon III's police for allegedly revealing state secrets and for being an outrage to morals.
[39] Edgar Leon Newman, '"I was born good, society corrupted me." Hippolyte Raynal, the Anti-Émile, Poet, Artisan and Thief', *Proceedings of the Western Society for French History*, 28 (2002), 76–85.

plots and characters in the underworld and among the police, and sought advice and information from the latter. Vidocq was known to Honoré de Balzac and Victor Hugo and he gave them both advice and storylines. In addition, his career and reputation were fictionalized and sensationalized into Balzac's sinister criminal and police detective Vautrin who first appeared in *Père Goriot* (1834–5) but went on to dominate *Splendeurs et misères des courtisanes* (1837–47). Like other journalists keen to portray the life of the lower and the criminal classes, Charles Dickens went on patrol with police officers. Inspector Field, whom Dickens described in journalistic essays, became the model for Inspector Bucket in *Bleak House* (1852). Dickens combined the common fears of the alien outsider and of the adult master of child pickpockets in his creation Fagin. There has been some debate as to whether this 'very old shrivelled Jew, whose villainous-looking and repulsive face was obscured by a quantity of matted red hair' was based on the notorious receiver Ikey Solomons, but the truth of this hardly matters.[40] Similarly with Bill Sikes, the brutal burglar and murderer also from *Oliver Twist* (1837–8), who may have been modelled on some individuals known to Dickens or simply constructed from offenders described in the press as he planned his story. The important point about Sikes is that with him, Dickens built upon fears of the criminal and in so doing established a fearsome, named, and hence readily known and identifiable, archetype. Dickens's friend William Harrison Ainsworth selected his criminals from well-known eighteenth-century offenders, the burglar Jack Sheppard and the highwayman Dick Turpin. In France, Eugène Sue took a storyline rather similar to some of those used by Ainsworth and by Dickens in *Oliver Twist*—the respectable child lost to its own parents and brought up rubbing shoulders with the criminal classes—and produced *Les mystères de Paris* (1842–43). The book was an instant success, running through fourteen editions before Sue's death, in 1857, and another nineteen re-editions from that date until the beginning of the First World War. In addition there were countless imitations, including Vidocq's *Les vrais mystères de Paris* (1844), as well as theatrical versions and songs.[41] Sue's grotesque setting and his violent characters became an international success and encouraged similar 'mysteries'. August Brass was among the first off the mark with *Die Mysterien von Berlin* (1844). A total of three dozen German cities had such mysteries

[40] Charles Dickens, *Oliver Twist*, ch. 8 for the description of Fagin. For Ikey Solomons see, J. J. Tobias, *Prince of Fences: The Life and Crimes of Ikey Solomons*, London: Vallentine Mitchell, 1974.
[41] Kalifa, *Crime et culture*, 40.

exposed in similar novels in the same year, while at the end of 1845 Germany even found its own Lacenaire in Christian Holtzwart, poet, playwright, and religious thinker, and murderer of his wife and five children.[42] In England the Chartist newspaper proprietor G. W. M. Reynolds followed Sue with the massive, rambling, but immensely successful *Mysteries of London*, published in weekly parts between 1845 and 1848.

The criminal characters of novels were never drawn solely from the working class. Press outrage over criminal behaviour was shrill when the offenders turned out to be respectable gentlemen defrauding people like themselves. The development of capitalism and the state bureaucracies that sought to replace the venal practices of the old regimes provided new and considerable opportunities for peculation, financial corruption, and fraud. What subsequently became labelled 'white-collar crime' was exposed among all social groups ranging from those who sold tickets for trains and omnibuses to company directors and supposedly reputable bankers. Balzac, Dickens, Trollope, and others picked up on such criminality illustrating it with some of their more odious characters. Yet while such offenders provided vicarious shocks for the reading public and sometimes real shocks for the small investor, they were generally perceived as isolated individuals and were never categorized among the criminal and dangerous classes.

The texts of policemen, the novels, and the reports of journalists combined with the statistics of crime and the occasional revolutionary outbreaks to create a picture for the propertied classes of their world under threat. In the aftermath of the Revolutions of 1848 a provincial French doctor, Bénédict Augustin Morel, developed the concept of *dégénérescence*—degeneration. His work came to fruition with the publication, in 1857, of *Traité des dégénérescences physiques, intellectuelles et morales de l'espèce humaine*. The book has been explained as a reflection of the concerns about the dangerous classes in the cities though, as Daniel Pick has convincingly argued, it is probably much more than this and reflects also concerns about the unpredictability of change and a loss of confidence in liberal progressivism. Morel's *dégénérescence* was a process of pathological change affecting society as a whole as well as individuals. He wove together a discussion of physical conditions and moral and social behaviour in an attempt to explain the pattern of heredity in society and to

---

[42] Rohr, *Origins of Social Liberalism*, 52; Christian Holtzwart, *Christian Holtzwart, der Mörder seiner Gattin und seiner fünf Kinder, als Mensch, Denker und Dichter, Bruchstücke aus seinem Tagebuche und vollständiger Bericht der Sudenburg-Magdeburg in der Nacht von 28–29 Dezember 1845 verübten sechsfachen Mordthat und Mordbrennerei (Mit dem Bildnisse des Mörders und des Schauplatzes der gräßlichen That)*, Brunswick, 1846.

demonstrate that physical degeneration might lead to intellectual and moral collapse and vice versa.[43] Morel's concept was not designed to explain criminality though it was to feed significantly into subsequent debates on the matter.

The representation of crime operates on a different level to crime itself. It is representations of crime in the press, in novels, in broadsides and prints that determine the cultural impact of crime rather than the relatively rare personal experience that individuals have as victims or perpetrators. The overwhelming majority of individuals brought before the criminal courts during the nineteenth century were accused of relatively minor offences, usually some form of petty theft. The crimes and the criminals that figured largest in the nineteenth-century literature, however, were of a much more serious variety. Victor Hugo's Jean Valjean was unemployed and desperate to feed his seven children when he broke the window of a baker's shop and stole a loaf of bread. For this offence the novelist had his hero sentenced to five years as a *galérien*. Valjean's reputation for poaching did not favour him with the court and various failed attempts at escape led to him serving a total of nineteen years. The public did not see Jean Valjean as the typical offender and Hugo, while noting the 'English statistics' that demonstrated four out of five thefts in London were occasioned by hunger, was keen to distinguish the unfortunate, but ultimately redeemed and redeeming, Valjean from the urban criminal: 'The towns make men ferocious because they make men corrupt. The mountain, the sea, the forest make men savage. They develop their fierce side, but often without destroying their humanity.'[44] In contrast while, as has already been noted, novelists keenly portrayed corrupt and evil financiers, the typical criminal as portrayed in fiction especially was a Bill Sikes or a Lacenaire. Moreover while, according to the statistics, most crime was petty and non-violent, the image of the criminal was the violent burglar who slipped easily into murder. Assumptions were made by the novelist, the social investigator, and the police expert about a steady progression from small theft to brutal violence as a man became more deeply involved in criminality. Achille Rabasse, a Parisian police officer seeking to ingratiate himself with his superiors and, probably, to gain promotion, described distinct types of offender in ways that better suited the imaginings of Eugène Sue than the reality of who was usually fished up in the nets of the night-time patrols on the streets of Paris. 'Within society', he wrote,

[43] Daniel Pick, *Faces of Degeneration: A European Disorder, c.1848–c.1918*, Cambridge: Cambridge University Press, 1989, 44–59.
[44] Victor Hugo, *Les Misérables*, bk. II, ch. 6.

there is another society, if it can be called such, which is made up of shadowy individuals, bandits who are hated without exception and who constitute the principal social peril. They are idle, liars, drunkards, murderers, and killers. They wait until the sky is black before showing themselves. In the evening they come out of their dens, the hovels that they entered before the feeble glimmers of day.[45]

Gender and class were important to the portrayal of criminals. Crime was a man's world—it was committed by male criminals and investigated by male policemen. Women were victims, and even when they were the perpetrators of offences—with the exception of prostitutes of whom more below—these offences were generally committed within the domestic sphere. Balzac's Cousine Bette ruined the Hulot family with her malice, but within the domestic sphere. Miss Gwilt, in Wilkie Collins's *Armadale*, was a voluptuous temptress who was involved in murder, theft, and forgery 'without any trace being left on her beauty'. But while she was 'fouler than the refuse of the streets' she was not a part of the criminal class that, for other writers, infested those streets.[46] Such women were not setting boundaries for female behaviour; they had crossed those boundaries by a considerable measure. Yet their behaviour might be said to have re-emphasized the idealized female roles of passivity and respectability. Similarly with the middle-class offenders portrayed by novelists. These were corrupt financiers and fraudsters and again they were sometimes based on actual individuals taken before the courts following criminal offences that owed much to the new opportunities provided by the growth of commerce and capitalist enterprise. But neither these actual offenders nor their fictional representations were seen as members of the criminal class; they were both portrayed as exceptions to the accepted behaviour of their own class.

Vivid literary images appealed to the emotions and were aggravated by the ways in which members of the propertied classes were ignorant of, or chose to ignore, the precarious economic position of those employed in casual labour in the towns and cities and the linked problems of underemployment and seasonal employment. It was not that some of the most popular commentators on the criminal classes always skipped over these problems. Ernst Dronke's *Polizei-Geschichten*, first published in 1847, foreshadowed Hugo's portrayal of Valjean by drawing attention to the way in which some individuals, after committing a petty offence, could be persecuted and stigmatized ever after.[47]

---

[45] APP 398/3, Achille Rabasse, 'Police Municipal' (1872), fo. 169.
[46] Review of *Armadale*, *Spectator*, 39 (1866), 638–9.
[47] Richard J. Evans, *Tales from the German Underworld: Crime and Punishment in the Nineteenth Century*, London: Yale University Press, 1998, 95–6.

And Mayhew and Binny wrote a vivid description of 'casual men' scrambling for work at fourpence an hour every morning in the London Docks. They also described how penury could prompt theft and argued that 'the poor shirt-makers, slop-tailors, and the like [who] have not the power of earning more than the barest subsistence by their labour' might be sucked into offending 'for "dear life"', on the occurrence of the least illness or mishap'. Such people, they insisted, should not be lumped together with habitual criminals, 'those who object to work'.[48] Yet, in general terms, the poor seem more often to have been seen as the philanthropist Mary Carpenter described the 'perishing and dangerous classes' who had not had the benefits of education and religion inculcated into them.

Look at them in the streets, where to the eye of the worldly man, they all appear as the scum of the populace, fit only to be swept as vermin from the face of the earth;—see them in their homes, if such they have, squalid, filthy, vicious, or pining and wretched with none to help, destined only, it would seem, to be carried off by some beneficent pestilence.[49]

If the poor were to be seen in large numbers on the streets, this was often because the street gave some respite from life in a teeming working-class tenement block. The streets and open spaces provided a setting for leisure, meeting and talking, and for buying both cooked and uncooked food. For men especially, the tavern still provided a site of leisure where friends and workmates might be met, entertained, and challenged to various games. The use of drink as a food substitute was unknown to those who were relatively well fed and who did not earn their living by manual labour. But it is important to appreciate that only fats provide more energy more efficiently than alcohol: the metabolism of one gram of alcohol produces seven calories of energy; protein or carbohydrates produce only four, while fats produce nine.[50] The anxieties generated by numbers of unemployed or underemployed men assembled in public places and by the working-class culture of drinking further aggravated the early and mid-nineteenth-century fears of economic, political, and social unrest that periodically broke into the foreground in the form of mass demonstrations and revolutionary action.

Alongside the occasionally blinkered understanding of why working-class men were on the streets could be found similar blinkered understanding

48 Mayhew and Binny, *Criminal Prisons of London*, 35–6 and 88–9.
49 Mary Carpenter, *Reformatory Schools for the Children of the Perishing and Dangerous Classes and for Juvenile Offenders*, London, 1851, 2–3.
50 Roberts, *Drink, Temperance and the Working Class* 17.

of the situation of children and juveniles. The decline in apprenticeships and of the number of children of the poor going into service was only marginally offset by the employment of children in factories and by other developing businesses in the burgeoning towns and cities of the early nineteenth century. But such changes meant also that children commonly stayed with their parents for longer and hence shared their problems of poverty, unemployment, and underemployment. At the same time, in keeping with the Romantic sensibility of the period, new concepts of childhood were being formulated that put great emphasis on the goodness and innocence of children. Street children, by their very existence, contradicted this comfortable notion. They looked 'suspicious and preternaturally sharp'; they possessed a *perversité précoce*.[51] Their presence on the streets was explained in two ways: like Sue's Fleur-de-Marie and Dickens's Oliver Twist, they were unfortunates often seen as betrayed by parents, guardians, or masters; or, like Dickens's Artful Dodger and, perhaps less clearly, Hugo's Gavroche, they were deviant and potentially dangerous, refusing to conform to the new norms of childhood. The contrast was made in Mary Carpenter's title referring to, on the one hand, the 'perishing' and, on the other hand, the 'dangerous' classes. Others preferred to contrast the 'deserving' with the 'undeserving'. There were also assumptions that the child offender moved from picking pockets to more serious offences as she, or much more commonly he, grew up. The Vicomte d'Haussonville began an article on abandoned children published in the *Revue des Deux Mondes* with the response to an assize judge made by a gang leader called Maillot accused of murdering an elderly widow.

What do you want me to say your worship? At the age of seven I found myself alone on the streets of Paris. I have never met anyone who took an interest in me. A child, I was abandoned to every danger, I was lost. I've always been unfortunate. My life's been passed in prisons and the *bagnes*. That's it. It's fate. I've finished up where you see me. I don't say that I committed this crime because of circumstances outside my control; but in the end (at this point Maillot's voice trembled) I've never had anyone to take my part. I've never known anything but theft. I stole. I ended by killing.

Haussonville claimed that this story was not exceptional and that others had made the journey from juvenile vagabondage to murder with prison stops

---

[51] Emsley, *Crime and Society*, 69; Cat Nilan, 'Hapless Innocence and Precocious Perversity: Constructions of the Child Criminal in Late Eighteenth- and Early Nineteenth-Century France', *Proceedings of the Western Society for French History*, 24 (1997), 81–91.

on the way.[52] In reality, however, there appears to be little evidence for this. Nor does the evidence suggest that offending children brought before the courts necessarily came from homes with feckless parents. Poverty, family disruption, general street-life with the availability of goods on open stalls or at shop fronts, and peer pressure all had an influence on juvenile offending.[53]

The blinkers also affected the understanding of female offending and of prostitution in particular. The model of femininity that emerged in the nineteenth century insisted that, together with their lack of physical strength in comparison with men, women had a natural passivity and even an innate moral superiority. In the private sphere allotted to the woman, she was expected to focus on the home, and on the bearing and nurturing of children. The female criminal and the prostitute challenged this ideal. The male criminal might threaten life, property, and prosperity, but the female offender was a danger to morality. There were always fewer women prosecuted for and convicted of crimes of theft and violence. But the prostitute became stigmatized as the female element of the criminal and dangerous classes. The life of the well-meaning, tragic Nancy in *Oliver Twist* had been 'squandered' on the streets and in the 'noisome stews' of London; and she was Bill Sikes's girl. The policeman Achille Rabasse insisted that Parisian criminals all lived with prostitutes. The final quarter of Giovanni Bolis's book on the police and the dangerous classes was devoted to prostitution, and Giovanni Gozzoli, the author of a book on prostitution in Italy, confidently asserted that 'Authors of crime often find refuge in houses of prostitution.'[54] By the turn of the century a group of German men could publish a joint analysis that linked prostitution with many of the other attributes that had been tacked on to criminality and the potential for revolution, particularly among the pimps.

Prostitution and pimping in the current regulation of their circumstances are the first and transitional step to common criminality. . . . How closely prostitution and crime are bound up with each other in Berlin can be judged from the fact that both speak the same language, the famous Berlin criminals' dialect which originally derived from Hebrew and subsequently became partly Germanized, partly adorned with German additions. That is the social danger of which we speak. And next to it there is also

[52] Vicomte d'Haussonville, 'L'enfance à Paris: 1, La criminalité—L'abandon', *Revue des Deux Mondes*, 17 (1 Oct. 1876), 481–511; 481.

[53] Lenard R. Berlanstein, 'Vagrants, Beggars and Thieves: Delinquent Boys in Mid-Nineteenth-Century Paris', *Journal of Social History*, 12 (1979), 531–52; Heather Shore, *Artful Dodgers: Youth and Crime in Early Nineteenth-Century London*, Woodbridge: Royal Historical Society/Boydell Press, 1999.

[54] APP 398/3, fos. 170–1; Bolis, *La polizia . . . e le classi pericolose*; Mary Gibson, *Prostitution and the State in Italy, 1860–1915*, 2nd edn., Columbus: Ohio State University Press, 1999, 21.

the sociopolitical danger. For if a time of serious hardship should ever come upon us, then we shall see unregulated prostitution, these thousands of vagabond pimps, standing on the side of the revolutionaries, not because of their bravery, but rather because of their blood-lust and their bestiality, and even more because of the limitless importunity with which they press themselves upon every group in society which is in any way accessible to them.[55]

The year 1836 saw the posthumous publication of *De la prostitution dans la ville de Paris* by Alexandre-Jean-Baptiste Parent-Duchâtelet, a French doctor and public health bureaucrat. The research, in which he combined statistical analyses with interviews, and the writing had taken Parent-Duchâtelet eight years; some believed that it had brought about his premature death at the age of only 45 years. In many respects the book produced a sympathetic portrait situating prostitutes within the poorer sections of the working class and drawing attention to what was commonly a desperate and helpless economic situation. The book encouraged similar investigations in other countries, most notably, perhaps, Dr William Acton's *Prostitution Considered in its Moral, Social and Sanitary Aspects in London and Other Large Cities* (1857). But even such relatively sympathetic accounts could not resist moral censure and the suggestion that indolence, licentiousness, and a misplaced love of luxury and fine clothes contributed to the decision to become a prostitute. Moreover while the male 'criminal' challenged civil society because he did not respect private property, deal honestly with others, or obey moral precepts, the female prostitute challenged the developing ideas of womanhood. The prostitute appeared sexually liberated and hence, for a woman, biologically abnormal. Here was a woman who chose not to fulfil her duty of restraining male sexuality. She was a street person and hence outside the middle-class expectation of a woman's place in the private sphere of home and family. Moreover, in addition to being a moral threat, the incidence of venereal disease that threatened the manpower of armies and navies meant that, in a very real sense, she was also a potential threat to the security of the state.[56] Zola's eponymous Nana (the novel was published in 1880) was the epitome of the prostitute as a moral threat to society. The daughter of degenerate

---

55 Quoted in Evans, *Tales from the German Underworld*, 188.
56 Becker, *Verderbnis und Entartung*, ch. 3. There is a considerable and growing literature on prostitution in the nineteenth century. See e.g. Alain Corban, *Les Filles de noce; misère sexuelle et prostitution aux XIX et XX siècles*, Paris: Aubier, 1979; Gibson, *Prostitution and the State*; Jill Harsin, *Policing Prostitution in Nineteenth-Century Paris*, Princeton: Princeton University Press, 1985; Judith R. Walkowitz, *Prostitution and Victorian Society: Women, Class and the State*, Cambridge: Cambridge University Press, 1980.

parents, Nana triumphs as an actress and courtesan, destroying men as her career progresses. At the end of the novel, as her suppurating corpse decays on a hotel bed, the French army marches to destruction at Sedan. In the understanding of respectable society it was the prostitute who was the blameworthy individual for her preparedness to sell her body rather than the client who was prepared to pay for it.

Anxieties about the criminal and dangerous classes had an impact in the courts when juries deliberated upon their verdicts. It seems that appropriate tears from an accused child or offers of assistance from a third party could benefit a child offender standing before the court. French juries were all male and, up until the beginning of the twentieth century, whether they were urban or rural, they were composed of members of the liberal professions, of property owners, and of men engaged in business and commerce. The detailed evidence contained in the *Compte général* suggests that these juries could be tolerant of some violence but were likely to show little mercy to any beggar, prostitute, rag-picker, or vagrant who came before them accused of theft. This tended to distort the conviction rates for felonies. The statistics from England are insufficient to reveal whether or not there were similarities in such rates. The qualitative assessment of trials for violence, however, suggests that English juries, also all-male institutions until the twentieth century, often took a much more lenient attitude to some forms of violence than did the judges and magistrates to whom they reported their verdicts. Moreover, in both England and France the juries commonly took a lenient line with young women accused of infanticide.[57] The guilt-ridden, tearful apologetic child and the guilt-ridden, tearful, unfortunate young woman appeared redeemable. There was hope that they had not yet slipped into that incorrigible criminality that would link them irretrievably with the criminal class and propel them on the downward slope into worse and worse actions.

The hope of eradicating criminality still existed among many thinkers during the mid-nineteenth century. But quite how this might be achieved remained the vexing question. The destruction of the institutions of the criminal world such as rookeries and brothels appeared one way ahead; but there was the fear that this might serve also to disperse criminality within the rest of society. The isolation, regulation, and supervision of such institutions was seen by others as a preferable alternative; in the words of a Commissioner of London's Metropolitan Police: 'We look upon it that we are watching

[57] James M. Donovan, 'Justice Unblind: The Juries and the Criminal Classes in France, 1825–1914', *Journal of Social History*, 15 (1981), 89–107; Weiner, *Men of Blood*.

St James and other places while we are watching St Giles and bad places in general.'[58] Other reformers considered that the incarceration of offenders in prisons or in workhouses was the way to inculcate proper behaviour and to break the bonds between criminals, beggars, vagabonds, prostitutes, and the other threats to society. But both the regulation and the supervision of the institutions of the criminal class and the implementation of a strict carceral regime required the further development of policing organizations and penal establishments.

[58] *Parliamentary Papers*, 1834, (600) xvi. 600, *Select Committee on the Police of the Metropolis*, q. 166.

9

Protection, Punishment, and Reformation

WHIG historians have interpreted the creation of police forces as a rational and effective response to a real threat from increasing crime and disorder, and the creation of prisons with reformative regimes as a rational and humane replacement for brutal and violent punishments. Anxieties about crime and disorder, and about threats to social and political stability, were genuine in the late eighteenth and early nineteenth centuries. And while the bleak Foucauldian interpretation has an internal logic, the dismissal or, at best, the marginalizing of genuine humanitarian aspirations among penal reformers that can emerge from it fly in the face of much contemporary evidence and thus constitute an unhistorical moral judgement. There are two additional issues that also warrant consideration. First, while ruling elites had the power to create police institutions, it was not ruling elites that would always benefit from them. And, while the police might have been felt as a pressure by the poor who were suspected of committing most offences, a public institution focused on the alleviation of threats from crime, from disorder and, when these occurred, from natural calamities was also a potential benefit to the poor and those without an articulate and audible voice within the state. Secondly, even if the notion of a surveillance society had been the motivating force behind many changes, no nineteenth-century European state had either the financial ability or the political independence to establish what the most ardent of the moral entrepreneurs advocated.

Whig historians of police in England liked to stress the difference between the 'new police', that they considered to have been first established in London in 1829, and their continental counterparts. A comparative perspective, however, suggests that there were much greater structural similarities between the police institutions across nineteenth-century Europe than this traditional English view would allow.[1] Peel's Metropolitan Police was a centralized body

---

[1] The following two paragraphs draw heavily on Clive Emsley, 'A Typology of Nineteenth-Century Police', *CHS* 3, 1 (1999), 29–44.

that had no links with local government. The ultimate political authority to which the police commanders were responsible was the home secretary. In this respect, London's new police were similar to the police of other European capitals. The Prefect of Police in Paris reported to the ministry of the interior; the Police President in Berlin was responsible to the king. These institutions were what might be called state civilian police given that the ultimate authority to which they were responsible was a key element of the central state. The people who were policed and protected by these police paid for them out of local taxes, often somewhat grudgingly and resentfully since they had no say in deployment, policies, or priorities. *Gendarmeries* might best be characterized as state military police since they were generally responsible, at least in part, to ministries of war. These corps had spread across Europe in the wake of French Revolutionary and Napoleonic armies. On Napoleon's fall many of his former satellites and allies, and even some of his oldest enemies, decided to keep the model and even, on occasions, to introduce it. Gendarmes generally policed rural areas and were especially useful on peripheries where, in addition to their basic police duties, they were a physical manifestation of the state showing the flag to the population. They brought the promise of protection from brigands and wild animals as well as assistance in times of natural disaster. But they also ensured reciprocity in a bargain with the citizenry. In return for assistance and protection, the gendarmes maintained passivity in, and a surveillance of, the rural areas, and they guaranteed that the citizens provided the state with its taxes and the annual quotas of young conscripts. Even the British government, still suspicious of European and especially French policing methods, developed a paramilitary, *gendarmerie*-style institution in the shape of the Irish (subsequently Royal Irish) Constabulary. Moreover, this was an institution that was to be developed in various ways across vast expanses of the British Empire.[2]

A third type of policing continued to evolve in the municipalities. The states of early nineteenth-century Europe were jealous of their authority. They successfully continued the policies of the princes of the Enlightenment

---

[2] British imperial policing employed a variety of models; the towns and cities, particularly in the white dominions, generally opted for variants of the London or provincial urban models; see e.g. Greg Marquis, 'Power from the Street: The Canadian Municipal Police', in R. C. Macleod and David Schneiderman, eds., *Police Powers in Canada: The Evolution and Practice of Authority*, Toronto: University of Toronto Press, 1994; Stefan Petrow, 'The English Model? Policing in Late Nineteenth-Century Tasmania', in Barry Godfrey and Graeme Dunstall, eds., *Crime and Empire, 1840–1940: Criminal Justice in Local and Global Context*, Cullompton: Willan Publishing, 2005; David Taylor, 'Melbourne, Middlesbrough and Morality: Policing Victorian 'New Towns' in the Old World and the New', *Social History*, 31, 1 (2006), 15–38.

and generally succeeded in reducing still further the power of the nobility, the gentry, and the church. Municipal power had long been on the wane but it was given something of a fillip by the broad requirement that municipalities maintain their police powers and develop police institutions. The English example is striking. The new borough forces that emerged out of the Municipal Corporations Act of 1835 were not, as some of the Whig historians maintained, based on the London model—at least not administratively. Local watch committees that were part of local government recruited the borough police and the committees had the last word in matters of discipline, recruitment, and police policy until well into the twentieth century. The English county forces, created following legislation of 1839 and 1840, were similarly under the direction of local government, first in the shape of a committee of magistrates from the county bench and then (from 1888) under committees of local magistrates and elected county councillors. All of this was a far cry from the centralized system advocated by the earnest utilitarian reformer Edwin Chadwick and the other members of the Royal Commission on Rural Police that reported in 1839.

In French municipalities the local *commissaire* was appointed by the ministry of the interior, but the number of individuals who worked under him as patrolmen, together with decisions as to whether or not they wore a uniform and, often, how they were deployed, were all matters determined by local government. The municipality also continued to control the purse strings not only for the subordinate agents but also for the pay of the *commissaire* himself. There were plenty of opportunities in the system for the mayor and the *commissaire* to clash and for the *commissaire* to be caught up in clashes between a municipality, which wanted a specific focus on street cleaning and crime, and a local prefect who wanted attention given to matters of *haute police*.[3] In Prussia the clashes were between the royal government and the municipalities when, in the aftermath of the Revolution of 1848, the central government attempted to establish an urban policing system that would be appointed from Berlin but paid for by the localities. The municipalities, incensed by the idea of having to pay for a police over whom they had no control, took the state to court over the financial provisions and won their case.

[3] John M. Merriman, *Police Stories: Building the French State, 1815–1851*, New York: Oxford University Press, 2006, esp. ch. 7. For a regional example see Jean-François Tanguy, 'Autorité de l'État et libertés locales: le commissaire central de Rennes face au maire et au préfet (1870–1914)', in Philippe Vigier et al., *Maintien de l'ordre et polices en France et en Europe au XIXe siècle*, Paris: Créaphis, 1987.

Police reformers and other commentators often lionized the state police officer as being a self-sacrificing defender of the public. Praise for the English Bobby—idealized as civilian, tolerant, unarmed, and a non-political manifestation of an impartial law—is, perhaps, the best known of this kind of thing. As crowds thronged the Great Exhibition of 1851 with the minimum of disorder and, apparently, of pocket picking and petty theft, the Metropolitan Police gained enormous credit. *Punch* suggested that the police constables were becoming 'national favourites' like the sailors of Nelson's fleet half a century before. The author of an article in the *Quarterly Review* praised the steady, unruffled police constable on his beat appearing as 'an institution rather than a man'.[4] In Paris the *sergent de ville* was similarly described as 'the guardian angel of peaceful citizens, and the terror of criminals'.

Without him, your wives, your mothers, your sisters would, at every moment, be exposed to the rudeness of the first villain. In the streets, in your absence, to whom can they address themselves to have these loose insults halted? To the *sergent de ville* alone, for this man is the law in official uniform.

For these men labour, trouble, unpleasantness; for us pleasures and joy.[5]

Similar comments were made about the *commissaires* and the gendarmes, though it was also recognized that some of the men on the ground did not measure up to the ideal.[6] In the early years of the Second Empire a version of 'Punch and Judy' was written that went out of its way to emphasize the heroic role of the gendarmes to the plebeian audiences of the puppet shows.

MAN OF THE PEOPLE   Gendarme, you have saved this woman and this child.

GENDARME   I did my duty!

MAN OF THE PEOPLE   But to do your duty, it's good.

GENDARME   My friends, the gendarme is the strong man who aids the weak!

CHILD   Yes, he is the law in uniform!

MR PUNCH   Out of my way; you're oppressing me.

GENDARME   I'm arresting you. . . . I don't attack, I defend. Understand that, and come along.

MR PUNCH   Help me!

---

[4] *Punch*, 21 (1851), 173; [Andrew Wynter], 'The Police and Thieves', *Quarterly Review*, 59 (1856), 160–200; 171.

[5] Alfred Rey and Louis Féron, *Histoire du corps des gardiens de la paix*, Paris, 1894, 116–17, quoting A. Durantin, *Les Français peints par eux-mêmes*.

[6] Clive Emsley, *Gendarmes and the State in Nineteenth-Century Europe*, Oxford: Oxford University Press, 1999, 136–7 and 263–4; Merriman, *Police Stories*, 12, 48–9, and 53.

MAN OF THE PEOPLE   I understand! Go away, Punch!. . . I'm not so stupid as to
help you! The gendarme protects us, but you, you hit our wives and our children.
MR PUNCH   All is lost! The people are standing up for justice and the law!

The important point about the didactic nature of this play, however, is the
fact that most popular puppet plays from this period involving Punch and
the Lyons weaver, Guignol, portrayed the police in a much less sympathetic
light.[7] The manifestation of the law in uniform often meant something
different for those who had nothing or next to nothing.

At times some of what might be termed the public police blurred with
private police. In France the *gabelous* had disappeared with the tax farms,
but here, and elsewhere, a police officer in a small municipality could easily
become the creature of the mayor and be used to enforce the mayor's interests.
The *gardes-champêtres*, for example, were commissioned by a sub-prefect and
could only be dismissed by a prefect, but they were nominated by mayors
and were often seen as the men of the mayor and his council.[8] In Andalusia
the post of municipal policeman was commonly given as a political favour,
changing every time that the municipal government changed.[9] In England
such blatant favouritism did not exist, but the level of police enforcement
of, for example, licensing regulations might depend on the influence either
of brewers or of temperance advocates on the watch committee. Business
concerns in England could fund new, temporary police officers for the local
borough or county force. This was done, for example, by some railway
companies so as to provide increased protection when the notorious gangs
of navvies were pushing a new line through a district. In Prussia, from the
mid-century until the early 1880s, industrialists offered benefits to gendarmes
in the shape of cheap housing and work for their children, and they took
over the full costs of any gendarmes that they could have stationed on
their premises.[10] In Andalusia private estate guards wore grey uniforms, were
armed and mounted, and had to be registered and sworn in by local and

---

[7] Aurélien Lignereux, 'Rosser le gendarme dans les spectacles de marionnettes au XIX siècle:
une école de rébellion?', in Jean-Noël Luc, ed. *Figures de gendarmes, Sociétés et Représentations*, 16
(2003), 97–113; quotation at pp. 108–9.
[8] Fabien Gaveau, 'De la sûreté des campagnes. Police rurale et demandes d'ordre en France
dans la première moitié du XIXe siècle', *CHS* 4, 2 (2000), 53–76; 64–6.
[9] Henk Driessen, 'The "Noble Bandit" and the Bandits of the Nobles: Brigandage and
Local Community in Nineteenth-Century Andalusia', *Archives européennes de sociologie*, 24 (1983),
96–114; 99–100.
[10] Maureen Scollan, *Sworn to Serve: Police in Essex, 1840–1990*, Chichester: Phillimore, 1993, 20;
Roy Ingleton, *Policing Kent: Guarding the Garden of England, 1800–2000*, Chichester: Phillimore,
2002, 59; Emsley, *Gendarmes and the State*, 221.

provincial authorities. Nevertheless, the boundary between estate guard and bandit appears often to have been a hazy one.[11] Gamekeepers in England remained private enforcers of the law on their employer's land, but the public police were also sucked into assisting them. Some chief constables tried to keep their men out of poaching conflicts, though the assumptions that poachers also committed other crimes complicated the issue. But then the Poaching Prevention Act of 1862, that authorized officers to stop and search anyone that they suspected of poaching, drew in even those forces whose chiefs had sought to remain aloof.[12]

Poaching, however, remained one of the areas where victims might find difficulty with the local police. Rural policemen, recruited from the local community, often ignored this offence and there were other acts of wrongdoing where their response might be less than energetic. As one Belgian official put it in 1852: 'the family relationships or intimate relations between these officers and persons from the commune where they are employed, lead them to a blameworthy leniency in the matter of recording offences.'[13] A rural mayor might also restrain his local police in this respect if he was sympathetic to the poachers. Controlling state police, however, was more difficult. In some instances of poaching, as with the pursuit of recalcitrant conscripts, gendarmes came into conflict with the local mayor. 'I know you well', complained one Gascon mayor to a local brigade, 'you would rather spend four nights waiting to catch a poacher in the act than catch a thief.' On other occasions, recognizing that they were likely to meet with a wall of silence and no help at all, even the gendarmes appear to have ignored some offences.[14]

Policemen were also still regarded as merely one option among several for the victim of an offence. Some victims and some communities, especially, it would seem, more remote rural communities, still preferred instant shaming or violent justice if an offender was known. They might also prefer an

---

[11] Driessen, 'The "Noble Bandit" and the Bandits of the Nobles', 100.

[12] David Jones, *Crime, Community and Police in Nineteenth-Century Britain*, London: Routledge, 1982, 78; John E. Archer, *'By a Flash and a Scare': Arson, Animal Maiming, and Poaching in East Anglia, 1815–1870*, Oxford: Clarendon Press, 1990, 240–2.

[13] Axel Tixhon, 'Police and Social Control in the Belgian Country Areas (1840–1885)', in Maria Ägren, Åsa Karlson, and Xavier Rousseaux, eds., *Guises of Power: Integration of Society and Legitimisation of Power in Sweden and the Southern Low Countries, c.1500–1900*, Uppsala: Opuscula Historica, 2001, 158.

[14] Emsley, *Gendarmes and the State*, 92–3 and 134; Regina Schulte, *The Village in Court: Arson, Infanticide, and Poaching in the Court Records of Upper Bavaria, 1848–1910*, Cambridge: Cambridge University Press, 1994, 112 and 117 and part III.

arrangement whereby a family's honour was protected from the trauma
of a court case and whereby amicable relations could be patched up and
preserved between the families of victims and perpetrators. Even homicides
and attempted homicides might be covered up in this way. In February
1824, for example, the *gendarmerie* brigade in Figeac heard a rumour of an
attempted murder in the small community of Fourmagnac. The subsequent
investigation by the gendarmes revealed that an elder brother had stabbed
a sibling over the inheritance of a family mill and the younger brother's
affair with a servant. The whole matter had been complicated further by the
recent death of the mother. The local mayor had played a significant role
in the attempted cover-up.[15] In some places a local mayor or a priest could
still act as an arbitrator. As late as 1866 a *curé* in the Pyrenees described
'doing a little policing' (*je fais un peu de police*) among the local shepherds.
Some people, he feared, might take his activities amiss 'but the intent was
commendable and for the best'.[16] On occasions the clergy responsible for a
religious festival or a travelling mission might set out to encourage confessions
to petty offences, which could then be pardoned with suitable amends being
made. Such occasions were popular with clerical authorities, for enhancing
their prestige. They were equally unpopular with the secular authorities and
when they dared to take on political overtones, notably before elections, the
authorities sought to forbid them.[17] There were also still instances where
rural dwellers, or particular groups among them, were reluctant to consider
certain forms of behaviour as meriting any criminal sanction. The men
in many local communities were inclined to show magnanimity to sexual
offenders, for example, particularly those with some standing and character.
Such magnanimity tended to be much less apparent when the victims of
the abuse were children.[18] Though in some remote regions even the rape of
children could be seen as normal and complaints on the child's part were
considered insolence. This was the case in the Gévaudon, for example, where
young orphans or illegitimate girls were hired out as shepherdesses and, alone
in the mountains with the flocks, became particularly vulnerable.[19] In those

[15] François Ploux, *Guerres paysannes en Quercy: Violences, conciliations et répression pénale dans les campagnes du Lot (1810–1860)*, Paris: Boutique d'histoire, 2002, 228–9.
[16] Jean-François Soulet, *Les Pyrénées au XIX siècle*, 2 vols., Toulouse: Eché, 1987, i. 191.
[17] Elisabeth Claverie and Pierre Lamaison, *L'impossible marriage: violence et parenté en Gévaudan, 17e, 18e et 19e siècles*, Paris: Hachette, 1987, 176–7.
[18] Geoffroy Le Clercq, 'Sexual Violence and Social Relations: The Survival of the Practices of Arrangement in Nineteenth-Century Rural Society', in Ägren, Karlsson, and Rousseaux, eds., *Guises of Power*.
[19] Claverie and Lamaison, *L'impossible marriage*, 241–5.

instances where the perpetrators of abuse were clergy the power of the church and the threats of damnation for making matters public could be brought into play, compelling silence or provoking other trouble. In 1838 the local *curé* was forced out of Endoufielle in Gers. He had got a girl pregnant, not a crime in itself but an act that divided the village. A shot was fired into the house of the doctor who had taken care of the girl; the mayor and his deputy were also targeted, and called in the *gendarmerie*.[20]

The settling of offences without recourse to the state's law and its agents continued to be found among traditional communities of workers. In his account of his tour of France as a tramping artisan during the mid-1820s Agricol Perdiguier described members of his brotherhood investigating a theft, organizing a trial of the offender amongst themselves, and then ritually expelling him from their company.

Lansargue was brought into the middle of the room. . . . We made him get down on his knees and beg forgiveness of God and men. We made him swear that he would never boast of having belonged in any capacity whatever to the Compagnons du Devoir de Liberté. The wine was brought. The compagnons and affiliates clinked glasses together, about ten at a time, and drank to the execration of rogues, swindlers, and thieves. Each time that a group of ten men clinked glasses and drank their wine, the convicted man had to swallow a glass of water. And when his stomach could hold no more, it was thrown in his face. . . . Lansargue had to swallow more water than he might have wished. Then the glass from which he had drunk was broken.

If he had been a full-fledged compagnon, we would have broken his cane and burned his colours. The roller [i.e. the local registrar responsible for the daily operations of the brotherhood in the district] made him rise, took him by the hand, and led him round the room, making him pass before each of us. Each gave the thief a light slap. He had to make a second round. A cane was passed from hand to hand as quickly as he advanced, and each man had to touch him lightly on the back. Finally the door was opened and Lansargue was allowed to leave. At that moment, the roller gave him a kick in the behind with the end of his foot. Justice had been done.

Lansargue had not been physically harmed, and besides he was free. Yet I must say that I have never seen a harsher punishment. Those who have participated in a *conduite de Grenoble* are not tempted to do anything that would earn one for themselves. Because of Lansargue's unparalleled effrontery, this one was executed in all its rigor. More often—in fact, almost always—they are cut short. . . .

[20] AN F⁷ 4010, Rapports de *Gendarmerie*, Gers, 1835–42. For examples of clergy or of the church using their authority to suppress complaints of abuse see Claverie and Lamaison, *L'impossible marriage*, 179; and, D. J. O'Connor, *Crime at El Escorial: The 1892 Child Murder, the Press and the Jury*, San Francisco and London: International Scholars Publications, 1995, 104–6.

After expelling a guilty party in this way, the compagnons send his description to all points on the Tour of France. In each town, it is recorded in the register of thieves, and the malefactor can no longer show his face anywhere, for he would be driven away.[21]

The *compagnons* could fight viciously with members of another brotherhood and this, like industrial action, could bring them into confrontation with the police. The police could also demand to see a workman's *livret* or any other kind of travel permit. But hostility from and towards the police was not an automatic feature of the tramping artisan's life. Indeed, Perdiguier recounts having a drink with a gendarme who was also the local 'roller'.[22]

It is impossible to indicate a precise cause for the eclipse of community sanction and the preference for the police and the formality of the courts. Over time it appears that the respectable individuals that had been called upon to supervise non-judicial settlements became increasingly reluctant to continue this role, acknowledging that the state's functionaries were the better arbiters. Local men with less social standing may have been found to take on the role, but a settlement arranged by a local tavern keeper, for example, carried less weight than one arranged by a priest or a mayor. At the same time, the growing presence and clear permanency of the police and local courts in itself gave the state's system an increasing recognition; moreover, as individuals used this system, so it gained legitimacy. The British protectorate over the Ionian Islands provides an interesting and dramatic example. The British assumed control in the aftermath of the Napoleonic Wars. They placed considerable emphasis on reforming the criminal justice system and made legal reform the centrepiece of their rule and their attempt to establish legitimacy. Their new courts began to be used in ways that they did not expect. Ritual knife-fights over matters of honour ended in the courts with charges of assault, but the plebeian Greeks began to use the courts to play out an additional act in the conflict. Witnesses emphasized who had fought well, and who had not, who was to blame and who had, or had not, got his just deserts. The winner used his moment in court to scorn his opponent further. The loser paraded his excuses: he was drunk; he was tricked or taken advantage of. Yet while Greek men used the courts for their own ends, they also began to legitimate the British system. New regulations about the carrying of knives in public were obeyed; punishments for knife

---

[21] Agricol Perdiguier, *Memoirs of a Compagnon*, in Mark Traugott, ed. *The French Worker: Autobiographies from the Early Industrial Era*, Berkeley: University of California Press, 1993, 152–3.
[22] Ibid., 132.

fighting became more severe, and the problem declined. Greek women used and legitimated the new courts in rather different ways. Gossip and sexual slander began to be brought into the public sphere of the court. By bringing a case of slander the victim put her reputation on the line but, at the same time, she also exposed that of her alleged slanderer who had to justify the gossip. When the British ceded the islands to Greece in 1864, however, the courts became fewer and less open. Knife fights over honour resumed their predominance in the male world of the tavern and the wine-shop. Women's gossip and sexual slander returned to the private sphere and to whispers in homes and streets.[23]

The Greeks of the Ionian Islands did not share a language with their British protectors, but then the range of patois and even different languages spoken within the boundaries of single nation states in nineteenth-century Europe created problems for policing.[24] One of the principal weapons or refuges of a recalcitrant peasantry was to speak in a language unknown to the authorities. *Cavaliers* of the pre-revolutionary *Maréchaussée*, gendarmes and *commissaires* were often appointed to the region of their birth precisely because they knew the local dialect or language. But the central government functionaries also saw a need to balance this use of local men against concerns that such individuals might show favour towards members of the local community and fail to enforce unpopular laws and regulations. In Ireland any member of the Irish Constabulary who married a local woman was promptly posted away from her native district. In England some police authorities favoured the appointment of local men while others preferred to appoint outsiders, and the wives of policemen were forbidden from taking employment on the grounds that their husbands could favour their business or their clients. Some local authorities urged that it was the duty of the police to seek conciliation before turning to the law. But when a community punishment became rough and public, the police, and particularly the state police who were less and less tied to the communities in which they served, were likely to step in to protect the accused. At the same time, they could enforce the law on behalf

[23] Thomas W. Gallant, *Experiencing Dominion: Culture, Identity, and Power in the British Mediterranean*, Notre Dame, Ia.: University of Notre Dame Press, 2002.

[24] This topic has been best covered with reference to the French experience, see Eugen Weber, *Peasants into Frenchmen: The Modernization of Rural France, 1870–1914*, Stanford, Calif.: Stanford University Press, 1976, esp. ch. 5 and 6; and for regional examples see e.g. Jean-Pierre Jourdan, 'Les juges de paix de l'Aquitaine méridionale (Landes, Basses-Pyrénées, Hautes-Pyrénées) de 1870 à 1914', *Annales du Midi*, 100, 183 (1988), 287–306, and idem, ' Les magistrats de la Cour d'appel de Pau au XIXe siècle (1811–1914): éléments de sociologie', *Revue de Pau et de Béarn*, 15 (1988), 233–60.

of a victim when the local community was prepared to leave the matter alone. There is evidence, for example, of gendarmes in Belgium enabling rape victims to use the law when local burgomasters and the other all-male leaders of communities were prepared to ignore offences or to allow them to be settled quietly out of court.[25]

Members of rural society were still inclined to regard a missing article of property in the same way that they sometimes regarded sickness among the family or among their livestock, or a blight on their crops, as the work of a sorcerer or witch. Such a problem had to be dealt with by seeking out another sorcerer or witch, and such individuals, sometimes deriving their powers from their parents, sometimes by a 'grace' acquired at birth or by stigmata on their palms, could attract clients from a considerable distance.[26] If, by counter-spells or other magic, sorcerers and witches could end sickness and find missing property so too, it was reasoned, could they find out thieves and other offenders. In the early 1840s while travelling in Russia, Franz von Haxthausen-Abbenburg witnessed an old woman called in to a village to find a thief. Surrounded by villagers, she threw balls of bread into a bowl of water. Each ball was named after a villager and, the *babushka* promised, the ball named after the offender would immediately sink. Usually, von Haxthausen was told, the offender confessed before the ball with their name was thrown.[27] This seeking out of 'cunning' men or women to solve 'crimes' was not confined to the more remote areas of Europe; country folk in mid-nineteenth-century Britain also believed in witches and sought such help when the victim of a crime.[28] Such behaviour may, at times, have been a result of the victim pursuing every avenue and coupling the visit to the cunning person with a visit to the police. Historians have yet to uncover in

[25] Merriman, *Police Stories*, 26–9 and 50; Clive Emsley, *The English Police: A Political and Social History*, 2nd edn., London: Longman, 1996, 193–7 and 210–11; idem, *Gendarmes and the State*, 114 and 248; Geoffroy Le Clercq, 'Violences sexuelles, scandale et ordre publique: le regard du législateur, de la justice et d'autres acteurs sociaux au 19ème siècle', *Belgische Tijschrift voor Nieuwste Geschiedenis/Revue Belge d'histoire contemporaine*, 1–2 (1999), 5–53.

[26] Willem de Blecourt, 'Witch Doctors, Soothsayers and Priests: On Cunning Folk in European Historiography and Tradition', *Social History*, 19 (1994), 285–303; and for some individual examples see J. A. Pitt-Rivers, *The People of the Sierra*, London: Weidenfeld and Nicolson, 1954, 190; J. C. Sebban, 'La sorcellerie en Berry au XIXe siècle', *Cahiers de l'institut d'histoire de la presse et de l'opinion*, 2 (1974), 137–59.

[27] Franz von Haxthausen-Abbenburg, *The Russian Empire: Its People, Institutions and Resources*, 2 vols., London: Chapman and Hall, 1856, i. 228–9; see also Samuel C. Ramer, 'Traditional Healers and Peasant Culture in Russia, 1861–1917', in Esther Kingston Mann, *Peasant Economy, Culture and Politics in Russia 1800–1921*, Princeton: Princeton University Press, 1991, 223.

[28] Clive Emsley, *Crime and Society in England, 1750–1900*, 3rd edn., London: Longman, 2005, 119.

any detail what appears to have been the very gradual decline of supernatural beliefs within European society.

Historians have been much more ready to trace the ideas behind the emergence of the penitentiary. Foucault particularly put considerable emphasis on Bentham's Panopticon as an architectural metaphor for the new disciplinary society; the Panopticon unquestionably presents a powerful image of control and surveillance. Yet the development of prisons, and particularly of the new penitentiaries, often advanced with only passing reference, if any, to Bentham's plans. Millbank Prison in London was finished in 1816. It was England's first national prison with inmates selected from those considered most likely to be reformed. The design incorporated a system of surveillance, but rather than the Panopticon this was a series of pentagons clustered around a chapel in a plan that resembled a flower with six symmetrical petals. It was extremely expensive to build, extremely expensive to run, and the surveillance system failed to fulfil the expectations. In addition to the marginalizing of the Panopticon when it came to building prisons, it could be argued that the decisions to reduce capital and corporal punishment had been taken and the new liberal legal codes had begun to be introduced without any clear ideas of what new penitentiaries might look like and what the new penal regimes might actually entail. Both the new French and the Bavarian penal codes set no precise guidelines, and it was not until after these legal changes had been made that the issue of prisons and penitentiary regimes began to be debated with any urgency at government level. Moreover, the experiments that provoked most interest at the close of the eighteenth and the beginning of the nineteenth centuries were not based on Bentham's plans but were those tried out in the infant United States. These had developed in the transatlantic interchange between penal reformers drawing heavily on the ideas of John Howard.

The state constitution drawn up for Pennsylvania in 1776 promised to provide a building where those convicted of non-capital crimes could be set to hard labour that might reform them. The prison of Walnut Street, Philadelphia, opened its doors in 1790, planning to reform offenders through a regime of coarse clothing, coarse food, and hard labour in isolation. One of its earliest European visitors described the system in glowing terms.

The end proposed in punishment, ought to be the correction of the guilty, and should include the means of amendment. The managers have connected with it a great political truth; that the confinement of a convict being a reparation made to a community, the society ought to be burdened as little as possible, with the expense attending such detention; whence it follows, that a chief object of the regimen of these prisons ought to be, first, to break off the old habits to which the convicts have become accustomed, and induce them to self-reflexion, and consequent amelioration; secondly, to proscribe all arbitrary ill-treatment of prisoners; and thirdly, to keep them constantly employed in some species of productive labour, with a view to make them contribute to the expenses of the prison, preserve them from idleness and inaction, and enable them to lay up some kind of fund against the termination of their capacity.[29]

The regime was tough and there were, as perhaps in any penal system, opportunities for overzealous harshness and even just plain cruelty. But, in the context of the period, the Walnut Street prison appeared both modern and progressive. It appealed to both rational secularists and evangelical Christians. It was an institution aiming at reform and redemption, inspired by the notion of the offender as a rational being who should not be brutalized but encouraged to consider and to improve his behaviour and situation. In 1819 a rather different penitentiary model was established at Auburn, New York. Here there was solitary confinement only by night; by day the convicts were engaged in silent work in groups with all communication between them by word or look forbidden. Ten years later the silent system of Walnut Street was extended behind the massive walls of Cherry Hill in Pennsylvania; here the convicts' identities were further suppressed by the requirement that they wear hoods whenever they left their cells. The reports of these American experiments that filtered across the Atlantic fed into European debates and also encouraged some to take ship and view these institutions for themselves.

In 1831 two young French public prosecutors, Gustave de Beaumont and Alexis de Tocqueville, set off to the United States to study the new prisons and penal practices. Their intention was to produce a book based on their observations that could be used for developing policy in France. *Du système pénitentiare aux États Unis* was published in 1833, the year after their return. Beaumont and Tocqueville wanted reform, but their starting point was rather different from that of most of the philanthropists who were calling for change. They were pragmatists who doubted some of the ideas floated by philanthropic theorists. 'Theories', they wrote, 'upon the reform of convicts are vague and uncertain; it has never been ascertained to what degree the law-breaker can be regenerated.' They substantiated this by quoting, in

[29] Duc de La Rochefoucauld Liancourt, *A Comparative View of Mild and Sanguinary Laws; and the good effects of the former exhibited in the present economy of the Prisons of Philadelphia*, London, 1796, 9–10.

English in a footnote, the comment of the former superintendent of the Maryland Penitentiary: 'from a closer and more intimate view of the subject, I have rather abandoned a hope I once entertained, of the *general reformation of offenders* through the penitentiary system. I now think that its chief good is in the prevention of crimes, by the confinement of criminals.' Beaumont and Tocqueville took a similar view but they believed that the new penitentiaries in the United States had some positive effects on the convict.

Perhaps he does not leave the prison a very honest man, but he has contracted honest habits; he was lazy, he is now a workman; his ignorance was a hindrance to him, he can now read and write, and the trade he has learned in prison will furnish him with the means of existence which he wanted formerly. If he does not truly love goodness, he can however, detest crime of which he has tasted the bitter fruits. If he is not quite virtuous, he is at least rational; his morality is not of honour but of interest.[30]

The book was rapidly translated into other European languages, sometimes by the kind of philanthropists about whose aspirations Beaumont and Tocqueville had doubts. William B. Sarsfield Taylor, for example, Honourable Secretary of the Society for Diffusing Information on Capital Punishment, made a considerably abbreviated English translation in 1833 urging the development of penitentiaries in England. But Sarsfield Taylor played down some of the criticism that Beaumont and Tocqueville made of philanthropists. He also insisted that the kind of whippings that were conducted in the American prisons could not be part of any English system. Such whipping existed in America, he suggested, only because of the continuance of slavery to which flogging was integral. Moreover, with no evidence from the original book, he stated that Beaumont and Tocqueville would not favour flogging in France.[31] A German translation also appeared in 1833. It was published by Nicolaus Heinrich Julius, a noted doctor and philanthropist, who is credited with galvanizing the penal reform movement in Germany by a series of lectures which he gave in Berlin in the late 1820s.[32]

---

[30] Gustave de Beaumont and Alexis de Tocqueville, *Du système pénitentiaire aux États-Unis et de son application en France,* Paris, 1833, 89. I have used the English translation here in William B. Sarsfield Taylor, *Origin and Outline of the Penitentiary System of the United States,* London, 23 and 25. For an important discussion of Tocqueville's thoughts on prison reform see Sheldon S. Wolin, *Tocqueville between Two Worlds: The Making of a Political and Theoretical Life,* Princeton.: Princeton University Press, 2001, ch. 20.

[31] Sarsfield Taylor, *Origin and Outline,* 21–2, fn. On p. 21 he quotes Beaumont and Tocqueville to the effect that that flogging in the penitentiaries 'does not appear to have produced any bad effects'.

[32] Beaumont and Tocqueville, *Amerika's Besserungs-System, und dessen Anwendung auf Europa,* Berlin, 1833. For Julius see Thomas Nutz, 'Global Networks and Local Prison Reforms: Monarchs,

In the wake of Beaumont and Tocqueville a number of other European investigators crossed the Atlantic to view the American systems and to write reports for their governments and for reform groups. Julius tried, and failed, to get the Prussian government to fund a trip. He was more successful in finding support from the government of Hamburg but on his return the Prussian authorities engaged him as an adviser. William Crawford, a philanthropic businessman and leading figure from the Society for the Improvement of Prison Discipline, travelled to the United States at the behest of the Home Office. On his return, and following his report, he became a forceful member of the Prison Inspectorate created in 1835 to make annual visits to local prisons and to report on these to parliament. But penal reformers and governments did not just look across the Atlantic for their ideas. In 1817 the British Society for Diffusing Information on the Subject of Capital Punishment and Prison Discipline reprinted a glowing account of the *Maison de Force* in Ghent. Here 100 inmates worked in 'perfect silence' manufacturing textiles.[33] Other Dutch prisons (Belgium was then part of the Kingdom of the Netherlands) gave their inmates work and sought to make profits from the institutions. During the 1830s and 1840s they were visited by more English philanthropists, by the French Inspector General of prisons, and by a delegate from the Spanish Cortes.[34]

In 1842 the British government opened Pentonville Prison in London. Again this was not a Panopticon but its architecture was developed with surveillance in mind. At the prompting of Crawford and his similarly forceful kindred spirit on the Prison Inspectorate, the Revd. Whitworth Russell, Pentonville also incorporated the solitary system; and Pentonville, in turn, became a focus for penitentiary tourism. Tsar Nicholas I ordered a study of the establishment as plans were drafted for the new Russian Criminal Code of 1845. The lack of any existing prisons and insufficient money to embark on a major building programme, however, meant that the Russians continued to rely principally on corporal punishment and exile.[35] Dr Julius translated and published first Crawford's account of the American system, and second

Bureaucrats and Penological Experts in Nineteenth-Century Prussia', *German History*, 23, 4 (2005), 431–59; and Richard J. Evans, *Tales from the German Underworld: Crime and Punishment in the Nineteenth Century*, London: Yale University Press, 1998, 63

[33] Anon., *An Account of the Maison de Force at Ghent*, London, 1817; the tract was first published as an article in *The Philanthropist*, May 1817.

[34] Herman Franke, *The Emancipation of Prisoners: A Socio-Historical Analysis of the Dutch Prison Experience*, Edinburgh: Edinburgh University Press, 1995, 36–7.

[35] Bruce F. Adams, *The Politics of Punishment: Prison Reform in Russia, 1863–1917*, DeKalb.; Northern Illinois University Press, 1996, 34 and 39.

Joshua Jebb's report, as Surveyor General of Prisons, of the construction details of Pentonville.[36]

During the old regime it had been common for all kinds of individual to be held in prisons—the convicted, those awaiting trial, men and women, first offenders and hardened recidivists, young and old. By the early nineteenth century it was generally accepted that prisons should segregate these different groups, and few doubted that different kinds of institutions were needed for juvenile offenders. The informal English policy of sending juveniles to philanthropic institutions for their reform has already been described. A rather similar policy had been developed even earlier in some Spanish cities.[37] In Paris in 1816 the first, formal attempt was commenced to separate those under 16 years of age from older offenders. Over the next twenty-five years a series of houses for correctional education were built, the most notable of which was La Petite Roquette in Paris. The Ministry of the Interior urged provincial administrators to adopt similar policies and there was a notable development in 1838 when Frédéric-Auguste Demetz established the agricultural colony of Mettray near Tours. Demetz was a judge, but Mettray began as a private philanthropic venture for the improvement of young male offenders. The Law of 5 August 1850 proposed sending all such youths to agricultural colonies and girls were to go to penitentiary establishments. The overwhelming majority of these two kinds of reformatory remained private ventures but with supervisory councils made up of a mixture of state, church, and local appointees. The institutions for girls were aimed at training them for domestic service and for motherhood. By the late 1860s the agricultural colonies, of which there were thirty-three with only five under state control, catered for 8,000 offenders or about half of the youths in correction regimes. The colonies were seen as a way of reducing the urban dangerous classes and transforming difficult urban youths into productive rural workers.[38]

The farming colony at Mettray, which had itself been inspired by the *Raue Haus* set up near Hamburg in 1833, attracted considerable interest far beyond the frontiers of France and there was a flurry of interest across Europe in developing similar colonies. An 'English Mettray', adapted with reference

---

[36] William Crawford, *Die amerikanischen Besserungs-System, erörtet in einem Sendschreiben*, Leipzig, 1837; Joshua Jebb, *Englands Mustergefängniss in Pentonville, in seiner Bauart, Einrichtung und Verwaltung, abgebildet und beschrieben*, Berlin, 1846.

[37] Valentina K. Tikoff, 'Before the Reformatory: A Correctional Reformatory in Old Regime Seville', in Pamela Cox and Heather Shore, eds., *Becoming Delinquent: British and European Youth, 1650–1950*, Aldershot: Ashgate, 2002.

[38] Patricia O'Brien, *The Promise of Punishment: Prisons in Nineteenth-Century France*, Princeton: Princeton University Press, 1982, 131–44.

to the 'national character', was established at Redhill in Surrey in 1849. At the same time related institutions were set up to care for and to resocialize young people who were not necessarily guilty of any criminal offences, but who were considered to be in danger or at risk. Funding for the colonies and the educational institutions generally depended upon philanthropists and, in consequence, were subject to the decisions of their benefactors. The first institution created in the Netherlands on the lines of Mettray, for example, was forbidden by its principal benefactor from taking any boys who had been in trouble with the police or taken before the judiciary. Interested parties also held national conferences to discuss the problem of rescuing juvenile offenders and those at risk. They also participated in a variety of international assemblies that met to discuss matters ranging from medicine to poor relief, and from statistics to penitentiaries.[39] The first international congresses dedicated to a public exchange of ideas about penitentiaries were held in Frankfurt in 1846 and in Brussels in 1847.

The exchanges, investigations, and translations, or at least précis of what were seen as important texts, focused on a wide variety of penal issues. The Frankfurt and Brussels congresses, for example, also considered penal legislation, preventive measures, and the treatment of children and minors. What developed in the second quarter of the nineteenth century was a belief among penal reformers across Europe and also in the United States that they belonged to an international movement. Whether secular or evangelical Christians, they saw themselves employing rational, scientific methods of observation and analysis. In many instances, too, they pushed their way into official positions where they might experiment and develop their ideas in practice. Crawford and Whitworth Russell in Britain and Julius in Germany have already been mentioned. In France as a young lawyer in 1826 Charles Lucas won a prize offered by the *Société de Morale Chrétienne* for an essay on the penal system and capital punishment. Four years later he became the first inspector general of Departmental Prisons and he went on to explore and publish comparative studies of prisons and penal policies. In Belgium the philanthropist Éduard Ducpétiaux published widely on penal issues, quoted

---

[39] Leon Radzinowicz and Roger Hood, *The Emergence of Penal Policy in Victorian and Edwardian England*, Oxford: Clarendon Press, 1990, 155–61; Chris G. T. M. Leonards, 'Border Crossings: Care and the "Criminal Child" in Nineteenth-Century European Penal Congresses', in Cox and Shore, eds., *Becoming Delinquent*; idem, 'Priceless Children? Penitentiary Congresses Debating Childhood: A Quest for Social Order in Europe, 1846–1895', in Clive Emsley, Eric Johnson, and Pieter Spierenburg, eds., *Social Control in Europe, 1800–2000*, Columbus: Ohio State University Press, 2004.

liberally from Bentham and Lucas and became inspector general of both prisons and welfare institutions. Carl Mittermaier provides one of the best examples of a mid-nineteenth-century cosmopolitan, and in his case highly influential and significant, penal analyst and reformer. Born in Munich in 1787, he studied law at the University of Landshut before acting as an assistant to Feuerbach by translating for him extracts from French and Italian laws during his preparation of the Bavarian Penal Code. His first teaching post was at his old university but in 1819 he moved to Bonn, in Rhenish Prussia, where he studied the continuing French system at first hand. He then became professor at Heidelberg in Baden. Mittermaier was active in politics as President of the Lower House in Baden and as chair of the *Vorparlament* in Frankfurt during the German Revolution of 1848. But his dominant interest was always the criminal law and penal policy. During the 1830s his was one of the voices expressing caution about what might be gleaned from criminal statistics. In the mid-1840s he was a leading figure at the international penitentiary congresses. He drew extensively on what he considered to be best practice from beyond German frontiers. He admired much in the English criminal procedure and advocated public trials using oral evidence and the jury system for Germany. Partly as a result of this he was made a corresponding member of both the Juridical Society and the Association for the Promotion of Social Science in Britain. He was heavily involved in the penal congresses in Frankfurt and Brussels and edited the proceedings of the former. His ideas also spread out from Germany since his work was translated into other European languages. His critique of capital punishment, for example, was translated into English in 1865, three years after the original German publication.[40] It was glowingly reviewed by the Swedish jurist Knut Olivecrona, who dedicated his own critique of the death penalty, *Om dödsstraffet*, published in 1866, to Mittermaier. And through Mittermaier, in turn, Olivecrona linked with Charles Lucas and became involved with a Europe-wide network of abolitionists.[41]

But even when these cosmopolitan reformers reached positions of authority within the penal system, they never had unlimited budgets and they continued to face suspicion and criticism from those who considered them to be

[40] Carl Joseph Anton Mittermaier, *Capital Punishment, based on Professor Mittermaier's 'Todesstrafe'*, ed. John Macrae Moir, London, 1865; idem, *Débats du Congrès penitentiaire de Franckfort-sur-le-Mein*, Paris, 1847.

[41] Martin Bergman, 'The Swede in Nineteenth-Century Capital Punishment Abolition: Knut Olivecrona and his *Om dödsstraffet*', Paper presented to the ESSH Conference, Amsterdam, March 2006.

creating regimes that were insufficiently tough and punitive. Prison, their critics insisted, was not there to moralize but to punish.[42] And there were other issues that the reformers had failed to appreciate. Whether advocating silence or separation, they assumed that the punishment and reformation within prison would accustom the offender to honest labour. But in so doing they failed to address the stigma of prison which often militated against a former prisoner finding and maintaining steady employment. Moreover the requirements regarding the residence and supervision of released prisoners could aggravate the situation. Exiling offenders from their city of origin had a long pedigree. Liberals and democrats in early nineteenth-century Germany were highly critical of the system that saw petty offenders exiled from their town of origin, returning because they had nowhere else to go, flogged and exiled again, only to return again and again to new floggings and new exiles. In early nineteenth-century France people who had served sentences for major offences were forbidden from residing in major urban centres, and in Paris in particular. The restrictions were relaxed during the July Monarchy but then tightened up under Napoleon III and extended still further at the beginning of the Third Republic. In Britain, serious offenders when released from prison were subject to police surveillance and many protested about police harassment and victimization.[43] Such problems continued as, in the final third of the nineteenth century, new medical and scientific approaches shifted the way in which criminals were perceived to a much sharper focus on heredity and environment.

[42] Gordon Wright, *Between the Guillotine and Liberty: Two Centuries of the Crime Problem in France*, Oxford: Oxford University Press, 1983, 65–7.

[43] Evans, *Tales from the German Underworld*, 91–7; O'Brien, *The Promise of Punishment*, 231–5; Emsley, *Crime and Society*, 179–80.

PART IV

THE APPLICATION OF SCIENCE

10

'Scientific' Criminology

AT the beginning of the nineteenth century the favoured explanation for criminal behaviour focused principally on the moral weakness of offenders. Poverty, drink, or feckless parents were considered by some commentators as playing a significant part, but the underlying problem was the criminal's desire for an easy life of luxury avoiding hard, but honest, labour. Towards the end of the nineteenth century the usual suspects were still being lined up and stigmatized as society's 'criminals'—beggars, vagabonds, prostitutes, the day-labouring poor of the cities, and their children. But there was a shift in accounting for their criminal behaviour. The notion of the criminal as a moral failure gradually gave way to the notion of the criminal as social wreckage. As Peter Becker has described it, 'fallen men' were replaced by 'impaired men'. Again, poverty, drink, and feckless parents, together with the social environment, were seen as playing parts, but the underlying problem was increasingly perceived as some kind of mental weakness within the criminal, requiring therapeutic intervention. There remained concerns about criminal and dangerous classes, but the new emphasis on the mental make-up of the individual offender explained why, at a glance, it could be difficult to tell some criminals from respectable, well-behaved citizens. It also helped to explain why some offenders committed crimes that were not only bestial but also, to the 'normal' person's eye, quite irrational. Murder and violent sexual assault were relatively rare offences yet, after 1850, in Germany at least, there was a significant growth of texts exploring such crimes and, by implication, suggesting that they were central to criminal behaviour. And across Europe the policemen, judges, and social reformers who had dominated as professional among the authors of texts about crime in the early and mid-nineteenth century gave way to anthropologists, medical men, and scientists. The crime-fighting professional changed, in the words of Martin Wiener, 'from a model of character to a model of intelligence, from a knower of the human heart to a master interpreter of circumstances'.[1]

Scientists and medical men had been offering their expertise to those seeking to detect offenders and to those concerned with prosecuting and defending them from the end of the eighteenth century. Early detection had often deployed the relatively simple techniques of taking casts of footprints or measuring the length of axles. Expert witnesses were increasingly deployed from the early nineteenth century particularly when scientific analysis could be deployed in, for example, cases of poisoning. Research by several chemists, in particular in the early nineteenth century James Marsh in England, Jöns Jacob Berzelius in Sweden, and Hugo Reinsch in Germany, provided a series of tests by which the presence of arsenic could be detected in cases of suspected poisoning. Arsenic was cheap and as a result of its wide use in some medicines, in paint, in fertilizer, and to control vermin and insects, it was also relatively available. Unfortunately none of the tests for arsenic poisoning were conclusive. Doctors, responsible for autopsies, and analysts were rarely the same persons. Some medical experts—sometimes academics and sometimes hospital-based surgeons—gained a reputation as expert witnesses in trials where the use of poison was suspected. But there was always the problem of experts being deployed by both the prosecution and the defence and hence against each other. Moreover, in the adversarial practices of the British courts, experts were required who could stand up to tough questioning by barristers.[2]

Medical men and men from the new science of psychiatry were also employed as expert witnesses when an accused appeared to be insane, or entered a plea of insanity. Doctors had appeared in courts during the eighteenth century. Kant urged that defendants whose sanity was doubted should be referred to members of philosophy rather than medical faculties, though the proposal does not appear to have been taken very far.[3] In eighteenth-century England doctors were regarded as not greatly different from character witnesses. Both judges and jurors tended to take a common-sense view of insanity accepting that a bang on the head or a war-wound might easily lead to an individual being 'out of their senses'. The Napoleonic

[1] Peter Becker, *Verderbnis und Entartung: Einer Geschichte der Kriminologie des 19. Jahrhunderts als Discurs und Praxis*, Göttingen: Vanderhöck und Rupprecht, 2002; Martin J. Wiener, *Reconstructing the Criminal: Culture, Law and Policy in England, 1830–1914*, Cambridge: Cambridge University Press, 1990, 224.

[2] Katherine Watson, *Poisoned Lives: English Poisoners and their Victims*, London: Hambledon, 2004, esp. pp. 16–21, 32–8, and 166–73.

[3] Richard R. Wetzell, *Inventing the Criminal: A History of German Criminology*, Chapel Hill: University of North Carolina Press, 2000, 40.

Criminal Code authorized magistrates to call on the evidence of medical experts. And as, in the early nineteenth century, the classical ideas of absolute mental responsibility yielded ground to new, scientific approaches to insanity, so the role of expert opinion grew about the extent to which certain offenders could be said to have known, clearly and rationally, what they were doing. But the doctors' appearances in court, and their fees, always depended on the presiding judge.[4] In 1835 half a dozen medical men gave evidence in the trial of the young Norman peasant, Pierre Rivière, who had murdered his mother and two siblings with a pruning-bill. Three testified to his sanity; three testified that he was insane. The jury found him guilty and he was sentenced to death but, when the sentence was appealed, seven well-known Paris doctors, including the king's principal physician, presented a report supporting the madness defence. Rivière's death sentence was commuted to life-imprisonment. For Foucault and a group of colleagues the interventions in the Rivière trial were an example of the practitioners of medical medicine demonstrating their growing power as experts within the penal system. It was also a key moment in the progress towards legislation of 1838 that gave them more input into committals to asylums in cases of insanity.[5] Yet it is not necessarily the case that the growth of such witnesses depended primarily on members of the profession pressing their claims to expertise. In France, while it is fair to see a collusion of two forms of authority, the magistrates ensured that it was they and, as they saw it, the law that maintained ultimate authority.[6] In England, as jurors became more and more the audience of the expert barrister so, it has been argued, the expert barrister brought in the expert doctor to present a scientific categorization for the jury. Here again was a fusion of different forms of expertise and authority. But it appears to have been the barristers' flattery of the doctors, their eagerness to fashion cases, and their emphasis on the doctors' special scientific knowledge, rather than any insistence on expertise by the doctors themselves, that fostered the development of the expert medical witness.[7] One group of experts developing their own professionalism and paying court to another can, of course, fit

[4] Robert A. Nye, 'Heredity or Milieu: The Foundations of Modern European Criminological Theory', *Isis*, 67 (1976), 335–55; 346.

[5] Michel Foucault, ed., *I Pierre Rivière, having slaughtered my mother, my sister, and my brother...: A Case of Parricide in the 19th Century*, Harmondsworth: Peguin, 1978.

[6] Laurence Guignard, 'L'expertise médico-légale de la folie aux assises, 1821–1865', *Le Mouvement social*, 197 (2001), 57–81; and see, in general, Frédéric Chauvaud, *Les experts du crime: la médecine légale en France au XIXeme siècle*, Paris: Aubier, 2000.

[7] Joel Peter Eigen, *Witnessing Insanity: Madness and Mad-Doctors in the English Court*, New Haven: Yale University Press, 1995.

the Foucauldian perception. A more potent challenge to the Foucauldian approach, and an area that would benefit from more research, is the extent to which restrictions were imposed upon the power and independence of the expert by bureaucratic structures and financial stringency. As noted earlier, in England at least, limits on the expenses available to coroners appears to have been one reason for so little investigation of the large numbers of baby and infant corpses found in streets, drains, privies, and rubbish tips.[8]

Doctors and psychiatrists increasingly discussed cases in their professional journals. The case of Pierre Rivière, for example, was extensively reported in *Annales d'hygiène publique et de médecine légale*. The extent and content of this report may have been unusual, but then so was the case. As this kind of professional analysis grew more and more common, so the professionals began to develop theories about particular forms of madness provoking particular offences. At the end of the eighteenth century there were some who believed that certain forms of theft were the result of insanity. In 1816 a Swiss doctor, André Matthy, published in Paris his *Nouvelles recherches sur les maladies de l'esprit précédées de considérations sur les difficultés de l'art de guérir*. Matthy's work announced his discovery of the concept of kleptomania. The concept was developed further during the July Monarchy by Louis Philippe's physician, C. C. H. Marc, but it was with the emergence of the department store during the last quarter of the century that the concept became particularly popular. It was used to explain why respectable, bourgeois women who lacked for nothing were tempted to steal from the new form of retail outlet. A series of case studies were made from roughly 1880 to 1905 in which psychiatrists and medical men across Europe explained the problem generally by finding what they were looking for in assumptions about female weakness and frailty. Thus kleptomaniacs stole as a result of irregular menstrual cycles, difficult pregnancies, the menopause, bad marriages, dead husbands, and so forth. The few male kleptomaniacs were identified as having similar sorts of frailties.[9]

While medical men and scientists offered the benefits of their expertise to both the courts and the police, some police officers also sought to develop their own personal experience into systematic means that would enable others more

---

[8] Mary Beth Emmerichs, 'Getting Away with Murder? Homicide and the Coroners in Nineteenth-Century London', *Social Science History*, 25, 1 (2001), 93–100. And see above p. 130.

[9] Patricia O'Brien, 'The Kleptomania Diagnosis: Bourgeois Women and Theft in Late Nineteenth-Century France', *Journal of Social History*, 17, 1 (1983), 65–78; Dorothy Rowe, *Representing Berlin: Sexuality and the City in Imperial and Weimar Germany*, Aldershot: Ashgate, 2003, 120–1.

easily to identify offenders. The value of physical descriptions of criminals
in the hope that these could be used to identify recidivists and suspects had
long been recognized. The disappearance of the punishment of branding an
offender so that he or she might be known in future, made such descriptions
even more important. But, even if descriptions were to be circulated far and
wide, there remained the problem of how such information might readily be
retrieved. This was aggravated by the general lack of uniformity in the way that
descriptions were made and of any agreement on what specific details should
always be included. During the Restoration period in France two junior
police officials drafted proposals for precise forms of categorizing different
distinguishing marks. The first of these officials, whose name is unknown,
appears to have been a former policeman who had been purged following
Napoleon's fall and who was keen to get some sort of employment back. The
other, Jean-Jacques Millot, was a gendarme serving in Alsace who seems to
have aspired to becoming a *commissaire de police*. Millot's plan was particularly
sophisticated, proposing a system of letters and numbers for distinguishing
marks on the face and body. Neither plan was adopted. It is possible that
the Ministry of the Interior regarded the cost of manuals and printed forms
as too high Ministerial employees may also have been prejudiced against
proposals from an anonymous individual and a simple gendarme. Moreover
both of these men were resident far from the centre of power and, in spite
of local endorsements of both their ideas and their zeal, they could easily
be ignored. German police appear to have been rather better organized in
developing similar ideas. In January 1828 the Prussian Ministry of Internal
Affairs and Police issued an order requiring that, in future, all descriptions
drawn up by police officials conform to a specific checklist. At the same time
networks emerged among police officers through professional publications
such as the *Allgemeiner Polizei-Anzeiger* that began to harmonize practices and
the content of different forms of document among the professionals.[10] But
for all that descriptions became more uniform, the problems of storage and
retrieval remained. It was the same with the new technology of photography
that held out new promise for the identification of offenders.

   The first individuals linked to criminal justice systems to use photography
were prison officials. Photographing convicts appears to have been done

---

[10] Vincent-Jérôme Denis, 'Inventeurs en uniforme. Gendarmes et policiers face à l'amelioration
des feuilles de signalement sous la Restoration', and Peter Becker, 'Classifier, communiquer,
confondre: l'histoire du "regard pratique" dans les services de police en Allemagne au XIXe siècle',
both in *Les Cahiers de la Securité*, 56 (2005), 271–89 and 225–50 respectively.

first on a regular basis in Belgian prisons during the 1840s; British and French prison officials followed suit during the following decade. In none of these countries, however, was the photographing of offenders established as government policy to record and detect criminals; an experiment commissioned by the Swiss attorney general in 1852 to photograph vagrants lasted only two years. No major European police organization had a photographic department before the 1870s and they usually began by commissioning commercial photographers to picture the most dangerous offenders. The number of photographs taken was another statistic to be added to annual reports to emphasize police modernity and, by implication, efficiency. But there was no notion of photographing all offenders as a means of identifying recidivists since, without a system of classification, it was recognized that a police force could finish up with a large number of images and no way of finding specific individuals among those images.

The problems of identification and retrieval were partially solved by the work in Paris of the French police official Alphonse Bertillon. In 1879 Bertillon established his system of anthropometry which involved the measurement of several sections of the adult offender's body. These measurements were carefully categorized and classified, stored, and used to identify recidivists. Initially Bertillon believed that his system made the photograph irrelevant but from the 1890s police forces across Europe began to consider a combination of the two, and Bertillon himself came round to seeing the judicial photograph as a useful supplement. Even so, there could still be problems of retrieval and, as Bertillon's own instructions put it:

Photographs are undoubtedly a great aid in establishing the identity of the criminal. But it is very difficult, almost impossible, to find in a large collection the picture of a person without knowing his name. A photograph is valuable in *verifying* the identity of an individual, but it is altogether impotent to help you *discover* the identity if you have no other means but your eyes to search for the photograph among the thousands in an ordinary collection.[11]

Sir Francis Galton, the eminent anthropologist and cousin of Charles Darwin, attempted a more ambitious experiment with photography. Galton invented a composite photography machine with which he hoped, by superimposing

[11] Jens Jäger, 'Photography: A Means of Surveillance? Judicial Photography, 1850 to 1900', *CHS* 5, 1 (2001), 27–51; Richard W. Ireland, 'The Felon and the Angel Copier: Criminal Identity and the Promise of Photography in Victorian England and Wales', in Louis A. Knafla, ed., *Policing and War in Europe, CJH* 16 (2002), 53–86; 77.

the images of different criminals upon one another, to identify the inherent physiognomic features of both race and criminology.[12]

While Galton's experiment with composite photography yielded no positive results, his interest in fingerprints had a more long-lasting impact. In 1892, building on the work of others, Galton presented a strong scientific case for the unique nature of an individual's fingerprints. He subsequently devised a complex system of classification. In 1893 a committee established by the Home Office in Britain recommended that the Metropolitan Police collect and keep fingerprints as an adjunct to its adoption of the Bertillon system of anthropometry. Again, however, there were problems of classification and retrieval; Galton's system was far too complicated. A solution was eventually found in British India by Edward Henry, Inspector General of the Bengal Police and, more particularly, by the head of his identification department, Azizul Hacque. At the turn of the century Henry returned to London as Assistant Commissioner of the Metropolitan Police and in 1901 he established a fingerprint bureau at Scotland Yard. The bureau was able to identify ninety-three recidivists in its first six months and in June 1902 fingerprints were used for the first time in a criminal trial, when they helped to convict a London burglar.[13] But for the ten years or so after the development of fingerprints the Metropolitan Police appears to have been quite unreceptive to further scientific developments in detective work. On the eve of the First World War Raymond B. Fosdick, an American police officer making a comparison of European police systems, considered Scotland Yard to have been 'passed and outclassed in the further extensions of criminal identification and crime detection by its more scientific and painstaking neighbors across the North Sea'.[14]

As medical men increasingly appeared in court and wrote articles and books on various problems of criminality, and as policemen and prison officials, rather more slowly, began to consider the use of scientific method and technological developments in their work, so the academic discipline of criminology also began to make an appearance. The boasts of expertise made by police officers like Rabasse already had a scientific underpinning with the work on phrenology and physiognomy that was done in the first

---

[12] Daniel Pick, *Faces of Degeneration: A European Disorder, c.1848–c.1918*, Cambridge: Cambridge University Press, 1989, 123 and 163–5.

[13] For a good popular account see Colin Beavan, *Fingerprints: Murder and the Race to Uncover the Science of Identity*, London: Fourth Estate, 2001.

[14] Raymond B. Fosdick, *European Police Systems* (first published 1915), Montclair, NJ: Patterson Smith, 1969, 313.

half of the nineteenth century. But the work of alienists, as the early students of psychiatry were known, as well as that of anthropologists and biologists interested in the contrasts between races and the potential impact of, for example, miscegenation, all contributed to debates on crime and criminals. The journals of these groups and their international congresses commonly had papers that addressed such debates.[15] The first recognizable group of academic criminologists proper, however, was the school that developed in Italy around Cesare Lombroso in the closing decades of the century.

Cesare Lombroso graduated as a doctor of medicine in 1858 and, in the following year, he volunteered for military service in the wars that unified Italy. Before his discharge in 1863 he served with the army fighting the Brigands War in Calabria. It seems probable that, during this conflict, Lombroso acquired the same perceptions of the people of the *Mezzogiorno* as other officers from the north of the peninsula. But it was not until 1871, according to his own, apparently embellished, testimony that he had the flash of inspiration that led to his concept of the born criminal. While conducting an autopsy on the body of a notorious brigand, Guiseppe Villela, Lombroso claimed to see a similarity between the brigand's skull and the typical skulls of the 'inferior races'. Combining his empirical work with ideas drawn from the French positivist philosopher Auguste Comte, from the German biologist and evolutionist Ernst Haeckel, and from phrenology and degeneration theory, in 1876 he published the first version of *L'uomo delinquente* (Criminal Man). Over the next twenty years the book went through five editions and grew considerably in size from 250 pages to three volumes and 2,000 pages. As the book grew, so Lombroso's ideas developed. He classified criminals into more and more distinct categories such as alcoholic, hysteric, passionate, and occasional. He was reluctant to give up his notion of the born criminal carrying the atavistic tendencies of ancient and savage peoples. Increasingly, however, he came to argue that criminals were born as such, not only because of heredity but also because of degeneracy brought about by alcoholism, malnutrition, venereal disease, and so forth. Finally, he modified his ideas on punishment. Since criminals acted out of compulsion rather than through a clear and simple rationality, he urged that punishment should be flexible and that judges should be relatively free to determine sentences according to

---

[15] Claude Blanckaert, 'Des sauvages en pays civilisé: l'anthropologie des criminels (1850–1900)', and Jean-Christophe Coffin, 'La "folie morale" figure pathologique et entité miracle des hypothèses psychiatriques au XIXème siècle', both in Laurent Mucchielli, ed., *Histoire de la criminologie française*, Paris: L'Harmattan, 1994.

the danger that the criminal presented to society. Most significantly this led him to shift his early liberal hostility to the death penalty and to advocate its use for the atavistic offender who had committed brutal and bloody crimes, particularly as part of a gang of brigands or *mafiosi*.[16]

As he continued to develop his ideas about criminal man, so Lombroso also turned his attention to the question of why the rates of offending were so much lower among women than men. In 1893, together with his son-in-law Guglielmo Ferrero, he published *La donna delinquente* (Criminal Woman). Here he blended his own developing theories of atavism with the research of others and a wide range of contemporary assumptions about gender differences. Lombroso began by assessing the 'normal' woman and, deploying his eclectic baggage of assumptions, he concluded that women in general were less evolved than men. They were smaller; they felt and thought less; and their moral sense was inferior. This was because their passive role in courtship, their reproductive abilities, and their maternal functions had retarded their development. When women were criminal, however, they were truly monstrous. Like so many of his predecessors he made the prostitute the equivalent of the male criminal; here, after all, was a woman who, by her deviant behaviour, rejected the things that were normal in women, namely monogamy and sexual frigidity.[17] Lombroso's ideas on female criminality struck a chord with those who, across Europe, had long considered the female offender as, above all, a threat to morality and who were keen to attribute any crimes committed by women to female biology.

Lombroso rapidly acquired a school. Enrico Ferri who, rather than Lombroso, actually coined the term 'born criminal', subsequently took over the leadership of the Italian school and proclaimed its work to be 'criminal sociology'. Ferri interwove criminal statistics and medical theories; he also coloured his views with ideas drawn from Charles Darwin, Karl Marx, and Herbert Spencer. The criminal was the product of environment and heredity. Ferri developed Lombroso's ideas into a positivist system that pooh-poohed notions of an offender's moral responsibility. He found his parallels in medicine. Once convicted, only one question about the offender would remain:

[16] Mary Gibson, *Born to Crime: Cesare Lombroso and the Origins of Biological Criminality*, Westport, Conn.: Praeger, 2002, esp. ch. 1. There is now an excellent translation drawing together extracts from the five editions of *L'uomo delinquente* that demonstrates the development of Lombroso's ideas: Cesare Lombroso, *Criminal Man*, tr. and intro. Mary Gibson and Nicole Hahn Rafter, Durham, NC: Duke University Press, 2006.

[17] Cesare Lombroso and Guglielmo Ferrero, *Criminal Woman, the Prostitute and the Normal Woman*, tr. and intro. Nicole Hahn Rafter and Mary Gibson, Durham, NC: Duke University Press, 2004.

To what anthropological category does the accused belong? Consequently, at this point, a new possible argument between the prosecution and the defence would arise to establish the personal and real qualities determining whether the delinquent should be held insane, incorrigible from birth, habitual, occasional, or swayed by passion.[18]

In the new circumstances the judicial police, criminal lawyers, and judges would not need legal training as much as the technical knowledge provided by criminal sociology. Juries could be abolished since they were 'the exact opposite of special knowledge'.[19] The convict, like patients in hospitals and the insane in asylums, should never be sentenced to a fixed term in prison since there was danger in releasing him until it was clear that he would not offend again. Ferri divided his time between a succession of university posts, a legal practice, and politics. He became a socialist deputy in 1886 and, ten years later, he founded the socialist journal *Avanti*, serving as its first editor.

While Ferri wrote and enthused over the prospects for positivist criminology, other members of the Italian school sought to put the ideas into practice. Notable among these was Salvatore Ottolenghi, who was Lombroso's assistant at the University of Turin and who firmly established himself as a disciple with a detailed study of 200 criminals and prostitutes published in 1896. But more significant in practical terms was Ottolenghi's creation of courses in scientific policing for police officers. He began by offering a free course on the subject at the University of Siena in 1896. The course, which included elements of anthropology, psychology, other subjects that fed into criminal sociology and some training in the methods of Bertillonage, became compulsory for administrative ranks of the *Pubblica Sicurezza* in 1903. Subsequently, taking his course with him, Ottolenghi transferred to Rome as Professor of Legal Medicine and established himself in a wing of the city's Regina Coeli Prison. Here he brought offenders into the classroom, where he interrogated them about their offences and indicated their physical characteristics to his students.[20]

Lombroso and his ideas had little influence on the new Criminal Code promulgated for Italy in 1889. Nor were his ideas universally accepted in

---

[18] Enrico Ferri, *Criminal Sociology*, Boston: Little, Brown, 1917; repr. New York: Agathon Press, 1967, 462–3.

[19] Ibid. 473.

[20] Gibson, *Born to Crime*, 9–11; Ilsen About, 'Naissance d'une science policière de l'identification en Italie (1902–1922)', *Les Cahiers de la Securité*, 56 (2005), 167–200. Ottolenghi's study of criminals and prostitutes, published with a preface by Lombroso, was *Duecento criminali e prostitue studiate nei laboratori di Clinica psichiatrica e di antropologia criminale di Torino*, Turin: Fratelli Bocca, 1897.

his native country. The determinism and materialism of his theories were strongly condemned by the Catholic church, but then the church largely opted out of the newly united Italy until the agreement with Mussolini in the 1920s. Napoleone Colajanni and Filippo Turati made more telling criticisms; they were particularly critical of Lombrosian biological determinism and they put a much greater stress on social conditions as a cause of offending. Yet Lombroso and his disciples remained dominant in Italy and, the reconstruction of the criminal law aside, their influence on the politics of penal practice and discourse in the country was profound, if sometimes pragmatic. An army recruit, claiming to be an anarchist, shot his commanding officer while his regiment prepared to embark for the invasion of Libya. The recruit could have been court martialled and shot but, as a leading anarchist put it, the prime minister 'thought of Cesare Lombroso' and had the man confined to an asylum. This decision defused the potential for an international outcry, unlike the response to a similar occurrence in Spain. Here also Lombroso's work had a significant impact on academics and lawyers, and both Liberals and Conservative-Reformists backed the training of penal personnel in the latest criminological theories. Following riots as troops embarked for Morocco, however, the Spanish government, in contrast to its Italian counterpart, allowed the death sentence passed by a military court on a well-known anarchist educator to stand. This was in spite of the fact that there was no solid evidence against the man, that the governor of the prison where he was held, Rafael Salillas, dubbed Spain's 'little Lombroso' (*pequeño Lombroso*), depicted him as a near lunatic, and that the case provoked huge protests across the Western hemisphere.[21]

While Salillas was 'little Lombroso', he was no simple imitator. Salillas and other early Spanish criminologists considered the Spanish race to be a fusion of different peoples forged in the country's unique history. In considering Lombroso's theories they saw their task as being to explain how criminality had developed among some individuals in contrast to the majority of the population. Thus ideas were floated about Gypsies as being resistant to mixing with other groups and maintaining their criminal propensities. And those regions of Spain notorious for their violence or where separatist groups fought for autonomy were seen as areas where the fusion had been limited and where, in consequence, ancient passions and violence were preserved

[21] Richard Bach Jensen, 'Criminal Anthropology and Anarchist Terrorism in Spain and Italy', *Mediterranean Historical Review*, 16, 2 (2001), 31–44.

in greater purity.[22] But in addition to the ideas of Lombroso, at the turn of the century Salillas and his contemporaries had a cluster of other new criminological theories upon which they could draw.

The last ten to fifteen years of the nineteenth century witnessed a ferment of criminological theories across Europe. Crime was perceived overwhelmingly as social pathology, though it has to be emphasized that this was not a universal perception. One of the most notable sociologists of the period, Émile Durkheim, took a line significantly different from most of those who considered themselves students of the new science of criminology. Rather than seeing crime as abnormal behaviour committed by social wreckage at war with society, Durkheim insisted on the normalcy of crime. Crime might change its forms, he argued, but it was nevertheless present in each and every society. Moreover, in Durkheim's analysis, crime was both useful and necessary. It could foster change; challenges to authority in the past, for example, had brought about freedom of thought and of expression. Similarly criminal laws and sanctions defined the acceptable boundaries of a society and, by bringing together and concentrating upright consciences, crime also encouraged social cohesion and solidarity. Yet like many of his contemporaries in France he was also convinced that social phenomena contributed to crimes. Thus he pointed to murder rates rising at moments when passions ran high, such as during wars or political crises, while suicides appeared closely linked with what he saw as a key characteristic of modern industrial societies, the lack of social cohesion.[23]

While Durkheim took a distinct path, other academics, jurists, and legal-medical experts in France combined to mount a major challenge to the Italian school. They drew on a long tradition of theoretical approaches that touched on the questions of crime and criminality, heredity and the impact of the social milieu. At the same time, defeat at the hands of the new Germany in 1871 and fears about a falling birth rate and 'racial' decline had revived interest in Morel's *dégénérescence*. In 1885 the Lombrosian school appeared at the height of its powers and sought to outshine the Third International Penitentiary Congress by holding the First International Congress of Criminal Anthropology

---

[22] Joshua Goode, 'Corrupting a Good Mix: Race and Crime in Late Nineteenth- and Early Twentieth-Century Spain', *European History Quarterly*, 35, 2 (2005), 241–65.

[23] Durkheim's key texts here are *De la division du travail social: étude sur l'organization des sociétés supérieures*, Paris, 1893 (numerous translations, usually under the title *The Division of Labour in Society*), and *Le suicide*, Paris, 1897 (again, numerous translations). His comments on murder are to be found in a series of lectures written and revised between 1903 and 1916, but not published until 1950 in *Leçons de sociologie: physique des mœurs et du droit*, Paris: Presses Universitaires de France.

in Rome. After the Italians, the largest national group at the conference were the French. From the outset the French made direct criticism first of the way in which Lombroso and his disciples used ill-defined words and terms such as 'atavism' and 'larval epilepsy' in their work, and then, more fundamentally, on the whole idea of supposedly primitive anatomical characteristics being an indication of a pathological predisposition to criminal behaviour.[24] Among the principal French critics were Alexandre Lacassagne and Gabriel Tarde, both of whom had made the shift from practitioner to academic. Lacassagne, like Lombroso, had been a military doctor. He had made two tours of duty in Algeria before taking up the post of Professor of Legal Medicine in the Medical Faculty at Lyons.[25] Tarde had begun his career as a provincial magistrate; he moved on from there to run the Bureau of Statistics in the Ministry of Justice, before becoming Professor of Sociology at the Collège de France.

The divisions between the French and the Italians were never as great as the ferocious debates suggested but national pride and professional jealousy were at stake, and this provoked petty attempts at scoring points. In 1886 Tarde published *La Criminalité comparée*, in which he took the measurements of criminal morphology made by various Italians and others and demonstrated both wide variations and considerable disagreements between them. At the 1889 congress held in Paris the eminent French psychiatrist Valentin Magnan took delegates to a reformatory and showed them the juvenile offenders who, he insisted, had no physical signs of degeneracy. Whereupon Lombroso took measurements and insisted that while there might not be any signs visible to the naked eye, abnormalities were unquestionably present. An empirical, comparative study was proposed involving 100 criminals and 100 'honest' men, the results of which were to be presented at the congress scheduled for Brussels in the following year. The comparison never took place following a French challenge to the methodology, to which the Italians responded with a boycott of the congress.[26]

[24] Nye, 'Heredity or Milieu', is a useful account of the formulation of French opposition to the Lombrosian school and of the debates at the early Criminal Anthropology congresses. For a broad analysis of the congresses up to the First World War see Martine Kaluszynski, 'The International Congresses of Criminal Anthropology: Shaping the French and International Criminological Movement, 1886–1914', in Peter Becker and Richard F. Wetzell, eds., *Criminals and the Scientists: The History of Criminology in International Perspective*, New York: Cambridge University Press, 2006.

[25] Marc Renneville, 'Alexandre Lacassagne: un médecin-anthropologue face à la criminalité (1843–1924)', *Gradhiva—Revue d'histoire et d'archives de l'anthropolgie*, 17 (1995), 127–40.

[26] Leon Radzinowicz and Roger Hood, *The Emergence of Penal Policy in Victorian and Edwardian England*, Oxford: Clarendon Press, 1990, 20; Marc Renneville, 'La réception de Lombroso en France (1880–1900)', in Mucchielli, ed., *Histoire de la criminologie française*.

It was not until 1890 that a translation of Lombroso's *L'uomo delinquente* into German was finally published. His work was known, however, not least though articles written by the psychiatrist Emil Kraepelin and published in the *Zeitschrift für die gesamte Strafrechtswissenschaft*. Franz von Liszt, a cousin of the great composer, had founded this journal in 1881; the first edition contained articles by Lombroso and also by the Lutheran moralist and student of criminal statistics Alexander von Oettingen. Liszt played the key role in the formulation of criminological thinking and research in Germany but, in the perceptive assessment of Richard Wetzell, as an 'impresario' rather than as a 'performer'. Born in Vienna, Liszt had trained in law and had taught at a variety of Austrian and German universities before establishing his own criminology institute when he moved to Halle in 1881. The following year he published *Der Zweckgedanke im Strafrecht*, in which he outlined his belief that punishment should be less concerned with revenge and more with the systematic protection of society. For Liszt the new science of criminology had three elements. The first of these was pedagogic and practical and concerned the training of lawyers and judges in jurisprudence and what was termed criminalistics—forensics and scientific methods of getting evidence. The second, the scientific element of criminology, addressed the causal explanations for crime and the utility and aims of punishment. The third element, the political, focused on penal policy and its formulation. By 1889 Liszt's reputation in Germany was second to none. In that year he and his institute transferred to Berlin and, keen to develop links with like-minded thinkers and reformers elsewhere, he founded the *Internationale Kriminalistische Vereiningung*, the International Union of Penal Law.[27]

In Liszt's native Austria criminology took a more practical slant. The principal figure here was Hans Groß who in 1883, after thirteen years as an examining magistrate, published a manual for his profession, *Handbuch für Untersuchungsrichter*. Examining magistrates in continental Europe were essentially criminal investigators responsible for scrutinizing the evidence of a crime presented by victims and witnesses and collected by the police. Groß's book was the result of his personal experience in dealing with offenders, his wide reading in medicine and psychology, and his belief that his legal training had left him ill-prepared for establishing the facts of a case. And his book was to have an appeal beyond the continental European institution of the examining magistrate, as is testified by the successive English language editions

---

[27] Wetzell, *Inventing the Criminal*, ch. 1, *passim*.

that were used even by detectives who grew up in the fiercely artisan culture of British police institutions.[28] In addition, in 1898 Groß launched the *Archiv für Kriminal-Anthropologie und Kriminalistik* which, while it had 'criminal anthropology' in its title, was no vehicle for the ideas of the Italian school. Indeed, Groß and his principal contributor on matters of criminal psychology Paul Näcke, a doctor with a long experience of working in asylums, were highly critical of Lombroso's formulations. And while the *Archiv* explored a range of criminological subjects, it was the practical, *Kriminalistik*, side that was favoured.[29]

In Britain the study of offenders had a long practical tradition among doctors and psychiatrists who worked in prisons and appeared as expert witnesses in the courts. Indeed, the British response to Lombrosian ideas was often couched in terms of the practitioners' day-to-day experience of working with convicts as opposed to those who theorized without getting their hands dirty.[30] This tradition led to an empirical study on a much greater scale than that proposed by the criminology congress in Paris in 1889. In 1902 Dr Charles Goring, recently appointed to the prison medical service, embarked on a study of English convicts. Over the next six years Goring developed and applied ninety-six variables to nearly 4,000 convicts and compared them with a mixture of soldiers, hospital patients, schoolboys, undergraduates, and university staff. He concluded that there was no physical evidence to confirm the existence of any criminal type though offenders, notably thieves and burglars, appeared to be shorter and lighter. In general offenders also appeared less intelligent. Faults can be found in Goring's methodology; in particular, he did not rigorously assess the social environment and experience of his offenders and he tended to take his convicts' behaviour as representative of all criminal behaviour without going any deeper into the possible causes of crime. Nevertheless *The English Convict* contributed significantly to the demise of an academic criminology dependent on assumptions about the physiological distinctions shared by criminal types.[31]

---

[28] Hans Groß, *Criminal Investigation: A Practical Textbook for Magistrates, Police Officers and Lawyers*, London: Sweet and Maxwell, 1st. edn. 1906; 2nd. edn. 1924; 3rd. edn. 1934; 4th edn. 1949. It is interesting to note, however, that the first editions declared that the translation had been 'prepared for the benefit of Indian and Colonial magistrates, lawyers and Police Officers'.

[29] Wetzell, *Inventing the Criminal*, 61–2.

[30] Neil Davie, *Tracing the Criminal: The Rise of Scientific Criminology in Britain, 1860–1918*, Oxford: Bardwell Press, 2005, 149–50.

[31] Charles Goring, *The English Convict: A Statistical Study*, London: HMSO, 1913; Radzinowicz and Hood, *The Emergence of Penal Policy*, 20–7, provides a useful summary of the origins of the work and its content.

In the process of demolishing the remnants of a theory that even Lombroso had increasingly side-stepped, Goring showed himself to be sympathetic to Sir Francis Galton's theory of eugenics. Galton had coined the word 'eugenics' from the Greek *eugenia*, meaning 'well born', in 1884. He defined it as 'the study of those agencies under social control which may improve or impair the racial qualities of future generations, either physically or mentally'. While he did not envisage his new science as related specifically to the understanding of crime and criminality, his work echoed ideas already being advanced by some of the prison doctors who, earlier, had commented on the pattern of offending. It also reflected some of the fears that were being voiced about the threat to the nation's racial stock by what was perceived as an inferior but burgeoning population in the urban slums. In *The English Convict*, Goring touched on eugenicist theory when he advocated the segregation and supervision of the 'unfit'. He even contemplated regulating the reproductive opportunities of those suffering from deficient social behaviour, alcoholism, epilepsy, feeble-mindedness, and other shortcomings that he categorized as being found in criminals.

At the close of the nineteenth century similar fears for racial stock were to be found across continental Europe. In Wilhelmine Germany a few began to advocate sterilization to prevent inherited mental disease and criminality. The Jena Prize Competition Essay announced at the turn of the century posed the question: 'What can we learn from the principles of evolution for the development and laws of states?' The winner, out of some sixty entries principally from Germany, was Friedrich Wilhelm Schallmayer, who argued that hereditary biology should provide the basis for social reform.[32] Measures to prevent the unfit from reproducing were part and parcel of his plan. But German criminologists and doctors were by no means the first or the only individuals to consider the sterilization of offenders and they were not the first to take action. In 1911 the Seventh International Congress for Criminal Anthropology meeting in Cologne heard a paper presented by a Zurich doctor involved in the recent sterilization of degenerate offenders in Switzerland. Many delegates expressed doubts and disquiet about the Swiss procedure. Not least amongst these was Gustav Aschaffenburg, a psychiatrist who was emerging as a leading figure in German criminology. Aschaffenburg thought that sterilization might have some merit with regard to sex offenders but, since he remained uncertain about the role of heredity as a cause of criminality, he was

---

[32] Paul Weindling, *Health, Race and German Politics between National Unification and Nazism*, Cambridge: Cambridge University Press, 1989, 101 and 115–18.

uncertain about its applicability elsewhere.[33] In the following year there was more extensive discussion of sterilization at the First International Eugenics Congress held at London University. The appeal of eugenics was apparent from the range of delegates who attended from Belgium, France, Germany, Greece, Italy, Spain, Japan, Australia, New Zealand, and the United States. Crime was not the key focus of the congress, but several of the papers reflected upon the problem. Not least of these was Bleeker van Wagenen's presentation of the 'Preliminary Report of the Committee of the Eugenic Section of the American Breeders' Association to Study and to Report on the Best Practical Means for Cutting Off the Defective Germ-Plasm in the Human Population'. Van Wagenen explained that, since 1907, eight states (Indiana, Connecticut, California, Iowa, Nevada, New Jersey, Washington, and New York) had introduced laws authorizing sterilization. Moreover, in some institutions in another five states (Pennsylvania, Kansas, Idaho, Virginia, and Massachusetts) some individuals had been sterilized 'for purely medical or for a combination of medical and Eugenic reasons, usually with the consent of parents or guardians'.[34] Leading European criminologists, however, continued to refrain from advocating such legislation as a significant means of reducing crime. And, at least among the administrators and doctors working in British prisons, concerns were expressed that enforced sterilization might worsen some forms of sexual crime and turn offenders still further into outcasts.[35]

Like the moral entrepreneurs of the earlier part of the century, the medical men and scientists believed that they could work towards solutions to the problems that they delineated. There is no reason to doubt the sincerity of their thinking, although there were careers to be made in the academic world and as professionals giving expert advice to the police and the courts, and doing further research as well as 'treating' those incarcerated in various penal institutions. But if the policeman, the judge, and the penal administrator now needed to defer, on occasions, to this new kind of expert, their own distinct forms of expertise were still in demand. Moreover, particular kinds of offender prompted some police officers and their political masters to develop links and information exchange across national frontiers akin to those already common among philanthropists and those interested in theorizing systems of punishment and criminality in general.

[33] Wetzell, *Inventing the Criminal*, 105.
[34] *Problems in Eugenics: First International Eugenics Congress, 1912*, London: Eugenics Education Society, 1912, 467. (Repr. New York: Garland, 1984.)
[35] Davie, *Tracing the Criminal*, 257.

Political police institutions had always taken an interest in those critics of the regime that they served who had sought refuge in another country. In the aftermath of the revolutions of 1848 large numbers of refugees had moved to liberal Britain, sometimes as a way-station for the United States, but sometimes to continue their political activity in safety close to home. The British invited some foreign police to attend the Great Exhibition of 1851 to watch for and to advise upon foreign criminals. European police saw this as an opportunity to take a closer look at some of the political exiles in London, and some police attended apparently without invitation. In the aftermath of 1848 the police chief of Berlin, Karl von Hinckeldey, established a police union among the German states that exchanged information about political radicals. It held annual meetings from 1851 to 1866 when the break between Austria and Prussia significantly reduced its reach. Other countries made agreements to exchange information; even the British government acquiesced in some instances, though it kept such exchanges from its population and continued to be seen by its European neighbours as insufferably smug about its boasted liberty.[36]

The murderous activities of anarchists in the closing years of the nineteenth century and at the beginning of the twentieth encouraged extensions to such links. The assassination of Empress Elizabeth of Austria by an Italian anarchist in Geneva in September 1898 followed more than a decade of outrages that had seen a bomb thrown in the French legislature, the killing of a French president, of a Spanish prime minister, and of other less exalted individuals, as well as people wounded or narrowly escaping injury. Two months after the assassination of the empress, and as a direct response, an international conference met in Rome with delegates from twenty-one countries including all of the major powers of Europe. The conference concluded with practical agreements to maintain surveillance over anarchist activists and to exchange information. It also issued a declaration to the effect that anarchism could not be regarded as a political doctrine and that anarchist activity was nothing more than violent criminality. A second conference, less well attended, was held six years later in St Petersburg.

---

[36] Phillip Thurmond Smith, *Policing Victorian London: Political Policing, Public Order, and the London Metropolitan Police*, Westport, Coan.: Greenwood Press, 1985, 89–95. For European developments, and for the issues discussed in the following two paragraphs see, Hsi-Huey Liang, *The Rise of the Modern Police and the European State System from Metternich to the Second World War*, Cambridge: Cambridge University Press, 1992, esp. pp. 62–76 and 153–69; and, Mathieu Deflem, *Policing World Society: Historical Foundations of International Police Cooperation*, Oxford: Oxford University Press, 2002, ch. 1.

Concerns about anarchists coincided with concerns about 'white slavery' and the movement of women across frontiers for prostitution. The momentum for international police action in this area began with an international conference organized in London in 1899 by a private body, the National Vigilance Association. A second international meeting 'On the International Fight against the White Slave Traffic' was held in Frankfurt in 1902 but, rather more importantly for international police co-operation, in the same year an intergovernmental gathering in Paris agreed practical arrangements aimed at suppressing the problem. These arrangements, which involved the surveillance of suspects and of railway stations and ports, were given greater shape by an international agreement signed two years later, again in Paris. In the late spring of 1914 the Prince of Monaco organized the First International Congress of Judicial Police with the aims of improving the apprehension and identification of suspects and fugitives across national borders. The prince's vision of co-operation was undermined by the absence of representatives from several major European powers, most notably Britain and Germany. The congress concluded with plans for an international bureau of criminal identification, but world war terminated any progress.

Anarchist outrages and young virgins being swept away to foreign brothels by sinister aliens made good headlines. The numbers of individuals physically affected by such instances was tiny, but it was good for politicians and policemen to be seen to be doing something. At the same time the practicalities of policing were never going to enable opportunities for international exchange nor the leisure for anything like the wide-ranging, if sometimes acrimonious, theoretical debates of philanthropists or criminal anthropologists. The tasks of a police officer at the close of the nineteenth century were not greatly different from those of his predecessors a century before. But ideas about the state and its relationship with its citizens were changing with a concomitant impact upon policing.

11

New Professionals: Old Problems

At the turn of the century three broad varieties of knowledge were in circulation about the criminal each based on a selection of empirical evidence. The new theoretical criminologists debated problems drawing on their attempts to study the bodies, minds, and environments of offenders. The expanding popular press marshalled material from the most shocking occurrences to sell its wares and, in so doing, it helped to mould and possibly re-emphasize the fears and prejudices of its readers. The practical men—police and prison officers, magistrates and judges—were exposed to all of the above. But they also had their own expertise based on day-to-day experience and shaped by the structures of their institutions as well as by broader changes in economy and society and by the aspirations and directives of legislators and governments. The three types of police institution described earlier—state civilian, state military, and municipal—remained in place across Europe. But in many regions the economic, social, and political environments in which they functioned in 1900 had changed enormously in the preceding half century. The developments in policing institutions, their impact on, and inter-relationships with these shifting environments in the second half of the nineteenth century are the focus of this chapter.

In 1856 the British government established an inspectorate to inquire annually into the efficiency and effectiveness of the police forces across England, Wales, and Scotland. The inspectorate, and the requirements that all counties and boroughs establish police forces, was only secured in parliament by the promise of a Treasury grant of one-quarter the cost of pay and clothing for those forces that were approved as efficient. The inspections and the grant gave central government some potentially significant involvement with local police, yet it still fell far short of a centralized system. Towards the end of the century, particularly with reference to labour disorders and requirements that forces provide mutual aid for each other, Home Office officials began occasionally to bypass the civilian police committees and to communicate directly with chief constables. This form of central state supervision of local forces was unique to nineteenth-century Britain. In France a new policing law passed in 1884 left ambiguity about where the principal authority was situated. It maintained the old system of mayors being the chief of police and the municipalities being responsible for funding; but it also gave a superior authority, in certain circumstances, to prefects and sub-prefects. In the booming industrial districts of the west of Germany, the increasing economic disorder towards the end of the century did not encourage the municipalities to invest significantly in their police. State officials wrote to Berlin expressing disquiet that the pressures of local politics dissuaded mayors from finding the enthusiasm and more especially the money for the kind of policing that was necessary. But the state held back from any system of central inspection let alone finance, and responded to major disorder by dispatching gendarmes and troops.[1] In Italy, where Liberals in the newly united state were impressed by many British practices, parliament decided against establishing a police system on the model of the Bobby on the grounds that the ordinary Italians were not yet ready to be policed by an unarmed officer of this type.[2] There was a long and proud tradition of municipal independence in Italy, and this ensured that towns and cities maintained their own police. But this municipal pride and independence may also have been significant in the decision not to allow the towns to run the only police institutions other than the military *Carabinieri*. While the latter force was responsible to the Ministry of War, in 1850 the Savoyard monarchy had also created the *Guardia di Pubblica Sicurezza* (PS) which was also spread down the peninsula with unification. The PS was answerable to the Ministry of the Interior yet it was not a state civilian force in the sense of the London Metropolitan Police, the Paris Police, or even the Royal Police of Berlin. Rather it was another militarized force that was deployed not only in the capital, but also in urban areas across the country.

By the end of the century the municipal police in Italy were restricted to carrying out simple management responsibilities such as the supervision of traffic, markets, slaughterhouses, and some aspects of public health. Matters of public order and crime required the intervention of the *Carabinieri* or the PS, and there was tension and jealousy between these bodies. Commanders of the former prided themselves on their force's close relationship with the

---

[1] Elaine Glovka Spencer, *Police and the Social Order in German Cities: The Düsseldorf District, 1848–1914* DeKalb; Northern Illinois University Press, 1992, 82–7.

[2] Steven C. Hughes, 'Poliziotti, *Carabinieri* e "Policemens": il *bobby* inglesi nella polizia italiana', *Le Carte e la Storia*, 2 (1996), 22–31.

monarchy, their role in Italian unification, and their military traditions. The institution portrayed itself as a family and new recruits were urged to consider themselves as joining a body that stood apart from the rest of society but that worked for the benefit of that society. The result was that the corps rarely responded to criticism and sometimes ignored their civilian superiors. While there were proposals for rationalizing and restructuring the police in Italy, these never got beyond proposals. It was apparent that, had they done so, a clutch of proud generals would have vigorously resisted any change.[3] There was a similar, if less acute, rivalry between the French *Gendarmerie* and the civilian police. The tensions of the days of Fouché and Moncey had subsided but police representations of the gendarme portrayed him as an unimaginative military man lacking the flair necessary for police work. Gendarmes, in turn, considered the police as the dubious heirs of Vidocq. The *Gendarmerie* was feted in the early years of the Second Empire but, once the regime was secure, it slipped down the government's and the public's list of priorities. Then, in the early years of the Third Republic, as it found itself required to enforce anticlerical legislation, it began to lose its traditional support and praise from conservatives.[4]

Although different police institutions were beginning to employ some new scientific aids such as Bertillonage, fingerprinting, and photography, the basic *modus operandi* for most policemen remained unchanged. In Russia urban police officers were assigned to static posts that were in theory, though for a variety of reasons rarely in practice, in hailing distance of each other. These officers rarely ventured far from their posts.[5] In most European towns and cities, however, policemen patrolled designated beats on foot sometimes alone, sometimes, in the more dangerous districts, in pairs. These men were scarecrows for petty thieves though more determined and practised offenders

[3] Raymond B. Fosdick, *European Police Systems*, 1915; repr. Montclair, NJ: Patterson Smith, 1969, 91–8; Clive Emsley, *Gendarmes and the State in Nineteenth-Century Europe*, Oxford: Oxford University Press, 1999, 202–04.

[4] Laurent López, 'Les relations entre policiers et gendarmes à travers leurs représentations mutuelles sous la Troisième République', in Jean-Noël Luc, ed., *Figures des Gendarmes, Sociétés et Représentations*, 16 (2003), 213–27; and, Edgar Egnell, 'Le renversement de l'image de la *gendarmerie* dans l'opinion conservatrice entre l'*Ordre moral* et le *Bloc des Gauches*', ibid. 147–52. Elsewhere López suggests that the use of scientific aids, and the need for training in these, had the unexpected repercussion of fostering closer co-operation between the police and the *Gendarmerie*. See Laurent López, 'Policiers, gendarmes et signalement descriptif. Représentations, apprentissages et pratiques d'une nouvelle technique de police judiciaire, en France à la Belle Époque', *CHS* 10, 1 (2006), 51–76.

[5] Robert W. Thurston, 'Police and People in Moscow, 1906–1914', *Russian Review*, 39, 3 (1980), 320–38; 325–6; Neil Weissman, 'Regular Police in Russia, 1900–1914', *Russian Review*, 44, 1 (1985), 45–68; 48–9.

learned how to avoid regular beat patrols. The patrolling policeman looked out for suspicious behaviour and for suspect persons; the latter were still most commonly situated among the poor working class, tramps, and vagabonds. Police officers knew some old offenders. Sometimes it was a requirement of an offender's release from prison that he or she remain for a period under police surveillance. Complaints came from ex-offenders in such circumstances that they were victimized by the police and prevented from finding honest jobs by intrusive surveillance. The police collected information from those willing to volunteer it, from those who were paid for it, and from those who could be pressurized into providing it. In the countryside police patrols commonly covered greater districts. Many of the state military forces continued to patrol on horseback but as the century drew to a close some were forced to exchange their horses for bicycles. In the countryside also the police looked for what was out of the ordinary. Here too, the tramp and the shabby traveller who could not give a good account of himself were suspect.

Police relations with the public continued to vary depending partly upon social class and partly upon incidents that brought police and public into contact or brought the police publicity. Across Europe the police were the first and often the only public institution to be deployed during economic and industrial unrest. Many senior policemen were suspicious of organized labour but, at the same time, they could see the value of neutrality in industrial trouble. As early as September 1832 the Prefect of Police in Paris pointed this out in one of his daily bulletins:

For the moment police action with reference to these workers' coalitions is limited to an unobserved surveillance and I think that this is the only suitable role unless material disorder should render repressive measures necessary. It seems to me *essential* to interfere as little as possible in the debates between masters and men. The administration cannot take the side of either without exciting protest and without the risk of making enemies among men who appear to have no ill intentions under the current political situation. The stopping of labour in a workshop and a coalition of workers is, without doubt, a problem; but the principal aim of the administration and even of justice should be to impede any worsening of the problem.[6]

The problem was that industrial disorders always had the potential for violence, especially if they dragged on for a long while. Frustrated strikers might seek to coerce employers by attacking their plant. Frustrated employers

---

[6] Quoted in Jean Tulard, *La Préfecture de Police sous la Monarchie de Juillet*, Paris: Imprimerie Muncipale, 1964, 94.

might seek to have strikers evicted from company housing. In an extended strike, as men wavered or even went back to work, the more determined strikers might seek to coerce the waverers and punish those who broke ranks. Finally, an employer's decision to recruit strike-breaking labour provided another potential for violence as strikers clashed with the blacklegs. In all of these incidents the police were likely to be drawn in to protect property and individuals and, given who owned the property and which individuals were likely to be threatened or attacked, police participation invariably appeared partial.

Police neutrality was an excellent idea for developing good relations between the police and the different ranks of society. But the situation of economic power across Europe meant that it could easily be compromised. In the West Riding of Yorkshire, for example, one of the things that impeded the creation of a county police was the existence of the Worsted Police established and funded by factory owners. This force continued to function even after the county police was set up in 1856. The legislation of 1840 that enabled the magistrates of any county that so wished to establish a police also authorized the appointment of what were called additional constables. These men were indistinguishable from other police officers but they were paid for by private individuals or businesses and were stationed principally to protect the property of those funding them. The recruitment of such officers in the mid-century to police the navvies building the railways has already been mentioned. Others worked for docks and harbour boards and a few were involved with the protection of factories.[7] In Prussia some industrialists entered into arrangements with municipalities to pay the salaries of additional police officers who were to patrol in the vicinity of their business premises. Similar arrangements were also made directly with the central state in Berlin to have *gendarmerie* posts established in factories in return for taking over the costs of pay, pensions, and equipment. Even though this practice was ended in 1883, industrialists still angled for gendarmes to be stationed close by their works and provided them with a variety of privileges.[8] Elsewhere, notably in Italy and even more so in Spain, even the rhetoric of neutrality at times was ignored by both senior police officers and their

[7] Barry Godfrey, '"Private Policing and the Workplace": The Worsted Committee and the Policing of Labour in Northern England, 1840–1880', in Louis A. Knafla, ed., *Policing and War in Europe, CJH* 16 (2002), 87–106; Carolyn Steedman, *Policing the Victorian Community: The Formation of English Provincial Police Forces, 1856–1880*, London: Routledge and Kegan Paul, 1984, 145–6; and see above, p. 164.

[8] Spencer, *Police and the Social Order*, 48; Emsley, *Gendarmes and the State*, 221.

political masters. *Carabinieri*, PS guards, and especially the Civil Guard all acquired reputations for arbitrariness and violence towards protesting workers and peasantry. In Italy, from the turn of the century, there was a change towards a greater use of moderation and mediation. But there were no such moves in Spain, where the Civil Guard was fully integrated with the army, where the army was increasingly relied upon to preserve public order, and where an insult by a civilian to a Civil Guard became an offence punishable under military law.[9] In Russia there appears to have been no notion of police neutrality. In Moscow, for example, thirteen police officers were assigned to factories where they were to 'observe the workers and the appearance among them of any ill-intentioned and trouble-making people with the object of preventing any disorders, disturbances, and strikes which might arise among them'.[10]

Police orders everywhere continued to require that they suppress rowdy and indecorous behaviour in the streets, at fairs or rural festivals. Such behaviour commonly involved the working class and the peasantry and, again, did little for police popularity among these groups. In Berlin from the turn of the century to the outbreak of war in 1914 it has been estimated that 40 per cent of street disorder, usually involving young men on warm summer nights, was directed against the police. At the same time, however, about 13 per cent of such disorder was directed against different kinds of criminal offender, sometimes in the absence of police but sometimes specifically in their support.[11] As members of families and, increasingly, as owners of property, the working class and the peasantry had a claim on the police roles as crime fighters, as the guardians of public safety on the streets, and as the men who might resolve a neighbourhood argument or punish unruly children. Moreover it was not unknown for some members of the respectable classes to experience rough and coercive behaviour on the part of the police. This appears to have been especially the case in Prussia where there was a plethora of rules and regulations involving different aspects of life and all of which were enforced by the police. In addition, in both state rhetoric and police training manuals there was little recognition that the citizen had any rights and especially where

---

[9] Jonathan Dunnage, *The Italian Police and the Rise of Fascism: A Case Study of the Province of Bologna*, Westport, Conn: Praeger, 1997, chs. 2 and 3; Adrian Schubert, *A Social History of Modern Spain*, London: Routledge, 1990, 178–82.

[10] Quoted in Thurston, 'Police and People in Moscow', 326.

[11] Thomas Lindenberger, *Straßenpolitik: Zur Sozialgeschichte der öffentlichen Ordnung in Berlin, 1900 bis 1914*, Bonn: Dietz, 1995, 121–49.

police action was involved.[12] In the years immediately before the First World War both big business and the Social Democratic Party agreed that there should be a new kind of police officer on the streets, a police officer who was non-military and who combined a variety of skills derived from judges, teachers, and even philanthropists and good Samaritans.[13] Liszt and the German branch of the *Internationale Kriminalistische Vereiningung* included the police in those elements of the German criminal justice system in need of reform and, at the turn of the century, they commissioned a study of the police in England where relations with the police appeared much better.[14]

The British Home Office considered Dr Carl Budding's book to be 'accurate', 'interesting and satisfactory'.[15] In England the deployment of police in industrial disorders and in some political demonstrations brought accusations of brutality. The old concerns about militarization surfaced from time to time, and especially between 1886 and 1888 when General Sir Charles Warren was Commissioner of the Metropolitan Police. Failure in major cases like the Ripper murders brought criticism, even mockery—'the defective police'. But in general the articulate members of the political nation celebrated the Bobby as a unique figure and central to the image of the model liberal, if unwritten, constitution. To such observers the Bobby was, quite simply, a member of 'the best police in the world'. This may have been an assertion rather than a claim capable of clear proof. Nevertheless, it was a claim that had potency at home and a general appeal to continental liberals who approved the concept of an unarmed, non-political police that respected rights and was not bound to enforce scores of pettifogging regulations.

Yet even if the idea of the Bobby was appealing, the interpretation of contemporary circumstances, probably combined with institutional inertia, fostered a general lack of commitment to introduce something similar. The attitude in Italy has already been mentioned. Not only did Italian Liberals think that their fellow Italians were not ready for *il Bobby inglese*, they also gave their police draconian powers. They talked of prevention (*prevenzione*) and in his study of the dangerous classes in Italy Giovanni Bolis argued that

[12] Anja Johansen, 'A Process of Civilisation? Legitimisation of Violent Policing in Prussian and French Police Manuals and Instructions, 1880–1914', *European Review of History* (forthcoming, 2007).
[13] Abrecht Funk, *Polizei und Rechsstaat: Die Entwicklung des staatlichen Gewaltmonopols in Preußen 1848–1914*, Frankfurt: Campus, 1986, 302–3.
[14] Carl Budding, *Die Polizei in Stadt und Land in Großbritannien*, Berlin: Guttentag, 1908.
[15] NA, HO 45.10352.148769, Memorandum on Dr. Budding's 'Police in Town and Country in Great Britain', A. B. Butler, 28 July 1908.

the quality of law enforcement might be gauged by how few arrests were made. But *prevenzione* meant rigorous and intrusive surveillance and it was backed up with the police authority to administer *ammonizione*, which was not simply a serious admonition but usually meant some severe restrictions being imposed on the personal freedom of the suspect. If the *ammonito* was unemployed he had five days to find work or to face a prison sentence. Any breach of the restrictions imposed could also lead to imprisonment. The *ammonizione* was widely used, and especially against the working classes and peasant groups. At the end of the 1870s perhaps as many as 100,000 were issued annually and in many instances their use appears to have been corrupt or sloppy. Yet while Italian governments periodically panicked when confronted with anarchist activity and popular disorder, and while they armed their police with extreme powers, the ideas of Liberalism still meant something. There was a serious commitment to the rule of law, to citizen's rights, and to individual freedoms and this was never mere window dressing.[16]

The manuals of the French police and the rhetoric of their political masters put greater emphasis on the rights of citizens than those in Germany.[17] But the French police, especially those in Paris, had acquired an unenviable reputation for roughness and brutality. In 1893 Louis Lépine was appointed Prefect of Police and he was determined to improve the quality of recruits, their behaviour on the streets, and hence their relations with the public.[18] Lépine's efforts, which were conducted with much publicity and also a welcome degree of success, were praised by the increasingly professional cadre of *commissaires*. Notable among these was M. L. Pélatant who, as *Commissaire central* in Grenoble, wrote a series of papers and published a 100-page pamphlet on the importance of the police role in society—'what it has been, what it is, and what it ought to be'. Pélatant acknowledged the French police's history of arbitrary authority, pushing people about, and injuring them. But those days, he insisted were past and had to stay in the past. 'It is important that, ultimately, the institution should appear to all what it truly is, and that it should never cease to be such—namely a wise

---

[16] Giovanni Bolis, *La polizia e le classi pericolose della società*, Bologna: Zanichelli, 1871, 19; see also Richard Oliver Collin, 'The Italian Police and Internal Security from Giolitti to Mussolini', D.Phil., Oxford University, 1983, 19–21; John A. Davis, *Conflict and Control: Law and Order in Nineteenth-Century Italy*, London: Macmillan, 1987, pp. 222–3, 245–6 and 249–50; Richard Bach Jensen, *Liberty and Order: The Theory and Practice of Italian Public Security Policy, 1848 to the Crisis of the 1890s*, New York: Garland, 1991.

[17] Johansen, 'A Process of Civilisation'.

[18] Jean-Marc Berlière, *Le Préfet Lépine: Vers la naissance de la police moderne*, Paris: Denoël, 1993.

and protective instrument, gentle and mild to the timid, formidable to the offender.'[19]

Rank-and-file police officers were also developing a professional identity. They were working-class men doing an unskilled job but required to behave, and to ensure that their families behaved as the respectable and skilled were considered to do. Whether or not the institution in which they served was military or municipal, they were subject to strict discipline and to tough, sometimes dangerous working conditions that required them to be out in all weathers. Professional journals, often eyed with suspicion by their superior officers and political masters, fostered the men's self-awareness and also provided organs for the discussion of common problems and complaints. There had been occasional manifestations of unrest over pay and conditions from relatively early on, but towards the end of the century policemen began taking steps towards forming trade unions.

While rank-and-file uniformed officers grumbled about their lot and contemplated unionization and while the academics of the new science of criminology argued about whether there was a criminal type and to what extent criminality was the result of nature or nurture, the figure of the criminal investigator began to acquire a new, eye-catching role. The investigator could be a police detective or a journalist. He was both real and fictional, and the lines between the two became blurred. From the 1880s especially a succession of detective police officers published thrilling memoirs describing the cases that they had solved during their careers and emphasizing the dangers as well as their skills, effectiveness, and dedication. Marie-François Goron, for example, former head of the Paris *Sûreté*, called the detectives an 'elite'; they were men who, for little remuneration, never queried 'nights under the stars' and 'dangerous missions'. Retired Detective Inspector Percy Smith wrote of men who were 'not unwilling slaves' to their job; of men for whom there were 'no such things as fixed hours or regular mealtimes.'[20] The popular press, especially in France, employed special correspondents (*envoyés spéciaux*) who delved into cases when the police were slow in giving details of evidence. At the same time a fictional genre developed with

[19] M. L. Pélatant, *Rapport sur la service de la police*, Grenoble: Imprimerie Générale, 1906, 14.

[20] Clive Emsley, 'From Ex-Con to Expert: The Police Detective in Nineteenth-Century France', and Haia Shpayer-Makov, 'Explaining the Rise and Success of Detective Memoirs in Britain', both in Clive Emsley and Haia Shpayer-Makov, eds., *Police Detectives in History, 1750–1950*, Aldershot: Ashgate, 2006, quotations at pp. 75 and 127. See also Paul Lawrence, '"Scoundrels and Scallywags, and Some Honest Men . . .": Memoirs and the Self-Image of French and English Policemen *c.*1870–1939', in Barry Godfrey, Clive Emsley, and Graeme Dunstall, eds., *Comparative Histories of Crime*, Cullompton: Willan Publishing, 2003.

police detectives, journalist investigators, and brilliant amateur sleuths, the most famous of which was Sherlock Holmes. This genre had some ancestry in the older traditions of ballads, broadsides, and chapbooks, but it was overwhelmingly modern and urban. The detective novels sometimes dealt with middle-class thieves and fraudsters, but the more populist serial novels and the press generally concentrated on violent crime by a professional underworld. The novels, if not the press stories, generally concluded with the highly intelligent, technical sleuth detecting the offender. In a reversal of the usual and expected relationship between fiction and the real world, Edmond Locard, who became the first head of the *Laboratoire de police criminelle* in France, publicly acknowledged a debt to Sherlock Holmes and, more particularly, to his creator Sir Arthur Conan Doyle. Locard urged his readers and students to recognize, as Holmes had shown, that every contact that an offender made with an object left a trace that might be detected and provide some clue. Non-violent, petty, and opportunist property crime remained the principal form of offending that came before the courts and that appeared in the published criminal statistics. But a cheap, fast-growing popular press knew what the public wanted to read and consequently offered its readers thrilling, sensational stories of true crime. Vicious crimes against the person, especially those that could be seen to have some sort of sexual connotation, were meat and drink to the popular press.[21]

It is difficult to assess whether or not violent crimes and sexual crimes were increasing, but the latter in particular appear to have become more and more of interest in the thinking of criminologists.[22] And more important, with respect to the general public, it made excellent copy and sold newspapers. Everywhere conservative and respectable critics condemned the expanding popular press for satisfying the demands of the uncultivated masses by providing them with squalid, sordid tales of crime and violence. Some of the radical and socialist press took a rather similar line, but the principal problem in their reading of the situation, was a capitalist system that produced stories designed to appeal to the worst in people. As the Madrid-based Marxist weekly *El Socialista* put it in 1894:

---

[21] Dominique Kalifa, *L'encre et le sang: récits de crimes et société à la Belle Époque*, Paris: Fayard, 1995, esp. pt. 1. For Locard's ideas see Edmond Locard, *L'enquête criminelle et les méthodes scientifiques*, Paris: Flammarion, 1920, and for one of his acknowledgements to Conan Doyle made in English, see idem, 'Dust and its Analysis: An Aid to Criminal Investigation', *Police Journal*, 1 (1928), 177–92.

[22] Peter Becker, *Verderbnis und Entartung: Eine Geschichte der Kriminologie des 19. Jahrhunderts als Diskurs und Praxis*, Göttingen: Vandenhoeck und Ruprecht, 2002, esp. ch. 5.

The uncultivated public, which constitutes the majority, wants to satisfy its unhealthy curiosity, and the press, more interested in business than in education of the people, satisfies its gross appetites by providing it with spiced-up fare.

Business interests oblige newspapers to cater to the public rather than to educate it; similarly, they oblige the reporter—who has to participate in a factory—to employ his mental energy in the confection of dishes which revolt his stomach and his conscience alike.[23]

It is a moot point as to whether reporters were revolted by what they wrote, but unquestionably the press fed a fascination with the sexual sadist. The British press, most notably, used the savage murders of Jack the Ripper in the autumn of 1888 to push back the frontiers of what was decent to report in terms of wounds and descriptions of the female body.[24] Also, at least from the middle of the century, the British press used foreign terms to describe violent criminals—they were 'thugs', employing the word for Indian bandits, or 'garotters', employing the Spanish technique of throttling. Where possible there was also an emphasis on the alien nature of violent criminality; such behaviour was seen as something unEnglish.[25] The Spanish press latched on to Lombroso's notions of atavism and to images of wild animals to describe Julián Garciá, accused of sodomizing and murdering a 3-year-old boy.[26] In France *Le Petit Journal* and *Le Petit Parisien* produced supplements and colour illustrations on notorious cases that involved 'monsters' or 'ogres' who had murdered women and children. Lurid crimes of passion, anarchist bombings, and the heroic deaths of gendarmes or police agents - 'victims of duty' - were equally popular.[27]

The popular press did not merely report crime to excite and secure its existing readership and sell more papers. It began also to use incidents and to structure sensational narratives so as to pursue political campaigns. *The Times* structured its reporting of the garrotting panic of the early 1860s so as to encourage parliament to endorse a greater use of flogging for violent

[23] Quoted in D. J. O'Connor, *Crime at Escorial: The 1892 Child Murder, the Press and the Jury*, San Francisco and London: International Scholars Publications, 1995, 22

[24] L. P. Curtis, Jnr., *Jack the Ripper and the London Press*, New Haven: Yale University Press, 2001.

[25] Clive Emsley, *Hard Men: Violence in England since 1750*, London: Hambledon, 2005, esp. 15–17.

[26] O'Connor, *Crime at El Escorial*, 121–2.

[27] Frédéric Chauvaud, 'Les figures du monstre dans la seconde moitié du XIX siècle', *Ethnologie française*, 21, 3 (1991), 243–53. See e.g. from *Le Petit Journal*, 'L'enfant martyr: Pauvre petit!!', 3 January 1897, and the follow-up 'L'affaire Grégoire: L'enfant martyr—trois monstres'; 'L' "ogresse" Jeanne Weber: Crime ou fatalité', 12 May 1907, and the follow-up 'Le dernier crime de l'ogresse', 24 May 1908; and various, 'Victime du devoir' 1 May, 1898, 29 January 1899, and 2 April 1899.

offenders.[28] Early in 1885 W. T. Stead, the editor of the *Pall Mall Gazette*, shocked his readers with four consecutive front-page articles headed 'The Maiden Tribute of Modern Babylon'. His aim was to expose the scale of child prostitution and pressurize parliament to raise the age of consent from 13 to 16 years. Stead's political aims were successful, though he was prosecuted and imprisoned for the abduction of the girl that he had purchased. In the short term, moreover, the story lost the newspaper money since he had his legal expenses, some shocked gentlemen's clubs refused to purchase future copies of the *Gazette*, and some news vendors refused to sell it at their railway station outlets.[29] A generation later *Le Petit Parisien* seized upon a series of violent incidents, particularly the rape and murder of 11-year-old Marthe Erbelding by Albert Soleilland, to launch a popular referendum on the death penalty. In part the referendum was a complex promotional scheme designed to boost the paper's already enormous sales. It appears also to have been structured to ensure a resounding vote against the abolition of the death penalty then being proposed in the National Assembly.[30]

The German newspapers, arguably, were rather more restrained than those in Britain and France. The assault and murder of 9-year-old Lucie Berlin in the working-class Berlin district of Wedding, however, not unlike the killing of Marthe Erbelding, was reported in lurid fashion across the Reich.[31] In Germany, even with crime stories, different newspapers selected their stories and described them with a clear bias towards their political and ideological persuasion. For the liberal press violence became ever more newsworthy as the nineteenth century gave way to the twentieth; while readers of the conservative press must have gained the impression that a violent threat—worker, socialist, Polish, Lithuanian, Jewish—lurked on every street corner. In German literature, as in the British, it was the foreigner who, whenever convenient, was emphasized as constituting the principal menace.[32]

---

[28] Rob Sindall, *Street Violence in the Nineteenth Century: Media Panic or Real Danger?*, Leicester: University of Leicester Press, 1990, esp. ch. 3.

[29] Deborah Gorham, '"The Maiden Tribute of Modern Babylon" Re-examined', *Victorian Studies*, 21 (spring 1978), 361–8; Judith Walkowitz, *City of Dreadful Delight: Narratives of Sexual Danger in Late-Victorian London*, Chicago: University of Chicago Press, 1992, 96–7 and 122–7.

[30] Jean-Marc Berlière, *Le crime de Soleilland: les journalistes et l'assassin*, Paris: Tallandier, 2003.

[31] Peter Fritzsche, 'Talk of the Town: The Murder of Lucie Berlin and the Production of Local Knowledge', in Peter Becker and Richard F. Wetzell, eds., *Criminals and their Scientists: The History of Criminology in International Perspective*, New York: Cambridge University Press, 2006. Fritzsche makes the point that the reporting, and subsequent investigation of the district in which the murder happened, served to challenge notions that 'criminals' were somehow significantly 'different'.

[32] Eric Johnson, *Urbanization and Crime: Germany 1871–1914*, Cambridge: Cambridge University Press, 1995, 55–95.

The city continued to be a significant focus for most worries about crime. As the *Deutsche Tageszeitung* put it, crime did better, 'much better, on the asphalt than in the fields . . . the rural population has kept itself much freer of the effeminate degeneration than have urban people, whose nerves are assaulted by so much that is wearing and corrosive.'[33] The city appeared especially dangerous by night and a cliché-ridden literary genre developed as different commentators, escorted by police guides, followed paths trodden by Dickens in mid-century London. They stepped into streets and alleyways which, by night, were occupied by a 'different' population, where gas lanterns 'flickered', 'sinister figures scurried', and 'unfortunate women' shunned the light.[34] It was in the city that the Ripper had found his victims, where Jean-Baptiste Troppmann had slaughtered the Kinck family—husband, pregnant wife, and six children. The Ripper's murders prompted the London press to engage in discussion of the wretchedness of the city's East End. In Budapest in 1885 Imre Balentic's savage murder of his mistress, Verona Végh, and her 8-year-old niece, prompted the press to embark on an exploration of the moral polarities of urban life, the problem of prostitution and the complexities of what constituted the criminal. Verona Végh was described by some as dangerous, since she prostituted herself outside the system of regulation established in the late 1860s, while others saw her as a victim of the hedonism of the privileged. Portrayals of Balentic himself ran the gamut from cruel and savage monster to mental deviant. During his trial he was stigmatized as a cannibal and a monster, but the court declared him to be insane and confined him in an asylum. When he died shortly afterwards a public autopsy revealed what was termed a 'biologically deformed brain'.[35]

Youth gangs began to be singled out as a threat, now with novel names. There had been a fascination with the dangerous native American in France dating back to the July Monarchy and the popularity of James Fenimore Cooper's novels. Arguably the respectable French bourgeois equated their situation, surrounded by the dangerous classes, with that of early white settlers in America. During the Mexican adventure of Napoleon III and his unfortunate nominee as Emperor of Mexico, Maximilian, the Apache came

---

[33] Quoted in Benjamin Carter Hett, 'The "Captain of Köpenick" and the Transformation of German Criminal Justice, 1891–1914', *Central European History*, 36, 1 (2003), 1–43; 34.

[34] Joachim Schlör, *Nights in the Big City: Paris, Berlin, London, 1840–1930*, London: Reaktion Books, 1998, 124–30.

[35] Mónica Mátay, 'The Slaughter of a Prostitute: Discourse on Femininity, Crime and Urban Degeneration in late Nineteenth-Century Budapest', IAHCCJ Colloquium, 'Crime and the Media', 4–5 June 2004.

to be singled out in the French popular mind for their pride, violence, and cruelty. At the turn of the century the name Apache began to be applied to violent offenders who were believed to lurk in parts of French cities ready to assault and rob the respectable.[36] In England, as elsewhere, the youth gang had a long pedigree and towards the end of the nineteenth century there were different names for such gangs—or the fanciful belief in such gangs—in different cities. There were the Peaky Blinders in Birmingham, the Scuttlers in Manchester and Salford, the High Rip in Liverpool, and gangs with a variety of names in London. Then, following a series of disorders over the August Bank Holiday of 1898 the London press picked upon the word 'hooligan'. The word appears to have been first popularized at the beginning of the 1890s in a music hall song by two Irish comedians.

> Oh, the Hooligans! Oh, the Hooligans!
> Always on the riot,
> Cannot keep them quiet,
> Oh, the Hooligans! Oh, the Hooligans!
> They are the boys
> To make a noise
> In our backyard.

There followed a panic about the gangs who allegedly assaulted policemen, loitered in the streets, abused passers-by, and attacked and robbed them. Most youth gangs appear to have been organized to fight similar gangs, to defend territory, personal honour, and girlfriends. The press perception, however, was different, stigmatizing the hooligan as a new and dangerous criminal phenomenon.[37] In Russia the popular press appropriated the term 'hooligan'. *Peterburgskii Listok* (the *Petersburg Sheet*) took upon itself an unspoken mission to describe the limits of acceptable and respectable behaviour for its readers. This encouraged the paper to highlight criminal behaviour and to seek to mould perceptions of what was happening in the city even when this incurred condemnation by, and fines from, the imperial censors. The Revolution of 1905, however, occasioned the virtual end of this censorship and the press, using statistics of increasing crime alongside its reporting of

---

[36] Dominique Kalifa, *Crime and Culture au XIXe siècle*, Paris: Perrin, ch. 2. The fullest and most penetrating analysis of the Apache phenomenon is C. Bettina Schmidt, *Jugendkriminalität und Gesellschaftskrisen: Umbrüche, Denkmodelle und Lösungsstrategien im Frankreich der Dritten Republik (1900–1914)*, Stuttgart: Franz Steiner Verlag, 2005.

[37] Geoffrey Pearson, *Hooligan: A History of Respectable Fears*, London: Macmillan, 1983, ch. 5; see also Andrew Davies, 'Youth Gangs, Masculinity and Violence in Late-Victorian Manchester and Salford', *Journal of Social History*, 32 (1998), 349–69.

lurid stories of violence and robbery on the streets, fed increasing fears about danger in the city.[38] Elsewhere at the turn of the century the fear of revolution led to a linkage between the criminal and the revolutionary. Foreign-born anarchists in London shot police officers and were besieged in Sidney Street by police and soldiers. In France the gang that clustered around Jules Bonnot, a mechanic, hijacked cars, robbed banks, shot police officers and anyone else who got in their way during a short criminal spree in and around Paris. Police and soldiers eventually caught up with them in a series of shoot-outs in the early summer of 1912. The *bande à Bonnot* was composed of native-born Frenchmen, but while most of them cannot be said to have been politically conscious in any meaningful sense they had developed close links with the circle responsible for the newspaper *L'Anarchie*.[39]

In Italy too there were fears about anarchists and revolutionaries and growing concerns about the new urban working class, but the countryside also continued to be seen as dangerous, particularly the *Mezzogiorno* and the islands of Sardinia and Sicily. To the literate urban dweller the peasant was romantically picturesque, but also wolfish and dangerous. Illustrations of shoot-outs with brigands filled the illustrated press, often in bright colours. In February 1914 the deputy prefect of Barletta lamented that the population that he supervised in Apulia was 'almost totally composed of impulsive peasants who have not yet evolved'.[40] If this smacked of Lombroso's ideas it was not surprising since Lombroso had been happy to popularize his thinking for a non-academic audience. In 1902, for example, following the capture of a notorious Calabrian brigand, Giuseppe Musolino, he published an article in the widely circulated popular magazine *Nuova Antologica*. On the basis only of photographs that he had seen, Lombroso explained how Musolino's face manifested all the signs of anatomical degeneration.[41] But this was not the only contemporary perception of Musolino.

As late as the beginning of the twentieth century brigands like Musolino could sometimes attract a degree of popular sympathy and be the subjects

[38] Joan Neuberger, *Hooliganism: Crime, Culture, and Power in St. Petersburg, 1900–1914*, Berkeley: University of California Press, 1993.
[39] Benjamin F. Martin, *Crime and Criminal Justice under the Third Republic: The Shame of Marianne*, Baton Rouge: Louisiana State University Press, 1990, 275–317.
[40] Quoted in Frank M. Snowden, *Violence and Great Estates in the South of Italy: Apulia, 1900–1922*, Cambridge: Cambridge University Press, 1986, 141.
[41] Mary Gibson, 'Science and Narrative in Italian Criminology, 1880–1920', in Amy Gilman Srebnick and René Lévy, eds., *Crime and Culture: An Historical Perspective*, Aldershot: Ashgate, 2005, 40–2.

of popular folk songs in the communities from which they came. Even the London *Times* picked up on Musolino's reputed Robin Hood-like image: 'He never robbed, generally paid for what he took, often did generous deeds and sometimes acted as executioner of other brigands who had presumed to rob peasants in his name. While he was at large, ordinary crime in Calabria is reported to have declined by 50 per cent.'[42] In Andalusia it was the same. Here an impoverished peasantry were squeezed more and more in a monoculture run by landowners on ever-expanding *latifunda*. The landowners had no inclination to modernize their estates so long as they could rely on cheaper and cheaper peasant labour. The peasantry responded with occasional local uprisings that were directed against a proprietor's property, and that were brutally suppressed. One such uprising, in the early 1880s, provoked a more widespread panic around fears of a national, even international, peasant-anarchist/socialist insurrection.[43] More constant than the occasional uprisings was the problem of banditry that also fed on the misery and desperation of the peasantry. While it would be wrong to see the bandits as Robin Hood figures, they were often regarded sympathetically by the peasantry, as was reflected in the popular saying: *Gracias a Dios que los bandidos roban para todos* (Thank God that the bandits rob for the benefit of all).[44] For many years even the tough, military police, the Civil Guard, was undermined by local political bosses in Anadalusia. These bosses often used bandits for their own purposes and protected them. It seems to have been similar in parts of Extremadura where the landowners' strong-arm men administered brutal and sometimes lethal summary punishment on offending labourers. If the Civil Guard did begin to have some impact on banditry towards the end of the nineteenth and at the beginning of the twentieth centuries, this, in turn, was undermined in the peasants' perception by the Guard's role in suppressing the peasants' own protest.[45]

---

[42] Gaetano Cingari, *Brigantaggio Proprietari e Contadini nel Sud (1799–1900)*, Reggio Calabria: Editori Meridionali Riunti, 1976, 211–12; *The Times*, 26 Oct. 1901, 15.

[43] Glen A. Waggoner, 'The Black Hand Mystery: Rural Unrest and Social Violence in Southern Spain, 1881–1883', in Robert J. Bezucha, ed., *Modern European Social History*, Lexington, Mass.: D. C. Heath, 1972.

[44] Henk Driessen, 'The "Noble Bandit" and the Bandits of the Nobles: Brigandage and Local Community in Nineteenth-Century Andalusia', *Archives Européenes de Sociologie*, 24 (1983), 96–114; idem, 'Heroes and Villains: Images of Bandits and Banditry in Nineteenth-Century Andalusia', in Gherardo Ortalli, ed., *Bande armate, banditi, banditismo e repressione di giustizia negli stati Europei di antico regime*, Rome: Jouvence, 1986, 191.

[45] Dreissen, 'The "Noble Bandit" ', 109; Martin Baumeister, *Arme 'campesinos': Überleben und Widerstand in der Extramadura 1880 bis 1923*, Berlin: Duncker und Humblot, 1994, 154–6.

Elsewhere the passage of time continued to lead to significant distortions in the history of individual bandits. Jean Pélot had been a singularly nasty individual. At the beginning of the nineteenth century he appears to have been implicated in an arson attack on a Gascon neighbour. Thereafter he, his siblings, and a group of friends were involved in a succession of progressively more serious offences culminating in violent attacks on houses and rape. In April 1816, following a shoot-out with the *Gendarmerie*, Pélot had died of his wounds in the prison at Tarbes while awaiting execution. Yet, forty years later, in his native Gascony he had been transformed into a mythical hero resisting the encroachments of the state based faraway in Paris. So much so, in fact, that a functionary in one of the courts in Tarbes thought it important enough to publish a short history to counter 'the incorrect versions that daily and for a long time [made Pélot] a noble soul who pushed his generosity even to the extent of giving up everything to aid humanity'.[46] On the other side of Europe a Hungarian bandit, Jóska Sobri, went through a variety of transformations. Unlike Pélot, it seems possible that there was an element of the Robin Hood or at least of the showman about the original Sobri. This is reflected in his band's dramatic raid on Hunkár Castle in December 1836. The castle was the home of a pompous, retired military officer who had served in the wars against Napoleon and the raid led to a determined manhunt by young noblemen and police. Sobri's band was wiped out when its pursuers caught up with it in some woods in February 1837. Sobri was reported to have killed himself rather than be taken, but there was no autopsy and no registration of his death, both of which helped to feed the myth. Within a decade Sobri was a romantic national hero who had challenged Habsburg law and domination. He was also, to the authorities, a barbarous descendant of Attila's Huns, and this image was taken up in elements of the foreign press that portrayed Hungary as an exotic land where the bandits made a point of robbing and killing travellers from abroad. Following the *Ausgleich* of 1867 that established the dual monarchy of Austria-Hungary the image of Sobri as a Hungarian hero became dominant. He was now credited with loyalty to the king as well as being the enemy of traditional enemies of the people such as 'the shark Jews'.[47]

---

[46] José Ramón Cubero, *Pélot: 'bandit d'honneur'. Un clan Gascon face au pouvoir central, 1800–1816*, Toulouse: Privat, 1992, 19.

[47] Mónika Mátay and György Csepeli, 'The Multiple Lives of the Hungarian Highwayman', in Amy Gilman Srebnick and René Lévy, eds., *Crime and Culture: An Historical Perspective*, Aldershot: Ashgate, 2005. The reference to 'shark Jews' is from Imre Sárosy, *Sobri Jóska a bakonyi rablóvezér* (Jóska Sobri the Brigand Leader of the Bakony), Budapest, 1903.

Bandits in the nineteenth-century Balkans had begun to acquire the trappings of national heroes in the struggle for independence from the Ottomans. It was a shock for the Philhellenes who travelled to fight for Greek independence when, instead of noble warriors resembling Achilles and Alexander, they came across the shaggy, bearded, brutal peasants and shepherds who switched from *klefts* and *armatoloi* to the military muscle of the insurgency. But as the newly independent states spread their authority, so the way of life that supported the bandit came under threat. In Greece, for example, independence put a new frontier across the land that the migratory shepherds, from whom many bandits came, were used to travelling. With the frontier came state officials demanding passports and various financial payments and taxes. There was a growth in cultivated holdings and the Greek state was determined to bring order to its advancing periphery. The political situation remained fraught for many years and irredentist dreams led to the border regions becoming militarized. This enabled some bandits to hire themselves out as guards to caravans and merchants that wanted to smuggle goods across the frontiers. It also allowed the bandits to sign up as irregulars, crossing into Ottoman territory to stir up unredeemed Greeks and fighting the Albanian irregulars sent in the other direction by the Ottomans. By the beginning of the twentieth century the bandit of the mountains in continental Greece was disappearing, though his presence continued to be both an embarrassment and a headache for the authorities well into the inter-war period.[48]

Moving from shepherd bandits to horse thieves, it is a semantic point as to whether organized gangs of horse thieves can properly be called bandits or brigands. In many parts of rural Europe towards the end of the nineteenth century the horse remained a vital draught animal. The theft of horses could have a serious effect on a community. At the same time the theft of horses was profitable for those who undertook it, especially in border areas where the animals could easily be sold off across a frontier. In Russia horse thieves sometimes operated in large gangs; sometimes they were in league with the few, poorly paid police; sometimes they were in league with a peasant village, or demanded protection money from villages. But a horse thief, caught by villagers who had no faith in the police and legal system, could be savagely

[48] John S. Koliopoulos, *Brigands with a Cause: Brigandage and Irredentism in Modern Greece, 1821–1912*, Oxford: Clarendon Press, 1987; for the inter-war period see the brief comments in Mark Mazower, 'Policing the Anti-Communist State in Greece, 1922–1974', in Mark Mazower, ed., *The Policing of Politics in the Twentieth Century: Historical Perspectives*, Providence, RI: Berghahn Books, 1997, 134–7.

and cruelly killed.[49] Other suspects might also be dispatched brutally by the community. In January 1879 Agrafena Ignat'eva, known as Grushka, who lived in a village in the province of Novgorod, was suspected by her neighbours of making many of her fellow villagers ill with a spell. The community responded by sealing her up in her house and burning it down. Sure that they had done the right thing, but possibly sensing that there might be repercussions, the villages sent 22 roubles to a local official requesting that he forget the case. He refused. Sixteen villagers were tried before a local court; the three that confessed were given a church penance while the others went free. *Samosud,* as popular peasant justice was called, was often less violent than the punishment inflicted on Grushka. It commonly took the form of a charivari with a criminal offender paraded and shamed through the village.[50] There were many in Russia who dismissed such behaviour as primitive, barbaric lynch law. But it remained a custom-based counter-narrative to the more refined and restrained forms of legal process and punishment lauded and advocated by the educated classes. And it was not greatly different from the justice that had been, and in some instances continued to be, meted out in other communities across Europe.[51]

Significant legal and penal reforms were carried out in Russia in the wake of peasant emancipation in 1861, but they took a unique form. The educated, city-dwelling elite were keen to establish their credentials as Europeans and considered the continuing and extensive use of corporal punishment as anachronistic, barbarous, and reflecting badly on their country. The law of 17 April 1863 abolished branding and considerably reduced the availability of various forms of whipping as punishments. The intention was to establish a prison system similar to that elsewhere in Europe, though exile for members of the elite and the gentry, and *katorga* for everyone else, were also maintained as options.[52] At the heart of the legal reform was the provision of trial by jury with jury selection based on a very broad franchise. Conservative critics protested that this would introduce mob rule not least because the ordinary people lacked the moral and intellectual development necessary for the role of jurors. As the system bedded down the well-to-do learned how to avoid

[49] Christine D. Worobec, 'Horse Thieves and Peasant Justice in Post-Emancipation Russia', *Journal of Social History,* 21 (1981), 281–93.

[50] Stephen P. Frank, 'Popular Justice, Community and Culture among the Russian Peasantry, 1870–1900', *Russian Review,* 46, 3 (1987), 239–65; 239–40 for the story of Grushka.

[51] John Carter Wood, *Violence and Crime in Nineteenth-Century England: The Shadow of Our Refinement,* London: Routledge, 2004, traces the fading of such customary behaviour in England.

[52] Bruce F. Adams, *The Politics of Punishment: Prison Reform in Russia 1863–1917,* DeKalb: University of North Illinois Press, 1996, 33.

what they considered to be a burdensome task and, in consequence, the overwhelming majority of jurors were drawn from the peasantry. Again the critics protested. Not only were the peasants poor, often having great difficulty surviving in the towns where they had to travel for the duration of trials, but the juries also acquitted large numbers of those brought before them. The authorities became so concerned at this that they removed juries from trials for offences against the state. However, when statistics began to be collected and published in the final decade of the century, the evidence suggested that while the Russian juries might have been acquitting rather more than their equivalents elsewhere, they followed very similar patterns in the way that they convicted for types of crimes. Supporters of the jury argued that it would teach peasants respect for the law and would help them develop a proper sense of justice.[53] But at the same time that the jury system was introduced, together with new public courts, judges, and lawyers, the Tsarist state made a move very different from developments in the West.

While some of the reformers pointed to legal systems in the West and while the changes of the mid-1860s included many of the institutions and personnel to be found in the West, the Tsarist state authorized the development of a two-tier court and legal system. As described in previous chapters, princes and governments in the west of Europe had long been jealous of alternative power structures. Towards the end of the old regime the princes had hedged the powers of feudal and church courts; the process was extended in the early nineteenth century. More and more the courts of the state became the only legitimate courts functioning within national or imperial boundaries within Europe. With the emancipation of the peasantry in 1861 the Tsarist regime abolished the judicial powers of the gentry and landlords but, recognizing the potential cost and complexity, it was unwilling, and probably felt itself unable, to establish the new legal system across the entire Russian Empire. The solution was to legitimate elements of peasant justice by incorporating them into the state's more refined and restrained system. The *volost'* was the lowest unit of administration in rural areas. It usually included several villages with a total adult population of between 300 and 2,000. Under the reforms of the 1860s *volost'* courts, presided over by emancipated serfs, were authorized to hear petty cases both criminal and civil and to pass verdicts according to local tradition.[54] The *volost'* courts could

53 John W. Atwell Jnr., 'The Russian Jury', *Slavonic and East European Review*, 53 (1975), 44–61.
54 Jane Burbank, 'A Question of Dignity: Peasant Legal Culture in Late Imperial Russia', *Continuity and Change*, 10, 3 (1995), 391–404.

order up to twenty strokes of the birch for a male peasant offender and, in general, the peasantry appears to have favoured corporal punishment over fines and imprisonment. Anatole Leroy-Beaulieu, a French traveller, noted how popular beatings remained as a punishment with those elders who acted as judges in the peasant courts. Other difficult offenders were sent into the army, and this, like the exiles decreed by the higher courts, could amount to a life sentence in Imperial Russia.[55] Legal reformers were critical of the *volost'* courts and so too were some of the men who served in them as clerks, rural lawyers, or justices of the peace. The critics with first-hand knowledge wrote of intimidation and of the well-to-do buying verdicts with supplies of vodka.[56] In the end the *volost'* courts provided little basis for transforming the peasant into a citizen, and they appeared too often to adjudicate according to the wishes of local men of influence and to maintain the traditions of *samosud*.

Russian peasants were also left much to their own devices with regard to policing. The Imperial *Gendarmerie* was closely tied to the political policing requirements of the Third section of the Imperial Chancellery. It was never in a position to make the regular rural patrols of its namesakes in the West. The post of constable (*stanovoi pristav*) had been established for rural areas in 1837 and a body of sergeants (*uriàdniki*) was created to assist them in 1879. The latter took their name from *uriàd*, meaning order. But in 1900, for a rural population approaching 90 million, there were only about 1,500 constables and 7,000 sergeants. Leroy-Beaulieu considered the *uriàdniki* to be a failure and reported how, among the peasantry, their name was corrupted to *kuriàtniki* or chicken stealers, a reflection of the reputation that they acquired for dishonesty and graft.[57] After emancipation village policemen were no longer the landowner's appointee but were drawn from the local community, and sometimes they appear to have played integral parts in the various forms of ritual and shaming punishment that were part of *samosud*.[58] In 1903 the government attempted to put a central presence in villages with the creation of a state guard of 40,000 men. But there was confusion about the best

[55] Adams, *The Politics of Punishment*, 33 and 37–8; Anatole Leroy-Beaulieu, *The Empire of the Tsars and the Russians*, 3 vols., New York: Putnam, 1902, ii. 278–9; Rodney D. Bohac, 'The Mir and the Military Draft', *Slavic Review*, 47 (1988), 652–66.
[56] Cathy A. Frierson, *Peasant Icons: Representations of Rural People in Late Nineteenth-Century Russia*, New York and Oxford: Oxford University Press, 1993, 71–4.
[57] Weissman, 'Regular Police in Tsarist Russia', 46–9; Leroy-Beaulieu, *The Empire of the Tsars*, ii. 122–4.
[58] Frank, 'Popular Justice, Community and Culture', 247.

method of deployment until the rural unrest of 1906 saw them turned into mounted squadrons designed for punitive action.[59]

Elsewhere in Europe, at times even members of the elite military police decided that the best policy was to fit in with the local community. In the Royal Irish Constabulary this system of live and let live became known as 'home rule', a satirical reference to the political campaign for at least some degree of autonomy for the Irish. At the same time, as noted earlier, there were some state policemen took a stand against the community where they were stationed and courageously enforced the state's law, sometimes protecting individuals from the wrath of an angry crowd, such as violent, and hence 'unnatural', parents.[60] Some offences, poaching for example, continued to receive a degree of community sanction, making investigation and suppression difficult for the police when faced with a wall of silence and even deliberate obstruction.[61] But there was an alternative viewpoint. When it was suggested that, since there appeared to be relatively little crime in Wales, then the major courts should be centralized away from county towns, S. H. Parry Jones raised another significant issue about rural communities that preserved their own language. Centralization, Parry Jones warned, might make men less likely to prosecute since the trial would be away from their locality where they knew no one and where a different language was spoken. In addition, he suggested, there was the fear of being bullied by lawyers and treated as a simpleton by judges when far from any kind of community support.[62]

Small and not so small communities also still rejected the ways in which the authorities wanted to deal with an offence or offender and acted in accordance with their own fears and assumptions. On occasions such popular reaction compelled the authorities to act in a manner about which they had reservations. During the 1890s there was a wave of accusations about Jews ritually slaughtering young gentiles. The Association against Anti-Semitism based in Berlin counted seventy-nine such between 1891 and 1900 and, in addition, there were others planted in the press by anti-Semitic politicians that brought no popular response. Almost half of the accusations were in the Austro-Hungarian Empire; around a fifth were in Germany. In the Rhenish town of Xanten a local Jewish butcher, Adolf Buschoff, was blamed when a

59 Weissman, 'Regular Police in Tsarist Russia', 50–1.
60 See above pp. 169–70; see also *Le Petit Journal*, 30 May 1897, 'Parents dénaturés'.
61 Regina Schulte, *The Village in Court: Arson, Infanticide, and Poaching in the Court Records of Upper Bavaria, 1848–1910*, Cambridge: Cambridge University Press, 1994, pt. III.
62 S. H. Parry Jones, 'Crime in Wales', *Red Dragon*, 3, 1 (1883), 522–30; 528–9.

five-year-old boy was found with his throat cut. Popular agitation, whipped up by local anti-Semites, forced the authorities to arrest Buschoff. He was released for lack of evidence but renewed agitation forced his re-arrest and trial. Buschoff was acquitted, but he and most of the Jews resident in the town thought it best to leave.[63] But popular reactions to offences were not simply, and not predominantly, reflections of anti-Semitism. In Don Benito, Extremadura, for example, in the summer of 1902 a notoriously dissolute young nobleman and his friend attempted to rape a young woman. The assault ended with the murder of both the woman and her mother. The nobleman was the scion of a powerful local family and the local community mobilized to ensure that he was arrested and tried in Don Benito. The community also compelled the local priest who heard the accused's confession to break the tradition of secrecy. Following the conviction of the accused the community tried, unsuccessfully, to ensure that the executions be held in public, but crowds forced their way into the prison yard to view the bodies once the two offenders were executed and to ensure that the sentence had been carried out.[64]

Some communities might also simply reject the state's law at least with respect to certain offences. Ireland provides a good example here with respect to the indigenous population's acceptance of the English law regarding property rights. At certain times aspects of this law became unenforceable, even when in theory it was given additional sanction by the criminal law.[65] Some magistrates decided against prosecutions for certain rural disturbances on the grounds that they would fail because of a lack of witnesses and partial juries. They believed that a failed prosecution would do only damage and discredit the law still further. But while some among the authorities considered that not pressing the law was the most sensible way ahead, some of the rural activists adapted some of the forms of the state's law to their own purposes. Mass poaching and 'people's hunts' were ways of challenging the right of landowners to ride across the fields of tenant farmers while, at the same time, insisting on the protection of hares, rabbits, and game birds on their own land. It was also known for some of the more violent

[63] Helmut Walser Smith, *The Butcher's Tale: Murder and Anti-Semitism in a German Town*, New York: W. W. Norton, 2002, 123 and 127–32. The main focus of Smith's book is another murder in Konitz, West Prussia, in March 1900, where serious rioting followed the discovery of a dismembered high school student and subsequent accusations of ritual slaughter.

[64] Baumeister, *Arme 'campesinos'*, 178–80.

[65] Both the Prevention of Crime (Ireland) Act of 1882 and the Criminal Law and Procedure (Ireland) Act of 1887 sought to use criminal sanctions to prevent boycotting and both signally failed.

protesters to establish their own, alternative courts where land agents and similar 'offenders' were tried in their absence and condemned. Notices of the verdicts of such alternative courts were then publicly posted to advise a convicted individual and others of the verdict according to the popular law.[66]

It is difficult to assess the extent of this rejection or bypassing of the state's functionaries and laws at the close of the nineteenth century. Almost certainly it was much less significant than it had been a hundred years earlier. Many may have remained suspicious of the state, especially in remote rural areas and in stigmatized slum districts in the cities, but the promise of protection and of the pursuit and prosecution of offenders at the state's expense had an attraction even in such areas. Police officers, jurists, and those who presided in the courts appear to have maintained the belief that criminals came from the poorer sections of society. But criminals, at least those thought capable of reform, were now considered to need the treatment of medical penal experts rather than a Bible and the encouragement to acquire a work ethic. These ideas, together with others gleaned from the conclusions of the new criminal anthropologists, fostered new sentencing policies and penal reforms as the twentieth century dawned. Such ideas still followed the progressive ideals and rational assumptions of the Enlightenment, though the political events of the first half of the new century were seriously to dent such ideals and assumptions.

[66] Heather Laird, *Subversive Law in Ireland, 1879–1920: From 'Unwritten Law' to the Dáil Courts*, Dublin: Four Courts Press, 2005.

PART V

THE FACES OF PENAL WELFARE

12

Penal Policies and the Impact of War

ACROSS much of Europe in the generation before the First World War the ideas of the new science of criminology began to filter down into court practice and into legislation. Although the criminologists argued amongst themselves, especially over heredity and environment, the ideas led to a shift away from the classical school of Beccaria that had sought a system of punishments designed to fit the crime regardless of the social rank of the offender, to a perspective that advocated individual punishment designed to fit the specific offender. The shift was as much to be found in liberal Britain as it was in the more authoritarian Imperial Germany. And while there were moves towards the lengthy incarceration of recidivists and the discussion of eugenics policies, there were also new moves to moderate punishment and to encourage the reformation of offenders. This emerging system, characterized by David Garland as 'penal welfarism', assumed that social reform and economic improvement would eventually bring about a reduction in crime. It built on the developments of the eighteenth and nineteenth centuries and took it as axiomatic that the modern state had, first, a contractual obligation to ensure the security of law-abiding citizens, and second, was responsible not only for the punishment and control of offenders but also for their care and rehabilitation. In each case the state's responsibility was a specialist undertaking entrusted to professional experts.[1]

Societies can be schizophrenic and such was the case with many European societies at the end of the nineteenth and beginning of the twentieth centuries. On the one hand there was a continuing belief in progress and an assurance that European civilization, however fragmented, was at the forefront of this. But, at the same time, there were prophets of doom. In 1886 Richard von Krafft-Ebing published *Psycopathia Sexualis* cataloguing sexual aberrations and warning of their potential for the material and moral ruin of societies.

---

[1] David Garland, *Punishment and Welfare: A History of Penal Strategies*, Aldershot: Gower, 1985. The thrust of Garland's work, however, is Anglo-American.

Six years later Max Nordau published *Entartung*, a sensational diagnosis of European civilization's degeneration that was dedicated to Lombroso, rapidly translated (as *Degeneration* in English) and avidly read and debated across the continent. These books, and Krafft-Ebing and Nordau, were merely the tip of a very large iceberg, and fed concerns within the most powerful states of Europe for what was understood as the national stock or race. Public scandals such as the trial of Oscar Wilde and revelations about homosexual activity among the Kaiser's entourage became indicators for some of decadence and decline at the highest levels. The urban working class appeared to many to be enfeebled by its slum existence and it was feared also to be lurching towards socialism. The link between revolution and crime continued to be made with the new ideologies of anarchism and socialism superimposed upon existing fears and blurring the distinctions still further. Lombroso, and one of his collaborators Rodolfo Laschi, however, sought to differentiate between the honest idealists behind genuine revolutions, such as the *Risorgimento*, and the political delinquents who attempted sedition and revolt. Here they found common ground with their French contemporaries.[2] Feminism appeared to be threatening respectable womanhood, and some of its critics considered that greater female emancipation and independence were forcing women away from their vital maternal duties and encouraging them into crime. In assessing the scale of crime and 'debauchery' in Paris, Charles Desmaze considered it relevant to publish the statistics of the number of women that had achieved university degrees between 1870 and 1878.[3] Some commentators took heart from what appeared to be declining statistics of crime. But there were also pessimists who put more gloomy interpretations on the figures, lamenting that crime was not going away, that there seemed to be a hard core of irredeemable criminals, and that large numbers of juveniles, especially young men, continued to commit offences.

In Britain concerns about how to handle the incorrigible offender had come to the fore in the middle of the nineteenth century when, faced with increasing criticisms and objections from the Australian colonists,

---

[2] Cesare Lombroso and Rodolfo Laschi, *Il delitto politico e le rivoluzioni in rapporto al diritto, all'antropologia criminale ed alla scienza di governo*, Turin: Baccu, 1890. For the French response and concern about the criminal-anarchist see Robert A. Nye, *Crime, Madness and Politics in Modern France: The Medical Concept of National Decline*, Princeton: Princeton University Press, 1984, 178–80.

[3] Lucia Zedner, *Women, Crime, and Custody in Victorian England*, Oxford: Clarendon Press, 1991, 68–73; Ann-Louise Shapiro, *Breaking the Codes: Female Criminality in Fin-de-Siècle Paris*, Stanford Calif.: Stanford University Press, 1996,. 205–16. Desmaze's book, published in 1881, was called *Le crime et la débauche à Paris: le divorce*.

transportation ceased to be an option. A succession of acts of parliament sought to maintain surveillance of offenders released from prison and to control those who became labelled as 'habitual offenders'. The Habitual Criminals' Act of 1869 shifted the burden of proof from the accuser to the accused where former offenders, notably those on parole with what was called a ticket of leave, became liable to a year's imprisonment if a police officer could convince a magistrate sitting summarily that the offender was behaving 'suspiciously'. But the system of surveillance, with its registration and identification requirements, also produced more information on recidivists and served to emphasize the problem. Governments continued to revisit the problem, always arguing that the innocent had nothing to fear even though evidence was presented time and again of the problems of getting and maintaining a job that were faced by individuals released from prison and subject to police surveillance. The Prevention of Crime Act of 1908 moved on further the policy against habitual offenders (the term 'professionals' was used in the debates) by the creation of preventive detention. This enabled the higher courts to impose a discretionary sentence of preventive detention of not less than five and not more than ten years on such an offender. Release was to be at the discretion of an advisory board.[4]

While the British government had given up transportation, and while Imperial Germany specifically rejected it as a policy, other states maintained it and pushed it in new directions. The Tsarist courts continued to exile a few offenders each year to the wastes of Siberia. In Italy forced domicile (*domicilio coatto*) was used for a variety of offenders. This involved administrative detention and exile to a region or to a penal settlement far from the offender's home. A cluster of penal settlements was established, but without full legal status, on various islands scattered off the Italian coast. By the mid-1890s some 5,000 persons were being held in this way on the islands around Sicily alone.[5] The Napoleonic Code had reserved transportation for political offenders in France but by the middle of the nineteenth century some of the perpetrators of serious non-political offences were also being shipped to penal settlements overseas. The growing awareness and growing fear of the recidivist led to new legislation in 1885. This authorized the transportation not only of those sentenced to hard labour for serious crimes, but now also

---

[4] Leon Radzinowicz and Roger Hood, *The Emergence of Penal Policy in Victorian and Edwardian England,* Oxford: Clarendon Press, 1990, ch. 8.
[5] John A. Davis, *Conflict and Control: Law and Order in Nineteenth-Century Italy,* London: Macmillan, 1988, 223–6.

of recidivists who were to be exiled to the penal colonies in New Caledonia or Guiana after they had served their prison sentence. Technically the law perceived a difference between the former, still called *bagnards*, and the latter, labelled *rélégués*, though, apart from them being placed in different camps, this appears to have meant little in practice. Proponents of the new act had spoken of removing some 5,000 recidivists from France annually as *rélégués*, but in the event the peak was never more than around 1,700 and that only briefly. In the decade before the First World War the annual number was about 500, roughly half the number of *bagnards*. After 1897 New Caledonia ceased to receive convict convoys, and after 1907 female recidivists were no longer transported.[6]

The fear of the recidivist, the extreme measures that this generated, and shrill demands for what in several countries was described as 'social defence' went side-by-side with liberal welfare measures designed to encourage the first-time offender and the juvenile away from stigmatization and a life of crime. The French legislation authorizing the transportation of recidivists, for example, was followed almost immediately by a liberal parole law. In the decade before the First World War a succession of legislatures came up with new laws to treat juvenile offenders as problem children rather than to punish them as young criminals. Some of the inspiration for this came from across the Atlantic, specifically from a law passed in Illinois in 1899 that applied to delinquent and neglected children in the suburbs of Chicago. But it built also upon a more general sensibility that was growing towards childhood. As a result of the new legislation children were increasingly kept out of the adult courts, and care was taken to ensure that, when a custodial sentence was deemed necessary, their education was entrusted to individuals with appropriate qualifications.[7] But not all of the new ideas were workable, not all of the juvenile institutions measured up to the standards hoped for, and for a variety of reasons the implementation of legislation could take time. Seven years after the passage of the 1907 law for developing the provision of reformatories in Italy there was still insufficient space for half of the

---

[6] Nye, *Crime, Madness and Politics*, 95–6; for the French penal colonies in general see Patricia O'Brien, *The Promise of Punishment: Prisons in Nineteenth-Century France*, Princeton: Princeton University Press, 1982, ch. 8.

[7] See e.g. Jenneke Christiaens, 'A History of Belgium's Child Protection Act of 1912: The Redefinition of the Juvenile Offender and his Punishment', *European Journal of Crime, Criminal Law and Criminal Justice*, 7, 1 (1999), 5–21; Ido Weijers, 'The Debate on Juvenile Justice in the Netherlands, 1891–1901', ibid. 65–78; Mary Gibson, 'The Criminalization of Youth in Late Nineteenth- and Early Twentieth-Century Italy', in Louis A. Knafla, ed., *Crime, Punishment and Reform in Europe CJH* 18 (2003), 121–44.

children and juveniles sentenced to reformatory education and supervision. In 1912 legislation was passed in France establishing new tribunals for cases against children together with a new system of punitive options for 13- to 18-year-olds. It was assumed, somewhat fancifully, that these tribunals would be able to differentiate easily between those who knew their actions to be wrong, hence deserving of punishment, and those who were innocent of such awareness. In Britain a new kind of detention centre was established for serious young offenders at Borstal in Kent in 1901. After seven years the experiment was considered a success and similar institutions were sanctioned elsewhere. But while the Borstal held out promise for the future, the industrial and reformatory schools to which children under 14 years had been sent since the days of Mary Carpenter were criticized for being old-fashioned and repressive, and for stunting the mental and moral growth of their charges.[8] In the courts, magistrates, judges, and jurors could be severe with the recidivist, but more and more they appear also to have taken the circumstances of an accused into consideration. In France the courts found a variety of ways to avoid transportation sentences for petty offenders. In Britain shorter prison sentences generated a fall in prison numbers. This may have contributed to the belief that crime was falling, and this, in turn, conceivably encouraged the shorter prison sentences. In 1907 a new practice was introduced that also reduced prison numbers. The Probation of Offenders Act was the first formal system of probation. Its intention was to keep first offenders, though not necessarily just first offenders, out of prison, to encourage reformation, and hence to prevent further criminal behaviour, by providing advice, assistance, and supervision.

Assumptions have commonly been made, particularly following the Nazi period when the idea of Germany's erroneous *Sonderweg* was popular, that the authoritarian nature of Imperial Germany fostered illiberal criminal policies. At the turn of the century conservatives in Germany were concerned about social and moral decline resulting from urbanization, industrialization, and the rise of mass society. These concerns led some to call for the use of corporal punishment as an antidote to violent crime. But such concerns were not unique to Germany, and while the rulers of Imperial Germany had been determined to ensure a place for capital punishment in their new criminal code, they did not insist on the restoration of flogging. In Liberal Britain, in contrast, flogging as a judicial punishment had been given a new lease

---

[8] Victor Bailey, *Delinquency and Citizenship: Reclaiming the Young Offender 1914–1948*, Oxford: Clarendon Press, 1987, 47–8 and 186–7.

of life during the Garrotting Panic of the early 1860s, and the number of offences liable to such sanction had been added to over the following thirty years or so.[9] Rather than being an exception, in the generation before the First World War Imperial Germany was in the mainstream of liberal penal sanctions and court decisions. Under the Kaiser's patronage an association for youth welfare (*Deutscher Zentralverein für Jugendfürsorge*) was set up and the Prussian government established a system of education for young offenders which, after a custodial sentence, saw such offenders sent out to selected families for training.[10] Defence counsel took an independent and assertive line. The courts were increasingly prepared to consider psychological and social factors as prompts to criminal behaviour and to respond with mild sentences. Both courts and government were increasingly prepared to take note of public opinion as mediated by the press. A particularly notable incidence of this is to be found in the lenient punishment handed down to Wilhelm Voigt, the so-called Captain of Köpenik, a petty offender who tricked soldiers into following him and assisting him in rifling a municipal treasury on the outskirts of Berlin. The court hearing Voigt's case, and the authorities in general, acknowledged previous harsh treatment handed down to him. They were also concerned about a negative public response to any severe sentence.[11]

But similarities in the manner in which penal policies were developing across Europe were no impediment to international rivalries and to the outbreak of war in 1914. For the combatant nations the First World War appeared initially to bring about a decline in crime and then to foster a new wave of criminality. In February 1915 *The Times* reported a significant decline in offences that the police of the southern counties in England attributed to three causes: 'First, the keeping of better hours, after the darkening of the streets and the early closing of public houses; second, the new consciousness of national duty and the impulse of patriotism; and third, the greatly increased prosperity of many of the poorer classes and the absence of unemployment.'

---

[9] Richard J. Evans, *Tales from the German Underworld: Crime and Punishment in the Nineteenth Century*, London: Yale University Press, 1998, 126–33; Clive Emsley, *Hard Men: Violence in England since 1750*, London: Hambledon, 2005, 157–9.

[10] Paul Weindling, *Health, Race and German Politics between National Unification and Nazism*, Cambridge: Cambridge University Press, 1989, 212.

[11] Benjamin Carter Hett, *Death in the Tiergarten: Murder and Criminal Justice in the Kaiser's Berlin*, Cambridge, Mass.: Harvard University Press, 2004; see also idem, 'The "Captain of Köpenik" and the Transformation of German Criminal Justice, 1891–1914', *Central European History*, 36, 1 (2003), 1–43.

A 90 per cent drop in crime was reported at the Middlesex Sessions.[12] There was also a significant decline in France, though detailed evidence from Bordeaux suggests that this was relatively short-lived and that the decline varied from offence to offence.[13] In Russia a drop in crime at the beginning of the war was attributed both to mobilization and to the prohibition of the manufacture, sale, and consumption of alcoholic drinks.[14] But before long, as wartime inflation and privation hit on the home fronts, across the combatant powers there were concerns about increasing crime. In particular it was feared that juveniles, without the controlling hand of fathers who had gone to the front, were running wild. 'Workers in the interests of child welfare,' reported *The Times*,

Police court missionaries, and others, regard the increase in the number of young offenders as a disturbing result of war conditions. To some extent they say the situation is due to a slackening of parental control. Many fathers are on active service, and often the unruly boy who roams the streets and is open to all their temptations is not very amenable to a mother's discipline.[15]

Nine months after the armistice *Le Petit Parisien* continued to lament *les petits vagabonds de la guerre* whose criminal behaviour it attributed to 'the father in the trenches, the mother in the workshop, the child alone'.[16] But the British and the French could take heart from reports that crime, particularly juvenile crime, had worsened, perhaps even more so, within the Central Powers.[17] In Austria and Germany, as the war progressed, serious concerns were expressed about crime, and especially about young offenders. By 1918 the German statistics showed a doubling of juvenile offenders from the pre-war levels; in Austria the increase was even greater. Wartime measures were identified as contributing to the problems. By 1916 more than half of Prussia's male schoolteachers had been drafted, some lessons had been cut, and school buildings had been requisitioned by the army. Training courses and apprenticeships were also cut and youths were encouraged to enter war industries, with resulting concerns about the independence and lawlessness

12 *The Times*, 6 February 1915, p. 11, and 8 February 1915, p. 3.
13 Yocas Panagiote, 'L'influence de la guerre européene sur la criminalité', thèse de la Faculté de Droit, Université de Paris, 1926; Philippe Chassaigne, 'War, Delinquency, and Society in Bordeaux, 1914–1918', *CJH* 15 (1994), 189–208.
14 George E. Snow, 'Perceptions of the Link between Alcoholism and Crime in Pre-Revolutionary Russia', *CJH* 8 (1987), 35–51; 46.
15 *The Times*, 3 February 1916, p. 5; for similar concerns in France, see Chassaigne, 'War, Delinquency and Society', 196.
16 *Le Petit Parisien*, 6 August 1919, p. 1.
17 *The Times*, 29 November 1917, p. 5; 9 February, 15, 25, and 28 June 1918, all p. 5.

fostered by the money in their pockets.[18] How much these fears reflected a reality remains difficult to assess. In Italy, for example, a similar panic about a rise in juvenile delinquency occurred precisely as the statistics for such delinquency were falling. The deployment of the *Carabinieri* to the front could have had an impact on the figures since there were less of them around to make arrests. Equally their very absence, by fostering the anxiety that there were fewer policemen available to keep offenders in check, may have contributed to the panic.[19]

In Belgium the wartime situation led to a resurgence of old-style banditry. In August 1914 the Belgian *gendarmerie* was ordered to march with the army and when the front stabilized the following November the survivors of the corps were confined in the small corner of western Belgium that remained under Belgian authority. As a consequence, unlike the towns where the structure of municipal policing remained more or less intact and under the control of the local burgomasters, the Belgian countryside was denuded of police. The privations of war, together with large numbers of deserters and stragglers, encouraged some to raid and pillage farms in a style reminiscent of the old regime and the Revolutionary and Napoleonic period. The German army present in Belgium was unprepared for occupation and was not prepared to involve itself in internal policing. Only with the restoration of peace and the return of the *gendarmerie* was the countryside pacified once again.[20]

Squeezed between Belgium, Germany, and the sea, the Netherlands maintained neutrality throughout the war. But the war had a profound impact and provided opportunities for smuggling on a scale unknown since the Napoleonic wars. Some three-quarters of the country was put under military jurisdiction by the promulgation of state of siege regulations. This led to friction between military and local civilian authorities that, at the lowest street level, prompted soldiers to rebuff police admonitions about their behaviour on the grounds that soldiers could do as they pleased since the army was now in charge. In the early stages of the war the fighting was so close that some wounded were picked up and treated by the Dutch Red Cross. Refugees and deserters crossed the border; and some military units

---

[18] Richard Bessel, *Germany After the First World War*, Oxford: Clarendon Press, 1993, 23–6; Holger H. Herwig, *The First World War: Germany and Austria-Hungary 1914–1918*, London: Arnold, 1997, 295.

[19] Gibson, 'The Criminalization of Youth', 126.

[20] Xavier Rousseaux, Frédéric Vesentini, and Antoon Vrints, 'Figures of Homicide. Belgium between Peace and Wars: Official Data on Homicide 1900–1950', paper presented to the conference 'Assaulting the Past', Oxford, July 2005.

accidentally strayed across the border. But it was smuggling that created the biggest problem for the Dutch army and the criminal justice system. Britain and France were insistent that the Dutch should not land goods in their ports destined for the Central Powers. The Germans, in turn, put pressure on the Dutch to sell them as much locally grown produce as possible. German agencies also dealt covertly with Dutch suppliers and smugglers. According to one government minister 'the temptation [to smuggle] became so great that the population along the border became one great smuggling band.' Smuggling cases declined in 1917 and 1918 mainly because of an overall dearth of goods. But in the earlier years of the war the Dutch courts could not cope with the numbers charged. This meant that many of those accused never faced a judge, but even so more gaols and correction centres had to be built to house the offenders. Two of these new institutions were established simply to house the soldiers that were convicted of smuggling.[21]

The Dutch soldier-smugglers prompt an important observation about war and crime that appears often to be lost, given the way that history is compartmentalized into sub-disciplines. Armies can never be entirely separated from the cultural behaviour and understanding of their societies. During the First World War it seems clear that senior officers made decisions about which men condemned to death for desertion should be shot, based at least partly on some popularly held notions drawn from eugenics.[22] The demands of war commonly siphon off from their civilian lives thousands of young men, and young men are generally the most crimogenic individuals within a society. This is not to follow the Quetelet argument that they must therefore have committed their crimes somewhere else. Rather it is to suggest that they might have been tempted to commit crime when somewhere else, especially when that somewhere else was far from home, when they were quartered among an alien population, but living with a peer group whose members, in the context of the war, felt that they had little to lose. Moreover, crime in a theatre of military operations fell under different legal jurisdiction and, as yet, there has been very little work on military crime and military justice.

Most of the men who served in the armies during the First World War probably regarded their military experience as transitory; they were keen to

---

[21] Maartje M. Abbenhuis, 'In Fear of War: The First World War and the State of Siege in the Neutral Netherlands, 1914–1918', *War in History*, 13, 1 (2006), 16–41; quotation at 33.

[22] Gerard Oram, *Worthless Men: Race, Eugenics and the Death Penalty in the British Army*, London: Francis Boutle, 1998, 80, 82–3, and 117–18.

get home and put the memory of terrible sights, sounds, and possibly deeds behind them. Most appear to have slipped back into civil life. Nevertheless, the returning veteran was an object of concern. For a century and more the respectable in European society had increasingly prided themselves on their restraint, their increased sensitivity, their civilization. But the war veterans were men who had seen and done terrible things; over an extended period they had witnessed and engaged in both industrial-scale killing and also its more intimate forms. They were feared as angry men, whose anger was irrational and a regression from mature civilized society. They had been trained in the use of arms. Some came back with their arms. Many had varying degrees of trauma. This concern about former soldiers taking to violent crime at the end of a war had been apparent at least since the early modern period. In eighteenth-century Britain the concern was probably linked with a common dislike of and suspicion about the soldiery. It is significant that a succession of major inquiries into the police of London occurred as the wars against Napoleon drew to an end and in the immediate aftermath of those wars.[23] Nineteenth-century Kent had a large number of military bases; it also had a disproportionate number of soldiers brought before its courts for criminal offences, and then filling its prisons.[24] There is more than a hint of concerns about rough, drunken soldiers in Kipling's *Barrackroom Ballads*. Danny Deever was to be hanged in the morning for shooting a sleeping comrade. And as Kipling's 'Tommy' explained:

> We ain't no thin red 'eroes, nor we aren't no blackguards too,
> But single men in barricks, most remarkable like you;
> An' if sometimes our conduck isn't all your fancy paints,
> Why, single men in barricks don't grow into plaster saints.

The nineteenth-century British army, unlike the armies of continental Europe, continued to be made up of volunteers rather than conscripts. David Hopkin has suggested that in France the image of the dangerous, marauding French soldier declined during the nineteenth century. In place of the view that the soldier and the bandit were closely linked came the idea that the soldier who indulged in a bit of thieving and trickery was demonstrating his Gallic flair, something that was more generally manifested in the skills of a quick wit and bravura. Of course, when German soldiers invaded in 1870

---

[23] J. M. Beattie, *Crime and the Courts in England, 1660–1800*, Oxford: Oxford University Press, 1986, 213–37.

[24] Carolyn A. Conley, *The Unwritten Law: Criminal Justice in Victorian Kent*, Cambridge University Press, 1991, 10–11, 60, 66, 109, and 154–5.

and indulged in marauding, in French eyes they were brutal bullies.[25] But when, in 1884, Wilhelm Starke noted the decline in the statistics of crime in Prussia and France during the war and an increase in violence thereafter, he echoed some of the British fears by suggesting that a brutalization associated with young men's participation as soldiers may have had repercussions in the shape of violent offences in peacetime society.[26]

The anxieties about dangerous veterans were almost certainly more widespread and more pronounced during and immediately after the First World War than they had been before. Such fears have been incorporated into subsequent historical interpretations of the inter-war period. In particular, it has been suggested that the violence of both the Italian *fascisti* and of the Nazi *Sturm Abteilung* also owed something to the training for, and the experience of war, as well as its brutalization. George Mosse, in particular, has argued that, unlike Germany and Italy, Britain and France 'were able to keep the process of brutalization largely, if not entirely, under control'.[27] But there is a problem with such an argument. Fascists in the 1920s and 1930s may have included veterans of a war of unprecedented scale and intensity, and they may have drawn on the experience of this war in their ideology and made reference to it in their propaganda, but this does not demonstrate that the war created those fascists and their brutality. It would be very difficult to prove that where fascism did not have a significant impact, this was necessarily the result of the better control of battle-hardened veterans. Spain did not participate in the First World War with the corollary of brutalized veterans, yet it was to experience a variant of fascist revolution. But Spain, like Italy, had also experienced violent and murderous confrontations between organized labour and the forces of the state well before the 1914; and Spain, like Prussia before the war, had a proud army that considered itself central to the maintenance of the state. The kind of argument deployed by Mosse focuses upon political violence. Yet, if men were brutalized in war, then, presumably, the manifestations of such violence ought not to be found solely on the streets among political thugs; moreover, it was not political thugs that were the concern in wartime. There was revolution in Germany and

[25] David M. Hopkin, 'Military Marauders in Nineteenth-Century French Popular Culture', *War in History*, 9, 3 (2002), 251–78; idem, *Soldier and Peasant in French Popular Culture, 1766–1870*, Woodbridge: Royal Historical Society/Boydell Press, 2003, 236–9 and 303.

[26] Wilhelm Starke, *Verbrechen und Verbrecher in Preußen, 1854–1878. Eine kulturgeschichtliche Studie*, Berlin, 1884, 152.

[27] George L. Mosse, *Fallen Soldiers: Reshaping the Memory of World Wars*, Oxford: Oxford University Press, 1990, 159.

elsewhere in east and central Europe after the First World War with the kind of savage violence usually associated with internal conflict and civil war. But the violence here was less the brutalization of men by war and more the political changes wrought by that war and the economic, political, and social problems created by reordering and restructuring for peace.

Gangs of deserters were beginning to infest the borderlands between the Austro-Hungarian Empire and the Balkan states from at least the summer of 1916. Two years later these so-called 'Green Cadres' were operating in gangs ranging from ten to forty men, and by the autumn some 50,000 infested the hills and woods of Bosnia-Herzegovina, Croatia, Dalmatia, Istria, and Slavonia. Everywhere across central and east Europe at the end of 1918 and beginning of 1919 there were large numbers of men returning from the fronts with guns. They were returning to lands from which the old order had gone and where a new political legitimacy was often wanting. They were also returning to lands where the economy had been enfeebled by war, where people were hungry and often sick. It was easy for men with guns to take whatever they needed or wanted. Manifestly the old order had failed; the armed gangs, indistinguishable from brigands and bandits, could claim to be defenders of their communities; and even of a national order. They were also able to stigmatize scapegoats for their, and their communities', misfortunes. Rural Hungary appears to have experienced some of the worst examples of this banditry. Gangs of ex-soldiers, glorying in names such as the Ragged Guard (*Rangyos Gárda*) and wearing their threadbare, battle-stained Austro-Hungarian uniforms with pride, sought to justify their depredations by finding significant targets among outsiders. Communists who had backed the short-lived regime of Béla Kun were one such group. Jews, who ran a disproportionate percentage of commerce and banking in the country, were another. Stories of attacks on Jews had contributed to the heroic, pre-war myth of the bandit Jóska Sobri; and now Jews were accused of both fomenting the war and profiteering from it. From the early 1920s these armed groups found themselves given a degree of sanction by the conservative political regime; this was a relationship with echoes of that between the bandits and landlords in southern Europe during the nineteenth century.[28]

In northern and western Europe peace meant claims of victory for the old order and claims that society could now return to normal. There were no Green Cadres or Ragged Guards in Britain and France. Crime was something

---

[28] My thanks to my colleague Mark Pittaway for details on this.

committed by criminals, though there was the fear that the trauma of war might have created new criminals on the domestic front. Contemporaries wrote of 'war psychosis' and argued that men had become mentally and morally unstable because of their military experiences. This instability was, it was maintained, manifested by resentful veterans showing violent anger and hostility towards the women who had stepped into their jobs while they were at the front. Also, the argument continued, there were returning soldiers who committed brutal violence towards wives that were thought to have exercised too much economic and sexual independence during the war. There were, of course, instances of assault and domestic violence that appeared to fit this category. The most dramatic of these involved men who killed on their return in the belief that their wives had been unfaithful. And much has been made of a group of male artists in Weimar Germany, mainly war veterans, who produced a series of images portraying savage violence towards women and the dismemberment of their bodies.[29] The problem is to assess the scale of and novelty of the actual criminal violence of this sort and to move beyond assumptions in assessing the causes.

Reliable statistics might offer an answer to the question of how far the brutalities of war contributed to violence in peacetime, but the difficulties with the statistics of crime have already been discussed at length. In addition it can be very difficult to compare the crime statistics of different countries because of different categories of offences and different methods of recording them.[30] Murder is commonly taken as an indicator of the scale of violence in a society. In 1926 Thorsten Sellin posed the question: 'Is murder increasing in Europe?' Using the available national statistics in his analysis, Sellin also made a highly questionable assumption:

All the belligerent countries show a decrease in the murder rate particularly during the first year of the war. This decrease, which at least in some countries seems to have persisted during the entire struggle, has sometimes been attributed to a wave of ennobling patriotism, but it was more likely due to the temporary enrollment and

---

[29] Susan Kingsley Kent, *Making Peace: The Reconstruction of Gender in Interwar Britain*, Princeton: Princeton University Press, 1993, 97–101; Dorothy Rowe, *Representing Berlin: Sexuality and the City in Imperial and Weimar Germany*, Aldershot: Ashgate, 2003, 134–5. For examples of soldiers committing murder in the belief that their wives had been unfaithful see e.g. *Le Petit Parisien*, 31 May 1919, p. 3 (case of Alphone Pagis), and 25 Jan. 1920, p. 3 (case of Alfred Grotiens); *The Times*, 6 March 1919, p. 7 and 5 July, p. 9 (case of Henry Gashin). Gashin's wife had already sought a separation from him.

[30] Hermann Mannheim, *Social Aspects of Crime in England between the Wars*, London: Allen and Unwin, 1940, 48–9.

discipline of the young men of the age groups which furnish the chief contingents of criminals.

This was to elide 'criminals' and 'murderers' when the latter have only ever constituted a tiny minority within the former. Sellin found an overall increase in the incidence of murder in those countries that had what he regarded as reasonably reliable statistics. The increase was most pronounced in Italy, Germany, France, and Finland and, in the belligerent countries, it was most marked during the period of demobilization 'with the possible exception of England and Wales'. Sellin did his best to make England and Wales fit by emphasizing the 'economic distress and consequent social and individual maladjustments' in the years before the war. But in suggesting that economic distress fostered murder in this way, he was running counter to the traditional view that distress encouraged theft and that prosperity, by providing money for leisure and, consequently, more drinking, contributed to violence. In conclusion Sellin suggested that the 'abnormal political, economic and social conditions' engendered by the war contributed to an overall increase in murder across Europe, but he could not prove it.[31] More recently, and drawing on much wider cross-cultural and statistical evidence, it has been argued that violence increases in the immediate aftermath of war and conceivably because war legitimates violent behaviour. But statistically the increases, like those following the First World War, have been generally short-lived.[32]

Murder aside, Germany, like other defeated powers in the centre and east, suffered an increase in violent crime after the war. Some of this was political or was tied to the revolutionary violence that wracked the country in the years immediately following the armistice. But some had no such political fig leaf, most notoriously the deliberate derailing of a train near the Prussian town of Schneidemühl in January 1919 so as to rob the passengers. The derailment killed 18 people and injured over 300.[33] Everywhere in the months following the armistice gangs of heavily armed men prowled the country, sometimes robbing farms, food depots, or large shops. At least one military commander voiced fears that conditions were sinking to the dreadful situation of Germany

---

31 Thorsten Sellin, 'Is Murder Increasing in Europe?', *Annals of the American Academy of Political and Social Science*, 126 (1926), 29–34.

32 Dane Archer and Rosemary Gartner, *Violence and Crime in Cross-National Perspective*, New Haven Ct: Yale University Press, 1984.

33 Richard J. Evans, *Rituals of Retribution: Capital Punishment in Germany 1600–2000*, Oxford: Oxford University Press, 1996, 524.

during the Thirty Years War.[34] During the 1920s two former students of Franz von Liszt, Franz Exner and Moritz Liepmann, explored the wartime impact of crime on Austria and Germany respectively. They found a decline in the incidence of assault during the war in both countries. This they attributed to the removal of young men into the armed forces and to the women and the older men left at home being less inclined to violent behaviour because of malnutrition and the decline in alcohol consumption. In both countries there was a slight decline in homicides during the war and major increases afterwards. In Austria the increase was 50 per cent; in Germany the figures doubled. Exner deployed the brutalization theory to explain the Austrian increase. Liepmann believed that the German increase was fuelled by the large number of firearms that were available in the country after the war. In its withdrawal from France in 1918 the German army 'lost' nearly 2 million rifles, 8,400 machine guns, and 4,000 trench mortars.[35]

In both France and Britain contemporaries made the point that the real increase in offending immediately after the war was to be seen in the statistics of property crime.[36] But there were still concerns about the returning veteran. *Le Temps* feared that the wave of theft was all the fault of the war since it had ruined all of the soldier's 'principles of regularity, order, and forethought'.[37] Such French jeremiads may have been tempered by the nineteenth-century shift away from the equation of the soldier and the brigand, and there was also the significant difference that, unlike the veterans of Austria and Germany, the French veteran was victorious. Moreover, the demobbed *poilu* did not return to a disintegrating state and collapsing economy. The British veteran was in a similar situation, but there were still the shrill, traditional concerns about brutalized soldiers. Sir Nevil Macready, Commissioner of the Metropolitan Police and himself a former soldier, warned in May 1919:

that freedom in battle from the restraint of ordinary law lowered man's respect for fear and of that institution, with the result that an increase in crime invariably

---

[34] Bessel, *Germany after the First World War*, 242–3.

[35] Richard J. Wetzell, *Inventing the Criminal: A History of German Criminology, 1880–1945*, Chapel Hill: University of North Carolina Press, 2000, 109–15; Eric J. Leed, *No Man's Land: Combat and Identity in World War One*, Cambridge: Cambridge University Press, 1979, 198–201. For specific detail see Franz Exner, *Krieg und Kriminalität in Österreich*, Vienna: Holder, Pichler, Tempsky, 1927; Moritz Liepmann, *Krieg und Kriminalität in Deutschland*, Stuttgart: Deutsche Verlags-Anstalt, 1930.

[36] Otto Kirchheimer, 'Remarques sur la statistique criminelle de la France d'après guerre', *Revue de Science Criminelle*, 1 (1936), 363–96; 364; *Judicial Statistics of England and Wales for 1924*, Cmd. 2494, London: HMSO, 1925, 1–7.

[37] *Le Temps*, 31 December 1919, p. 1.

followed war. At the present time there was a big rise in the number of robberies, and the robber of to-day, grown callous after four years' experience of killing, was indifferent alike to the taking of life and to his own personal safety. . . .

Sir Nevil expressed the view that another result of the war would be an increase in the number of women murders [*sic*]. Before the war, he said, when a man quarrelled with his wife or the woman he lived with, he would 'just clip her under the ear', and everything would be all right the next day. But now, after four years of life-taking, he would hit her over the head with an iron bar or anything that happened to be handy, and there would be no next day for her.[38]

Similar comments were expressed in the provincial press. Following the report of the execution of some ex-soldiers for a murder, and under the headline 'Human Life Cheap', the *Sheffield Mail* lamented that:

The after effect of every war is the cheapening of the value of human life. . . . The monetary impoverishment entailed by war is severe, but never so great as the moral loss. In the terrible ordeal where a man is placed upon a pedestal the greater the number of lives taken by him, it is not easy, indeed it is not sensible, to expect to bring him back to the adequate appreciation of the standards compatible with order and civilisation.[39]

Such concerns were reflected in the official comments on the crime statistics for 1923 that saw a slight increase in violent crime by gangs and the use of firearms as 'characteristic of less settled communities'. In the following year, however, while suspecting that 'reckless attempts to live more or less luxuriously without rendering any services in return . . . may . . . be traceable to experience during the war', the analysts could not find any evidence that 'experience of warfare' had led to any increase in violent crime.[40]

By the mid-1920s across Europe the statistics of crime had generally settled back to roughly pre-war levels and patterns. At the same time, old concerns about various criminal stereotypes were picked up again, and variously embroidered by different commentators and forms of media. The sexual monster was rare, but made good headlines whether his crimes were on the small scale, like the pathetic but frightening individuals who snipped off the long plaits of women and girls in the streets or cut their clothes, sometimes in the dark of a cinema, or whether he was a serial killer such as Peter Kürten, 'the Düsseldorf vampire'. The tabloid press, the illustrated magazines, artists, and film-makers continued to emphasize such offences. Perhaps in some way

---

[38] *The Times*, 5 May 1919, p. 7.   [39] *Sheffield Mail*, 2 December 1920, p. 2.
[40] *Judicial Statistics of England and Wales for 1923*, Cmd. 2277, London: HMSO, 1925, 9; *Judicial Statistics of England and Wales for 1924*, Cmd. 2494, London: HMSO, 1925, 2 and 6.

as a reaction to the relatively restrained press of Imperial Germany and to the trauma of defeat, the media of the Weimar Republic appears to have been particularly obsessed with crime, and especially violent, sexual crime. Kürten, the last of a cluster of serial killers brought to justice in the republic—the others being Karl Denke, Wilhelm Großmann, and Fritz Haarmann—was made for such a media. A journeyman mason, in 1929 he was charged with nine murders and seven attempted murders. The press was urged to report his trial responsibly and it refrained from giving details of the savage, sexual injuries that he inflicted on his victims. But the events of the case were sufficient for the media to make the trial a major event.[41] The case also provided a heightened context and receptive audience for Fritz Lang's astonishing film about a serial child killer, *M*, which was released in 1931 and which served as the culmination of the Weimar Republic's fascination with crime.

As well as picking up on concerns about the sexual killer that had preoccupied the Weimar press, Lang's masterpiece reflected concerns about the biologically degenerate criminal who killed because he could not help himself and it drew on fears and assumptions about professional criminals. In *M* the child killer is hunted, captured, and tried in an alternative court by the *Ringvereine*, criminal counter-societies mirroring the conventional, hierarchical society that they preyed upon. The *Ringvereine* had begun in the 1890s as self-help associations of former prisoners though their numbers increased during the 1920s. They figured increasingly in the Weimar press as criminal organizations responsible for organized crime, particularly the organization of prostitution. Lang portrayed the *Ringvereine* as hierarchical institutions with a leader and with members specializing in different forms of criminality. The *Ringvereine* hunt the child killer since the police hunt for him is disrupting their normal criminal activity. The image of the hierarchical counter-society went back to the bandit gangs of the old regime and to descriptions of the criminal classes in the nineteenth century. And the idea of characterizing criminals as a distinct social group remained a comfortable way to distinguish those that committed crime from ordinary, hence law-abiding, members of society.

Professionals existed, often in the form of criminal entrepreneurs who organized prostitution and, as in Britain where there were strict rules on

---

[41] Maria Tatar, *Lustmord: Sexual Murder in Weimar Germany*, Princeton: Princeton University Press, 1995; Evans, *Rituals of Retribution*, 591–605; for hair snippers and dress cutters see the comments in Jan Bondeson, *The London Monster: A Sanguinary Tale*, Cambridge Mass.: Da Capo, 2002, 170–1.

betting and gambling, who acted as bookmakers. These entrepreneurs could be violent and vicious themselves, but they also recruited strong-arm men to protect their business and their territory. The enforcers often had criminal records for violence and property crime.[42] Some criminal gangs still came together on an ad hoc basis for a major theft. A few continued to be made up of family members like the Sass brothers in Germany whose burglaries and safe-crackings, and escapes from Weimar justice, so infuriated Himmler that, in March 1940, he had them shot.[43] But the overwhelming majority of offences across Europe in the inter-war period, as in earlier years, continued to be petty and opportunist, and appear principally to have involved young men.

The young offender continued to excite anxiety and condemnation. The celebrated and influential psychiatrist Cyril Burt might have considered juvenile delinquency as nothing more than an outstanding example, 'dangerous and extreme but none the less typical—of common childish naughtiness'.[44] But such views were rarely acceptable beyond the intellectual group responsible for penal welfarism, particularly in liberal democratic societies. Moreover, in authoritarian states where adherence to the national community was a central tenet of the regime, the category of youth delinquency could be significantly expanded. Thus, in Nazi Germany members of protest youth groups such as the *Edelweißpiraten* or the *Meuten* might engage in some of Burt's dangerous and extreme 'naughtiness', but their real delinquency lay in their resistance to and hostility towards the Hitler Youth and all that it stood for.[45]

Other traditional outsiders also continued to be eyed with suspicion as potential criminal offenders, notably the foreigner and the tramp. The economic depressions of the inter-war period aggravated these suspicions as more and more idle men in shabby clothes gathered on the streets looking for work, and even lived on the streets. Thousands of Italians, Poles, and others migrated to France during the 1920s to fill gaps in the labour force left by the war. Among many French people these new immigrants were seen as taking jobs and creating social problems and difficulties, not the least of which was crime. The statistics of crime showed a percentage of foreign offenders

[42] Clive Emsley, *Hard Men: Violence in England since 1750*, London: Hambledon, 2005, 32–5; Philip Jenkins and Gary W. Potter, 'Before the Krays: Organized Crime In London, 1920–1960', *CJH* 9 (1988), 209–30.

[43] Nikolaus Wachsman, *Hitler's Prisoners: Legal Terror in Nazi Germany*, New Haven and London: Yale University Press, 2004, 57 and 207–8.

[44] Cyril Burt, *The Young Delinquent*, 2nd edn., London: University Press, 1927, p. viii.

[45] Detlev J. K. Peukert, *Inside Nazi Germany: Conformity, Opposition and Racism in Everyday Life*, tr. Richard Deveson, Harmondsworth: Penguin, 1987, 154–66.

disproportionate to their number in the population.[46] This may have been a reflection of the reality of offending, but equally it might have been the result of suspicion leading to greater surveillance of the foreign-born, the result of the immigrant not finding the hoped-for work, or being the first to be laid off work in an economic downswing. Overall the economic depressions had some impact on the rates of crime as manifested by the statistics, yet the increase was rarely more than a blip and even the most sophisticated analysis had difficulty in finding a precise correlation between unemployment and an increase in, particularly, property crime.[47] The problems of homelessness and vagrancy were especially apparent towards the end of the Weimar Republic, with enormous numbers forced to live on the streets and passed by the authorities from town to town. There were brotherhoods of vagrants, magazines for vagrants and, in 1929, a vagrants' congress met in Stuttgart. The Nazis sought to win this constituency but, once in power, they turned against it with increasingly harsh methods. Reflecting the old concerns about those who would not work, the Nazis passed legislation against the 'asocial' and the 'workshy' (*Arbeitsscheu*) and swept them up with those defined as enemies of the national community.[48] In many respects this policy that filled workhouses and prisons, and then concentration camps and death camps, was another manifestation of the way in which the authoritarian regimes of the inter-war period took to extreme and brutal conclusions long-standing ideas about both criminals and certain penal welfare concepts.

[46] Paul Lawrence, ' "Un flot d'agitateurs politiques, de fauteurs de désordre et de criminels": Adverse Perceptions of Immigrants in France between the Wars', *French History*, 14, 2 (2000), 201–21; Kirchheimer, 'Remarques sur la statistique', 377.

[47] Mannheim, *Social Aspects of Crime*, ch. 5.

[48] Wolfgang Ayass, 'Vagrants and Beggars in Hitler's Reich', in Richard J. Evans, ed., *The German Underworld: Deviants and Outcasts in German History*, London: Routledge, 1988.

13
Policing and Punishing after the War

THE First World War has often been described as a watershed or seen as some kind of caesura in European history; books and history courses on political, economic, and social development commonly have ended in 1914 or started in 1918. The beginning, course, and end of the war were meaningless for many of the developments in early twentieth-century policing and penal policy. Yet, at the same time, the war did have an impact on police institutions, while the political regimes and cultural evolutions that followed, and often in considerable measure were shaped by, the war also had an effect on both policing and penal policies. In some instances, these effects of war meant propelling institutions and policies in directions already apparent. But different political ideologies could give very different shapes and outcomes to policies that employed similar discourse. The inter-war period in Europe saw new, extreme authoritarian states—sometimes labelled 'totalitarian'—developing alongside liberal democratic ones. The ideologies of these different kinds of state and their attitudes towards their citizens were very different, yet they used the same penal and policing discourses. In some instances, too, in the tradition of intellectual exchange dating back to the Enlightenment and beyond, they also considered that they might read and learn from, and exchange with, each others' academics, jurists, and practitioners.

Once the Great War began the men of the state military police institutions were, as soldiers, immediately involved in the conflict. In the eyes of the populations of France and Italy both the *Gendarmerie* and the *Carabinieri* became tainted by their wartime roles. For the only time in its history the *Gendarmerie* did not have a military unit in the front line engaged with the enemy. A *Carabinieri* regiment was hurled against the enemy on the Isonzo in the early months of Italian participation in the war. The regiment was all but destroyed and thereafter the principal role of the corps, like that of the French gendarmes, was immediately behind the front line. As the war developed the military duties of the *carabinieri* and the *gendarmes* were largely restricted to policing military transport, checking that troops were not out of bounds, and arresting deserters and men accused of inflicting wounds upon themselves to avoid the front. Worst of all, they were the enforcers of the military provosts. The *poilus* joked that the front line ended where you met the first gendarme and the *Gendarmerie* spent the inter-war years trying to live down the stigma. For the *Carabinieri* the situation became even more unpleasant since, in addition to serving in firing squads, they were authorized to keep men at the front by summary shootings—and the ferocity of certain Italian generals in ordering such was exceptional. A fierce hostility towards *carabinieri* developed among the front-line troops. This hostility seems to have been especially strong among the crack *arditi* units and as the war progressed individual *carabinieri* appear frequently to have been shot by Italian troops. In the aftermath of the war *carabinieri* were spat upon by socialist crowds and condemned by socialist politicians who drew up plans to disband the institution. As a result of the war experience and the growing hostility some men resigned from the corps.[1]

The manpower demands of the First World War meant that large numbers of municipal and state civilian police officers were withdrawn from the streets and countryside and sent into the trenches. The policemen in continental Europe were commonly ex-servicemen who had served for longer than the required period of conscription. Even in Britain, where there was no conscription until halfway through the war, the outbreak of the conflict left holes in police ranks as reservists were called to the colours and as others volunteered. Across the continent, the police officers remaining at home were usually older men, and while there may, as noted earlier, have been a decline in criminal activity in the early stages of the war, the police were heaped with new tasks. It fell to them to enforce new wartime regulations on food supplies, to seek out subversives, to search on the home front for deserters and for military absentees. As one senior officer in Bordeaux put it to the local prefect in June 1917: 'It will not be long before the police services are physically unable to fulfil their duty, at a time when they will be most

---

[1] Louis N. Pinel, 'Cognes, hommes noirs et grenades blanches: les enjeux de la représentation des gendarmes dans la Grande Guerre', in Jean-Noël Luc, ed. *Figures de Gendarmes, Sociétés et Représentations*, 16 (2003), 167–82; Olivier Buchbinder, *Gendarmes prévôtales et maintien de l'ordre (1914–1918)*, Maisons-Alfort: Service historique de la *Gendarmerie* nationale, 2004; Richard Oliver Collin, 'The Italian Police and Internal Security from Giolitti to Mussolini', D.Phil., Oxford University, 1983, 106–10. For Italian summary executions see Irene Guerrini and Marco Pluviano, *Le fucilazioni sommarie nella prima guerra mondiale*, Udine: Gaspari, 2004.

wanted.'[2] There was also the problem of an apparent increase in prostitution as women, sometimes in desperation, were attracted to large military camps. In Britain this contributed directly to experiments in the use of women police officers. As the war dragged on and as both food shortages and wartime inflation began to bite, so the police everywhere found themselves faced with anger and sometimes rioting in markets and shopping districts. Women protesting over food shortages and high prices in the streets of wartime Berlin challenged policemen for not being with the military, and hence challenged both their ability to fight and their manhood. The police themselves were not immune to the shortages and the difficulties in feeding their own families. In some instances they turned a blind eye to the black markets that sprang up everywhere. In others, as is evidenced by several British examples, when large, angry crowds, sometimes backed by soldiers on leave, turned on shopkeepers and others, the police saw discretion as the better part of valour and stepped back. In Germany even the political police, not generally recruited from the working class, began to distance themselves from the state.[3]

Everywhere wartime inflation ate away at police pay, and the additional pressures of the job fostered the industrial militancy that had been emerging among police officers before 1914. As the war drew to a close, and even more so when peace was restored, rank-and-file police discontent became overt and serious. In Marseilles in July 1919 the majority of the police went on strike. Elsewhere in France, and particularly in Paris, the police demonstrated to demand the *droit syndical*, the right to form unions that could work for salary and pension increases and provide men with support in claims against disciplinary procedures or about being passed over for promotion. The demonstrations were larded with revolutionary rhetoric, but the police continued to be eyed warily by fellow workers, particularly since they were frequently deployed to break up demonstrations by those fellow workers. Indeed on 11 December 1923 3,000 off-duty Paris police demonstrating in Paris were attacked by on-duty officers; sixty of the demonstrators were arrested and dismissed from the service. The victory of the *Cartel des Gauches* in the election of the following May led to the

---

[2] Philippe Chassaigne, 'War, Delinquency and Society in Bordeaux, 1914–1918', *CJH* 15 (1994), 189–208; 200.

[3] See e.g. ibid.; Belinda J. Davis, *Home Fires Burning: Food, Politics and Everyday Life in World War I Berlin*, Chapel Hill: University of North Carolina Press, 2000, 14, 27, and 99–103; Clive Emsley, *The English Police: A Political and Social History*, 2nd edn., London: Longman, 1996, 121–32; David Englander, 'Police and Public Order in Britain, 1914–1918', in Clive Emsley and Barbara Weinberger, eds., *Policing Western Europe: Politics, Professionalism and Public Order, 1850–1940*, Westport, Conn.: Greenwood Press, 1991.

reinstatement of the sixty 'victims' and to the tacit acknowledgement that the police might unionise. But union activity on the part of the police remained suspect among many politicians. Those politicians that supported it appear often to have acted for their own ends, and to many labour activists the police still appeared to be 'on the other side'.[4] In England, and most significantly in London, police officers twice went on strike, first in August 1918 and then in August 1919. The first strike, confined to London, was largely successful, bringing promises of a pay increase and pension improvements. The second affected London, Birmingham, and Liverpool. It was essentially about the survival of the union and was a disaster leading to the dismissal of all those who had participated. The formation of the first Labour government in 1924 brought no reinstatements and a federation, denied any right to strike, was the only form of labour organization permitted to the Bobby.[5]

But not every country in Europe was involved militarily in the First World War. While the conflict imposed new pressures on police in the countries that did participate and provided an additional impetus to the labour activism emerging in some police institutions before 1914, not every police union was established as a direct result of war. In Scandinavia and in the Netherlands police unions had been authorized in the early years of the century. Even police in some of the states of Imperial Germany had been permitted a degree of labour organization before the outbreak of war.[6]

The war's effect on the centralization of police institutions and upon shifts in the ethos of policing in different national contexts was complex and varied. The restoration of the Belgian state provided the opportunity for the creation of a detective police run from the offices of the public prosecutors in Brussels, Liège, and Ghent. This was something that had been discussed since the 1880s and had seen legislation prepared in 1896 but which, in the event, required a major event such as the liberation to bring to fruition.[7] In France the ambiguities of the 1884 police law remained unchanged. At the turn of the century the state only had clear and direct authority over the police in

---

[4] Michel Bergès, *Le syndicalisme policier en France (1880–1940)*, Paris: L'Harmattan, 1995.

[5] Emsley, *The English Police*, 132–6.

[6] Archives privées de la CGT, typescript, 'Internationale Föderation der Polizeibeamten, Sitz Berlin, Mai 1931', dates the origins of other police unions as the Netherlands (1902), Norway (1905), and Sweden (1903); Saxony claimed 1908 and Prussia 1915. My thanks to Marie-France Vogel for this information.

[7] Benoît Majerus and Xavier Rousseaux, 'The World Wars and their Impact on the Belgian Police System', in Cyrille Fijnaut, ed., *The Impact of World War II on Policing in North-West Europe*, Leuven: Leuven University Press, 2004, 51.

Paris and in Lyons; long-standing anxiety over the militancy of labour in Lyons had led to the city's police being brought under the direct control of the local prefect in the 1850s. Many voices were raised about ineffectiveness and inefficiencies among the municipal police. But successive governments remained hesitant about centralization: it would cost money; it would run counter to the principles of decentralization espoused in the early years of the great revolution one hundred years earlier; and it would provoke serious opposition from the big towns.

Some steps were taken towards centralization and centralized coordination in the decade before the war. The prime mover here was the old radical republican, and long-term critic of illiberal behaviour by the French police, Georges Clemenceau. Radical and republican he might have been, but this did not deflect him, as minister of the interior, from sending troops against strikers. In 1907 he pushed through legislation to centralize and coordinate detective policing. He also encouraged his able executive agent in this, the career police officer Célestin Hennion, to establish mobile detective squads, *Brigades mobiles de police judiciare*, which during the 1920s acquired both a romantic and exalted reputation, and the nickname, after Clemenceau, of '*les brigades du tigre*'. In 1908, on the grounds that crime was rife in the city and that the municipal police were too few and quite ineffective, Clemenceau's ministry brought the police of Marseilles under state control. Early in 1914 plans were introduced for similar *étatisation* in the Briey-Longwy basin and in the towns of Toulon and La Seyne, where there were large numbers of foreign workers and sailors, allegedly attracting large numbers of prostitutes and also often engaging in serious, violent disorder. The war halted the plans. When peace was restored Briey-Longwy was no longer seen as a problem since, with the restoration of Alsace, the region was now not so close to the frontier. The conglomeration around Toulon and La Seyne, however, was a different matter and was brought under state control as the guns fell silent. The restoration of Alsace provided the opportunity to take over the police of the region's big towns—Strasbourg, Metz, and Mulhouse—in 1925. Ten years later all of the municipal police were also taken over in the departments of Seine-et-Marne and Seine-et-Oise that surrounded Paris. But, with governments still sensitive to the ideas of 1790 to 1791 and still wary of big-city opposition, further centralization had to await the Vichy government.[8]

[8] Jean-Marc Berlière, *Le Monde des polices en France, XIX–XX siècles*, Brussels: Éditions Complexe, 1996, 88–90.

British governments were always sensitive to charges of centralization and trampling over local independence, but they and their civil servants also had a vision of what constituted efficient and effective policing. In the middle of the nineteenth century governments had sought to force the amalgamation of the smallest forces, and when they had failed in this the inspectors of constabulary had been established to bring some uniformity and broad, comparable levels of efficiency. British governments were reluctant to deploy soldiers to deal with disorder and had no *gendarmerie*; in consequence they encouraged local police forces to enter into agreements with their neighbours to provide mutual aid in cases of emergency. The war served to bring chief police officers closer to each other in district conferences and under the military officers put in charge of the special administrative divisions that were created across the country. It also strengthened the links between senior police officers and the Home Office. Not all of these links were dismantled with the return of peace, and post-war concerns about industrial and political unrest particularly ensured the continuation of the links between local police and the Home Office. At the same time the Desborough Commission, that met in the aftermath of the first police strike in 1918, recommended greater uniformity between the different forces. Sensibilities and the potential of serious opposition from local government militated against forced amalgamations during the inter-war period, but the Second World War provided the opportunity for such. The inter-war period in general saw increasing links between the police and the centre and a growing tendency, at least at the centre, to see the police officer as a servant of the Crown rather than of local government.[9]

As police forces in Britain grew closer to the centre so, across Europe, there were also attempts to draw national police institutions closer together. There was statistical evidence to support the idea that crime had begun to rise in individual European states after the war but, among senior police officers, there appears also to have developed the idea that there was a simultaneous growth in international crime. The pre-war concern with white slavery was now expanded to include a new class of international criminal taking advantage of modern mobility and the disruption of war to cross boundaries forging cheques, currency, and passports, and trafficking in drugs. Such criminals appear to have existed more in popular fiction than in reality but the concerns were sufficient for senior police officers across Europe to come together to form the International Criminal Police Commission

[9] Emsley, *The English Police*, 129–30, 136–69.

(*Internationale Kriminalpolizeiliche Kommission*). The idea was proposed initially in 1919 by M. C. van Houten, a captain of the Dutch *Marechaussee*, but the driving force behind the commission was Johann Schober. Schober was a veteran of the police of imperial Vienna who had become police chief of the city in 1918, had served briefly as Chancellor and Foreign Minister in the new Austrian republic, and then returned to his policing post in the summer of 1922. At the beginning of September 1923 some 150 delegates answered a call from Schober and a German colleague, Robert Heindl, to attend an international police congress in Vienna. The congress led directly to the formation of the commission with its headquarters situated in Vienna and Schober as its president. The organization acted essentially as an information exchange available for members to assist in their common struggle against 'ordinary crime' (*gemeine Verbrechertum*). It saw itself as a body of police professionals who recognized and rejoiced in national differences and distinctions, and who were bound together in a common cause. The commission has been described as a political body designed to keep international communism in check though the evidence is debatable. The police of the Soviet Union appear not to have engaged with it, not because of the commission's political aims—these were not clearly outlined, but rather because the Soviets neither sought nor shared the formal separation of police and government boasted by the police experts who adhered to it.[10]

The creation of the Soviet Union out of the chaos of the Russian Revolution fed post-war fears of economic unrest and political upheaval across Europe. This, in turn, prompted an increased emphasis on the police role as protector of the state. Everywhere auxiliary and paramilitary police organizations were debated, established, or improved and the police role in political surveillance and repression was enhanced. In the new states created in central Europe, such as Czechoslovakia and Poland, police forces had an important role in ensuring political and national consolidation. The new forces were highly centralized and the dominant ethnic groups were favoured in all ranks. Unreliable ethnic minorities, especially in Poland, were commonly stigmatized as Bolshevik, and not always without reason.[11]

    [10] Mathieu Deflem, *Policing World Society: Historical Foundations of International Police Cooperation*, Oxford: Oxford University Press, 2002, esp. ch. 5. Cyrille Fijnaut, 'The International Criminal Police Commission and the Fight against Communism', in Mark Mazower, ed., *The Politics of Policing in the Twentieth Century: Historical Perspectives*, Providence, RI: Berghahn Books, 1997, stresses the anti-communist stance of many of the founder members.

    [11] Samuel Ronsin, 'Police, Republic and Nation: The Czechoslovak State Police and the Building of a Multinational Democracy', and Andrzej Misiuk, 'Police and Policing under the Second Polish

In Britain the means and extent of political policing had been significantly extended during the First World War, and the fear of Bolshevism ensured their continuance afterwards. There were also discussions for strengthening the Police Reserve and even for creating a Citizen Guard. In Belgium in 1919 the *Gendarmerie* was re-established across the whole country and its numbers were significantly increased. This was partly because of the concerns about rural crime and banditry, but also because of anxieties about revolutionary activity. Additional companies were recruited as a mobile force for rapid deployment and the *Gendarmerie* officers began to claim a distinct expertise in law and order maintenance. Mobile *Gendarmerie* companies were also created in France and, following the deaths of demonstrators during the 1930s, investigations were made into alternative methods of crowd control, specifically the use of tear gas, plastic bullets, and coloured dies that could be squirted from fire hoses. The Netherlands had not participated in the war; nevertheless the revolutionary disorders in Germany, coupled with food riots and fears of socialism at home, prompted the government to create a new militarized police unit, the *Korps Politietroepen*. But concerns about antagonizing police opinion and the rivalries between different police organizations sapped the political will to sort out what had been acknowledged since the close of the nineteenth century as an over-complex network of village constables, municipal police, and *Marechaussee*, the latter now rivalled by the *Politietroepen*. Spanish Republicans rose to the challenge of reforming the police, most notably with a new public order police that was designed to confront crowds with batons rather than the weaponry of the military Civil Guard. But again fear of antagonizing the old police order by abolition or complete reform limited the effectiveness of the changes before the army uprising that initiated the Civil War. In Germany, where military collapse prompted political revolution, various citizen militias were established to maintain some law and order and the new republican government recruited military units, the *Freikorps*, to enforce its will. In the summer of 1919 the Prussian Interior Ministry established a paramilitary 'Security Police', the *Sicherheitspolizei* or *Sipo*. But the rapid growth of this organization and its military characteristics suggested to the victorious allies that it was a body designed to bypass the strict limits imposed on the post-war German army. Under allied pressure the *Sipo* was disbanded in October 1920. The *Sipo*, in any case, did not fit with the new kind

Republic, 1918–1939', both in Gerald Blaney, Jr., *Policing Inter-War Europe: Continuity, Change and Crisis, 1918–1940*, London: Palgrave, 2006.

of police that the leaders of Weimar Germany wanted to create for the republic.[12]

The idea of the civil, unarmed and ostensibly non-political British Bobby remained a potent one with liberals across Europe in the inter-war period. And even though it was increasingly being undermined by new policies from the centre, the system of local government control of the police helped to maintain the image of the Bobby by stifling much critical investigation. Whenever a home secretary was asked to investigate police behaviour outside of London, he was able to respond that, since he was not the police authority, he could not sanction any inquiry. Metropolitan London was different. But here inquiries into high-handed police behaviour and parliamentary questions, often initiated by the infant National Council for Civil Liberties, about police behaviour at political meetings were commonly seen as irritants and politically motivated attempts to tarnish what was sincerely considered to be a fine institution. In 1929 a Royal Commission concluded that the police had a good relationship with the public and that, while any large public body was bound to have one or two disreputable individuals in its ranks, taken in the round there were no problems with the institution. The proceedings of the commission had shared newspaper pages with reports of a corruption trial at the Old Bailey involving a Metropolitan Police sergeant. The sergeant, George Goddard, had already been dismissed from the police and was found guilty as charged. It would be wrong to see the Goddard affair as typical of the police as a whole; but the full story never appeared in 1929 and it suggests a cover-up, the victimization of a whistle-blower, and, in some areas, systematic corruption involving police officers, restaurateurs, night-club owners, prostitutes, and various small traders. At the time, and subsequently, Goddard was labelled as a 'rotten apple'. In public throughout the inter-war years, British, and perhaps more specifically English, politicians, political commentators, and senior police officers still claimed that their police were the best in the world.[13]

The respectable image of the Bobby was something that liberal politicians hoped to see emulated in their own police. Moreover, they hoped to harness such an image to new technologies, something about which, during the

---

[12] These issues are explored extensively in the essays contained in Blaney, *Policing Inter-War Europe*.

[13] Clive Emsley, 'Sergeant Goddard: The Story of a Rotten Apple, or a Diseased Orchard?', in Amy Gilman Srebnick and René Lévy, eds., *Crime and Culture: An Historical Perspective*, Aldershot: Ashgate, 2005.

inter-war period, the police in Britain continued to be very lackadaisical.[14] As in Britain and France, much of the policing in the Weimar Republic was decentralized; police institutions remained largely under the direction of the separate, federated states. Fingerprint records were centralized in Berlin and missing persons searches were co-ordinated from Dresden, but further attempts at centralization were opposed by the individual states.[15] Prussia was the largest state in Germany and contained about two-thirds of the republic's population, hence its continuing importance. The key figure in reshaping the Prussian Police during the Weimar period was Wilhelm Abegg. A civil servant in Imperial Germany who had reorganized the Prussian Police towards the end of the war, Abegg became a leading figure in the Prussian Interior Ministry under the republic. He was keen to establish the kind of technocratic, liberal police officer increasingly advocated in the years immediately before the outbreak of war. In 1926, to coincide with the International Police Congress held in Berlin, Abegg and Carl Severing, the Social Democratic Interior Minister, organized a police exhibition that was intended to show the police officer as a dedicated friend and helper of the public. In the same year, under Abegg's editorship and with the support of the Prussian Interior Ministry, publication began of a series of short books on policing written by noted academics and senior police administrators. The books acknowledged the authoritarian nature of previous policing in Germany but stressed how things had changed and would change further, particularly with the adoption of modern ideas and technologies.[16]

There is commonly a gap between what politicians and commentators boast about their police and the behaviour of many patrolmen on the beat.

---

[14] In the provinces scientific aids to detection and police communications depended on the whims of chief constables and on what local government was prepared to finance. In the late 1930s a Home Office committee concluded that detective policing required a significant overhaul, but implementation of the report, most of which remained confidential, was interrupted by the new war. See e.g. *Report of the Departmental Committee on Detective Work and Procedure*, 5 vols., London: HMSO, 1939. Volumes ii, iii, and iv have, on their front pages: 'This Document is supplied for Official Use and the Contents should not be made public.' The committee was established in 1933 and reported five years later.

[15] For the police during the Weimar Republic see, in particular, Richard Bessel, 'Policing, Professionalisation and Politics in Weimar Germany', in Emsley and Weinberger, eds., *Policing Western Europe*; Peter Leßmann, *Die preußische Schutzpolizei in der Weimarer Republik. Streifendienst und Straßenkampf*, Düsseldorf: Droste, 1989; Hsi-Huey Liang, *The Berlin Police Force in the Weimar Republic*, Berkeley.: University of California Press, 1970.

[16] The dozen books included *Geschichte der Polizei*, by Karl Melcher, the Police Chief of Essen; *Polizei und Politik*, by Bernhard Wiess, the director of the Criminal Police section of the Berlin Police; *Polizei und Verbrechen*, by Robert Heindl, who collaborated with Schober in calling the International Police Congress in Vienna in 1923; *Polizei und Sitte*, by the noted psychologist and sexologist Albert Moll.

For commentators drawn from the British political elite the Bobbies may have constituted the best police in the world between the wars, but there were still some very rough policemen on the beat. In some of the rougher working-class districts of the big towns a policeman needed to be tough to secure a personal legitimacy and to stamp his authority. The development of the motor car also meant that, for the first time in Britain, the police were increasingly brought into conflict with the respectable, propertied classes. The latter began to learn that police officers were not always civil or deferential to their social superiors when they perceived a breach of the law.[17] In Weimar Germany and in the successor states of the Austro-Hungarian Empire, it was one thing for chiefs of police and their political masters to design a new police force in which the individual officer became a friend and helper of the public and a loyal supporter of the republic, but it was quite another to implement the design. The need to create a police institution rapidly in the aftermath of war meant that many of the old officer corps, with an ambivalent attitude to the new regime, remained in post in states like Czechoslovakia and Germany. And in Germany the difficulty in getting new recruits, at least before the Depression hit, meant that many of the new men were former soldiers with little experience of civilian life. Some of these appear to have moved from the army to the *Sipo* and thence to the new *Schutzpolizei*. And there were other problems. After the statistical upsurge of crime in the immediate aftermath of the war, levels of offending seem to have dropped back to roughly those of pre-war, but this did not halt the Weimar media's obsession with the topic. The growth of motor traffic brought new burdens and complications. Some people appear to have taken the idea of 'friend and helper' literally and they made increasing demands on police time, though the police never built successful relationships of trust with key sections of the urban working class. Quite the contrary, in fact, even when the police leadership was social democratic. Above all, however, and especially as the 1930s opened, there was a growing problem of maintaining order and coping with escalating political violence on the streets.

First in Italy and then in Germany political violence and disorder on the streets gave way to new authoritarian regimes. Liberal Italy's police legislation formed the basis for that of Fascist Italy, but there remains debate about the

    [17] Clive Emsley, *Hard Men: Violence in England since 1750*, London: Hambledon, 2005, ch. 8; idem, ' "Mother, what *did* policemen do when there weren't any motors?" The Law, the Police and the Regulation of Motor Traffic in England, 1900–1939', *Historical Journal*, 36, 2 (1993), 357–81.

extent of continuities and similarities. Some police officers were sympathetic to Mussolini before his March on Rome in October 1922. Afterwards, many more were content with the relatively free hand that was given to them when dealing with those considered as police property, particularly petty offenders and political radicals. It does not appear that many individual officers had any great commitment to Fascist ideology though, as the 1930s wore on, more and more police recruits had grown up under, and been indoctrinated by, Fascist rule. After 1932 it became a requirement that all police recruits were to be members of the Fascist Party. Initially on coming to power Mussolini had favoured the *Carabinieri* and he took steps to abolish the PS. But the *Carabinieri* always boasted that their first loyalty was to the king and in 1925 Mussolini revived the PS, gave it black shirts for its best uniform, and ordered the use of the Roman salute. From 1928 every October witnessed parades and celebrations in Rome celebrating the Day of the Police (*festa della polizia*). Nevertheless, the police forces of Mussolini's Italy are probably best understood as state fascists rather than necessarily being party fascists. They enforced government policy, but often with some elasticity and without fervent commitment to the party line.[18]

Although politics and the maintenance of the state were considered to be more important police tasks than the suppression of crime, the Fascist state continued the commitment to having police leaders instructed in criminological theory and practice. In his socialist period before the war Mussolini had been highly critical of Ottolenghi and his ideas of scientific policing. For Mussolini this was sterile positivism that made no sense. After the war, however, the Fascists and scientific policing embraced. Ottolenghi joined the Fascist Party before the March on Rome, possibly through expediency. Mussolini increasingly saw value in Ottolenghi's international reputation that brought both personal honours for the man and national honour for Italy. In addition, scientific policing appeared modern, progressive, and technocratic, thus fitting with the Fascists' view of their revolution. Its biological emphasis on the crime problem also suited the Fascists' ideology and their desire to use scientific discourse to underpin police regulations for the suppression of alcoholics, juvenile offenders, prostitutes, and so forth. In addition to police officers, the students taking the courses presented in the inter-war years by

[18] Jonathan Dunnage, 'The Policing of an Italian Province during the Fascist Period: Siena, 1926–1943', in Gerard Oram, ed., *Conflict and Legality: Policing Mid-Twentieth-Century Europe*, London: Francis Boutle, 2003; idem, 'Social Control in Fascist Italy: The Role of the Police', in Clive Emsley, Eric Johnson, and Pieter Spierenburg, eds., *Social Control in Europe: 1800–2000*, Columbus: Ohio State University Press, 2004.

Ottolenghi and, following his death in 1934, by his successors, included prison guards, officers and doctors from military prisons, and even members of the Fascist militia. In 1937 a special postgraduate course was announced to provide members of the judiciary with 'professional, technical knowledge'.[19]

In 1933 the police of the Weimar Republic made a smooth transition to become the police of the Third Reich. There were significant parallels with what had happened in Italy, but subsequently Nazi control of the police appears to have been much more rigorous.[20] The smooth transition was not because German police officers were authoritarian, right-wing, closet Nazis. There were Nazi sympathizers in the police ranks and there was tension between the police and their social democratic superiors over pay and also over the approaching end of the first set of twelve-year police service contracts introduced under Weimar. But the Nazis promised an accommodation with non-political professionals and a society within which the position of such professionals would be enhanced, where police budgets would be increased, and where pettyfogging democratic restrictions and emphases on the rights of the defendant would be subordinated to the professional tasks of fighting crime and maintaining order.

The Nazis took many of the ideas circulating about police and policing, crime and criminals and, infusing them with their own ideology, used them to curry favour with police and people.[21] For both home and overseas consumption, they also stressed their modernizing policies and the use of technology. For the first time in Germany the police were centralized. The detective police (*Kriminalpolizei* or *Kripo*) and the political police (*Geheime Staatspolizei* or *Gestapo*) became two divisions of a single Security Police under the command of Reinhard Heydrich. The Order Police (*Ordnungspolizei* or *Orpo*) was singularly unified under the command of Kurt Daluege. The unified *Orpo* consisted of four divisions: municipal policing, rural policing, fire fighting, and the technical services; the latter were originally created in 1919 to ensure the maintenance of water, gas, and electricity during strikes

---

[19] Mary Gibson, *Born to Crime: Cesare Lombroso and the Origins of Biological Criminality*, Westport, Conn.: Praeger, 2002, 140–4; Collin, 'The Italian Police and Internal Security', 70; for the 1937 course see *Bolletino della Scuola di Polizia Scientifica*, 27–9 (1937–9), 160.

[20] Jonathan Dunnage, 'Policing Right-Wing Dictatorships: Some Preliminary Comparisons of Fascist Italy, Nazi Germany and Franco's Spain', *CHS* 10, 1 (2006), 93–122.

[21] The following is drawn principally from Robert Gellately, *Backing Hitler: Consent and Coercion in Nazi Germany*, Oxford: Oxford University Press, 2001, esp. 43–7 and 91–4; and Philip Blood, 'Kurt Daluege and the Militarisation of the *Ordnungspolizei*', in Oram, ed., *Conflict and Legality*; see also Patrick Wagner, *Hitlers Kriminalisten: Die deutsche Kriminalpolizei und der Nationalsozialismus zwischen 1920 und 1960*, Munich: C. H. Beck, 2002.

and national emergency. Within a year the police were claiming enormous successes in the suppression of criminality and it was not long before detectives were publicly looking forward to being able to solve any and every crime. Foreign visitors were invited to visit the offices of *Kripo* and to be impressed by their modernity and technical equipment; and many went away suitably impressed. In 1934 the Nazis organized their first 'Day of the German Police' (*Tag der deutschen Polizei*). By 1937 this had become far more sophisticated than its Italian counterpart. It was a week-long event with bands, parades, charity collections; there was also an emphasis on the police officer as an 'expert', as the 'friend and helper' of the people, and as the 'enemy' of the criminal and those who threatened the state and the national community (*Volkesgemeinschaft*). The argument was made that it was worth giving up some rights to fight crime and maintain order; criminals and enemies of the state, after all, were 'degenerates' and, as Heydrich put it, many of the former had developed from an 'inherited disposition'. Daluege urged his men to think of themselves as the people's servants who would also help to develop a better sense of order among the people. A Nazi *Schutzman* was no longer to be one of the old, despised 'truncheon guards' (*Knüppelgarde*) but he was to be inspired by the military ideals of discipline, honour, and obedience. In 1939 Daluege's men were issued with their own Ten Commandments that, in addition to demanding loyalty to the Führer and ruthlessness to enemies of the state, urged:

Behave toward people as you would want them to behave toward you (Four).
Be true, be modest, lies are ordinary, bribes and the desire for pleasure dishonourable (Five).
Do not neglect your appearance because it is a picture of your inner self (Seven).
Train and improve yourself; respect should be your highest pride (Ten).

As the German armies moved east with the outbreak of the Second World War, Daluege's militarized, often middle-aged police officers followed to enforce Nazi policies that included mass executions. On the Day of the German Police in 1940 the principal Nazi newspaper, *Völkischer Beobachter*, explained that in Poland the German police battalions were re-establishing a clear legal order by putting an end to the 'unimaginable' amount of crime and by destroying 'bandits and criminal riffraff'. Overall, it would seem that the German police did not show, or perhaps were never allowed to consider, the differentiation between state fascism and party fascism of their Italian counterparts.

The penal system in Germany followed a somewhat similar trajectory to that of the police. During the Weimar period penal reformers, notably the group of university teachers, prison officials, and civil servants who formed the Study Group for Prison Reform (*Arbeitsgemeinschaft für Reform des Strafvollzugs*), urged that prisoners had the rights of citizens, and should receive education and training for useful jobs on their release. A few of the states adopted the progressive ideas. A model penitentiary was established at Untermaßfeld in Thuringia. Discussions were also begun for the preparation of a new criminal code with the fervent hope expressed by many reformers, that this would see the end of the death penalty. But there were problems. While Thuringia was progressive, other federated states of the republic maintained conservative prison regimes and the majority of people working as prison officers disliked the reformers' ideas. At Untermaßfeld the prison officers resented the introduction of social workers who appeared to encroach on their authority; even more, they resented being accountable to prison tribunals. Courses on the reformative prison service were boycotted, on one occasion in favour of attending courses on Japanese wrestling. Debates on the new criminal code and the death penalty stalled in the political shifts towards the end of the regime and under pressure generated by the trial and sentence of the notorious serial murderer Peter Kürten.

The transition to the Third Reich was as seamless in the prison service as it was in the police. The Nazis cashed in on Weimar's fascination with crime and on populist and right-wing protests that the prisons were becoming too much like hotels and that the reform programmes were soft. A few officials closely identified with the Weimar reforms were removed but the majority of prison officers, even those who had supported the SPD, kept their jobs. Prison officers began to join the Nazi Party as it seemed the right thing to do for their career, and some party activists joined the prison service. While it would be impossible to prove statistically, it seems that violent assaults on prisoners increased, though even during the Nazi period extreme violence by prison officers who were also party members might be punished. The Nazi understanding of modern penal policy was manifested in the development of prison camps in which the inmates performed hard physical labour on the land or on public works. Edgar Schmidt, a prison governor and subsequently a leading figure in the Nazi prison administration, summed up the intentions to a visiting delegation of British prison administrators in 1934: 'He who will not hear must feel'. In addition to the tougher prison policies, the Nazi regime granted wide powers of preventive detention to the courts and to the police. From 1936 recidivists and suspects could be incarcerated indefinitely on police direction and without any judicial scrutiny. The number of death sentences, and the number of executions that were carried out, began to rise steadily from the Nazi take-over.[22]

A fascist regime was not a prerequisite for the adoption of policies based on eugenics solutions, as is demonstrated by the sterilization practices of the liberal democratic Scandinavian countries—Denmark, Norway, and Sweden.[23] Nevertheless, the Nazis picked up on the biological notions of criminality and eugenics that had continued to circulate in Weimar Germany. Such ideas fitted well with their simplistic, populist Darwinian notions, and by looking back to the work of the German biologist Ernst Haeckel they were able to bypass any link with the ideas of Lombroso, a Jew. At the same time, however, there were a few theorists who seized the opportunities provided by Nazi attitudes to test their own theories of the biological origins of criminal behaviour.[24] During the Weimar Republic the sterilization of criminals had received support from among sections of the SPD. The Nazis introduced a Sterilization Law in the summer of 1933, though initially the Ministry of Justice limited its broad use against those labelled 'criminals'. Six years later 'criminally insane persons' were included in the categories listed for the euthanasia programme.

Nazi Germany inflicted terrible physical violence on the bodies of its victims, criminals as well as political and 'racial' enemies, particularly after its armies marched east in 1939. At first, those sentenced to be executed were commonly beheaded; gallows, gas, and guns increasingly took over, however, as, during wartime, the numbers sentenced to execution or catego-rized for 'special treatment' reached astonishing levels. But in Germany at least, the squeamishness and sensibility towards public punishment that has been associated with Elias's civilizing process was largely maintained until

[22] Richard J. Evans, *Rituals of Retribution:Capital Punishment in Germany 1600–2000*, Oxford: Oxford University Press, 1996, esp. chs. 13 and 14; Nikolaus Wachsmann, *Hitler's Prisons: Legal Terror in Nazi Germany*, New Haven and London: Yale University Press, 2004, esp. 27–9, 78–9, 85–6, and 101–6. Edgar Schmidt himself was a member of the Catholic Centre Party and did not join the Nazi Party until 1937. The British delegation was unimpressed and came away thinking that Germany's new penal system was using punitive measures to the detriment of education and reform.

[23] Patrick Zylberman, 'Les damnés de la democratie puritaine: stérilisations en Scandanavie, 1929–1977', *Le Mouvement social*, 187 (1999), 99–125. Zylberman includes Finland in his analysis, but makes the point that this had an authoritarian regime in the inter-war period.

[24] Patrick Wagner, *Volksgemeinschaft ohne Verbrecher. Konzeptionen und Praxis der Kriminalpolizei in der Zeit der Weimarer Republik und des Nationalsocialismus*, Hamburg: Hans Christian Verlag, 1996, 265–78.

the closing stages of the war when some offenders were executed in the streets. The stigma of public shame was not inflicted on criminals though, arguably, this was partly the intention behind the requirement that Jews wear a yellow Star of David. Nazi Germany was, perhaps, the closest that Europe had yet come to a full carceral society. Large numbers of offenders and enemies of the *Volkesgemeinschaft* were incarcerated in different forms of closed institution—asylum, prison, concentration camp—sometimes simply on the word of experts such as police officers or judges. Sometimes medical experts experimented upon them. Yet many German criminologists—also experts—continued research that was untainted by the crude genetic determinism or racism of the party. And once the Nazis decided to extend preventive detention to habitual criminals, to sterilize some and to kill others, their penal administrators were confronted with the complex problem of how, precisely, to assess which individuals were irredeemable. In addition, while violence could be employed as therapy on those who had the potential to return to their families, to take responsibility, and to behave in a law-abiding fashion, the Nazi penal bureaucracy and its advisers were again compelled to focus on specific individuals. Some criteria had to be established in each case so as to decide whether or not an individual's criminal behaviour was congenital or the result of circumstances, and this forced them to engage with the continuing debates of criminologists, psychologists, and others.

There is another issue here. The disciplined society of the Third Reich might be considered also to have spread beyond the asylum, the prison, and the camp as friends and relations were encouraged to inform upon the activities of others. Denunciation also played a role in Fascist Italy and Franco's Spain. In Germany most written denunciations were signed; in Italy most were anonymous. And the problem remains to assess how far denunciation to a modern authoritarian regime was significantly different from denunciation to earlier regimes, or from the intense scrutiny of neighbours, the gossip and the potential for ostracism or shaming through charivari that occurred earlier in ordinary village communities.[25]

An extreme form of carceral society also developed in the Soviet Union. Indeed, in 1935 flight from this society became a capital offence and the remaining adult members of such a fugitive's family became liable to five

---

[25] See *Practices of Denunciation in Modern European History, 1789–1989*, special issue of the *Journal of Modern History*, 64, 4 (1996); Dunnage, 'Policing Right-Wing Dictatorships', 116–17. For denunciation in earlier periods, see, Michaela Hohkamp and Claudia Ulbrich, eds., *Der Staatsbürger als Spitzel. Denunziation während des 18. und 19. Jahrhunderts aus eurpäischer Perspektive*, Leipzig: Leipziger Universitätsverlag, 2001.

years' internal exile. A Soviet law book explained the 'political significance' of this as merely 'the strengthening of the overall action of the criminal law for the purpose of averting so heinous a felony'.[26] After experiments with popular policing during the revolution the Soviet authorities established a new police institution, the militia. The militia was supervised by Communist Party commissars and was deployed to enforce the new economic, political, and social system. The Enlightenment dream of a citizen's life, liberty, and property being protected, which had come to dominate much thinking during the nineteenth century, acquired a new slant. In the Soviet Union the means of production was in the hands of the state and the party, and the criminal law was used with a new and greater emphasis against those stigmatized as idle or undermining production. A worker who arrived ten minutes late for work on two occasions could be sentenced to five years in a labour camp. A worker who bought a packet of cigarettes in one place and sold them in another could receive a similar sentence on a charge of speculation. The ordinary militiamen were poorly paid and poorly equipped, but the police could do no wrong within the understanding of the system. One victim claimed to have been told: 'we never arrest anyone who is not guilty. And even if you weren't guilty, we can't release you because people would say that we are picking up innocent people.' There was a Soviet legal code established in 1922–3; there were formal legal institutions, guaranteed judicial procedures and rules of evidence. But Soviet prosecutors, taking their cue from Andrei Vyshinsky, the Attorney General, Professor of Law and Vice Chancellor of Moscow University, felt free to dismiss these when they appeared to confuse or deflect from Soviet justice. In the trial of a group of people accused of bribery in 1923, for example, Vyshinsky protested that 'though the facts of the alleged actions . . . had not been demonstrated, nevertheless all the circumstances "cry out" that "something stinks".' And he demanded the death penalty.[27]

As in other authoritarian regimes, the Soviets drew on denunciation. There was a tradition of denunciation in Russian society. The Bolsheviks, along with other revolutionaries, had condemned this during the Tsarist regime, but rapidly adopted their own variant as virtuous and necessary. The forced, humiliating confessions made in the courts, particularly required

---

[26] Quoted in Robert Conquest, *The Great Terror: Stalin's Purges of the Thirties*, rev. edn., London: Macmillan, 1973, 128–9.

[27] Adam Bosiacki, 'Andrei Yanuarevitch Vyshinsky: Paragon of the Totalitarian Conception of the Law and Political Organization', in Jerzy W. Boreisza and Klaus Ziemer, eds., *Totalitarian and Authoritarian Regimes in Europe: Legacies and Lessons from the Twentieth Century*, New York and Oxford: Berghahn Books, 2006; quotation at p. 179.

from political offenders, may be considered as reminiscent of the old shaming punishments. The Tsarist *katorga* was vastly expanded under Stalin into the Gulag. Propaganda, often penned by intellectuals such as Maxim Gorky, took up the penal welfare discourse and insisted that the aim of the system was to transform offenders into good citizens and workers. In Nikolai Pogodin's play about convicts working on the White Sea Canal the convicts sing enthusiastically:

> I was a cruel bandit, yes,
> I stole from the people, hated to work,
> My life was black like the night.
> But then they took me to the canal,
> Everything past now seems a bad dream.
> It is as if I were reborn.
> I want to work, and live and sing . . .

But within the Gulag the authorities commonly allowed the toughest common criminals to maintain order and control through violence and intimidation.[28] And the form of the Gulag, like the form of Nazi incarceration, was of a completely different order to that of liberal democratic societies.

Liberal democratic societies debated many of the same issues, using much the same penalogical discourse as the authoritarian states.[29] A bill for the sterilization of 'mental defectives' was introduced into the British parliament in 1931. It received cross-party support; but the cross-party opposition was greater and the bill fell. The concept of preventive detention had been introduced into both Britain and France before the war, but it was never enforced with the determination of Nazi Germany or given political colouring in the manner of the Soviet Union. In Britain, where there were only just over 120 persons held in preventive detention during the 1930s, the judges were among those accused of sabotaging the concept by opting to pass

---

[28] Anne Applebaum, *Gulag: A History of the Soviet Camps*, London: Allen Lane, 2003. The two examples of men given five years in the labour camps are to be found on p. 272; the quotations are at pp. 140 and 82. For the militia see e.g. Louise I. Shelley, *Policing Soviet Society: The Evolution of State Control*, London: Routledge, 1996, ch. 2. For denunciation see Jeffrey Burds, 'A Culture of Denunciation: Peasant Labour Migration and Religious Anathematization in Rural Russia, 1860–1905', and Sheila Fitzpatrick, 'Signals from Below: Soviet Letters of Denunciation in the 1930s', both in *Practices of Denunciation* (n. 25 above).

[29] The two following paragraphs are based primarily on Gordon Wright, *Between the Guillotine and Liberty: Two Centuries of the Crime Problem in France*, Oxford: Oxford University Press, 1983, ch. 8; W. J. Forsythe, *Penal Discipline, Reformatory Projects and the English Prison Commission, 1895–1939*, Exeter: University of Exeter Press, 1991; Mathew Thomson, *The Problem of Mental Deficiency: Eugenics, Democracy, and Social Policy in Britain, c.1870–1959*, Oxford: Clarendon Press, 1998.

minimum sentences and by criticizing the idea of indeterminacy that was key to the policy. While prisons and labour camps expanded in the authoritarian states, in both Britain and France during the inter-war years many local prisons were closed and in 1938 the French finally put an end to the *bagne*. Mental institutions, hospitals for alcoholics, and carceral educational and training centres took some individuals brought before the courts. The Mental Deficiency Act passed in Britain in 1913, for example, was used to control the sexuality of young women and, especially, to control disruptive and criminal young men. In particular this act enabled an extension of the confinement for some 16- to 18-year-old males outside the adult prison. Forms of what contemporaries in Britain called 'care in the community' were developed that kept other individuals out of various penal institutions. At the same time stress continued to be put on educational and reformative treatment rather than on fierce discipline and the truncheon. Indeed, during the 1930s the Prison Commissioners in England had a clear ambition to replace the old Victorian prisons with more open institutions designed to encourage responsibility and self-control through greater freedoms. Violence existed within the system. Both Britain and France maintained the death penalty and in France executions continued to be public until just before the outbreak of the Second World War, though the lowering of the scaffold reduced the public's view. Flogging remained a sentence option available to British magistrates and judges in certain cases. There were opportunities for abuse and unofficial brutality behind prison walls. But the revelations of abuses and brutality could prompt reform. The exposure of scandalous behaviour by members of the staff at Mettray, for example, led the French government to order that offenders be sent there no longer and the institution was forced to close. It may be a truism, but it remains worth emphasizing that the penal systems of the liberal democratic states had a very different view of human worth to their authoritarian contemporaries.

The Nazi take-over of power in Germany brought international debate about policing and punishment to a new level. There had been serious divisions before between experts, notably in the clashes over Lombroso's ideas at criminology conferences towards the end of the nineteenth century. But during the 1930s German experts were commonly also party members and the party line became a central plank in their argument. Senior Nazi police officers, including Daluege, participated in the International Police Commission Conference in Copenhagen in 1935 and in Belgrade in 1936. They declined the invitation to the London Conference of 1937 since the invitation, apparently in an attempt to stifle Nazi pomp and spectacle, advised that uniforms would not be worn. The following year, as a corollary of the *Anschluss*, the Nazis took control of the commission anyway.[30] In the same year that Nazi police officers went to Copenhagen, Berlin was host to the 11th International Penal and Penitentiary Congress. Here delegates were lectured by Nazi penal experts, as well as by Joseph Goebbels, on Germany's position as a bulwark against communism and on the new system by which judges would be able to act from their knowledge 'of the uniform national view' that gave them 'a secure feeling of what was right and wrong' regardless of the formal law—he would, of course, have rejected the obvious parallel here with Vyshinsky. More significant, however, was the wide gulf that emerged over policies regarding an individual's defence in a major political trial, the sterilization of offenders, and the value of severity and 'humanization' in punishment. The gulf was accentuated by arguments about whether votes should be taken by head, which guaranteed a majority for the German side, or by nation state.[31]

During the inter-war years both authoritarian and liberal democratic states centralized their police, used much the same discourse about offenders and carceral solutions, and claimed to construct their penal systems on the advice of experts and on the basis of scientific research. The authoritarian states claimed to be pursuing many of the penal and policing ideas prevalent since the Enlightenment and they employed the discourse of penal welfarism. They promised to ensure the security of the law-abiding, to punish and control offenders, and even in a perverted sense to care for and rehabilitate them. It makes perfect sense to explore the authoritarian and the liberal democratic systems separately in their respective national contexts and to see them as manifesting strategies for greater control, discipline, and surveillance. But when set side-by-side in a comparative framework the outcomes looked, and the resulting practices were, vastly different. This does not preclude a unifying theoretical explanation. Rather it emphasizes that the idea of the carceral society, of the developing significance of the penal expert and of surveillance in general, must always be deployed with an awareness of human agency and of the political and economic context.

---

[30] Deflem, *Policing World Society*, 169–70.
[31] There were almost daily reports of the congress in *The Times*, 20, 22, 23, 24 and 26 August 1935; followed by two letters to the editor from participants, 27 and 30 August. The quotation is from the speech by Franz Gürtner, Reich Minister of Justice, to the first plenary session; *Times*, 20 August 1935, p. 11.

14

National Paths: Common Patterns

AT first glance it may seem perverse to end this survey around 1940, but there are good reasons. The Second World War signalled the end of the European domination of the world; it also signalled the end, or at least a significant moment, in the decline of the Enlightenment faith in progress that had informed so much penal policy since the mid-eighteenth century. The end of the war saw another panic about brutalized veterans starting a crime wave, but the most marked and lasting increase in the statistics of crime, at least across western Europe, came during the 1960s. Moreover, this increase, in a time of growing affluence and consumerism affecting all social groups, created a problem for the old paradigm that stigmatized the poor or the less integrated sections of society as the criminal threat.[1]

Over the period 1750 to 1940 in Europe there were both considerable changes and considerable continuities in the understanding of the criminal, in the development of police institutions, and in penal policies. Equally, while there were major national differences in laws and institutions, there were also broad similarities. Across the period, experts exchanged ideas and governments looked at what seemed to work elsewhere and sought to adapt institutions and practices to their own use. In very broad terms, offenders went from being perceived by state jurists, by self-proclaimed reformers, and by other commentators as members of social groups often on the fringe of ordinary society, to individuals that might be redeemed, to a dangerous class at war with society, to individuals with problems mental, social, and otherwise who might be helped by education, training, or treatment. These were generally broad shifts in emphasis rather than the obliteration of one set of notions by another. In the twentieth century, for example, it was still popular in some quarters, especially in the media, to portray criminals as

---

[1] Though the idea of a criminal 'underclass' was vigorously revived at the close of the twentieth century see e.g. Ruth Lister, ed., *Charles Murray and the Underclass: The Developing Debate*, London: IEA, 1996.

an identifiable group at war with society. This was a result of the cultural embroidery that sought to make sense of criminal offending and to mediate it for a variety of audiences.

Throughout the period covered by this volume moral entrepreneurs explained criminal behaviour in ways that suited their remedies and their careers. This is not to say that they conspired deliberately to mislead. Rather it was the case that the rational arguments that they used of pinpointing problems and then working out their solutions were not as linear and as logical as they liked to maintain and, almost certainly, as they believed. Their fixed focus led them to ignore, first, the mindset within which they appear to have stigmatized offenders and, second, the possibility that their solutions were already clear in their own minds before they had analysed the problem. The same might be said of the academics, the medical, and the legal experts who, from the late nineteenth century, developed the discipline of criminal anthropology and, later, criminology.

Media treatment of offenders and of crime shows considerable continuity over the period. Once there was a significant collection of statistics for the experts, both the moral entrepreneur and the criminal anthropologist were compelled to admit that most crime was petty. The media made a genuflection in this direction, at least in as much as some petty offences were usually reported in the small print of newspapers. But a significant proportion of the media was always involved with excitement and with hooking its audience as much as with reporting what was happening with any precision. Broadsides, ballads, chapbooks, then front pages, illustrated supplements, and the cinema all put their emphasis on spectacular and shocking criminal stories. Such emphases were significant for the ways in which the popular understanding of crime developed. It was not as victim or perpetrator that most people experienced crime, but through the media, and the media has always presented a distinctive, invariably colourful and sensational view of crime and criminals.

Criminal offending has never been restricted to a single social class. The end of the old regime saw the abolition of venal posts in state adminis-tration; henceforward profiteering from an official position acquired a more pronounced moral sanction and often also a criminal one. The growth of cap-italist enterprise in the late eighteenth century and throughout the nineteenth provided new opportunities for the offender who appeared well-to-do and respectable—the 'white-collar' criminal. Yet, in constructing the image of the criminal, moral entrepreneurs, journalists, novelists, and others—sometimes themselves former police officers or people with some position in the criminal justice system—had recourse to a series of recurring narratives that rarely considered the well-to-do offender. There was the assumption that 'the criminal' was not an ordinary member of society. In the eighteenth century, and earlier, there was some clear reality to this assumption in the way that, in continental Europe at least, bands of brigands or bandits sometimes recruited among people in stigmatized and ostracized trades or groups. But it also became a commonplace to chart an individual criminal's personal decline as a result of a lack of moral fibre or of appropriate role models. Hogarth's dramatic portrayal of the path that led the idle apprentice to the gallows is one particularly striking representation of this narrative, but it was not unique. There was a logical simplicity and a comforting morality in the description of a criminal career following a linear pattern from petty offences when the offender was a child to serious, violent crimes as he—and the majority of offenders were male—matured. There was a similar simplicity in the notion that criminal offenders were not like other, respectable folk, especially when they could be linked with groups that appeared to threaten the stability of society such as vagrants, revolutionaries, foreigners or, in the case of female prostitutes, women who could be accused of having rejected their 'natural' role. It was comforting, too, if the offender could convincingly be portrayed as a throwback or a monster. These narratives emerged and, with some tinkering, re-emerged across the period. Towards the end of the nineteenth century they began to be given a degree of scientific and theoretical underpinning; but they also always played to a common-sense populism.

There was another side to this. In some circumstances, and for some social groups, it was welcome if the offender was cocking a snook at authority. Everyone could admire a hero who robbed the rich to aid the poor. Even the rich could admire such a hero, as long as he was dead, or had lived a long time ago and was not being portrayed as a role model for the present. And, of course, for many respectable, liberal-minded people of wealth it was obvious that the good bandit would recognize their philanthropy and never consider them to be targets.

There were greater means of control and new levels of surveillance established during the period. Some of this control was internal and personal to the individual. The duel continued, especially among military personnel and within societies that exalted military prowess such as Imperial Germany and Fascist Italy. But from the Enlightenment there was a growing belief among the educated and respectable classes that a man's honour and reputation did not depend overwhelmingly on his physical strength or martial skills and on his preparedness to use violence. As Norbert Elias's subtle and nuanced civilizing process convincingly argues, this was not something imposed from above. Indeed, in some states and regions, notably in parts of southern Europe, attempts at such an imposition from above met with very little immediate success. Yet, broadly speaking, across the nineteenth century certain forms of customary behaviour, including the community punishment of offenders, were increasingly stigmatized by the educated as 'violent' and 'primitive'. And, increasingly, members of the plebeian classes, especially those in respectable trades and who aspired to inclusion in the political nation, began to acknowledge the new norms and themselves to marginalize behaviour that they considered violent. The new sensibility towards the public manifestation of physical violence was further reflected in the state's increasing turn towards private punishment, particularly in the regulated, reforming structure of the penitentiary.

The nineteenth-century European state established greater control and surveillance over its citizens in part by means of its new police and penal institutions. Earlier princes may have aspired to such control, but the nineteenth-century state had the ability as well as the aspiration so to do. The new fiscal and bureaucratic structures that emerged from the Revolutionary and Napoleonic period enabled an expansion of police and penal institutions that had been impossible under the old regime. Moreover in the changing political context policing was seen as desirable not only because it could help check threats to the state but also because it enhanced the legitimacy of the state. The police, it was argued, were present to protect and assist the citizen. The police may have been experienced principally as a pressure by much of the working class and the peasantry for much of the nineteenth century. In addition, the system may have allowed for the victimization of some innocent individuals by virtue of their ethnicity, social, or, in the case of female prostitutes, gender grouping. Yet the promises of assistance and protection had an appeal to those of modest property as well as to their social superiors. It was also something that had an appeal at least to some of those who were likely to be ignored under traditional forms of settling offences; female victims of rape in some rural areas provide an obvious example.

Alongside modern, bureaucratic police was developed also the modern prison. Again the new fiscal and bureaucratic structures provided money and administrative drive, though it is also important to recognize the continuing presence of private philanthropy, particularly in the running of reformatories for young offenders and for prostitutes. The structure of the prison has parallels with similar institutions that were also developed simultaneously over the period. Asylums, hospitals, and workhouses, like prisons, were often shaped by a mixture of private philanthropy and state involvement. And the idea of reforming as well as punishing offenders also had echoes in what went on within these other institutions. Reformers and liberals considered the penitentiary as a great improvement on extensive capital and corporal punishment and as a mark of humanitarian progress that they equated with civilization. Most of the individuals incarcerated in the prisons came from the poorer sections of society. But while the criminal justice systems of Europe may have assisted in the maintenance of a grossly unequal division of wealth, it is probably also true that most of the victims of those incarcerated were not drawn from the wealthiest and most powerful sections of society either.

There were always limitations to the development of the new policing and penal institutions. Some of these were cultural. The English tradition of liberty, for example, militated against the development of a military-style or an armed police. Across Europe some all-male juries lagged behind the judges, the jurists, and the law in their condemnation of violence, especially when it involved male honour or the 'disciplining' of a wife. Some of the limitations were political; and everywhere institutional change was limited by financial considerations. Politicians and others may have talked about a war against crime and criminals, but the brakes upon expenditure were rarely released to fight this war in quite the way that they were released to fight international or civil conflicts.

Contemporaries, from the Enlightenment to the aftermath of the First World War and even beyond, liked to link many of the changes in policing and penal policy to ideas of progress and to a growing humanitarianism. There were assumptions about the superiority of educated, rational European society and the possibilities for its social inferiors and even for the rest of the world when this civilization was spread through example and education. Many enthusiastic advocates of the new prisons saw in them the opportunity of reforming young, and even hardened offenders through the Bible, through work, and even by some education. At different times, and in different places, the penitentiary regimes swung between an emphasis on tough punishment and a meagre diet and an emphasis on reform and rehabilitation. But as the nineteenth century wore on the problem was highlighted not only of how to explain those who, it appeared, would not reform, but also of what to do with them. Even some liberals, fired by ideas of humanitarianism and progress, subscribed to harsh and fearsome policies in this situation, specifically life imprisonment and sterilization. Those societies that prided themselves on rejecting liberal scruples went even further.

During the Second World War a bestial nadir was reached in some of the concepts developed during the nineteenth century and used, in part, to describe criminal offenders. In the war's aftermath a bleaker view of Western societies emerged. The generation of 1968 read the Marxist philosopher Herbert Marcuse and recognized that, by demonstrating on the streets, they could force a bourgeois state to reveal a repressive nature. And working out from here Michel Foucault found it possible to describe a disciplined society under a surveillance that was epitomized by a merry-go-round criminal justice system. 'Police surveillance provides the prison with offenders, which the prison transforms into delinquents, the targets and auxiliaries of police supervision, which regularly send back a certain number of them to prison.'[2] Once on this merry-go-round it was (and is) difficult to get off. But this was recognized early on in the nineteenth century by those philanthropic bodies that sought both to discourage juveniles from repeat offending and to help discharged prisoners. It was also recognized at the end of the nineteenth century by a range of individuals, from academic criminologists to those who sat in judgment in the criminal courts, and who sought alternatives to prison for young and first offenders. Moreover, individuals who found themselves on the merry-go-round had often made a conscious decision that got them on it in the first place. Foucault's merry-go-round has no space for attempts to divert the offender. Nor does it have space for any consideration of the victims of those that are, allegedly, created and perpetuated as delinquents or deviants. Indeed, while victims have been increasingly the focus of contemporary criminology, with the exception of the battered woman and the abused child, victims have been sadly neglected by the recent historians of crime.[3]

A further problem with Foucault's notion of the carceral society is that it allows so little space for human agency and for differences between political contexts, forms, and structures. It is, perhaps, significant that he concluded *Discipline and Punish* in the mid-nineteenth century. There was a broad consensus in Europe and the United States on the need for penal change during these years and on the form that such change might take. By the end

---

[2] Michel Foucault, *Discipline and Punish: The Birth of the Prison*, London: Allen Lane, 1977, 282.
[3] But see Benoît Garnot, ed., *Les victimes, des oubliées de l'histoire*, Rennes: Presses Universitaires de Rennes, 2000.

of the century many prisons still did not have a cellular structure and medical and psychiatric experts were still struggling for full acceptance in parts of the criminal justice process. Nevertheless, on the eve of the First World War most European states were broadly in step with each other. Courts and penal policies were shifting away from a determination to impose equality of punishment with punishments dictated by the crime, preferring increasingly to impose a punishment tailored specifically to the offending individual. The rise of states directed by individuals who put state and ideology above the individual, however, meant that by the 1930s there were enormous differences in ideology and form between the penal institutions and policies of liberal democratic states such as Britain and France and the carceral archipelagos of Nazi Germany and Soviet Russia.

There was a great deal of continuity between policing, penal and medical discourses, practices and institutions across Europe during the inter-war years. The practices employed by the functionaries of the criminal justice systems to achieve their aims were also similar: patrols, surveillance, registration, the collection of information, incarceration, and so forth. The differences between these systems were not in their discourses or practices, but in their relationship with the political system within which they were situated. In liberal democratic societies, drawing particularly on Enlightenment traditions, the law was held to be politically neutral. Such neutrality was relative, since there was always an unequal division of wealth and political power. Yet within the liberal states the rule of law was held to be both non-partisan and one of the highest principles, if not the highest. In the authoritarian states, in contrast, the rule of law was subservient to the party and the party's perception of the people's good and will.

In some ways it is tempting to suggest that the great discrepancies between the liberal democratic penal and policing systems and those of the autocratic states during the inter-war years are such as to render useless both Elias's civilizing process and Foucault's carceral society. Yet the Gulag and the concentration and death camps were sufficiently removed from public gaze to salve any squeamishness within the population. Moreover functionaries from both kinds of state employed the same kinds of discourse and, admittedly in very different degrees especially once divided by war, many similar policies. The application of the theoretical concepts, in consequence, still helps to shape questions about penal and policing policies within these different entities. And when deployed sensibly, with an eye to the significance of political and social contexts, and the potential of human agency, these concepts might also provide a contemporary warning. The concepts, practices, and structures of the criminal justice systems developed in Europe since the Enlightenment are enormously powerful institutions. They are not neutral. They can be used for good or ill. The slide from Weimar Republic to National Socialist state provides a terrible example of what can happen to such institutions when political and ideological directions are changed and certain notions of justice, even popular justice, are given pre-eminence.

Bibliographical Note

EACH chapter has detailed references. This was not done to obviate the need for a bibliography but rather to supply a full guide to further reading both chronologically and thematically. The paragraphs that follow are designed to draw attention to the kind of work that has been done, the places where broad further reading might be pursued and, by the implication of the lacunae, where further research might usefully be undertaken. The emphasis here on books in English is deliberate.

The two most influential theorists for the current research into the history of crime and criminal justice are, as has been emphasized throughout, Michel Foucault and Norbert Elias. The former's *Discipline and Punish: The Birth of the Prison* (London, 1976) is an obvious starting point, though much more of Foucault's work is also relevant. And for all of its power, it has to be emphasized that much of *Discipline and Punish* draws on the French experience over a relatively short period. In some ways Elias's work is more difficult to deploy since very little of *The Civilizing Process: Sociogenetic and Psychogenetic Investigations* (Oxford, 2000) addresses crime and, chronologically, it ends roughly at the point where this book begins. Nevertheless, both authors have provided stimulating theories from which to develop questions and to marshal material in probing the history of crime and criminal justice.

The history of crime and criminal justice has generally been written up with distinct national or regional emphases. A broad introduction to different national experiences and to the different national trajectories of research is to be found in Clive Emsley and Louis A. Knafla, eds., *Crime Histories and Histories of Crime: Studies in the Historiography of Crime and Criminal Justice in Modern History* (Westport, Conn., 1996). Book-length studies of individual national experiences include Clive Emsley, *Crime and Society in England 1750–1900* (3rd edn., London, 2004), David Taylor, *Crime, Policing and Punishment in England, 1750–1914* (London, 1998), John A. Davis, *Conflict and Control: Law and Order in Nineteenth-Century Italy* (London, 1988), and Eric H. Johnson, *Urbanization and Crime: Germany, 1871–1914* (Cambridge, 1995). Richard J. Evans, *Tales from the German Underworld* (New Haven and London, 1998) is more a collection of linked, stimulating essays than a broad survey but constitutes a valuable and important introduction to different issues in crime and criminal justice in nineteenth-century Germany. Surprisingly, given the considerable amount of significant research that has been undertaken by historians such as Frédéric Chauvaud, Jean-Claude Farcy, Dominique Kalifa, Michelle Perrot, and Bernard Schnapper, to name but a few, there is no single study of crime in France from the eighteenth to the mid-twentieth centuries. Nor is there a book that focuses on a major part of that period for the country as a whole, though Benjamin

Martin, *Crime and Criminal Justice under the Third Republic: The Shame of Marianne* (Baton Rouge, La., 1990) is useful.

There are several important studies of particular kinds of offending. Interpersonal violence has generated a flurry of publications in the last decade or so, especially with reference to England. Clive Emsley, *Hard Men: Violence in England since 1750* (London, 2005), Martin J. Wiener, *Men of Blood: Violence, Manliness and Criminal Justice in Victorian England* (Cambridge, 2004), and John Carter Wood, *Violence and Crime in Nineteenth-Century England: The Shadow of our Refinement* (London, 2004) are three book-length studies. The last particularly, with its theoretical framework drawn from Elias, provides a useful model for work elsewhere. For France the topic has been explored by Frédéric Chauvaud in *De Pierre Rivière à Landru: la violence apprivoisée au XIXe siècle* (Paris, 1991). Stephen Wilson's *Feuding, Conflict and Banditry in Nineteenth-Century Corsica* (Cambridge, 1988) is an excellent study of the society that many in mainland France stigmatized as criminal, and John Dickie's *Cosa Nostra: A History of the Sicilian Mafia* is a highly readable, but also thoroughly researched and cogently argued, study of the 'institution' that has become a byword for organized crime. It is time, perhaps, for a new synthesis of banditry and criminal gangs in the period up to the Second World War that takes us beyond Eric Hobsbawm's ground-breaking but, in spite of various revisions, now dated extended essay *Bandits*.

Cultural representations of crime, particularly representations in the press, remains a fruitful area for research. Rob Sindall, *Street Violence in the Nineteenth Century: Media Panic or Real Danger?* (Leicester, 1990) poses some important questions about the press, notably its choice of stories and its use of letters to the editor, that remain central. L. Perry Curtis, Jr., *Jack the Ripper and the London Press* (New Haven and London, 2001) is a model of what can be done in analysing the press response to a major crime. Dominique Kalifa, *L'encre et le sang: récits de crimes et société à la Belle Époque* (Paris, 1995) vividly explores the portrayal of crime, primarily in Paris, at the close of the nineteenth century, raising the key questions about whether representations in 'ink' reflect a reality or fashion the imagination.

Policing and punishment have also been addressed largely within national contexts. For policing see, for example, Clive Emsley, *The English Police: A Political and Social History* (2nd edn., London, 1996), Jean-Marc Berlière *Le monde des polices en France* (Brussels, 1996), Elaine Glovka-Spencer, *Police and the Social Order in German Cities: The Düsseldorf District, 1848–1914* (De Kalb, Ill., 1992). Michel Aubouin, ed., *Histoire et dictionnaire de la police: du Moyen Âge à nos jours* (Paris, 2005) is enormous, contains an enormous amount of information, but is also an odd mixture of rather dated and more modern perspectives. Clive Emsley, *Gendarmes and the State in Nineteenth-Century Europe* (Oxford, 1999) attempts to explore the development of a particular form of policing across the continent from the late eighteenth century to roughly the beginning of the First World War. Recently there have also been some important essay collections seeking to address, comparatively, police reforms and police experiences at particular moments. Important here are Vincent Milliot ed., *Les mémoires policiers, 1750–1850: écritures et practiques policières du Siècle des Lumières au Second Empire* (Rennes, 2006), which looks at the debates and plans surrounding police reform in France from the Revolution to the Second Empire, and Gerald Blaney, Jr., ed., *Policing Interwar Europe: Continuity, Change, Crisis* (London, 2006), which contrasts the experiences and roles of different police institutions across Europe during the inter-war period.

Capital punishment is superlatively served by Richard J. Evans's massive *Rituals of Retribution: Capital Punishment in Germany, 1600–1987* (Oxford, 1996) and V. A. C. Gatrell's passionately argued *The Hanging Tree: Execution and the English People, 1770–1868* (Oxford, 1994). For France, Gordon Wright, *Between the Guillotine and Liberty: Two Centuries of the Crime Problem in France* (Oxford, 1983) looks at both arguments about capital punishment and the development of the prison system in France from the Enlightenment to the late twentieth century. Patricia O'Brien, *The Promise of Punishment: Prisons in Nineteenth-Century France* (Princeton, 1982) is important for exploring the nineteenth-century French penal system in greater detail, and for its emphasis on the experience of those incarcerated. The key book on French prisons, however, has to be Jacques-Guy Petit, *Ces peines obscures: la prison pénale en France (1780–1875)* (Paris, 1990). Two volumes by W. J. Forsythe, *The Reform of Prisoners, 1830–1900* (London, 1987) and *Penal Discipline, Reformatory Projects and the English Prison Commission, 1895–1939* (Exeter, 1991) are essential for the study of prison policy in England, and for a challenging engagement with Foucault's ideas. The development of the prison in Germany during Weimar and, particularly, under the Nazis is the topic of Nikolaus Wachsmann's impressive *Hitler's Prisons: Legal Terror in Nazi Germany* (New Haven and London, 2004).

The history of thinking about crime and, more specifically, of criminology has generated a considerable amount of work in recent years. Again the focus has commonly been on developments in a single country. Particularly important are: Neil Davie, *Tracing the Criminal: The Rise of Scientific Criminology in Britain, 1860–1918* (Oxford, 2005); Mary Gibson, *Born to Crime: Cesare Lombroso and the Origins of Biological Criminology* (Westport, Conn., 2002); Robert A. Nye, *Crime, Madness and Politics in Modern France: The Medical Concept of National Decline* (Princeton, 1984); Richard F. Wetzell, *Inventing the Criminal: A History of German Criminology* (Chapel Hill, NC, 2000); and Martin J. Wiener, *Reconstructing the Criminal: Culture, Law and Policy in England, 1830–1914* (Cambridge, 1990). There is also the wide-ranging and stimulating collection edited by Peter Becker and Richard F. Wetzell, *Criminals and their Scientists: The History of Criminology in Comparative Perspective* (New York, 2006). Drawing on Foucault, the collection addresses criminology as a 'discursive practice', and explores the topic from the perspective of the non-academic police officers and judges as well as that of academics and doctors. German readers ought also to consult Becker's *Verderbnis und Entartung: eine Geschichte der Kriminologie der 19. Jahrhunderts als Diskurs und Praxis* (Göttingen, 2002). Laurent Mucchielli's *Histoire de la criminologie française* (Paris, 1994) is an edited collection but is structured as a broad chronological account.

Anyone keen to pursue the subject needs to keep abreast of the journal literature; most academic journals concerned with cultural and social history or criminology regularly contain articles on various aspects of crime, policing, and punishment. There is also the bilingual (English/French) *Crime, Histoire et Sociétés/Crime, History and Societies*, which is essential for anyone interested in the topic.

Index

Wiener, Martin 181
Wild, Jonathan 72
Wilde, Oscar 228
William, Prince of Orange 89
Wirion, Gen. Louis 109
witchcraft 85–86, 170–71

Wolff, Christian 21
Wright, Sir Sampson 107

Zehr, Howard 127–30
Zola, Émile 157